WOMEN IN ANTIQUITY

GENDER AND ARCHAEOLOGY SERIES

Series Editor
Sarah Milledge Nelson
University of Denver

This series focuses on ways to understand gender in the past through archaeology. This is a topic poised for significant advances in both method and theory, which in turn can improve all archaeology. The possibilities of new methodological rigor as well as new insights into past cultures are what make gendered archaeology a vigorous and thriving subfield.

The series welcomes single authored books on themes in this topical area, particularly ones with a comparative focus. Edited collections with a strong theoretical or methodological orientation will also be considered. Audiences are practicing archaeologists and advanced students in the field.

EDITORIAL BOARD

BOOKS IN THE SERIES

Volume 1, *In Pursuit of Gender: Worldwide Archaeological Approaches*, Sarah Milledge Nelson and Myriam Rosen-Ayalon, Editors

Volume 2, *Gender and the Archaeology of Death*, Bettina Arnold and Nancy L. Wicker, Editors

Volume 3, *Ancient Maya Women*, Traci Ardren, Editor

Volume 4, *Sexual Revolutions: Gender and Labor at the Dawn of Agriculture*, by Jane Peterson

Volume 5, *Ancient Queens: Archaeological Explorations*, Sarah M. Nelson, Editor

Volume 6, *Gender in Ancient Cyprus: Narratives of Social Change on a Mediterranean Island*, by Diane Bolger

Volume 7, *Ambiguous Images: Gender and Rock Art*, by Kelley Hays-Gilpin

Volume 8, *Gender and Chinese Archaeology*, Katheryn M. Linduff and Yan Sun, Editors

Volume 9, *Gender in Archaeology: Analyzing Power and Prestige, Second Edition*, by Sarah Milledge Nelson

Volume 10, *The Archaeology of Childhood: Children, Gender, and Material Culture*, by Jane Eva Baxter

Volume 11, *Women in Antiquity: Theoretical Approaches to Gender and Archaeology*, Sarah Milledge Nelson, Editor

Volume 12, *Worlds of Gender: The Archaeology of Women's Lives around the Globe*, Sarah Milledge Nelson, Editor

SUBMISSION GUIDELINES

Prospective authors of single or coauthored books and editors of anthologies should submit a letter of introduction, the manuscript or a four- to ten-page proposal, a book outline, and a curriculum vitae. Please send your book manuscript/proposal packet to:

Gender and Archaeology Series
AltaMira Press
1630 North Main Street #367
Walnut Creek, CA 94596
(925) 938-7243
www.altamirapress.com

WOMEN IN ANTIQUITY

Theoretical Approaches to Gender
and Archaeology

EDITED BY
SARAH MILLEDGE NELSON

A Division of
ROWMAN & LITTLEFIELD PUBLISHERS, INC.
Lanham • New York • Toronto • Plymouth, UK

AltaMira Press
A division of Rowman & Littlefield Publishers, Inc.
A wholly owned subsidiary of The Rowman & Littlefield Publishing Group, Inc.
4501 Forbes Boulevard, Suite 200
Lanham, MD 20706
www.altamirapress.com

Estover Road
Plymouth PL6 7PY
United Kingdom

British Library Cataloguing in Publication Information Available

Library of Congress Cataloguing-in-Publication Data

Women in antiquity : theoretical approaches to gender and archaeology / edited by Sarah Milledge Nelson.
    p.   cm.
Includes index.
ISBN-13: 978-0-7591-1081-6 (cloth : alk. paper)
ISBN-10: 0-7591-1081-6 (cloth : alk. paper)
ISBN-13: 978-0-7591-1082-3 (pbk. : alk. paper)
ISBN-10: 0-7591-1082-4 (pbk. : alk. paper)
    1. Feminist archaeology.   2. Women—History—To 500.   3. Sex role—History.
I. Nelson, Sarah M., 1931–
CC72.4.W66   2007
920.72—dc22   2007000567

Printed in the United States of America

Contents

Introduction

SARAH MILLEDGE NELSON

THESE CHAPTERS were originally published as Part I of the *Handbook of Gender in Archaeology*. That large volume has been so well received that it seemed important to make the material available for classes at a reasonable price. For students of general archaeological theory, this book will prove particularly rewarding, as it covers all aspects of gender theory in archaeology. Some of the contributors helped to create the field, and others have specialized in a part of it, but all possess both a thorough knowledge of the history of gender theories and offer fresh perspectives about gender in archaeology.

Those of us who have been pursuing theories of gender in archaeology seriously through long careers have been discouraged to find that papers sent to us for review often lack any acknowledgment of the vast body of theory about gender in archaeology that has already been published. Is it a prevailing notion that anybody can "do" gender, now that the question of women in the past is on the table? Just mention women, and that takes care of it? It is careless and naïve to ignore what has already been written about any topic, but especially one as essential as gender for understanding all other facets of societies. These chapters will put to rest any lingering suspicion that no theories of gender exist, and will make it easy to understand both the practical side of "doing" gender and the variety of ways in which it can be approached.

One perspective that runs throughout these papers is that to study gender is not to discuss just women. The topic of gender concerns interactions, negotiations, and change. It includes negotiations about which gender did what in a particular time and place, setting aside stereotypes of gender derived, for the most part, from our own culture. Studying gender even in the present is not simple, and to derive knowledge about gender from archaeological remains is even more challenging. The chapters presented here demonstrate thoughtful and careful theory about how to discover and interpret gender in the past.

In this book readers will discover many approaches to theories of gender in archaeology. This topic has sky-rocketed from a "fringe" idea—sometimes considered a nice idea but not possible to put into practice, and sometimes as well beyond the pale of mainstream of archaeology—to a topic that all archaeologists need to consider seriously, no matter where they dig, what period they cover, or what paradigm they espouse. The topic of gender is not as simple as it may seem at first glance. A particular culture, for instance, may recognize more than two genders. Furthermore, gender intersects with other categories, such as class and ethnicity. There are many ways to approach it, but, as noted above, "finding the women" is barely the beginning.

The chapters cover a broad spectrum of archaeological ideas. Some are grounded in particular branches of archaeology (processual, post-processual), and some focus on subsets of topics (households, landscapes). Each author is in the forefront of the topic discussed. Each chapter is an important contribution to the ongoing project of putting gender into the heart of archaeology. Long ago, I wrote that adding a perspective on gender to archaeology is like using a prism, scattering light to allow one to see what was there before, but invisible. These chapters are all prisms of that sort. Each chapter is a new and articulate statement about a particular topic, including a review and critique of what has already been published on the topic, as well as creative ideas about new directions for research. Each chapter is written in accessible language, but the authors do not simplify that which is inherently complex.

In using the prism metaphor, I do not mean to suggest that gender studies are about making women visible in archaeology. For the most part, women have become visible in archaeology. What needs to be explored in a more sophisticated way is the relationship of genders to each other. Roles exist, not in isolation, but in contrast to other roles. They may be rigid or permissive, overlapping or strictly separate. The polarized gender stereotypes of the 1950s, which influenced so much of how we understood the archaeological past (whether prehistoric, classical, or historical archaeology) have been vanquished under new visions of gender roles.

The book begins with a chapter on feminist methods by Elizabeth Brumfiel. Her own work on Aztec gender has demonstrated exceptionally creative ways to use field data from both excavations and surveys in examining changes in gendered work through time. Numbers and types of spindle whorls indicate the amount and kinds of weaving, for example, and varieties of pots and pans reveal changes in cooking methods. In this chapter, Brumfiel discusses variability, the analysis of genders in relationship to each other, the uses of history and ethnography, bioarchaeology and burial data, art and representation, and gendered tools and spaces. She suggests that a return to comparisons within larger regions and between regions can help us understand how gender relates to other structural variables, and that following changes through time may reveal changes not only in particular kinds of work but in the meaning of that work. This chapter will reward several careful readings. Be sure not to miss the end note discussing the dialogic approach, which in a few words is a pearl beyond price.

Suzanne Spencer-Wood was one of the first to bring gender in historical archaeology to the attention of the field. Her chapter, "Feminist Theory and Gender Research in Historical Archaeology," includes a keen sense of the development of feminist theory in the field. She shows how feminist critiques have delved deeper and deeper into problems with how historical archaeology has been carried out and in the underlying theory. She calls this "peeling the androcentric onion." She considers topics such as mothering and child-rearing, public and domestic roles, ideas about the home, and reform movements aimed at gender roles. In looking to the future, she sees postmodern approaches playing a large part, but she warns that although class and other variables are important, they should not be allowed to eclipse the study of gender.

Gender and material culture is the topic examined by Marie Louise Sørenson. She discusses the reciprocal effects of material culture and people, in which objects both reflect the social structure and affect individuals within it. She defines material culture as beyond "things," to include conventions about how things are used and the potential for disrupting understood norms. Objects familiar to archaeologists, such as clothing and tools, reflect and affect gender in the present. This has led to questions about how gender is "constructed and negotiated." Sørenson takes up questions of appearance as constructing the social person and the gendering of space. One promising new direction, she points out, is to consider even the human body as part of material culture.

Bettina Arnold examines both the theory and practice of mortuary analysis. She discusses various approaches to mortuary analysis that have been used to study gender, and then uses some of her own work on Iron Age Europe as a case study. In looking to the future, she points out that text-aided archaeological analyses are able to construct a richer description of genders in burial contexts than can be done for prehistory. She worries that agendas of the present may distort our understanding of the past.

Julia Hendon writes about households and gender. Engendering the household seems obvious, since domestic groups usually include men, women, and children, but in fact a deeper understanding has required both theoretical and methodological innovations. Household archaeology involves people's daily lives and helps us to understand "social dynamics at multiple social scales." Archaeologists often have dwellings to study, and the theoretical perspectives examined in this chapter help define what constitutes a household and how it can be studied. These perspectives touch on social action, uses of space, household production and consumption, identity, and issues of prestige.

Wendy Ashmore considers how landscapes become gendered. Her inclusive definition of landscapes is helpful for archaeological interpretations, allowing for sky, water, and things underground to be perceived as part of the landscape. While there is nothing inherently gendered about landscapes, Ashmore discusses the ways in which cultures have indeed gendered landscapes, drawing on rock art research, cosmology, and history. She demonstrates four ways that landscapes have been understood as having a gender or related to gender: In terms of shapes perceived in a landscape, activities undertaken in a landscape, the construction of gendered images and monuments that alter the landscape, and the application of historical or cosmological ideas to landscapes. She suggests that it is in fact the norm for landscapes to be gendered, although they have other characteristics as well.

Heterarchy and hierarchy are proving to be useful concepts in archaeology, although specifically including gender in the analysis is an unusual venture. Nevertheless, Janet Levy is an archaeologist who has thought seriously about the implications of heterarchy for gender studies in archaeology. In this chapter, she describes the ways in which heterarchy has been used in archaeology and anthropology. After presenting some of those attempts and their critiques, she demonstrates that the inclusion of gender makes it possible to use the concept of heterarchy to highlight individuals as well as groups. Levy points out cogently that heterarchy and gender analysis share "the quality of disruption; disrupting implicit assumptions about human social systems, social complexity, and social change."

Kathryn Weedman frames her topic of ethnoarchaeology with the Flintstones, a cartoon that exploited every possible gender stereotype. She describes the fruitful addition of gender to studies in ethnoarchaeology. She first covers gendered theories in anthropology and archaeology that ethnoarchaeology has been able to deconstruct. She describes the methodologies of specifically gendered ethnoarchaeology, and then considers particular topics, such as division of labor and the use of household space, that have been particularly problematic for gender in archaeology. Occupations that are specialized by gender have been studied perhaps more than any other topic. She describes how difficult it is to find gendered ethnoarchaeological studies in print, and provides a full bibliography to aid those who would like to seek them out.

Research on gender in classical archaeology is not merely a mirror of historical archaeology, although they have in common the availability of textual material to aid in interpreting archaeological discoveries. Early on, classicists tended to see women with art-historical eyes, that is to say the masculine gaze. Suzanne Spencer-Wood describes the ways in which feminism has been introduced into classical archaeology, and the results of such critiques and studies. She frames her discussion in terms of first, second, and third waves of feminism, and then looks at postmodern studies of sexuality and bodies in classical archaeology.

These chapters together should be required reading for any class in archaeological theory. They represent the leading edge of scholarship in the field, demonstrating how important gender is to the interpretation of archaeological sites and regions, and to the understanding of the development of culture and cultures.

Methods in Feminist and Gender Archaeology: A Feeling for Difference—and Likeness

I

ELIZABETH M. BRUMFIEL

METHODOLOGIES FOR FEMINIST and gender archaeology have been sharpened by two decades of fieldwork with explicitly feminist and gender objectives, the diversification of theoretical approaches within feminist and gender archaeology, and the insights gained from twenty years of critical discussion. Feminist and gender archaeologists now ask a wider variety of research questions, draw on more forms of relevant evidence, and avoid a number of earlier pitfalls in data interpretation.[1]

Four methodological developments have been particularly important in feminist and gender archaeology: (1) increased attention to the variability in gender-relevant data; (2) increased concern with the inclusion of women, men, and other genders in a single frame of analysis; (3) increased caution in the use of ethnohistoric and ethnographic analogy in the study of gender; and (4) new methods for ascertaining how gender was experienced in the past. After reviewing these developments, I examine the strengths and weaknesses of four domains of archaeological evidence relevant to the study of gender: human skeletal remains, burials, representational art, and distributions gender-associated artifacts. I also examine some approaches to gender that do not require gender attribution.

Throughout this chapter, I highlight the contributions that archaeologists can make to the feminist goal of promoting social equality. Unlike Sørensen (2004), I do not believe that the presentist objective of achieving gender equality is in conflict with the disciplinary aim of developing a theoretically informed archaeology of gender. A scholarly archaeology of gender cannot be severed from politics because, implicitly or explicitly, all scholarship in the social sciences is rooted in political stances and has political implications (Shanks and Tilley 1987). Feminist archaeology is not exceptional in this regard. But even for the emotionally charged subject of gender, the material evidence maintains a degree of independence from the political and theoretical biases of the investigator so that feminist archaeology is much more than "just politics" (Wylie 1992, 1996; see also Brumfiel 1996b).

An empirically and theoretically informed archaeology of gender makes real contributions to the feminist goal of expanding social equality. An archaeology of gender can (1) promote self-confidence and pride for women and people of other genders, (2) create a sympathetic understanding of difference within genders and sameness across genders that will facilitate broad-based political movements capable of achieving social equality, and (3) enhance our understanding of how gender hierarchy is created and maintained so as to design effective policies for promoting equality in contemporary society.

Variability

Feminists of color have focused our attention on the existence of variability ("difference") within gender categories (Combahee River Collective 1977; hooks 1984; Mohatny 1988). These feminists argue that the meaning and consequences of gender vary, depending on the intersection of gender with other social identities, such as race, class, ethnicity, and age (see also Butler 1990; di Leonardo 1991; Sacks 1988). Inspired by this insight, archaeologists have searched for the ways that the intersection of gender with other social categories, such as age and civil status, has produced variability within gender groups. For example, Martin (1998) defines a subgroup of women at the Pueblo site of La Plata, New Mexico, with multiple skeletal trauma. Rather than interpreting this as undifferentiated "violence against women" or "wife beating," Martin suggests the existence of a special subclass of women subjected to violence, perhaps female war captives or servants. Membership in this subclass, then, would be determined by the intersection of gender with a distinctive civil status (war captive or servant). Similarly, on the basis of burial treatment, Robb (1994a) suggests that the most important division in Neolithic Italian society was not between women and men but between the subgroup of adult (initiated?) males on the one hand and subadult (uninitiated?) males and all females on the other. Both gender and initiated status (for men, a function of age) were the criteria for these social groupings (see also Joyce 2001a).

Gay and lesbian scholars have demanded that we not assume a norm of exclusive heterosexuality (e.g., Rubin 1984), and this has prompted archaeologists to search among burials sexed as male or female for individuals who represent third and other genders (Hollimon 1997; Weglian 2001). For example, Hollimon

(1997) identifies two Chumash male burials that differ in important ways from other male burials in her sample. These males show much greater degeneration in the spine as compared to other males, and they were buried with digging-stick weights and basket fragments. Hollimon concludes that these two individuals were third-gender, two-spirit undertakers known from ethnographic descriptions of Chumash culture rather than conventional men.

Archaeologists also search gender-relevant data to find variation in the expression of gender from one context to another. This is linked to the recent emphasis on the social construction and maintenance of gender through performance (Butler 1990, 1993; Morris 1995). Gender can be performed differently in different contexts, imparting a mosaic quality to gender rather than overriding consistency, and these different performances might be evident in different archaeological contexts (Cohodas 2002:28; Crown 2000; Gero and Scattolin 2002; Sørensen 2000:61). Gero and Scattolin (2002) suggest that at Yutopian, Argentina, specialized tasks such as corn grinding divided household members by age, sex, and space, while collaborative activities such as copper smelting were collaborative and erased the differences between household members.

Archaeologists also explore variation in the way that gender is represented in the different media of a single society. For example, women are often represented differently in household figurines and state-sponsored art, and the gender attributes emphasized in burial practices may be different still (Brumfiel 1996a; Cohodas 2002; Joyce 2000). These different presentations of gender often highlight the elements of gender ideology that were contested by different social groups (Cohodas 2002). Thus, by recognizing variation in the representation of gender rather than expecting uniform conventions, archaeologists can define the elements of gender that were contested and study how these disagreements were negotiated.

Archaeologists also recognize variability in the various indices of gender equality. The different measures of social well-being within a given society do not always coincide. For example, Crown and Fish (1996) found that Hohokam women who were members of high-status households could be judged advantaged by some criteria (e.g., they had access to high-prestige spaces at the tops of mounds) but disadvantaged by other criteria (e.g., their personal autonomy was limited by walls enclosing high-prestige domestic space). This suggests that gender status is a mixed bag: individuals may be offered higher standing in some areas of life (e.g., prestige) at the cost of low standing in other areas of life (e.g., autonomy). Such trade-offs are very common in social life, and rather than expecting any simple answer to the question "What was the status of women in ancient society X?," archaeologists should investigate the various dimensions of social well-being and what is gained and what is lost at each step of social change.

Women, Men, and Other Genders—Together

The consideration of men, women, and other genders in a single analysis distinguishes the newer feminist and gender archaeologies from the older feminist archaeology, which emphasized the roles and status of *women*. Studies of women in ancient societies tried to correct for the fact that women and women's activities were virtually ignored in earlier archaeological reports (Conkey and Spector 1984). Studies of women in prehistory continue to be published (Ardren 2002; Bruhns and Stothert 1999; Nelson 2003), and they continue to serve two important functions. First, these studies highlight the contributions of women in ancient societies, and, second, they demonstrate the variability of gender roles in ancient societies, with the implication that gender roles and identities cannot be attributed a universal, unchanging human biology laid down during the Paleolithic. However, it is increasingly recognized that the condition of women in past societies is best understood if women are placed in a frame of analysis that includes men and other genders. This is because different genders are defined in relation to one another through their paradigmatic relationships. That is, men and women and other genders are defined not only in terms of what they are but also in terms of what they are not. The contrasting properties between genders define the meaning of each gender. Thus, recent work in feminist and gender archaeology includes both women and men (e.g., Meskell and Joyce 2003).

In addition, different genders must be analyzed together in order to identify the extent of difference between gender categories. The degree of difference between genders provides a measure of the salience of gender as a social category, that is, the extent to which gender is an important organizing principle in any given society. Second-wave feminists were certain that gender was a universally important dimension of social differentiation, but, more recently, scholars have realized that the emphasis given gender differences varies greatly from culture to culture or even in the same culture according to different contexts. We are only beginning to explore the causes of cross-cultural differences in gender salience. Archaeologists can contribute much to this discussion by being cognizant of the areas of overlap between genders, the situations in which difference is highlighted, and how these change through history.

Cross-gender comparison is also important for assessing the relative fates of women and men and other genders during periods of cultural transformation, such as the adoption of agriculture or state formation (Peterson 2002; Pyburn

2004a). For example, if in the transition to state formation both women and men suffered parallel declines in well-being, this is very different from a situation where women but not men experienced decline.

The Uses of Ethnohistory and Ethnography

Feminist and gender archaeologists have begun to exercise increased caution in projecting ethnographic and ethnohistorical data into deep prehistory and to resist more vigorously "the tyranny of the ethnographic record" (Wobst 1978). They recognize that historical records and ethnographies often are unreliable guides to the gender systems of past societies because these records are colored by the culture, class, and gender biases of their Western authors (Pyburn 2004a; Stahl 2001). And even when these records accurately describe gender systems as they existed at the time of Western contact, the gender systems might be vastly different from their precontact predecessors, given the often cataclysmic changes wrought by the contact situation (Etienne and Leacock 1980). In addition, the unexamined projection of ethnography or ethnohistory into prehistory erases the record of culture change and thus promotes essentialist views of both gender and culture (Chance 1996; Luedke 2004; Robin, in press; Stahl 2001; Trigger 1980).

Aware of these problems, archaeologists are beginning to show more finesse in the application of ethnographic analogy. Ethnographic analogy is most convincing when archaeologists identify complexes of traits in the ethnographic record along with the functional or ideological circumstances that account for these complexes (Wylie 1985). For example, Robin (2002) examines the historical forces (e.g., nucleated settlements, schooling for children, and grants of agricultural land to village-based *ejido* committees) that have made farming an archetypically male task among contemporary Yucatec Maya. In the absence of these forces during the Classic period, Maya women and men may have collaborated on farming, which is the pattern for Maya women and men in the Lacandon area today. Robin argues that the dispersed households at ancient Chan Nòohol, Belize, are consistent with a pattern of collaborative farming during the Classic period.

Weismantel (2004) uses Melanesian and Amazonian ethnography to build a model of beliefs about sex, reproduction, lineage, and power in lineage societies. She then uses this model to convincingly explain many features of the iconography and depositional context of Moche pots. Her composite model avoids reliance on any single ethnographic case; in this way, Weismantel avoids collapsing historical change. By finding specific points of correspondence between the elements of her model and the Moche data set, Weismantel invites archaeologists to unpack the attributes of Moche style, to study the changing configurations of these attributes over time, and to track changes in Moche style and lineage ideology from the past to the present.

Experience

Phenomenology is concerned with the variable quality of human experience (Wilkerson 2000:269); it asks, "Who experienced what in prehistory?" (Gero 1991). Archaeologists have approached human experience in several different ways. One approach focuses on the *locations* of women and men and other genders on a site and the implications of these locations for gender-related statuses and roles, access to knowledge, experience, and motivation (e.g., Gero 1991; Gilchrist 1999; Hendon 1997; Sweely 1998; Tringham 1991). Another approach focuses on *embodiment,* the experience of gender and sexuality through the senses (Joyce 2004). Archaeologists study embodiment to explore how bodily experience can be used to lend an aura of naturalness and immutability to gender roles and identities (Joyce 2000; Sørensen 2000) and to demonstrate historical variation in definitions of sexuality and the body, thus undermining our belief that our conceptions of gender, sexuality, and the body are natural and self-evident (Gilchrist 1999:109–45; Meskell and Joyce 2003; Schmidt and Voss 2000; Weismantel 2004).

Phenomenological studies in archaeology have found a receptive audience. In part, this is because their concern with the individual, embodiment, identity, and agency resonates well with the ideas of the person in Western capitalist society. Phenomenological approaches can make intelligible the experiences of women or men or third genders in other times and other places and thus foster a sympathetic awareness and understanding of *differences.* This understanding of difference is important to feminist politics because it facilitates the building of political coalitions across groups, coalitions that are large enough to achieve institutional change (Hames-García 2000; Nguyen 2000).

However, interest in the experience of gender is sometimes associated with a distinct lack of interest in the organization of wealth and power that structures experience. An analysis of experience severed from its political and economic contexts runs the risk of essentializing people in the past because, in the absence of an understanding of political economy, gender subjectivity is often attributed to arbitrary sets of cultural definitions, values, and norms. To fully appreciate the experiences of others, these experiences must be related to the array of available possibilities and constraints that individuals face. Recognizing the economic and political structures that engaged individuals in past societies actually enhances our sense of them as active agents rather than cultural dupes.

I now turn to four types of archaeological evidence that are relevant to the study of gender: human skeletal material, burials, representational art, and distributions of gender-associated artifacts. I also examine some approaches to gender systems that do not require the identification of gender or the association of certain artifact classes with specific genders.

Bioarchaeological Approaches to Gender

Gender is a system of culturally defined differences that are ascribed to individuals on the basis of their biological sex. Bioarchaeology, the study of human skeletal material from archaeological contexts, has established fairly reliable methods for defining the sex of individuals on the basis of skeletal measurements.[2] Therefore, the association of particular types of grave goods and burial practices with male and female skeletons is a common point of entry into past gender systems (see the discussion later in this chapter). But of equal (or greater) interest is the fact that many types of behavior leave their marks on human bone. Since gender is socially constructed, it must be created and maintained through engendering performances, and these habitual performances result in skeletal alterations. Unlike burial ritual and art, which provide *representations* of gender, human bone records actual *enactment* of gender. Human bone is the closest thing that archaeologists have to the direct observation of gendered behavior in the prehistoric past.

Patterns of work are revealed in bone density, the size of muscle attachments, and wear on skeletal joints (Larsen 1997; Peterson 2002). Particular kinds of work are also indicated by some wear patterns on teeth (associated with the production of baskets, mats, and cordage; Molleson 1994), high rates of tooth decay (associated with the frequent intake of food and during cooking; Ardren 2002), and high frequencies of auditory exostoses (associated with deep-sea diving for shellfish; Allison 1984). Comparing indicators of sex with indicators of work, archaeologists can determine the presence of a gendered division of labor or, of equal importance, the *absence* of a gendered division of labor. They can assess changes in the work patterns of women and men during important cultural transitions, such as the adoption of agriculture (Peterson 2002), and they can provide independent assessments of the accounts of the division of labor left by Western observers (Hollimon 2000).

Archaeologists can explore variation in bone and joint alteration within sexes as well as between sexes to reveal the existence of third and other genders. For example, third genders can be identified by bone and joint patterning typically found on female skeletons but occasionally occurring on male skeletons (or vice versa) or by bone and joint patterns that are atypical for both males and females

(Hollimon 1997). Within sexes, differences in bone and joint alteration may also mark the intersection of gender with other social categories, such as age and class.

Bone can also reveal habitual participation in nonsubsistence activities. For example, ritual activities such as feasting may be evident in bone chemistry (Hastorf 1991), and sweat bathing may produce auditory exostoses (Lambert 2001). Healed fractures provide evidence of participation in warfare (Goodman and Armelagos 1985; Hollimon 2001) or exposure to violence (Martin 1998; Robb 1997; Walker 1989; Wilkinson and Van Wagenen 1993).

Bone can also distinguish native-born individuals from immigrants. Patterns of residential change are important aspects of past (and present) gender systems because social power is often a function of social alliances, and alliances are often disrupted by migration. Hence, women in societies with virilocal residence may have a more difficult time in maintaining social power than women in societies with uxorilocal residence. When individuals are buried in houses that persist over several generations, the distribution of genetic anomalies by sex can be used to identify patterns of postmarital residence (Spence 1974). Bone chemistry may also identify postmarital residence patterns and other patterns of migration (Price, Grupe, et al. 1994; Price, Johnson, et al., 1994), and it can reveal the existence of alien subgroups, such as female war captives (White et al. 2002, 2004).

Burial Data

Depositional contexts for human skeletons may provide direct evidence of behavioral patterns. For example, at least nine of sixteen skeletons recovered from precolonial gold mines in Zimbabwe were female, suggesting that the miners were women (Luedke 2004; Summers 1969). But usually, skeletons occur in burials, which are conscious creations that serve as a medium for the constitution of social relations (Arnold and Wicker 2001; Joyce 2001a). Burials reflect gender ideologies, which may or may not coincide with actual practice.

Differences in the burial programs for women, men, and other genders provide one measure of the salience of gender as a social category. For example, burials in the early levels of Çatalhöyük, Turkey, reveal no appreciable gendered differences in burial location, orientation, aspect, or grave goods. Heads were often removed from both female and male bodies and deposited in the foundations of house posts, which suggests that both females and males could qualify as honored ancestors (Meskell 2005). Gender at Çatalhöyük might have been marked in such perishable media as clothing, hairstyles, and tattoos, but archaeologists can provisionally accept the proposition that Çatalhöyük was a society where genders were not highly differentiated. Lack of gender differentiation probably indicates a condition of gender equality (see also King 2004).

When two or more contemporaneous burial programs exist in a single culture, they usually demarcate genders. When the distinctive burial programs include subadults, it is possible to define the age at which gender identity was imposed by society at large (Rega 2000). But different burial programs do not always demarcate genders, for example, in Neolithic Italy (Robb 1994a). Where men and women receive different burial treatments, gender inequality is usually implied since the whole purpose of creating gender difference is to legitimate differential access to resources and status (Sørensen 2000). But several archaeologists have argued that gender differences can signal parallel gender hierarchies rather than gender inequality (Gilchrist 1999; Hendon 1999; Moore 1993). The presence or absence of parallel gender hierarchies can be established using burial data: gender inequality is marked by differences in the labor invested in constructing female and male graves and by the quantity and quality of grave goods deposited in female and male graves (Chapman 1997; Crown and Fish 1996; Haviland 1997; Meskell 1998b).[3]

Since burials reflect gender ideologies, which may or may not coincide with actual practice, the assessment of gender equality based on burial data should be compared with skeletal indicators of material well-being in terms of health, nutrition, and violence (Ardren 2002; Cohen and Bennett 1993; Danforth et al. 1997; Gerry and Chesson 2000; Lillie 1997; Neitzel 2000; Rega 1997; Robb 1997; Savage 2000; Walker 1989; Wilkinson and Van Wagenen 1993). Archaeologists should also determine whether all members of a sex group were treated equally since only certain subgroups may have been disadvantaged. If not recognized as distinctive, a disadvantaged subgroup will drag down averages for a gender as a whole and make a special case of gender inequality appear to be a general condition (Ambrose et al. 2003; Martin 1998). Pyburn (2004a) argues that, almost always prior to Western contact, differences of class are much more salient than differences of gender in burial data, suggesting that the rise of class inequality did not uniformly entail marked gender inequality as suggested by Engels (1972 [1884]) and other gender theorists (e.g., Coontz and Henderson 1986; Gailey 1987; Leacock 1983; Sacks 1982; Silverblatt 1987; Zagarell 1986).

Grave goods have often been interpreted as indicating the activities of women, men, and other genders (Costin 1996). The persistent association of a specific artifact class with women or men or other genders implies a gendered division of labor or at least the ideology of a gendered division of labor.

In inferring activities from grave goods, archaeologists have shown a persistent tendency to invoke a double standard according to whether the patterns of activity suggested by the grave goods conform to Western gender roles (Conkey and Spector 1984; Nelson 1997; Pyburn 2004a). When the grave goods suggest activity patterns that parallel Western gender roles, the inferences are accepted as unproblematic. When the inferred patterns differ from Western gender roles, archaeologists seek alternative interpretations. For example, Winters (1968) inferred that grinding pestles found with female burials at Indian Knoll reflected women's food-processing roles but that grinding pestles found with male burials reflected male craft manufacture (Conkey and Spector 1984:11). It is always a good exercise in thought to imagine what interpretations archaeologists would give to grave goods were they strongly associated with the other sex and then to test for the likelihood of this alternate hypothesis by examining skeletal indicators of activity, the associations of this artifact with other tools and waste, or the representation of gendered activities in ancient art.

Finally, grave goods have been used to examine the life cycle in different cultures, particularly the way in which gender varies as it intersects with age and other social variables. Joyce (2001a) examines the burials of a dozen women at Early Formative Tlatilco, Mexico, showing the range of variation among them as gender intersects with age and household membership. Through this analysis, the Tlatilco women emerge as multidimensioned individuals rather than "faceless blobs" (Tringham 1991; see also Meskell 1998b).

Representational Art

Burials provide one form of gender representation; others forms include the presentation of human figures in rock art, figurines, murals, painted pottery, and sculpture. Human figures may or may not be gendered; that is, they may or may not bear anatomical features or styles of clothing suggesting gender difference. The prominence of gender difference in representational art is one indication of the salience of gender, which may change over time. For example, Hays-Gilpin (2000, 2004) has studied gender salience in the rock art of the American Southwest. In the preagricultural Archaic, only ungendered spirit beings were depicted, which Hays-Gilpin interprets as shamans' spirit helpers. During the Basketmaker era, a time of scattered, economically self-sufficient households, figures in rock art are clearly marked as male or female by anatomy or dress. In later, nucleated, Pueblo settlements, gender was no longer displayed on rock art; instead, it was enacted in public performances.

The public nature of representational art makes it a useful tool in enforcing gender norms. Thus, when representational art depicts women and men and other genders engaged in different activities, these depictions may constitute ideological statements about gender roles rather than direct reflections of reality. For example, in both Late Neolithic Italy and the Great Basin, the depiction of male figures in hunting scenes became more frequent just as hunting declined in economic importance (Robb 1994b; Whitley 1994). As in the case of gender patterns suggested by grave goods, the gendered activities depicted in representational art should be tested against skeletal indicators of activity and/or the distribution of associated tools in occupation contexts.

In addition to conveying norms of appropriate gender activities, artists may make ideological statements about gender through the differences in the sizes of female and male figures (as in Egyptian royal art) or through the relative positions of female and male figures: above/below, right/left, and front/back (Joyce 1996). The depiction of only one gender in art and the absence of the others has sometimes been interpreted as indicating gender dominance. However, like the interpretations of grave goods, the meaning of gender in art has sometimes been subject to a double standard. For example, the absence of women in Olmec art has been interpreted as an effort to exclude them from political negotiations and power (Joyce 2000), but the absence of males in Paleolithic figurines has been attributed to male fascination with the female body (Nelson 1990). In many cases, men have been considered the audience for art regardless of its content. For example, Meskell and Joyce (2003) interpret the depiction of the nude female body in ancient Egyptian art as serving male pleasure, but they also interpret the depiction of the nude male body in ancient Maya art as serving male pleasure. When women are depicted with little clothing and/or engaged in sexual acts, Western equations of nudity with sexuality and sexuality with the degradation of women lead to inferences of a low status for women. But Weismantel (2004) offers a convincing alternative reading of Moche depictions of sexuality connecting sexual acts with the nurturing of children.

Representational art provides an excellent opportunity to examine the negotiation of gender. Different art forms have different authors and different consumers. Archaeologists have begun to pay attention to differences in the way that gender is expressed in different contexts: state-sponsored art, such as monumental sculptures, versus commoner art, such as ceramic figurines, and so on (Brumfiel 1996a; Joyce 2000). In doing so, archaeologists hope to capture some of the tensions generated by the existing gender system. Cohodas (2002) distinguishes five separate strands of discourse in Maya art: sculpture in public spaces, sculpture in residential spaces, painted ceramics, mold-made figurine whistles from commoner households, and Jaina figurines from elite burials. The discourse generated by these different art forms has yet to be fully analyzed.

Gendered Tools and Spaces

Linking artifact types to one gender or another opens further avenues of inquiry by archaeologists. Changes in the frequency of gender-linked tools can be used to monitor changes in workloads and organization of labor that accompany social transitions such as emerging food production, imperial expansion, and colonialism (Brumfiel 1991; Costin 1993; Crown and Fish 1996; Deagan 2004; Hastorf 1991). The technical properties of artifacts can be used to examine the gendered dimensions of technological innovation or hidden forms of resistance in gendered labor (Brumfiel 1996a; Sassaman 1992). Artifact decoration may reflect the negotiation of gender status. For example, Hodder (1986:109) suggests that contemporary Ilchamus women decorate milk calabashes in order to call attention to the importance of women in reproduction in a society where reproduction is the central pivot of male power. Aztec women may have used decorated spindle whorls to call attention to the importance of women's production in the domestic and state economies (McCafferty and McCafferty 1991:31–32; 2000:47–48).

However, linking artifacts with gender, what Costin (1996) calls "gender attribution," is a tricky business. Ethnohistoric texts may describe the gendered division of labor in non-Western societies, but these descriptions cannot be taken at face value. The authors of these texts frequently skewed their observations to conform to their own Western, male expectations of the gendered division of labor. The association of grave goods with specific sexes in burials might represent a cultural ideal, but it might not coincide with the actual distribution of labor. The same could be true of the activities and tools associated with gender in representational art. Archaeologists have sometimes used the location of production areas to assign gender to one set of tools or activities or another. Usually, archaeologists attribute tools or activities within or adjacent to houses to women and tools or activities in more distant locales to men. But this seems to inscribe a Western, nineteenth-century "separation of spheres" ideology on all of human history (Pyburn 2004a).

The problems of gender attribution are so great that it is tempting to discard the enterprise entirely. But the valuable knowledge gained from studying gender-associated artifacts is an inducement to proceed cautiously to establish gender attributions. A gender attribution can be proposed when multiple lines of evidence (skeletal alteration, ethnohistory, burial data, and representational art) point consistently in the same direction. For example, Gero (1992) observes that *tupus* (clothes-fastening pins) and spindle whorls are consistently associated with women in ethnohistoric texts, representational art, and burials in the Andes from the Early Intermediate period to the present. Therefore, she argues, the recovery of *tupus* and spindle whorls from ritual feasting locales in Queyash, Peru, testify to the participation of women in those feasts. Her conclusion is strengthened by the fact that the spatial distributions of *tupus* and spindle whorls at Queyash overlap extensively.

Gender attribution must be argued separately for each historical case. For example, the association of spindle whorls with women in the Postclassic Basin of Mexico is strongly suggested by the ethnohistorical literature, burial data, and representational art. But the presence of spindle whorls in male graves at Cholula (McCafferty and McCafferty 2002) and Lamanai (Fekete 1996) indicates that the equation of spindle whorls with women cannot be taken for granted, even for pre-Hispanic Mesoamerica.

The distribution of gendered artifacts in different sorts of spaces has been used to infer power exercised by men and women in different social contexts (Gero 1992; Hendon 1997). Using artifacts to define gendered space is most effective for artifacts that are found in use contexts rather than trash or storage. Rapidly abandoned sites, such as Cerén, El Salvador, or Aguateca, Guatemala, are more likely to preserve artifacts in use contexts than sites that were gradually abandoned (Inomata and Stiver 1998). But even at rapidly abandoned sites, many artifacts will be found in storage spaces, and these do not necessarily represent the extent of gender segregation or blending that occurred in daily activity. Meskell (1998a) avoids problems of depositional context by basing her analysis of gendered domestic space on wall decorations and fixtures within New Kingdom Egyptian houses. Wall paintings pertaining to the sexual lives of mature women define rooms dominated by women; raised divans define the rooms devoted to men's sociability.

In general, a lack of spatial segregation by gender indicates a low degree of gender salience and inequality, as Gero (1992) argues for Queyash feasting and Hendon (1997) argues for domestic activity among the Classic Maya. The segregation of space by gender generally reflects gender inequality, although the argument has been made that the division of space by gender indicates parallel gender hierarchies (Gilchrist 1999). The scale, integration, and complexity of gendered spaces might also have implications for gender hierarchy (Blanton 1994; Hegmon et al. 2000; Hopkins 1987). Hendon (1997) and Robin (2004) suggest that Classic Maya royal courts were significantly more segregated by status, occupation, and gender than were the houses of lower-ranking nobles and commoners.

Finally, Gero and Scattolin (2002) consider the implications of a hearth at Yutopian, Argentina, that contains the debris of both food preparation (which they gender female) and copper working (which, they believe, would have engaged household members of different ages and genders). Gero and Scattolin conclude that a single household might engage in some tasks that segregate household members by age and gender and other tasks that involve the collaboration among household members of different ages and genders. In such situations, segregation and collaboration could act together to intensify household cohesion, and this would be missed if archaeologists sought only one overall measure of spatial segregation.

Beyond defining the spaces occupied by different genders, spatial distributions of gendered artifacts also suggest lines of vision that can used to reconstruct social relations. For example, Sweely (1998) uses the locations and orientations of grinding stones to establish personal interactions and relations of authority among women in the rural Maya village of Cerén. Lines of vision can also aid phenomenological analysis, as in Gilchrist's (1999) reconstruction of the experiences of noblewomen in their sequestered quarters in medieval castles.

Gender in the Absence of Gender Attribution

In a few cases, archaeologists have made inferences about gender relations without resorting to gender attribution. For example, Robin (2002) argues that the dispersion of rural Maya houses among agricultural fields at Chan Nòohol, Belize; the outdoor location of most activity areas; and the pole walls of houses that would have allowed people inside or outside the structure to peer at or talk to each other all facilitated a collaborative pattern of female and male labor among household members, with continuous communication throughout the day.

Hastorf (1991) argues that the extent of dispersion of debris from women's food-processing activities in Sausa, Peru, reflects the degree of contestation between genders. She observes that when Sausa came under Inca rule, an earlier pattern of relatively high dispersion of food debris was replaced by a pattern of decreased dispersion, suggesting that Inca dominance was accompanied by increased strain between women and men in local households. The interesting thing about this argument is that it applies equally even if food processing was not considered women's work. The heterogeneity or homogeneity of debris on household floors, regardless of their gendered affiliations, could gauge the degree of strain in household relations.

Dobres (1995:41) uses a similar line of argument to propose that site-specific technical variability in Magdalenian artifacts reflects the flexibility of social norms: "Flexibility in technical strategies practiced on a site-by-site basis may be interpreted as the embodiment of a general flexibility in social conduct situated to the specific settings in which people organized societies." Strictly defined gender roles, then, would be associated with low technical variability in artifacts; more flexible gender roles would be expected in cases of high technical variability.

Given the difficulties of gender attribution, these efforts to comment on gender without first linking artifacts to genders seem exceedingly worthwhile.

Using a Wider Lens: Proposals for Future Studies

Case studies are the most common form of research in feminist and gender archaeology. In part, this reflects the long-standing practice in archaeology of taking the site (or the region) as the unit of analysis. Archaeologists have frequently viewed themselves as the ethnographers of past societies, with a goal of reconstructing in as great a detail as possible the lifestyles, experiences, and worldviews of people in a particular time and place.

Recent efforts to avoid totalizing accounts of the past have reinforced this tradition. Many feminist archaeologists have rejected sweeping evolutionary models of prehistory because they utilize essentialized cross-cultural categories (such as "women," "progress," and "states") and mechanical models of culture change (Conkey and Gero 1991; Pyburn 2004a; Silverblatt 1988, 1991). These students of gender have emphasized the specificities of archaeological time, place, and culture, and their studies have been very useful. They have (1) refuted assumptions about the timelessness and invariability of women's roles, (2) heightened our sensitivity to gender difference, and (3) discredited evolutionary models of gender that were little more than projections of the gender biases of their Western authors (Nelson and Rosen-Ayalon 2002). Too often, however, these highly nuanced case studies leave unexamined the dynamic relationship between gender and other broad variables, such as ecology, economy, politics, and culture. The severing of connections between gender and these other broad variables threatens to marginalize the study of gender by reducing it to just another subfield of archaeology, leaving unrealized the full transformative potential of gender studies for archaeology. In addition, the case study approach in archaeology has frequently meant that archaeologists have adopted ethnographers' synchronic perspective for their own. But it was ethnography's shallow time depth that led early anthropologists to construe contemporary cultural variation as evolutionary development (Fabian 1983; Yoffee 1993), with all the essentializing and mechanistic qualities of unilineal evolutionist schemes.

The ties between gender systems and other broad variables are difficult to pursue in the absence of a comparative perspective. I suggest that we begin to broaden our focus in gender studies to include several neighboring regions and/ or long-term histories. Such controlled comparisons would enable feminist and gender archaeologists to study broad social processes without falling into the essentializing traps that are so objectionable.

Archaeologists have real sequences of development at their disposal, and these sequences have analytic potential that has not yet been realized. Archaeologists can begin to examine the intertwining of identity, agency, economy, politics, and gender over the long term: how shifts in one variable open new possibilities for change in the others. Working with real sequences of development in limited regions, archaeologists can provide accounts that are *comparative but also contextual* and that deal with *structural variables*, such as economics and politics, *but also subjective variables*, such as identity and agency. Let me provide an example of work that I think would be very productive.

In Mesoamerica at the time of European contact, cloth production was a female activity laden with symbolic meaning (McCafferty and McCafferty 1991; Sullivan 1982). Archaeologists could ask, How did cloth production emerge as a symbol of women's identity? Was weaving always a female activity, given its compatibility with women's child care responsibilities (Barber 1994), or did the changing economic and political circumstances of cloth production determine that spinning and weaving would emerge as women's activities? How did these changing circumstances alter the power and status of cloth producers, the ideological meanings of cloth production and of being a woman? A broad, comparative study of the 3,500-year history of cloth production and gender in Mesoamerica would provide answers to these questions but would avoid the essentializing and mechanistic qualities of more synthetic, less historical accounts (for an initial effort at such a history, see Brumfiel 2005).

The study of long-term change in the social relations of cloth production alerts us to the likelihood of changes in the meaning of cloth production for women's identity. It encourages us to search for change in gender ideologies, identities, and experiences over time, and it makes us more (not less) aware of how gender is socially constructed through the negotiation of issues that range far beyond gender. The study of long-term change is one of the unquestioned strengths of archaeology, and the study of economic and political relations over the long term will enrich our understanding of gender subjectivity.

Feminists need real histories of weaving and farming, nursing and state formation, warfare, gender identity, and gender symbolism in Mesoamerica and in other regions of the world in order to better understand both the general principles that guide the operation of gender systems and the specific possibilities and constraints that women face under varied political, economic, and cultural circumstances. *Archaeologists* need these real long-term histories so that they can better account for both the intimate details of specific finds (e.g., Hodder 2000; Joyce 2001a; Meskell 1998b) and for the broader sweep of social change.

Notes

1. This chapter does not deal with issues of feminist epistemology, which would include the construction of basic categories in archaeology such as cultures, phases, and types; androcentric bias in the processes of data recovery, interpretation, and hypothesis testing; and feminist approaches to archaeological writing and to the teaching of archaeology. For reviews of these issues, readers should consult Conkey and Gero (1991, 1997), Conkey and Tringham (1995, 1996), Gero (1996), and Romanowicz and Wright (1996). These archaeologists argue that unreflective empiricism is not likely to yield comprehensive and reliable understandings of past gender systems and that the development of critical and reflexive research categories and procedures is the most essential goal of feminist methodology. I agree with these authors that the continuing critical assessment of basic archaeological assumptions is crucial; however, I also believe that feminist critiques in archaeology have progressed to the point where it is possible to generate reliable information about past gender systems by using amended approaches to traditional archaeological data.

I disagree with feminist archaeologists who argue that the primary contribution of archaeology to gender equality is its ability to demonstrate the *irreducible ambiguity* of all knowledge about the past. This position has been most clearly articulated by Conkey and Tringham (1995:231):

> What is empowering, in our view, is the recognition and acceptance of ambiguity, which admits the role of constructedness and the possibilities for reconfiguring and renegotiating meanings, including what constitutes evidence. . . . The contemporary reader . . . must participate in and confront the entanglement of ambiguity, history, and the production of knowledge.

Instead, I prefer a *dialogic approach* to the presentation of archaeological data and interpretation. In a dialogic approach, investigators would present their own and others' interpretations of an archaeological data set along with the train of assumptions and inferences that underlies each interpretation. Investigators would then explain their preference for one interpretation over the others. I take as my model Warren's (1998:33–51) exposition of the arguments favoring and opposing the pan-Maya identity movement in *Indigenous Movements and Their Critics*.

The advantage of a dialogic approach is that it promotes the feminist goals of demystifying authoritative "facts" about the past and inviting readers to participate in the construction of knowledge (Longino 1994). At the same time, a dialogic approach makes it possible to argue against blatantly sexist and racist interpretations of the past, thus enabling feminists to mobilize the "emancipatory function of modern science" (Keller 1982). A dialogic approach also preserves the excitement of archaeological research, which is often carried out in the hopes of resolving at least some of the ambiguities in the archaeological record. Finally, a dialogic approach would build a reliable fund of knowledge about gender systems in the past that can be used by gender activists in the present to design effective strategies for promoting systems of gender equality.

2. In humans, biological sex is marked in several ways: by DNA, hormone levels, external genitalia, and skeletal structure. In any given individual, these may or may not coincide (Sørensen 2000:45).

3. Haviland's (1997) reconstruction of gender inequality at Classic Maya Tikal is the subject of vigorous criticism by Pyburn (2004b), but criticism seems warranted only of those who would use the Tikal data to generalize for "Maya culture" as a whole. During the Classic era, gender statuses seem to have differed from one Maya polity to the next.

References

Allison, Melvin J.
    1984   Paleopathology in Peruvian and Chilean Populations. In *Paleopathology at the Origins of Agriculture*. M. N. Cohen and G. J. Armelagos, eds. Pp. 515–30. Orlando: Academic Press.
Ambrose, Stanley H., Jane Buikstra, and Harold W. Krueger
    2003   Status and Gender Differences in Diet at Mound 72, Cahokia, Revealed by Isotopic Analysis of Bone. *Journal of Anthropological Archaeology* 22:217–26.
Ardren, Traci
    2002   Death Became Her: Images of Female Power from Yaxuna Burials. In *Ancient Maya Women*. T. Ardren, ed. Pp. 68–88. Walnut Creek, CA: AltaMira Press.
Ardren, Traci, ed.
    2002   *Ancient Maya Women*. Walnut Creek, CA: AltaMira Press.
Arnold, Bettina, and Nancy L. Wicker, eds.
    2001   *Gender and the Archaeology of Death*. Walnut Creek, CA: AltaMira Press.
Barber, Elizabeth Wayland
    1994   *Women's Work: The First 20,000 Years: Women, Cloth, and Society in Early Times*. New York: Norton.
Blanton, Richard E.
    1994   *Houses and Households: A Comparative Study*. New York: Plenum.
Bruhns, Karen Olsen, and Karen E. Stothert
    1999   *Women in Ancient America*. Norman: University of Oklahoma Press.
Brumfiel, Elizabeth M.
    1991   Weaving and Cooking: Women's Production in Aztec Mexico. In *Engendering Archaeology*. J. M. Gero and M. W. Conkey, eds. Pp. 254–51. Oxford: Blackwell.
    1996a   Figurines and the Aztec State: Testing the Effectiveness of Ideological Domination. In *Gender and Archaeology*. R. P. Wright, ed. Pp. 143–66. Philadelphia: University of Pennsylvania Press.

1996b   The Quality of Tribute Cloth: The Place of Evidence in Archaeological Argument. *American Antiquity* 61:453–62.

2005   Cloth, Gender, Continuity and Change: Fabricating Unity in Anthropology. Presidential Address presented at the 104th Annual Meeting of the American Anthropological Association, Washington, DC.

Butler, Judith

1990   *Gender Trouble: Feminism and the Subversion of Identity.* London: Routledge.

1993   *Bodies That Matter: On the Discursive Limits of "Sex."* London: Routledge.

Chance, John K.

1996   Mesoamerica's Ethnographic Past. *Ethnohistory* 43:379–403.

Chapman, John

1997   Changing Gender Relations in the Later Prehistory of Eastern Hungary. In *Invisible People and Processes: Writing Gender and Childhood into European Archaeology.* J. Moore and E. Scott, eds. Pp. 131–49. London: Leicester University Press.

Cohodas, Marvin

2002   Multiplicity and Discourse in Maya Gender Relations. In *Ancient Maya Gender Identity and Relations.* L. S. Gustafson and A. M. Trevelyan, eds. Pp. 11–53. Westport, CT: Bergin & Garvey.

Combahee River Collective

1977   *The Combahee River Collective Statement.* Reprinted in *Theorizing Feminism.* A. C. Herrman and A. J. Stewart, eds. Pp. 26–33. Boulder, CO: Westview.

Cohen, Mark Nathan, and Sharon Bennett

1993   Skeletal Evidence for Sex Roles and Gender Hierarchies in Prehistory. In *Sex and Gender Hierarchies.* B. D. Miller, ed. Pp. 273–96. Cambridge: Cambridge University Press.

Conkey, Margaret W., and Joan M. Gero

1991   Tensions, Pluralities and Engendering Archaeology: An Introduction to Women and Prehistory. In *Engendering Archaeology.* J. M. Gero and M. W. Conkey, eds. Pp. 3–30. Oxford: Blackwell.

1997   Programme to Practice: Gender and Feminism in Archaeology. *Annual Review of Anthropology* 26:411–37.

Conkey, Margaret W., and Janet D. Spector

1984   Archaeology and the Study of Gender. *Advances in Archaeological Method and Theory* 7:1–38.

Conkey, Margaret W., and Ruth E. Tringham

1995   Archaeology and the Goddess: Exploring the Contours of Feminist Archaeology. In *Feminisms in the Academy*, D. C. Stanton and A. J. Stewart, eds. Pp. 199–247. Ann Arbor: University of Michigan Press.

1996   Cultivating Thinking/Challenging Authority: Some Experiments in Feminist Pedagogy in Archaeology. In *Gender and Archaeology*. R. P. Wright, ed. Pp. 224–50. Philadelphia: University of Pennsylvania Press.

Coontz, Stephanie, and Petra Henderson
    1986   Property Forms, Political Power and Female Labour in the Origins of Class
            and State Societies. In *Women's Work, Men's Property*. S. Coontz and P. Hender-
            son, eds. Pp. 108–55. London: Verso.
Costin, Cathy L.
    1993   Textiles, Women, and Political Economy in Late Prehispanic Peru. *Research in
            Economic Anthropology* 14:3–28.
    1996   Exploring the Relationship between Gender and Craft in Complex Societies:
            Methodological and Theoretical Issues of Gender Attribution. In *Gender and
            Archaeology*. R. P. Wright, ed. Pp. 111–40. Philadelphia: University of Penn-
            sylvania Press.
Crown, Patricia L.
    2000   Gendered Tasks, Power, and Prestige. In *Women and Men in the Prehispanic South-
            west*. P. L. Crown, ed. Pp. 3–41. Santa Fe, NM: School of American Research
            Press.
Crown, Patricia L., and Suzanne K. Fish
    1996   Gender and Status in the Hohokam Pre-Classic to Classic Transition. *Ameri-
            can Anthropologist* 98:803–17.
Danforth, Marie, Keith P. Jacobi, and Mark Nathan Cohen
    1997   Gender and Health among the Colonial Maya of Tipu, Belize. *Ancient Meso-
            america* 8:13–22.
Deagan, Kathleen
    2004   Reconsidering Taíno Social Dynamics after Spanish Conquest: Gender and
            Class in Culture Contact Studies. *American Antiquity* 69:597–626.
di Leonardo, Micaela
    1991   Introduction: Gender, Culture, and Political Economy. In *Gender at the Cross-
            roads of Knowledge*. M. di Leonardo, ed. Pp. 1–48. Berkeley: University of Cali-
            fornia Press.
Dobres, Marcia-Anne
    1995   Gender and Prehistoric Technology: On the Social Agency of Technical Strat-
            egies. *World Archaeology* 27:25–49.
Engels, Frederick
    1972   [1884] *Origin of the Family, Private Property, and the State*. E. B. Leacock, ed. New
            York: International Books.
Etienne, Mona, and Eleanor Leacock, eds.
    1980   *Women and Colonization: Anthropological Perspectives*. New York: Praeger.
Fabian, Johannes
    1983   *Time and the Other: How Anthropology Makes Its Object*. New York: Columbia Uni-
            versity Press.
Fekete, Eva
    1996   Excavating Gender: Rethinking the Archaeology of Maya Mortuary Practice.
            Master's thesis, York University.

Gailey, Christine W.
  1987   *From Kinship to Kingship: Gender Hierarchy and State Formation in the Tongan Islands.*
          Austin: University of Texas Press.
Gero, Joan M.
  1991   Who Experienced What in Prehistory? A Narrative Explanation from Quey-
          ash, Peru. In *Processual and Postprocessual Archaeologies.* R. W. Preucel, ed. Pp.
          126–39. Carbondale: Southern Illinois University Center for Archaeological
          Investigations.
  1992   Feasts and Females: Gender Ideology and Political Meals in the Andes. *Nor-
          wegian Archaeological Review* 25:15–30.
  1996   Archaeological Practice and Gendered Encounters with Field Data. In *Gender
          and Archaeology.* R. P. Wright, ed. Pp. 251–80. Philadelphia: University of
          Pennsylvania Press.
Gero, Joan M., and M. Cristina Scattolin
  2002   Beyond Complementarity and Hierarchy: New Definitions for Archaeological
          Gender Relations. In *In Pursuit of Gender: Worldwide Archaeological Approaches.* S. M.
          Nelson and M. Rosen-Ayalon, eds. Pp. 155–71. Walnut Creek, CA: Alta-
          Mira Press.
Gerry, John P., and Meredith S. Chesson
  2000   Classic Maya Diet and Gender Relationships. In *Gender and Material Culture in
          Archaeological Perspective.* M. Donald and L. Hurcombe, eds. Pp. 250–64. New
          York: St. Martin's Press.
Gilchrist, Roberta
  1999   *Gender and Archaeology: Contesting the Past.* London: Routledge.
Goodman, Alan H., and George J. Armelagos
  1985   Disease and Death at Dr. Dickson's Mounds. *Natural History* 94(9):12–18.
Hames-García, Michael R.
  2000   "Who Are Our Own People?": Challenges for a Theory of Social Identity.
          In *Reclaiming Identity: Realist Theory and the Predicament of Postmodernism.* P. M. L.
          Moya and M. R. Hames-García, eds. Pp. 102–29. Berkeley: University of
          California Press.
Hastorf, Christine A.
  1991   Gender, Space, and Food in Prehistory. In *Engendering Archaeology: Women and
          Prehistory.* J. M. Gero and M. W. Conkey, eds. Pp. 132–59. Oxford: Black-
          well.
Haviland, William A.
  1997   The Rise and Fall of Sexual Inequality: Death and Gender at Tikal, Guate-
          mala. *Ancient Mesoamerica* 8:1–12.
Hays-Gilpin, Kelley
  1999   Beyond Mother Earth and Father Sky: Sex and Gender in Ancient Southwest-
          ern Visual Arts. In *Reading the Body.* A. E. Rautman, ed. Pp. 165–86. Philadel-
          phia: University of Pennsylvania Press.

2004   *Ambiguous Images: Gender and Rock Art.* Walnut Creek, CA: AltaMira Press.

Hegmon, Michelle, Scott G. Ortman, and Jeannette L. Mobley-Tanaka

2000   Women, Men, and the Organization of Space. In *Women and Men in the Prehispanic Southwest.* P. L. Crown, ed. Pp. 43–90. Santa Fe, NM: School of American Research Press.

Hendon, Julia A.

1997   Women's Work, Women's Space, and Women's Status among the Classic-Period Maya Elite of the Copan Valley, Honduras. In *Women in Prehistory: North America and Mesoamerica.* C. Claassen and R. A. Joyce, eds. Pp. 33–46. Philadelphia: University of Pennsylvania Press.

1999   Multiple Sources of Prestige and the Social Evaluation of Women in Prehispanic Mesoamerica. In *Material Symbols.* J. E. Robb, ed. Pp. 257–76. Occasional Paper 26. Carbondale: Center for Archaeological Investigations, Southern Illinois University.

Hodder, Ian

1986   *Reading the Past.* Cambridge: Cambridge University Press.

2000   Agency and Individuals in Long-Term Processes. In *Agency in Archaeology.* M. A. Dobres and J. Robb, eds. Pp. 21–33. London: Routledge.

Hollimon, Sandra E.

1997   The Third Gender in Native California: Two-Spirit Undertakers among the Chumash and Their Neighbors. In *Women in Prehistory: North America and Mesoamerica.* C. Claassen and R. A. Joyce, eds. Pp. 173–88. Philadelphia: University of Pennsylvania Press.

2000   Sex, Health, and Gender Roles among the Arikara of the Northern Plains. In *Reading the Body: Representations and Remains in the Archaeological Record.* A. E. Rautman, ed. Pp. 25–37. Philadelphia: University of Pennsylvania Press.

2001   Warfare and Gender in the Northern Plains: Osteological Evidence of Trauma Reconsidered. In *Gender and the Archaeology of Death.* B. Arnold and N. L. Wicker, eds. Pp. 179–93. Walnut Creek, CA: AltaMira Press.

hooks, bell

1984   *Feminist Theory from Margin to Center.* Boston: South End Press.

Hopkins, Mary R.

1987   An Explication of the Plans of Some Teotihuacan Apartment Compounds. In *Teotihuacan: Nuevos Datos, Nuevas Síntesis, Nuevos Problemas.* E. McClung and E. Rattray, eds. Pp. 369–88. Mexico City: Universidad Nacional Autónoma de México.

Inomata, Takeshi, and Laura R. Stiver

1998   Floor Assemblages from Burned Structures at Aguateca, Guatemala: A Study of Classic Maya Households. *Journal of Field Archaeology* 25:431–52.

Joyce, Rosemary A.

1996   The Construction of Gender in Classic Maya Monuments. In *Gender and Archaeology.* R. P. Wright, ed. Pp. 167–95. Philadelphia: University of Pennsylvania Press.

2000   *Gender and Power in Prehispanic Mesoamerica.* Austin: University of Texas Press.
2001a   Burying the Dead at Tlatilco: Social Memory and Social Identities. In *Social Memory, Identity and Death: Anthropological Perspectives on Mortuary Rituals.* M. S. Chesson, ed. Pp. 12–26. Archaeological Papers of the American Anthropological Association 10. Washington, DC: American Anthropological Association.
2001b   Negotiating Sex and Gender in Classic Maya Society. In *Gender in Pre-Hispanic America.* C. F. Klein, ed. Pp. 109–41. Washington, DC: Dumbarton Oaks.
2004   Embodied Subjectivity: Gender, Femininity, Masculinity, Sexuality. In *A Companion to Social Archaeology.* L. Meskell and R. W. Preucel, eds. Pp. 82–95. Oxford: Blackwell.

Keller, Evelyn Fox
1982   Feminism and Science. *Signs* 7:589–602.

King, Stacie M.
2004   Spinning and Weaving in Early Postclassic Coastal Oaxaca. Paper presented at the 69th Annual Meeting of the Society for American Archaeology, Montreal.

Lambert, Patricia M.
2001   Auditory Exostoses: A Clue to Gender in Prehistoric and Historic Farming Communities of North Carolina and Virginia. In *Archaeological Studies of Gender in the Southeastern United States.* J. M. Eastman and C. B. Rodning, eds. Pp. 152–72. Gainesville: University Press of Florida.

Larsen, Clark S.
1997   *Bioarchaeology.* Cambridge: Cambridge University Press.

Leacock, Eleanor
1983   Interpreting the Origins of Gender Inequality. *Dialectical Anthropology* 7:163–83.

Lillie, M. C.
1997   Women and Children in Prehistory: Resource Sharing and Social Stratification at the Mesolithic-Neolithic Transition in Ukraine. In *Invisible People and Processes.* J. Moore and E. Scott, eds. Pp. 213–28. London: Leicester University Press.

Longino, Helen
1994   In Search of Feminist Epistemology. *The Monist* 77:472–85.

Luedke, Tracy
2004   Gendered States: Gender and Agency in Economic Models of Great Zimbabwe. In *Ungendering Archaeology.* K. A. Pyburn, ed. Pp. 47–70. New York: Routledge.

Martin, Debra L.
1998   Violence against Women in the La Plata River Valley (A.D. 1000–1300). In *Troubled Times: Violence and Warfare in the Past.* D. L. Martin and D. W. Frayer, eds. Pp. 45–75. Amsterdam: Gordon and Breach.

McCafferty, Geoffrey G., and Sharisse D. McCafferty

2002   Boys and Girls Interrupted: Mortuary Evidence on the Children of Postclassic Cholula, Puebla. Paper presented at the 101st Annual Meeting of the American Anthropological Association, New Orleans.

McCafferty, Sharisse D., and Geoffrey G. McCafferty

1991   Spinning and Weaving as Female Gender Identity in Post-Classic Mexico. In *Textile Traditions of Mesoamerica and the Andes*. M. B. Schevill, J. C. Berlo, and E. B. Dwyer, eds. Pp. 19–44. Austin: University of Texas Press.

2000   Textile Production in Postclassic Cholula, Mexico. *Ancient Mesoamerica* 11:39–54.

Meskell, Lynn

1998a   An Archaeology of Social Relations in an Egyptian Village. *Journal of Archaeological Method and Theory* 5:209–43.

1998b   Intimate Archaeologies: The Case of Kha and Merit. *World Archaeology* 29:363–79.

2005   De/Naturalizing Gender in Prehistory. In *Complexities: Beyond Nature and Nurture*. S. McKinnon and S. Silverman, eds. Pp. 157–75. Chicago: University of Chicago Press.

Meskell, Lynn M., and Rosemary A. Joyce

2003   *Embodied Lives: Figuring Ancient Maya and Egyptian Experience*. London: Routledge.

Mohatny, Chandra

1988   Under Western Eyes: Feminist Scholarship and Colonial Discourses. *Feminist Review* 30:61–88.

Molleson, Theya

1994   The Eloquent Bones of Abu Hureyra. *Scientific American* 271(2):70–75.

Moore, Henrietta L.

1993   The Differences Within and the Differences Between. In *Gendered Anthropology*. T. Del Valle, ed. Pp. 193–203. London: Routledge.

Morris, Rosalind C.

1995   All Made Up: Performance Theory and the New Anthropology of Sex and Gender. *Annual Review of Anthropology* 24:567–92.

Neitzel, Jill E.

2000   Gender Hierarchies: A Comparative Analysis of Mortuary Data. In *Women and Men in the Prehispanic Southwest*. P. L. Crown, ed. Pp. 137–68. Santa Fe, NM: School of American Research Press.

Nelson, Sarah M.

1990   Diversity of the Upper Paleolithic "Venus" Figurines and Archeological Mythology. In *Powers of Observation*. S. M. Nelson and A. B. Kehoe, eds. Pp. 11–22. Archaeological Papers of the American Anthropological Association 2. Washington, DC: American Anthropological Association.

1997   *Gender in Archaeology*. Walnut Creek, CA: AltaMira Press.

Nelson, Sarah M., ed.

2003   *Ancient Queens: Archaeological Explorations.* Walnut Creek, CA: AltaMira Press.
         Nelson, Sarah M., and Myriam Rosen-Ayalon, eds.
2002   *In Pursuit of Gender: Worldwide Archaeological Approaches.* Walnut Creek, CA:
         AltaMira Press.
Nguyen, Minh T.
2000   "It Matters to Get the Facts Straight": Joy Kogawa, Realism, and Objectivity
         of Values. In *Reclaiming Identity: Realist Theory and the Predicament of Postmodernism.*
         P. M. L. Moya and M. R. Hames-García, eds. Pp. 171–204. Berkeley: Uni-
         versity of California Press.
Peterson, Jane
2002   *Sexual Revolutions: Gender and Labor at the Dawn of Agriculture.* Walnut Creek, CA:
         AltaMira Press.
Price, T. Douglas, G. Grupe, and P. Schrörter
1994   Reconstruction of Migration Patterns in the Bell Beaker Period by Stable
         Strontium Isotope Analysis. *Applied Geochemistry* 9:413–17.
Price, T. Douglas, C. M. Johnson, J. A. Ezzo, J. H. Burton, and J. A. Ericson
1994   Residential Mobility in the Prehistoric Southwest United States. *Journal of
         Archaeological Science* 24:315–30.
Pyburn, K. Anne
2004a   Rethinking Complex Society. In *Ungendering Civilization.* K. A. Pyburn, ed. Pp.
         1–46. New York: Routledge.
2004b   Ungendering the Maya. In *Ungendering Civilization.* K. A. Pyburn, ed. Pp. 216–
         33. New York: Routledge.
Rega, Elizabeth
1996   Age, Gender and Biological Reality in the Early Bronze Age Cemetery at
         Mokrin. In *Invisible People and Processes.* J. Moore and E. Scott, eds. Pp. 229–47.
         London: Leicester University Press.
2000   The Gendering of Children in the EBA Cemetery at Mokrin. In *Gender and
         Material Culture in Archaeological Perspective.* M. Donald and L. Hurcombe, eds.
         Pp. 238–49. New York: St. Martin's Press.
Robb, John E.
1994a   Burial and Social Reproduction in the Peninsular Italian Neolithic. *Journal of
         Mediterranean Archaeology* 7:27–71.
1994b   Gender Contradictions, Moral Coalitions, and Inequality in Prehistoric Italy.
         Journal of European Archaeology 2:20–49.
1997   Violence and Gender in Early Italy. In *Troubled Times: Violence and Warfare in the
         Past.* D. L. Martin and D. W. Frayer, eds. Pp. 111–44. Amsterdam: Gordon
         and Breach.
Robin, Cynthia
2002   Gender and Maya Farming: Chan Nòohol, Belize. In *Ancient Maya Women.* T.
         Ardren, ed. Pp. 12–30. Walnut Creek, CA: AltaMira Press.
2004   Social Diversity and Everyday Life within Classic Maya Settlements. In *Meso-*

american Archaeology. J. A. Hendon and R. A. Joyce, eds. Pp. 148–68. Oxford: Blackwell.

In press   Gender, Farming, and Long-Term Change: Maya Historical and Archaeological Perspectives. *Current Anthropology*.

Romanowicz, Janet V., and Rita P. Wright
   1996   Gendered Perspectives in the Classroom. In *Gender and Archaeology*. R. P. Wright, ed. Pp. 199–223. Philadelphia: University of Pennsylvania Press.

Rubin, Gayle
   1984   Thinking Sex. In *Pleasure and Danger: Exploring Female Sexuality*. C. S. Vance, ed. Pp. 267–319. London: Routledge and Kegan Paul.

Sacks, Karen B.
   1982   *Sisters and Wives: The Past and Future of Sexual Equality*. Urbana: University of Illinois Press.
   1988   *Caring by the Hour: Women, Work and Organizing at Duke Medical Center*. Urbana: University of Illinois Press.

Sassaman, Kenneth E.
   1992   Gender and Technology at the Archaic-Woodland "Transition." In *Exploring Gender through Archaeology*. C. Claassen, ed. Pp. 71–79. Madison, WI: Prehistory Press.

Savage, Stephen H.
   2000   The Status of Women in Predynastic Egypt as Revealed through Mortuary Analysis. In *Reading the Body*. A. E. Rautman, ed. Pp. 77–92. Philadelphia: University of Pennsylvania Press.

Schmidt, Robert A., and Barbara L. Voss, eds.
   2000   *Archaeologies of Sexuality*. London: Routledge.

Shanks, Michael, and Christopher Tilley
   1987   *Re-Constructing Archaeology*. Cambridge: Cambridge University Press.

Silverblatt, Irene
   1987   *Moon, Sun, and Witches: Gender Ideologies and Class in Inca and Colonial Peru*. Princeton, NJ: Princeton University Press.
   1988   Women in States. *Annual Review in Anthropology* 17:427–60.
   1991   Interpreting Women in States. In *Gender at the Crossroads of Knowledge*, M. di Leonardo, ed. Pp. 140–71. Berkeley: University of California Press.

Sørensen, Marie Louise Stig
   2000   *Gender Archaeology*. Cambridge: Polity Press.
   2004   The Archaeology of Gender. In *A Companion to Archaeology*. J. Bintliff, ed. Pp. 75–91. Oxford: Blackwell.

Spence, Michael W.
   1974   Residential Practices and the Distribution of Skeletal Traits in Teotihuacán. *Man* 9:262–73.

Stahl, Ann B.
   2001   *Making History in Banda: Anthropological Visions of Africa's Past*. Cambridge: Cambridge University Press.

Sullivan, Thelma D.
  1982   Tlazolteotl-Ixcuina: The Great Spinner and Weaver. In *The Art and Iconography of Late Post-Classic Central Mexico*. E. H. Boone, ed. Pp. 7–35. Washington, DC: Dumbarton Oaks.

Summers, Roger
  1969   *Ancient Mining in Rhodesia and Adjacent Areas*. Salisbury: Trustees of the National Museums of Rhodesia.

Sweely, Tracy L.
  1998   Personal Interactions: The Implications of Spatial Arrangements for Power Relations at Cerén, El Salvador. *World Archaeology* 29:393–406.

Trigger, Bruce G.
  1980   Archaeology and the Image of the American Indian. *American Antiquity* 45:662–76.

Tringham, Ruth E.
  1991   Households with Faces: The Challenge of Gender in Prehistoric Architectural Remains. In *Engendering Archaeology*. J. M. Gero and M. W. Conkey, eds. Pp. 93–131. Oxford: Blackwell.

Walker, P. L.
  1989   Cranial Injuries as Evidence of Violence in Prehistoric Southern California. *American Journal of Physical Anthropology* 80:313–23.

Warren, Kay B.
  1998   *Indigenous Movements and Their Critics*. Princeton, NJ: Princeton University Press.

Weglian, Emily
  2001   Grave Goods Do Not a Gender Make: A Case Study from Singen am Hohentwiel, Germany. In *Gender and the Archaeology of Death*. B. Arnold and N. L. Wicker, eds. Pp. 137–55. Walnut Creek, CA: AltaMira Press.

Weismantel, Mary
  2004   Moche Sex Pots: Reproduction and Temporality in Ancient South America. *American Anthropologist* 106:495–505.

White, Christine D., Michael W. Spence, Fred J. Longstaffe, Hilary Stuart-Williams, and Kimberley R. Law
  2002   Geographic Identities of the Sacrificial Victims from the Feathered Serpent Pyramid, Teotihuacan: Implications for the Nature of State Power. *Latin American Antiquity* 13:217–36.

White, Christine D., Rebecca Storey, Fred J. Longstaffe, and Michael W. Spence
  2004   Immigration, Assimilation, and Status in the Ancient City of Teotihuacan: Stable Isotopic Evidence from Tlajinga 22. *Latin American Antiquity* 15:176–98.

Whitley, David S.
  1994   By the Hunter, for the Gatherer: Art, Social Relations and Subsistence Change in the Prehistoric Great Basin. *World Archaeology* 25:356–72.

Wilkerson, William S.
  2000   Is There Something You Need to Tell Me? In *Reclaiming Identity*. P. M. L. Moya and M. R. Hames-García, eds. Pp. 251–78. Berkeley: University of California Press.
Wilkinson, Richard G., and Karen M. Van Wagenen
  1993   Violence against Women: Prehistoric Skeletal Evidence from Michigan. *Midcontinental Journal of Archaeology* 18:190–216.
Winters, Howard D.
  1968   Value Systems and Trade Cycles of the Late Archaic in the Midwest. In *New Perspectives in Archaeology*. S. R. Binford and L. R. Binford, eds. Pp. 175–222. Chicago: Aldine.
Wobst, Martin
  1977   The Archaeo-Ethnology of Hunter-Gatherers and the Tyranny of the Ethnographic Record in Archaeology. *American Antiquity* 43:303–9.
Wylie, Alison
  1985   The Reaction against Analogy. *Advances in Archaeological Method and Theory* 8:63–III.
  1992   The Interplay of Evidential Constraints and Political Interests: Recent Archaeological Research on Gender. *American Antiquity* 57:15–35.
  1996   The Constitution of Archaeological Evidence: Gender Politics and Science. In *The Disunity of Science*. P. Galison and P. Stump, eds. Pp. 311–43. Palo Alto, CA: Stanford University Press.
Yoffee, Norman
  1993   Too Many Chiefs? (or, Safe Texts for the '90s). In *Archaeological Theory: Who Sets the Agenda?* N. Yoffee and A. Sherratt, eds. Pp. 60–78. Cambridge: Cambridge University Press.
Zagarell, Allen
  1986   Trade, Women, Class, and Society in Ancient Western Asia. *Current Anthropology* 27:415–30.

Feminist Theory and Gender Research in Historical Archaeology

2

SUZANNE M. SPENCER-WOOD

I N THIS CHAPTER, I use the development of feminist theory as a framework
to survey gender research in historical archaeology. My aim is to increase
awareness, overt expression, and disciplinary dialogue concerning the application of feminist theoretical approaches in gender research. To this end, I analyze
the feminist theoretical approaches that are implicit in much gender research in
historical archaeology. In the final section of this chapter, I consider issues in
feminist theory and how they may be addressed by synthesizing different feminist
approaches.

This chapter selects from a wide variety of gender research in historical
archaeology to outline the scope of the field. Although technically historical
archaeology includes all societies with written records, this chapter is limited to
Deetz's (1977:5) definition of historical archaeology as the archaeology of European colonies, particularly America and Australia. Despite the continued predominance of ungendered discourse in historical archaeology, the amount of gender
research in America and Australia has grown rapidly since groundbreaking feminist publications in the late 1980s (Bickford 1987; Spencer-Wood 1987a).

All feminist research is concerned with gender, but not all gender research
applies feminist concepts, theories, or methods. Feminists are unified by the theoretical standpoint that gender is a foundational social structure that always needs
to be analyzed in archaeological research as much as class has been and ethnicity
and race increasingly are. The feminist standpoint that gender must be analyzed
leads to new questions that push archaeological research, method, and theory
beyond existing epistemological assumptions about what kinds of archaeological
knowledge can be created (e.g., Conkey and Gero 1991; Gero 1991; Linton
1971; Wylie 1991a, 1991b).

A core difference between feminist and nonfeminist archaeology is the definition of the concept of gender. Early gender research in historical archaeology

followed the traditional practice of equating gender with biological sex. In the 1970s, feminist theory distinguished biological sex from the cultural construction of gender as a social structure (Spencer-Wood 1992). The feminist conceptualization of gender—and, more recently, sexuality—as separate from biological sex reveals the foundational role of feminist critique as the first step in the development of feminist concepts, theories, frameworks, methods, and research. If the process of feminist critique of androcentrism is not first undertaken, then gender is uncritically explained using received male-biased theoretical perspectives, frameworks, concepts, and methods (Spencer-Wood 1995).

Another major distinction is that feminist research *analyzes* gender power dynamics, while nonfeminists uncritically accept the dominant patriarchal gender ideology as universally descriptive of past gender practices. Nonfeminist gender research assumes and reifies stereotypic asymmetrical constructions of gender roles and power dynamics as innate and unchanging, naturalizing and legitimating the devaluation and subordination of women in modern patriarchal society. Feminist critique has exposed the androcentrism involved in legitimating Western gender inequalities by projecting them onto other cultures as universal (Spencer-Wood 1992).

This chapter is presented according to the historical development of feminist theories, although these theories have been simultaneously applied and sometimes combined in historical archaeology. Feminist theory developed as a process of critique of androcentric biases and reflexive critique that can be metaphorically understood in analogy with the process of peeling an onion, in this case the androcentric onion of male bias. Peeling away one layer of androcentrism reveals deeper layers of male bias that need to be critiqued and corrected. Male biases in different layers support and reinforce each other, creating a complex androcentric structure of knowledge that is internally consistent and difficult to critique from within the framework (Spencer-Wood 1991c, 1995).

Feminist critique first revealed male biases in the surface layer of ungendered paradigms, frameworks, method, and theory that have been traditionally used to construct supposedly ungendered pasts that often generalize men's experiences as universal and disappear women. This critique led to remedial feminist research making visible the importance of women's public and/or domestic roles. However, sometimes women's stereotypic domestic roles were just added to androcentric constructions of the past, using what has been called the "add women and stir" approach (Bunch 1987:140). Postmodern feminist theory critiques binary constructions of gender and has instead researched the diversity and fluidity of gender ideologies, identities, roles, relationships, and power dynamics due to the complex intersections of gender, class, race, ethnicity, and other social dimensions (Spencer-Wood 1995).

Feminist Critiques of Male Biases in Historical Archaeology

Correcting male-centered bias requires a critical paradigm starting from feminist standpoint epistemology rather than an androcentric epistemology. Feminist critiques developed as a process of asking critical questions, from the standpoint of a feminist analysis of women's experiences, about what was missing or androcentric in ungendered and stereotypic constructions of the past.

Androcentric Paradigms and Models

Feminist critiques in fields with predominantly ungendered discourse, including archaeology, have asked why and how such a fundamental social structure as gender has been excluded from the research paradigm (e.g., Conkey and Spector 1984; Englestad 1991; Spencer-Wood 1992; Wylie 1991a, 1991b). Social stratification had always been considered important to research. In historical archaeology, race relations on plantations had been analyzed since the 1970s (Singleton 1990), and ethnicity was highlighted as a topic in 1980 (e.g., Schuyler 1980).

Much of historical archaeology had followed the predominant practice in anthropology analyzing cultures as monolithic wholes with some level of social stratification. Gender systems were seldom analyzed because they were assumed to involve the same innate tasks worldwide, so there was no variation through time or between cultures that required explanation with archaeological theory or research (Wylie 1991b:34).

Historical archaeology in America developed into a field in the late 1960s and was first taught in Australia in 1974 (Lydon 1995:73). In the 1960s, the rise of Binford's new archaeology included the systems theory model of culture that either excluded gender entirely or subsumed it within the social system. Wylie (1991a, 1991b) critiqued systems theory for excluding gender as a foundational subsystem that cannot be reduced to any other subsystem. Further, feminist archaeologists critiqued how the scientific focus on large-scale patterns and processes led to ignoring the importance of small-scale internal variables, particularly gender and ethnicity (Conkey and Spector 1984; Spencer-Wood 1995, 2000; Wylie 1991a, 1991b).

Binford (1962) also theorized a hierarchical ladder of inference in which ideological and social information were more difficult to analyze from archaeological data than information about technology or subsistence. This widely accepted hegemonic model of inference effectively took gender ideology and gender power dynamics off the historical archaeological research agenda until feminists began to reclaim them (e.g., Spencer-Wood 1987a, 1989a, 1991b; Weber 1991; Yentsch 1991a, 1991b, 1991c).

Historical archaeology drew on the dominant ungendered cultural paradigm reified in both anthropology and history in which elite white men's roles, activities, and viewpoints were represented as the genderless norm. Because white men are the dominant cultural group, their accounts of historic men's ideas and behaviors were considered representative of the entire culture. The underlying assumption of this paradigm is that men have always been the significant members of society who made the important public history, while women's domestic roles and activities were not significant to history. The disappearance of women and other minorities from the past was facilitated by the low frequency of their voices in historical documents, which were written mostly by elite white men and a few elite women (Spencer-Wood 1992, 1995).

Feminist Critiques of Androcentrism in Ungendered Constructions of the Past

Historical archaeologists have often uncritically adopted historians' unitary ungendered overgeneralizations of men's viewpoints as *the* American colonial mind or universal meanings of material culture (e.g., Boorstin and Boorstin 1989; Glassie 1975). Drawing on Glassie (1975), Deetz (1988) constructed a supposedly ungendered structural analysis of the stylistic evolution of Anglo-American architecture, ceramics, and gravestones from the seventeenth century to the nineteenth century. He described these styles as evolving progressively from chaotic, irrational, natural colors in the seventeenth century to orderly, cultural, intellectual, white-colored architecture and artifacts in the nineteenth century. This supposedly ungendered evolutionary construction in fact de-genders and masks the well-known ideological dichotomy between irrational, chaotic, natural, inferior women in opposition to cultural, rational, orderly, superior men. In addition, Deetz's framework also carries racist undertones in the evolutionary progress from colored artifacts to white ones (critiqued by Spencer-Wood 1993, 1995). Deetz was no doubt unaware of the sexist and racist dichotomies underlying Glassie's construction of architectural evolution that Deetz applied to other kinds of artifacts.

Androcentric Biases in Ungendered Theoretical Frameworks, Epistemology, and Language

Deetz (1988) justified his construction of the evolution of American colonial culture in dichotomies with a structuralist argument that binary thinking is universal and natural. In the paradigm of structuralism, the principal contention that all thought and culture can be reduced to a set of binary oppositions is based on the heterosexist binary construction of gender and biological sex in mutually exclusive *either* male *or* female opposed categories, ignoring other genders such as berdache or transvestites and the biological diversity that includes hermaphrodites. Structuralism is deeply embedded in Western thought and belief, as represented in the ungendered paradigm of logic that insists on categorizing something as *either* P *or* not P (Spencer-Wood 1992, 1995). Hodder and Hutson (2003:68, 90) have critiqued how structuralism constructs cultures in ahistorical dichotomies that cannot analyze or explain processes of culture change.

Feminist epistemological critiques have unmasked purportedly objective and ungendered paradigms such as structuralism to show that they actually represent men's interests, perspectives, questions, and experiences. Similarly, at the deeper level of supposedly generic language, the use of androcentric nouns such as "mankind" or "man" and the male pronoun "he" often represent a male-biased view as universal (Spencer-Wood 1992). Scientific methodology and language predominantly used in archaeology have misrepresented archaeological research as completely objective, masking the subjectivity involved in what research theories and questions are considered important, the methods used to select and analyze data, and the resulting conclusions (Longino and Doell 1983).

The use of the scientific omniscient third-person passive voice stating what the facts or data show masks the subjective processes of interpretation and inference, making them more difficult to challenge (Spencer-Wood 1992, 1995). Thus, feminists argue for including the researcher as a person, as the I who explains how s/he made the subjective decisions in the research process (Longino 1989; Spencer-Wood 1995:130). It is particularly important for archaeologists to reveal their subjective decisions because interpretations are often underdetermined by data (Wylie 1992). Janet Spector's 1993 book *What This Awl Means* exemplifies the value of the use of the first-person active voice by archaeologists to reveal how gendered narratives about people's lives in the past can be imaginatively constructed from ethnohistorical and archaeological evidence.

The storytelling school in historical archaeology, inspired by Spector's book, shows how telling the stories of real people in the past requires addressing the

complex intersections of gender identities, roles, relationships, and power dynamics with class, age, race, religion, and other social dimensions (e.g., Costello 2000;
Praetzellis and Praetzellis 1998; Yamin 2004). While storytelling may require
some imagination when documentary data are lacking, this school has increased
the reconstruction of *documented* individual life histories that are at least as interesting as the more imaginative stories (compare Cook 1998 with Heck and Balicki
1998).

Feminist Critiques of Androcentric Methods

Methodologically, women have been disappeared from the past by the practice of
using male-defined ungendered categories of analysis. For instance, a male viewpoint was evident in calling brothels "sporting culture" or "entertainment" sites,
when for the prostitutes brothels were primarily workplaces and secondarily
domiciles (e.g., Baker 1983, critiqued in Spencer-Wood 1991c:238; Kennedy
1989; Lawrence-Cheney 1991). Deetz (1977) used supposedly ungendered language in discussing the yeo*man's* dairy but did not discuss the normative importance of women's roles in dairying, as did Yentsch (1991b). Henretta (1971)
presented an ungendered account of the socioeconomic structure of Boston based
on men's occupations without even mentioning women. Classes defined by men's
occupations reify in modern discourse the historic Western legal practice of the
male head of household representing his wife and children in the public sphere
(Millett 1970).

The patriarchal dominance of men as a group has also been reified by the
usual practice of naming domestic sites and gardens for the surname or whole
name of the male head of household. While it is perfectly valid to research the
male head of household's relationship to his house and garden, feminists have
critiqued the exclusive androcentric focus on men. They call this the "male
power-garden syndrome" of interpreting gardens as expressing the prestige of
only the male head of household, ignoring his wife's prestige and the work of
servants or slaves who created the garden (Spencer-Wood 1991c:237). Weber
(1991) critiqued the neglect of elite women's gardens and gardening expertise in
historical archaeology.

Some feminist historical archaeologists have critiqued the androcentric practice of constructing the past in the shape of essentialist binary gender stereotypes
(Seifert 1991a; Spencer-Wood 1989a, 1989c, 1991a, 1991c:237, 1992, 1995).
The dominant gender dichotomy has led to the tendency to dichotomize the
classification of sites into *either* female-domestic *or* male-public sites. Women's
roles have been ignored at "public" sites occupied predominantly by men, such as

military sites (Clements 1993; Starbuck 1994), mining camps (Hardesty 1989), and lumber camps (Brashler 1991) in America and a railroad construction camp and telegraph station in Australia (Bickford 1993:198). On the other hand, men are often overlooked at domestic sites that are associated with women in the gender dichotomy. Further, sites where women are prominent have often been labeled domestic sites even if they also held public significance for women. For instance, brothels have been stereotypically labeled primarily domestic sites because they were associated with women (e.g., Seifert 1991b, 1994), ignoring or downplaying the fact that they were women's public entrepreneurial businesses.

Many historical archaeologists use South's (1977) ungendered classification system of artifacts into functional categories such as architectural, kitchen, and personal artifacts. Spencer-Wood (1991c:236, 1995:126) has critiqued the androcentrism in South's ungendered personal and kitchen categories. Yentsch (1991a:254) further unpacked South's kitchen artifact group, showing that it lumped together in a meaningless category ceramics used in very different gendered activities, ranging from food preparation and storage usually by women in the kitchen, pantry, or basement to food service tableware used by women and men in the dining room.

Although South's categories appear ungendered, implicit assumptions gendering these categories may have contributed to androcentric analyses. For instance, Seifert (1991b) followed South's classification of cosmetics as personal artifacts, although she was analyzing a brothel site where cosmetics held their most significant meanings as work-related artifacts. She failed to analyze cosmetics as work-related artifacts because she uncritically accepted and used South's categorization of cosmetics as personal artifacts (Spencer-Wood 1995).

Feminist Theories in Historical Archaeology

The historical development of feminist theory is often simplified into three "waves." However, these three waves do not capture the full range of diversity in feminist theories or their frequent use in complex combinations. Further, the wave metaphor gives the incorrect impression that each wave of theory was replaced by the subsequent wave. In actual fact, each wave of theory has continued to be developed as subsequent waves of theory were created, often through reflexive critique of previous theories (Nelson 2002). What the wave image does correctly represent is that the most recent wave of feminist theory is the most prevalent.

Another problem is that different feminists define the waves of feminist theory in a variety of ways. This chapter resolves this issue by using the framework that includes the widest range of feminist theories that have been developed throughout history. This framework is the most widely accepted and used because it is most inclusive of the variety in feminist theory. In this framework, the first wave of feminist theory started in the Enlightenment, the second wave began with Betty Friedan's *Feminine Mystique* in 1963 (although it has precedents from the mid-nineteenth century), and the third wave started in the 1980s (Donovan 2001; Lorber 2001).

First-Wave Feminist Egalitarian Liberal Theory

Liberal egalitarian feminist theory critiques the patriarchal gender ideology that devalues women and their domestic roles and conducts research demonstrating that women exercised social agency in a variety of important roles in both public and domestic spheres. Liberal feminist theory and research demonstrates that gender stereotypes were not universally practiced through three different kinds of research paradigms concerning the ways that women have been social agents as much as men (Donovan 2001).

Research on Women's Public Roles

The first egalitarian feminist paradigm critiques sexist stereotypes of a biologically determined universal dominance of men in public roles. Instead, this corrective paradigm involves asking about and seeking evidence that historic women had important public roles, even in patriarchal societies (e.g., Lorber 2001:25–28, Nelson 2003; Valian 1998; Wertheimer 1977). This paradigm measures women against the standard of public men and does not challenge the status hierarchy in which public roles are judged to be more important than domestic roles. However, neither this paradigmatic limitation nor the persistence of patriarchy can be used to dismiss the significance of women's social agency in public roles.

In America, archaeologists have researched native women who had important public positions in the European fur trade (Frink 2005; Hollimon 2005; Jackson 1994). Archaeologists have researched some Euro-American women who managed plantations (Anderson 2004), founded and led utopian communes (Spencer-Wood, in press), overcame legal restrictions to own land as wives (e.g., Bell 2001; Lewis 2003), or operated merchant businesses or shops with their husbands or as widows (Elliott 1977; Goodwin 1999; Jamieson 2000:146; Little 1994; Spencer-Wood 1987b:336–37; Wheeler 2000). Research has also been undertaken on white women who were doctors (Sipe 2003; Spencer-Wood 1994b, 2003); ship captains and navigators (Smith 1989); schoolteachers and principals (Gibb and Preston 2003), hotel operators (Hardesty 1994); day care workers, dietitians, social workers, nurses, librarians, and street inspectors (Spencer-Wood

1987a, 1991b, 1994a, 1994b); prison matrons (Spencer-Wood 2001b); crafts-women (Hautaniemi and Rotman 2003); seamstresses, laundresses, and entrepre-neurs (Hardesty 1994); and factory workers (e.g., Beaudry and Mrozowski 2004). Archaeologists have further researched slave women who produced pot-tery (McEwan 1991:33–34) and agricultural produce and cooked food that they took to markets in southern cities (Franklin 2001; Yentsch 1994:243, 246). Postbellum African American women have been researched who worked as mid-wives (e.g., Wilkie 2003), laundresses, domestic servants, shop owners (Davidson 2004:88–102), beauty salon owners, and entrepreneurs, such as the famous Madame C. J. Walker, founder of a major company selling African American skin whitening and hair straightening products (Mullins 1999:63–64).

Excavations in the Five Points area of New York City have revealed occupa-tion-related artifacts discarded by women as well as men of different ethnicities working in the needle trades (Griggs 2001). A very large deposit of materials and tools from a Jewish commercial tailoring business was found, including thimbles inscribed "Forget Me Not," "Love," "A Present," and "From a Friend" that were usually given to women by men (Griggs 2001:82). Griggs (2001:77–78) ana-lyzed how gender stereotypes resulted in discrimination against women, including requiring more work for lower wages than men and exclusion of women from the better-paid needlework undertaken by men.

Groups of elite philanthropic reform women in both America and Australia founded and operated a wide variety of public institutions and landscapes. Among the earliest were female orphan asylums in the early 1800s and industrial schools for girls, which trained predominantly poor girls for domestic service. In Sydney, Australia, the first governor's wife founded the earliest female orphan asylum, and the second governor's wife designed its grounds. The governor's wife in Tasmania designed the island's first museum and gardens (for Australia, see Bickford 1998:196–97; for the United States, see Spencer-Wood 1994a). In Boston, Spencer-Wood (1987a, 1994a, 1996) located sites of public charitable cooperative homes founded by Anglo-American, African American and Jewish, Catholic, and Protestant middle-class women, such as homes for working women, aged women, intemperate women, "fallen" girls and women, and unwed mothers. De Cunzo (1995, 2001) researched the site of the Philadelphia Magdalen Asy-lum for fallen women.

Liberal egalitarian research on the importance of women's domestic roles derived from cultural feminist theory valorizing women's domestic roles. Andro-centric devaluations of women's domestic work have been corrected with feminist analyses demonstrating the importance of women's social agency in domestic roles (Donovan 2001). Feminists seek and find evidence that women's domestic roles are in many cases either as important as men's public roles or significant to the culture in general. If women's domestic roles are measured against the importance of men's public roles, then this paradigm does not challenge the dominance of public men in the gender status hierarchy. However, in some cases the importance of women's domestic roles to the culture in general is discussed.

Feminist historians and archaeologists have found evidence that native American women and American colonial women shaped domestic lifeways and sites as social actors, even in male-dominated situations (e.g., Deagan 1983:181–85, 234; Jackson 1994; McEwan 1991; Wheeler 2001; Woodhouse-Beyer 1999; Yentsch 1991b, 1994). Some research has involved finding evidence that historic white women's domestic roles were important in maintaining lifeways at a variety of male-dominated types of sites (Brashler 1991; Clements 1993; Purser 1991; Smith 1989; Starbuck 1994).

Yentsch (1994:196–217) researched the documentary and archaeological evidence that slave women maintained African lifeways and also altered white foodways with imported African squashes, birds, and spices. Slave women were domestic social agents in manufacturing African-style colonoware cooking pots, wattle and daub cooking huts, and hearthstones (Armstrong 1990:266). The importance of slave women's cooking in separate kitchen buildings has been researched in relation to American white urban house site layout (Stewart-Abernathy 2004). In Connecticut houses, caches of amulets, charms, bones, and so on found buried at kitchen thresholds or in corners have been interpreted as part of magical rituals by slave women (Woodruff 2005). On the Oakley Plantation in Louisiana, Wilkie (1996) found that women were often in charge of the medical care of the African American community, shifting from homemade concoctions to patent medicines as the plantation labor system evolved from slavery to tenant farming and sharecroppers.

In some household research, women's life cycle in the household has been important in changing the use of household space as well as in creating archaeological deposits. Archaeologists researching consumer choice have long related family life cycle to household consumer choices of ceramics (e.g., Garrow 1987; Leedecker et al. 1987). At two house sites of white people near Boston, Massachusetts, Wheeler (2001) identified the construction of new kitchens with new female heads of household. Further, at one site two separate discard areas were identified with the old and new kitchen locations. Women's role in maintaining the hearth provided them with social agency to construct new kitchens and discard previous tableware in order to acquire their own.

Spencer-Wood (1996:418–25, 1999d:181–85) researched how white middle-class reform women developed new gender ideologies to justify designing household spaces to raise the status of women in a number of ways. The central importance of women's domestic roles was symbolized by raising the kitchen from the basement, where it had been used by servants, to the main public floor in the center of the house, permitting surveillance by mothers of children's and adults' activities in the two first-floor parlors, while working in the kitchen. As the "sovereign of her empire," mothers were to organize their children's cooperative labor. Further, potted plants were to be brought into the conservatory to morally educate children through contact with God's nature that was associated with women's sphere.

In an excavation of an Australian sheep station household in the outback, Allison (2003) found evidence under floorboards of women's uses of different rooms, verandas, and outbuildings. Similar to urban households in the American south (e.g., Stewart-Abernathy 2004), a separate kitchen building was identified. However, in the late nineteenth century, a kitchen was built in the main house when meal preparation devolved from servants to the wife of the station owner. This process of loss of ability by the middle class to afford servants was important in the Beecher sisters' design of a potentially servantless house with its central kitchen in 1869 (Beecher and Stowe 1975:22). Allison (2003) found archaeological evidence that in the summer women had tea and coffee on the veranda and also sewed there as they watched their children playing with dolls.

Gendering the Historical Archaeology of Mothering and Child Rearing

In *The Archaeology of Mothering*, Wilkie (2003:6–7) notes the neglect of mothering in historical archaeological analyses and cites three out of a number of publications that have addressed child rearing and mothering or parenting (see Clark and Wilkie, this volume). Contextual differences at three sites affected the parenting interpretations of similar children's toys, particularly white dolls. Yamin and Bridges (2002) analyzed working-class parenting practices from nineteenth-century children's toys at working-class house sites in Paterson, New Jersey, and in the poor Five Points neighborhood of New York City. Yamin concluded from slate pencils and writing slate fragments that parents were teaching children to write at home since documentary data recorded working-class objections that public schools taught their children middle-class values. Yamin usually considers the working class and reformers as monolithic opposed groups and does not address how differences in income, number and gender of children, or parenting styles within her working-class sample could account for the diversity that she found in amounts of children's toys, such as dolls and marbles. Yamin glossed over these differences in order to make universal generalizations about the working class, rejecting the possibility that some might be upwardly mobile. In contrast, Brighton (2001:27–28) interprets children's artifacts found at Five Points, such as children's mugs with names as well as doll parts and cloth remnants, as indicating an upwardly mobile parenting style that emulated middle-class respectability and gentility. In Wilkie's (2003:107–9) analysis of mothering in the African American Perryman family living in Mobile, Alabama, she concluded that remains of four white dolls and a toy tea set expressed the family's desire for upward mobility as well as the sanctity of motherhood rather than the emulation of whites.

Research on the Importance of Women's Combined Domestic and Public Roles

Some research has combined both of the egalitarian feminist approaches to show that women's domestic and public roles were both culturally significant. Further, in some cases women's roles or activities combined aspects of the traditional domestic and public spheres. This feminist approach shows that the ideology of gender dichotomy between *either* female-domestic *or* male-public roles did not accurately express the complexity of actual gender practices (Spencer-Wood 1991a, 1992, 1995, 1996, 2003).

During the American contact period in the Spanish American colonies, McEwan (1991) analyzed the importance of Native American women's roles as public traders of their domestically produced pottery and foodstuffs as well as the cultural importance of the domestic roles of Spanish women and female African slaves who may also have produced pottery. Jackson (1994:47–48) found in records of the Russian American trading company that native Alaskan women were paid both for domestic work such as making clothes and for public work stringing trade beads and as translators.

Gardens at domestic sites have been analyzed as expressing the public prestige of men at some sites and women at other sites. Feminist historical archaeologists countered the previously exclusive construction of gardens as expressing male power with evidence of elite European and American women who publicly displayed their prestige or public image through ornamental household gardens in the eighteenth and nineteenth centuries (Spencer-Wood 1991c, 1999a; Weber 1991, 1996). Others have researched how wives were involved in designing gardens for the public image of elites at house sites in America (e.g., Bescherer Metheny et al. 1996), including President Jackson's plantation (McKee 1996), and at the Australian governor's estate (Casey 2002).

Research in Australia and America has revealed the significance of women's domestic roles in household production not only for household consumption but also for public markets. In particular, the importance of women's household dairy products has been researched both for the Australian colonial system by Casey (1999) and for the American international cheese and butter markets by Yentsch (1991b:136). Women frequently conducted underpaid waged labor in their homes, such as seamstresses and laundresses. By the twentieth century, African American women also frequently set up hair-straightening and manicure businesses in their homes (Mullins 1999:63). Excavations of households conducting outwork have yielded both work-related artifacts and domestic artifacts providing information about lifeways and consumer choices. For instance, in New York City's Five Points area, a domestic deposit included jewelry, pottery, and children's toys with a few sewing-related items, in contrast to another deposit with a large number and variety of discarded sewing materials from thirteen poor Irish women in the tenement who were documented working in the needle trades from 1850 to 1880 (Griggs 2001:80).

Women could gain income and status by operating boardinghouses in their homes. Archaeologists have excavated nineteenth-century American boardinghouse sites in Harper's Ferry, West Virginia (Lucas 1994); Lowell and Lawrence, Massachusetts (Mrozowski 2000:288–89); and Portsmouth, New Hampshire (Agnew 1995:68–71) and an Australian one in Sydney (Lydon 1993a, 1993b). Lucas (1994:84) has pointed out that boarders' tableware consumer choices were made by the boardinghouse keeper and represent the meaning of meals to the keeper. In addition, keepers were conducting a business in which they had to weigh the costs of tableware and food against the quality of boarders they wished to attract as customers. The boardinghouses at Harper's Ferry (Lucas 1994:89–90) and in Sydney (Lydon 1993b:143, 1993a:38) both signaled their respectability with unmatched transfer-printed breakfast sets plus additional special tableware at Harper's Ferry. Plain white tableware predominated at all the boardinghouse sites, possibly symbolizing women's domestic morality and surveillance since most had rules against alcohol consumption. However, at Lowell numerous hidden alcohol bottles, as well as patent medicines at all the sites, testified to the ability of boarders to circumvent the rules, although the medicines were connected to children's diseases at Harper's Ferry (Larsen 1994:70). The Sydney boardinghouse served beef, the preferred meat (Lydon 1993a:37–38, 1993b). The Lowell textile company boardinghouse was also documented as serving mostly beef, but parasitological analysis of the privies revealed that horse meat was also being served. A further contrast was found between company propaganda about the cleanliness of their boardinghouses and the documented objections of the "millgirls" to the crowding in Lowell boardinghouses (Beaudry 1993:96–100).

Some gender research has found that women's domestic roles were important in linking households into a public community. For instance, excavations at two eighteenth-century Spanish colonial house sites near the Rio Grande in Texas yielded identical chocolaterias that could have been from the same set, suggesting that the households were kin (Bonine 2004:31). At President Jackson's nine-teenth-century Hermitage plantation, slave women and men created community by sharing yards between their houses that hid their activities from surveillance by whites in the plantation house (Battle 2004). Wilkie (2003:119–42) has shown how African American midwifery not only was an occupation but also provided symbolic mothering for a community and taught each young mother child-rearing practices after she gave birth to her first child (Wilkie 2000; for further details, see Voss, this volume).

American reform women constructed new kinds of connections to resolve the perceived conflict between individual households and the public sphere in the nineteenth century. The predominantly middle-class reform women sought to increase women's powers by combining and conflating the domestic and public spheres in two ways. Some reformers applied men's scientific-industrial technol-ogy to raise the status of housework to a profession, arguing that women should control the domestic sphere (Spencer-Wood 1999d:181–85). Second, reform women transformed private domestic mothering and housekeeping tasks into a variety of female public professions in public cooperative housekeeping institu-tions, from orphan asylums and public kitchens to day nurseries, kindergartens, playgrounds, and children's gardens. In the municipal housekeeping movement, reform women argued that they were the symbolic mothers and housekeepers of the community, gaining appointments from male government officials to posi-tions from juvenile parole officers to school committee members, elementary school teachers, playground supervisors, and factory inspectors. Reform women living cooperatively in social settlements in working-class neighborhoods further acted as community mothers by offering a wide variety of after-school programs for children of working mothers, organizing local children to clean up the streets, and provided hot-water showers, baths, child clinics, and laundries for the major-ity of working-class families living in cold-water tenements (Spencer-Wood 1991b:234, 1994a:179–80, 1994b:126, 2002b, 2003).

Public institutional community mothering was evident from turn-of-the-century deposits excavated at the Daughters of Charity Catholic orphanage for white children at Schuyler mansion in Albany, New York. Middle-class child-rearing practices were indicated from the variety of middle-class doll parts and miniature tea set fragments found along the south wall of the mansion, indicating that girls played there. Few other toys were found, including buff clay marbles, jacks, and a pocketknife, which may have been associated with boys' play (Feister 1991). Feister (2003) concluded that boys played farther away from the house.

Second-Wave Feminist Theoretical Approaches to Analyses of Patriarchy

The second wave of feminist theory, starting in the 1970s, is concerned with explaining and analyzing how patriarchy, as a culturally constructed ideology and societal institution, maintains gender inequalities (e.g., Ortner 1974; Rosaldo 1974; Rosaldo and Lamphere 1974). Second-wave feminist theory was developed by white Western middle-class women and essentialized their experiences in the dichotomy between domestic women and public men (Gilchrist 1999:6; Spencer-Wood 2002a:207).

Second-wave feminist theory has been critiqued for essentializing men's and women's actual behaviors as universally conforming to patriarchal gender ideology (e.g., Rosaldo 1980). Women's public roles were either categorized as domestic or dismissed as exceptions that prove the rule of women's domesticity. Such constructions of other cultures reify gender stereotypes and fail to show the diversity in actual gender practices.

Second-Wave Analyses of Dominant Gender Ideology and Women's Social Agency

Some second-wave research has not overgeneralized gender practices as universally conforming to dominant binary gender ideology but has instead analyzed the specific situations and circumstances in which historic patriarchal gender ideology was or was not materially expressed. Some of these analyses, exemplified here, have also considered the possibility of women's social agency or resistance to patriarchy.

At the nineteenth-century Magdalen Asylum for fallen women in Philadelphia, De Cunzo (1995) researched how inmates' lives were controlled using the dominant patriarchal ideology that blamed women rather than men for sexual promiscuity. The institution sought to reform women by isolating them in a walled institution with convent-type cells. Inmates were forced to perform domestic work, ostensibly to learn their appropriate role so they could be transformed into domestic servants. However, a number of inmates demonstrated social agency by escaping over the walls. Although higher walls were continually constructed, some inmates continued to escape.

Spencer-Wood's (2004) research analyzed how the social agency of mid-nineteenth-century Harvard faculty wives in establishing the Cambridge Cooperative Housekeeping Society was thwarted by their husbands, who exerted their patriarchal male dominance to prevent their wives from participating in the cooperative. However, Melusina Fay Peirce, who founded the cooperative, divorced her husband after a number of years and became renowned as the leading theorist of housekeeping cooperatives, which became one of the most numerous types of domestic reform sites.

In a case study from early twentieth-century Deerfield, Massachusetts, patriarchal male dominance was found to be expressed in the location of municipal water spigots near barns rather than houses at some sites after local women had raised the money to pay for the municipal water system. Married women seldom got a water spigot at the house because their husbands had it installed near the barn to facilitate tending hogs and other livestock. However, financially independent widows with income from participating in the Arts and Crafts movement were successful in getting water spigots at the back of the house to facilitate washing laundry (Huateniemi and Rotman 2003).

Marxist-Feminist and Postcolonial Feminist Approaches to Gender Research

In the 1970s, Marxist-feminism emerged by making an analogy between the way the bourgeois capitalist class exploited the oppressed working classes and the ways men as a class and capitalism as a whole benefited from exploiting women's unpaid domestic labor (Delphy 1984; Guettel 1974; Hartsock 1983; Kuhn and Wolpe 1978). In contrast to the essentialist/structuralist analysis of dominant gender ideology as congruent with actual practice, Marxist-feminist theory was concerned with women's actual gender practices that resisted the gender ideology legitimating public men's domination over subordinate domestic women. Thus, feminists adopted the Marxian framework of domination and resistance and applied it to gender relationships.

Marxism and Marxist-feminism have been useful in analyzing some of the structural sources of sexism and discrimination against women. However, Marxism and Marxist-feminism are essentializing in considering only the dominant gender ideology and overgeneralizing about women and men as homogeneous groups. Marxist-feminism focused on women's domestic work and tended to neglect women's public wage labor aside from proposing it as the solution to the devaluation of women's domestic labor (Engels 1884:148, cited in Donovan 2001:88). These limitations stemmed from the development of Marxist-feminism as part of the second-wave feminist focus on the experiences of white middle-class women, most of whom only worked at home in the 1960s and 1970s (Donovan 2001:79–105).

Postcolonial feminist theory relates the Western devaluation of women's unpaid domestic labor to the devaluation of and lower wages in women's paid work in Western capitalist enterprises in Third World countries. Postcolonial feminist theory critiques the imposition of Western gender categories and values to often degrade women's traditional precolonial status, roles, economic independence, and identities. It is also concerned with women's resistance to their exploitation and the breakdown of their traditional subsistence economy (Lorber 2001:55–73).

Marxist-feminist theory was first advocated for historical archaeology gender research by Elizabeth Scott in a paper presented at the 1991 Society for Historical Archaeology conference in a miniplenary titled "Shaken, Not Stirred" organized by Margaret Purser. In the introduction to her edited volume, Scott (1994) discussed the application of the Marxist paradigm of domination and resistance to gender research.

Contact-period gender research in historical archaeology frequently addresses changes in native American gender systems due to colonization, although feminist postcolonial theory has not yet been applied. Change toward more patriarchal gender roles due to indigenous interaction with western European culture was researched by Bassett (1994) for the Apache, Devens (1991) for the Cree, and Birmingham (1993) for Australian aborigines. The fur trade undermined Eskimo women's traditional status in clothing manufacture (Frink 2005), and the Russian American company required native women to produce food for them, resulting in starvation for native families (Woodhouse-Beyer 1999:141).

Some Marxist-feminist research in historical archaeology has speculated on women's resistance to European patriarchy, including Australian aboriginal women resisting Victorian missionaries' gender ideology of a clean, neat, Christian home (Birmingham 1993:122–23); native American women retaining matrilineal tribes (Clements 2005) and traditional powers (Frink 2005); African American free women retaining their land despite capitalist pressures (Muller 1994); white women keeping forbidden personal items in an Australian asylum (Piddock 2001); American white women in Shaker communes resisting the men's attempts to get women to undertake work traditionally accomplished by men (Savulis 2003:180–84); and white women resisting the appropriation of their household cheese production by men's factories in the second half of the nineteenth century (Yentsch 1991b). However, in some cases women did not retain their household cheese production by choice, according to interviews with them (McMurray 1987).

Marxist-Feminist Postmodern Analyses

Scott (1991a) applied Spector's (1983) task differentiation framework to conduct an explicitly Marxist-feminist analysis of who did what for whom in gender relationships at eighteenth-century British Fort Michilimackinac in Michigan. Scott used Spector's (1983) Marxist analytic framework to analyze the complexity of gender roles and interactions among English, French, and native Americans. Spector's framework holds implications for power dynamics that have yet to be explicitly addressed.

Delle (2000) combines a Marxist analysis of colonial slave labor on Jamaican coffee plantations with a postmodern comparison of idealistic writings and actual gender practices. Idealistic writings advocated methods by which plantation owners could control slave women's sexual behavior and reproduction. Delle compares these idealistic writings with evidence for actual gender practices such as infanticide, which Delle interprets as slave women's resistance to white men's attempts to control women's reproduction.

Third-Wave Postmodern Feminist Theoretical Approaches to Gender Research

Postmodern feminist theory critiques and corrects essentialist second-wave feminist theory that constructed actual gender practices as a heterosexist dichotomy (Spencer-Wood 1992, 1997a). Postmodern feminist theory constructs gender and sexuality as diverse, complex, fluid performances that cannot be monolithically described for any social group. The heterosexist construction of biological sex as a dichotomy is critiqued with evidence of biological diversity in physical sexual characteristics and hormones. Diversity and flexibility in gender identities, roles, performances, relationships, practices, and power dynamics are related to the complex intersections of gender, race, class, ethnicity, and other social dimensions. Sexism is related to racism and classism. Finally, postmodern feminism theorizes performances and representations of gender and sexuality as texts and discourses that can be understood through the process of deconstruction (Lorber 2001:147–63, 203).

Inclusive Feminist Theory and Continuum Models in Historical Archaeology

Spencer-Wood (1991a, 1991c, 1992, 1995, 1997a) drew on postmodern feminist theory to critique binary structuralist either/or thinking used to classify a range of variation in phenomena into two opposed categories. Instead, she argued for the use of feminist "both/and" thinking to create inclusive models of the actual range of variation and nuance of meanings in social dimensions, including but not limited to the two opposed binary categories that are constructed by structuralism as the only categories. Spencer-Wood (1995:130, 1997a) proposed replacing structural dichotomies with continuum models of social dimensions to represent their entire range of variation.

The diversity of an individual's identity can be represented as the intersection point of a number of continuum lines for different social dimensions. The situational fluidity of identity can be dynamically represented as the potential for movement along each continuum and the extent to which the intersection point between different continuums can move dynamically (Spencer-Wood 2002a:207, 1997a).

Diversity in Historic Women's Gender Ideologies of the Home

In the Cult of Female Invalidism, elite and middle-class white women used the dominant ideology of women's inherent physical weakness as a way to control their sexual relationships with their husbands. In the Cult of Republican Motherhood, middle-class white women emphasized the importance of women's child-rearing skills and morality for raising the next generation of male leaders of the new republic of the United States. The Cult of Republican Motherhood transformed child rearing from a supposedly simple innate female function into scientific child rearing, a complex learned behavior that required special tools, advice books, and higher education, leading to the growth of the academic fields researching child development and education (Beecher and Stowe 1975:13–14, 275–86; Spencer-Wood 1996:421, 1999d:172–79). Wilkie (2003:11, 177–204) has followed historians who further divide "republican mothering" ideologies into "intensive mothering" accompanying the separation of the domestic and public spheres and "scientific mothering" due to the development of male-dominated medicine and childbirth, accompanied by advertising of mass-produced mothering products.

Wilkie (2003:70–74) analyzed a different ideology of motherhood developed among African American slaves that stressed love, nurturing, protection, and strength in adversity. African American women often came from matrilineal African societies and developed strong roles and an ideology of female strength in slavery that seems incompatible with the Cult of Female Invalidism (e.g., Muller 1994). However, distrust of white male medicine also led to the use of patent medicines (Wilkie 2000) that often contained labels illustrating delicate white women. Since patent medicines illustrating African American women were not available, African American use of these patent medicines is not necessarily evidence that African American women ascribed to the Cult of Female Invalidism, as has been argued by Hautaniemi (1994).

The Cult of True Womanhood or Domesticity claimed that white middle-class and elite women were innately more pious, moral, modest, and domestic than men (Larson 1994; Wall 1994; Welter 1966) and, by assumption, African American women (Wilkie 2003:84). The Cult of True Womanhood or Domesticity was used to elaborate and increase the significance of women's domestic roles as a source of power (Spencer-Wood 1989a:114, 1991b:237, 250–55, 1991c:240). Wall (1991:78–79, 2000:111) identified the Cult of Domesticity with mid-nineteenth-century Gothic white paneled ceramics that were interpreted as symbolizing the sanctity of the home and community at meals and tea taken by the family, in opposition to capitalist competitive status display.

In the Cult of Home Religion, middle-class white domestic reformers further argued that women's housework should be equivalent in status to the male ministry because women sacrificed for their family flock just as ministers sacrificed for their religious flock. Women's role as home ministers was symbolized in the Gothic house style, ceramics, glassware, and furnishings as well as a round table with a Bible. Cut flowers and potted plants were ideally used in household conservatories to symbolize women's innately higher piety due to the closeness of their domestic sphere to God's nature, removed from men's sinful capitalistic sphere (Spencer-Wood 1994a, 1996:418–19, 1999d:181–83).

Wilkie (2003:56–59) discusses how elite white gender ideology depended on the opposite stereotypes of African American women as oversexed Jezebels and dominating matriarchs, who by definition were unnatural mothers for supposedly not exhibiting the unsexed purity and higher morality of white mothers in the sanctified home of the cult of domesticity. These negative stereotypes of African American women were compounded with the stereotype of the oversexed promiscuous working woman that was applied to all working-class women but especially African American working women, who were considered "public women," akin to prostitutes for transgressing men's sphere and walking public streets without a male protector and guarantor of her purity (Ryan 1990:67; Stansell 1986:125–27, 148). This was part of the dominant elite gender ideology that domestic reformers significantly manipulated to make it acceptable for women to have public professions (Spencer-Wood 1991b, 1994a).

Archaeologists and historians have defined the Cult of Gentility in diverse ways. A few archaeologists have identified the cult with eighteenth-century men (e.g., Crass et al. 1999), but most identify it with nineteenth-century women. Wall (1991:79; 2000:111, 122, 135–36) has identified the Cult of Gentility with competitive status display using secular gilt and floral tea sets and tableware. In contrast, Linda Young (2003) has included the Cult of Domesticity in the Cult of Gentility, and Fitts (1999:53–55) further associates the two cults with Gothic paneled ceramics.

Lawrence argued that the desire to display middle-class domestic respectability led Euro-Australian miners and their wives to line their tents or cabins with decorative cloth or wallpaper, construct whitewashed fireplaces, and display some fashionable middle-class artifacts, such as a gilt clock, transfer-printed ceramic teawares and tablewares, glass tumblers, and pressed-glass stemmed bowls. In addition, a few remains of women's jewelry were found, and Christian temperance was indicated by low numbers of alcohol bottles (Lawrence 1999:1129, 1133). The decorated tablewares may be an expression of respectability involved in the Cult of Gentility more than the sanctity of the home symbolized by undecorated white ceramics. Purser (1991) found the Cult of Gentility expressed in western American mining household decoration and the practice of women visiting each others' homes.

Public Domestic Reform Ideologies

Women's domestic reform ideologies transformed Western culture by making it acceptable in the dominant gender ideology for women to have public professions and be economically independent. In the communitarian ideology of domestic reform, women argued for the socialization of women's household tasks in public cooperative housekeeping institutions in order to eliminate the isolated repetitive labor of women in individual households (Spencer-Wood 1994a). The ideology and practice of cooperative housekeeping was adopted by urban reform women from American utopian communes, which often called themselves families (Spencer-Wood 1987a, 1999d, 2006).

Domestic reformers further used a cultural feminist ideology in municipal housekeeping and City Beautiful movements to argue that women's innately superior domestic morality was needed to reform men's sinful capitalist cities, where youth were corrupted by dirty streets and the lack of contact with God's nature, which was associated with women (Spencer-Wood 2003). Based on this ideology, reform women used their feminine powers of moral suasion to gain the assistance of government officials in establishing urban green spaces and park playgrounds (Spencer-Wood 1994b, 1999c, 2003).

In other ideologies, women developed justifications for having public professions. The Cult of Single Blessedness (1740–1910s) advocated that women not marry men but instead marry their professions as religious callings, in analogy with nuns who became celibate brides of Christ (Chambers-Schiller 1984, cited in Spencer-Wood 1999c:172). The Cult of Real Womanhood, starting in the 1890s, advocated that women marry carefully, undertake exercise for health, and be trained in a profession in case they needed to work to support their family (Cogan 1989, cited in Spencer-Wood 1999d:172).

Diversity and Change in Gender Ideologies and Practices in Different Religions

Postmodern gender research analyzes the polyvocal nature of women's and men's actions in constantly renegotiating gender ideologies and actual gender practices (Spencer-Wood 1991c:239). Religious beliefs can have a major effect on negotiations over consumer choices. For instance, Kruczek-Aaron (2002) found unusual letters documenting negotiations concerning gender ideology and practice between Gerrit Smith and his wife and daughter. Gerrit was a prominent abolitionist and temperance reformer who experienced an Evangelical Protestant conversion and sought to present himself as a plain man who eschewed ostentation. His wife and daughter wished to display fashionable Victorian gentility, especially at dinner parties. Negotiations resulted in the compromise of fancy decorated ceramics but not matched sets (Nickolai 2003:154) for the dinner parties in a house that was plainly furnished. It may be that the unmatched decorated ceramics were justified for use because they were secondhand or heirlooms. In any case, during the 1850s, when Gerrit was a congressman in Washington, D.C., he materially betrayed his religious beliefs by adding an ostentatious two-story Greek Revival porch with Doric columns to his Federal-style mansion.

Different Jewish sects developed distinct gender ideologies and practices as they moved across Boston's landscape from 1840 to 1930. In poor, orthodox eastern European communities, women were segregated in screened balconies in synagogues, were provided ritual bath buildings called *mikvehs*, and practiced kosher foodways with separate pots and dishes for meat and milk. In contrast, over time middle-class western European Reformed Jews increasingly adopted Protestant mixed-gender seating and singing in synagogues and stopped building *mikvehs* and practicing kosher foodways (Spencer-Wood 1999b).

Postmodern Research Contrasting the Dominant Gender Ideology with Household Gender Practices

A major theme in postmodern feminist historical archaeology are analyses separating and comparing dominant gender ideology with the diversity and fluidity in actual gender practices due to the complex intersections of gender, class, race, ethnicity, religion, and other social dimensions. This approach contrasts with the second-wave structuralist approach of uncritically projecting the dominant gender ideology as the universal reality of actual practice.

Some historical archaeological research shows that "separate spheres" gender ideology often contrasted with actual practices that combined domestic and public spheres. In both America and Australia, colonial homes often housed women's as well as men's businesses. Gibb and King (1991) found little evidence of segregation in the deposition of traditionally gendered artifacts around seventeenth-century houses in Maryland, in contrast to the ideology of gender dichotomy in the use of household spaces (Yentsch 1991c). Further, neither American, African American, nor Australian colonial or working-class houses of one to three multipurpose rooms had the separate dining room and gender-segregated rooms required for the cult of gentility, although Australian photos show that part of a room could be used for women's genteel ritual of tea using decorated ceramics, though usually not the tea sets used by the middle class (Baker 1980; Deetz 1977; Karskens 2003:41; Russell 1993:30). In the Sydney Rocks neighborhood, a working-class house site yielded middle-class decorated ceramics for genteel dining but inexpensive cuts of meat (Karskens 2003:45–50). Mullins (1999:174–75) found that tableware at an African American house site in Annapolis, Maryland, did not fit the genteel ideal but instead consisted of a variety of old, worn, unmatched ceramics.

Gendered household research in historical archaeology has progressed from a second-wave structuralist construction of household spaces as universally conforming to the elite gender ideology of fixed mutually exclusive male versus female spheres (e.g., Yentsch 1991c) to postmodern contrasting of this dominant separate-spheres gender ideology with the actual diversity and fluidity in the use of household spaces. Research on nineteenth-century house sites in western Michigan contrasted the elite ideology of separate domestic spaces for women and men with actual practices involving different degrees of gender mixing and segregation in household spaces due to class. Generally, more mixed-gender use of domestic spaces was found in the working-class households and more gender segregation in the use of spaces in upper-class houses (Nassaney et al. 2001:251–52; Rotman and Nassaney 1997). In contrast, fewer gender segregation tasks were found on middle-class farm landscapes employing hired hands (Rotman and Nassaney 1997; Sayers and Nassaney 1999).

Postmodern Historical Archaeological Research on Diversity, Fluidity, and Negotiations in Gender Systems

A variety of publications in historical archaeology have conducted postmodern analyses of diversity in gender roles, behaviors, practices, and identities due to complex intersections of gender, class, race, and ethnicity. In America, archaeologists have analyzed how gender roles in the colonies varied among native Americans, African Americans, and white colonists as well as how these groups related to each other (e.g., McEwan 1991; Scott 1991a).

Class differences in ability to practice the cult of gentility have been found in both Australia (Russell 1993) and America (Wall 1991, 1994, 2000). Two archaeological studies of the use of household spaces for the performance of gentility, one each in Australia and America, have found documentary evidence of negotiations between elite women and servants over the proper performance of elite dining rituals and housecleaning (e.g., Kruczek-Aaron 2002; Russell 1993).

Some historical archaeologists have analyzed the complex intersections between gender, race, and class. Wilkie (2000:56–58, 96) argues that unmatched plain white ironstone tableware, a white porcelain set, and sets of pressed-glass goblets, tumblers and bowls found at the turn-of-the-century African American Perryman house site in Mobile, Alabama, do not indicate simple middle-class emulation but rather symbolize the purity of sacred motherhood in the cult of domesticity in order to counteract negative stereotypes of African American women as oversexed immoral Jezebels who were unnatural bad mothers. A "Rebekah at the Well" pitcher and two white cherub figurines are also interpreted as domestic symbols of the importance of full-time mothering and domesticity, displaying not only middle-class domesticity but also the freedom from previous work in plantation fields that limited slave women's time for mothering their children (Wilkie 2003:106, 113–14). It is interesting to note that the earlier tableware set is blue, suggesting, along with the recovery of numerous blue bottles, materialization of African American ideology of hoodoo magic, in which using blue is believed to bring good luck (pointed out by Wilkie 2000).

Brandon (2004) analyzed the gendered racial identities and relationships symbolized in one artifact, the topsy-turvy doll that was popular in nineteenth-century America. Brandon (2004:197) states, "It is effectively two dolls in one—one end an elegant white 'missy' and the other a manifestation of the well-used stereotype of the 'wild-eyed pickaninny.'" The skirt on this doll covered the head of one manifestation when the other was in view, making it a horrific metaphor for racialization in America: the two are inextricably attached and cannot exist without the other, while simultaneously they are unarguably in two different worlds as they cannot be seen together." Stewart-Abernathy (2004) is one of the few historical archaeologists who has interpreted race relations between slave women and their white mistresses from the separation of the elite house from the kitchen, where slave women had some independence in preparing meals for both the slave and white residents of the house site.

Intersecting gender, class, and ethnic inequalities can be expressed in cultural landscapes. Archaeological investigations of the grounds of Sailor's Snug Harbor on Staten Island found that the prestige and wealth of the white Anglo male benefactor was expressed through a formal public front lawn with his tomb in front of a row of five Greek temple building facades. The institution's inmates constructed an elaborate garden landscape, including a fish pond, around the large fashionable Italianate house of the white Anglo male governor of the institution. The lower-status white doctor's house was adjacent to a corner of the front lawn of the institution. The lowest-status maintenance workers lived behind the institution in closely spaced buildings with no lawns and dumps in back, including the Irish women who were domestic servants for the institution. The landscape expressed the low status of these women in terms of both their gender and their ethnicity (Baugher and Baragli 1987).

Some research has shown how women were social agents in using gender solidarity to create connections across cultural, ethnic, and class differences. At the nineteenth-century Locust Grove plantation near Louisville, Kentucky, excavations yielded ceramics of the same patterns in different slave houses, which were interpreted as gifts between slave women to create community solidarity among women who may or may not have been kin. Community solidarity was important in resisting the oppressions of slavery (A. Young 2003:108–13). Research at an early twentieth-century mining town in Berwind, Colorado, found that women's networks linked miners' households both within and across ethnic boundaries, permitting them to organize a strike that was suppressed by the 1914 Ludlow massacre of miners' families by the Colorado National Guard (Wood 2004). A survey of women's domestic reform sites in Boston from 1865 to 1925 found that annual reports of social settlements and other organizations expressed the middle-class reformers' goal of reaching across social barriers separating women (Spencer-Wood 1994a:197; 1996).

Documentary and archaeological data have revealed the gendered social agency of children in using play landscapes. For instance, at the early twentieth-century racially integrated Cambridge Pine Street playground for young children, older girls did not passively accept their exclusion, but instead successfully negotiated to be admitted in order to "mind baby in the sand" (Spencer-Wood 1994b:133). In excavations at a turn-of-the-century orphan asylum site in New York and at a state home for older children in Rhode Island, evidence of children's social agency was expressed through gendered differences in children's use of institutional landscapes for play. Excavations revealed that girls played close to the buildings and lost toys such as dolls there, while boys played in the woods farther away from the buildings and lost toys identified with boys, such as marbles or toy soldiers (Feister 2003; Morenon 2003).

Spencer-Wood (1994a, 1996) has researched complex class and ethnic dialogues between Boston reform women and program participants who were not passive but negotiated with reformers over the content and material culture of programs. Some reform women viewed their programs as social experiments rather than social control and therefore recorded and responded to participants' reactions to programs. For instance, in the Denison House settlement annual reports, Anglo reform women recorded their response to the voices of immigrant women who complained that their production of ethnic textiles for sale ought to be put on a business basis instead of a charitable basis. In 1881 at the North Bennet Street Industrial School for Girls in Boston, boys did not passively accept their exclusion but instead successfully argued with reform women to provide the boys with a carpentry class taught by a man who worked for the women, inverting the normal gender hierarchy (Spencer-Wood 1996:433–34).

Reform women were not a monolithic group. While some worked for women's unions and had programs to create a pluralistic society by preserving ethnic cultures, others attempted social control with classes to train domestic servants, which nonpassive working-class women refused to attend (Spencer-Wood 2002b:121). In contrast to the secular college women's settlements in Boston, the New York Ladies' Home Missionary Society of the Methodist Episcopal Church sought to morally reform the poor working class living in Five Points by converting immigrant Catholics to Methodism and the cult of domesticity, requiring material expression in middle-class genteel consumer choices. The missionaries produced three publications characterizing Five Points as the most notoriously dirty and immoral slum, rife with crime, violence, and promiscuity. Working-class lifeways, including mixed-gender crowded sleeping quarters, open sexuality, drinking, smoking, and racial and ethnic miscegenation, were viewed by the middle-class missionaries as immoral. These reports justified the mission and neighboring House of Industry in boasting that they had "rescued" 60,000 children by the early 1890s, separating them from their natural (usually Catholic) parents and sending them to a Protestant family in the country (Fitts 2001).

Methods in Postmodern Feminist Historical Archaeology

Feminists have analyzed archaeological data in new ways to establish the gender identity of site occupants as well as the diversity in distinctive gendered behavior patterns at different types of sites. The gender identity of site occupants was found to be best determined from personal artifacts. Gendered differences in consumption patterns were compared at different types of sites, finding the highest alcohol consumption at brothels, a police station, and a hotel, where single men apparently ate and drank since their tent sites did not include these types of artifacts (Spude 2001). Households were found to vary in alcohol consumption, but their generally lower rates of consumption than brothels and hotels has been related to the influence of wives subscribing to the cult of domesticity and temperance (Blee 1991; Lawrence-Cheney 1991, 1993). However, a priest's privy revealed hidden alcohol bottles, although he vocally supported the local temperance law (Spude 1999).

Beaudry and Mrozowski (2004) analyzed how consumer choices of Lowell factory operatives indicated their intersections of gender, ethnic, and class identities. Costume jewelry and fancy imitation jet buttons were interpreted as expressions of female factory operatives' identities as working-class women (Ziesing 1989:141–68). Irish pipes that were found were associated with men's ethnic identities (Beaudry and Mrozowski 2004) since women who smoked were considered "loose," and working women were more likely to smoke cigarettes than pipes when they did smoke (Cook 1997). Thus, consumer choices were shown to be affected by intersections of gender, class, and ethnic identities.

Postmodern Queer Theory and Masculinity Theory

The most recent development of postmodern feminist theory is the critique and correction of heterosexist biases in feminist theory in order to analyze the diversity and fluidity in sexual orientations and performance, masculine identities, and bodily identities. Historical archaeological research has found a variety of sexual ideologies, practices, and identities at different sites, from utopian communes (Spencer-Wood, in press) to brothels (see Voss, this volume; Andretti, this volume).

The Future

Postmodern approaches appear to be developing most in part because this approach facilitates extending research into the diversity and fluidity among cultural subgroups and individuals in gender ideologies, identities, actual gender roles, practices, behaviors, and performances. Postmodern feminist theoretical approaches to gender research have progressed from considering complex inter- sections with class, ethnicity, and age in 1991 (e.g., Scott 1991a, 1991b; Spencer- Wood 1991b; Whelan 1991), to further analyzing their intersections with race, religion, and sexual orientation (e.g., Delle et al. 2000; Knapp 1998; Scott 1994; Spencer-Wood 1999b, 1999d, in press). Marxist-feminist theoretical approaches have been and will continue to be important in the analysis of gender power dynamics and social agency among subcultural groups (e.g., Delle 2000).

Postmodern feminist theory has synthesized the first and second waves of feminist theory by separating the analysis of patriarchal gender ideology from the analysis of actual gender practices. This paradigm can also be useful in analyzing how gender ideologies and practices are mutually constituted and constantly rene- gotiated between individuals, cultural subgroups, and social institutions.

There are a number of theoretical and methodological issues concerning gen- der research in historical archaeology that are gaining increasing attention. One fundamental concern is that the analysis of gender become as prevalent as analyses of class. In the past two Society for Historical Archaeology conferences (2004, 2005), the number of papers on gender research has declined. While no one would fail to consider class in historical archaeological research, it is still accept- able to conduct and publish ungendered research, even in analyzing households, where gender is a primary organizing principle.

At the deeper level of epistemology, it is essential that postmodern feminist theory's concern for diversity not be extended into a nihilistic relativistic episte- mology in which all claims to knowledge are considered equally valid, as has been claimed in postprocessual archaeology by Hodder (1991b). The consideration of feminist and androcentric interpretations of the past as equally valid dismisses the feminist critique of androcentric archaeology and the feminist claim to more inclusive analysis and resulting knowledge (Spencer-Wood 1992). The claim that feminist and androcentric constructions of the past are equally valid reveals how relativism is a tool of the dominant group used to discredit claims to more valid knowledge by subordinate groups (Harding 1993). Both Hodder (1991a) and Englestad (1991) have noted that the dominant male elite in archaeology decides which interpretations are most valid, given that interpretations are underdeter- mined by data (Wylie 1992).

Feminist philosophers have written about the need to balance postmodern theories of gender diversity with the feminist epistemological standpoint argu- ment privileging feminist knowledge as more inclusive and less partial than andro- centric knowledge (Harding 1987). Harding (1993) has created the term "strong objectivity" to express the argument that recognition of the researcher's political standpoint creates more objective knowledge than the impossible attempt in traditional science to eliminate all researcher biases (Spencer-Wood 1992). The postmodern diversity of perspectives due to class, race, ethnicity, and other social variables can be reconciled with feminist standpoint theory by retaining a feminist theoretical approach starting from women's lives that critiques and corrects androcentrism.

Feminist historical archaeology needs more conscious choice and justification of the appropriateness of a feminist theoretical approach to a research project. The field would benefit greatly from more overt discussion about the value and limitations of different feminist theoretical approaches for a variety of gender research projects in historical archaeology. Postmodern feminist theory can assist archaeologists in the construction of frameworks for interpreting material culture from the standpoint of women in a variety of classes, races, and ethnic groups. Bickford (1998); Brandon (2004); Franklin (2001); Lawrence (1999); Mrozowski et al. (2000:xviii–xx); Scott (1991a, 1994); Spencer-Wood (1989a, 1989b, 1991a, 1991b, 1991c, 1992, 1994a, 1995, 1996, 1997a, 1997b, 1999a, 1999b, 1999c, 1999d, 2000, 2001b, 2002a, 2004, 2005, in press); Wilkie (2003); and Yentsch (1991c) have been among the minority in overtly discussing different feminist theoretical approaches to gender research in historical archaeology. It is hoped that this volume will lead more archaeologists researching gender to overtly discuss their theoretical approach. Discussions of feminist theory can only lead to more informed and nuanced analyses of historic gender systems by archaeologists.

Acknowledgments

I would like to thank the following colleagues for their generous assistance in providing me with information on gender research in historical archaeology of Australia: Penelope Allison, Judy Birmingham, Annie Bickford, Mary Casey, and Jane Lydon. My thanks to Sherene Baugher for sending me references from Northeast Historical Archaeology. My deepest thanks to Sarah Nelson for her thoughtful editing. Of course, any errors are my own.

References

Agnew, Aileen B.
   1995   Women and Property in Early 19th Century Portsmouth, New Hampshire. *Historical Archaeology* 29(1):62–75.
Allison, Penelope M.
   2003   The Old Kinchega Homestead: Doing Household Archaeology in Outback

New South Wales, Australia. *International Journal of Historical Archaeology* 7(3):161–94.

Anderson, Nesta
2004   Finding the Space between Spatial Boundaries and Social Dynamics: The Archaeology of Nested Households. In *Household Chores and Household Choices: Theorizing the Domestic Sphere in Historical Archaeology.* Kerri S. Barile and Jamie C. Brandon, eds. Pp. 109–38. Tuscaloosa: University of Alabama Press.

Armstrong, Douglas V.
1990   *The Old Village and the Great House: An Archaeological and Historical Examination of Drax Hall Plantation, St. Ann's Bay, Jamaica.* Urbana: University of Illinois Press.

Baker, Vernon G.
1980   Archaeological Visibility of Afro-American Culture: An Example from Black Lucy's Garden, Andover, Massachusetts. In *Archaeological Perspectives on Ethnicity in America.* R. L. Schuyler, ed. Pp. 29–38. New York: Baywood Publishing.

Baker, Steven
1983   A Quantitative Archaeological Study of the "Sporting Subculture": The Victorian Brothels of Ouray, Colorado. Paper presented at the 16th annual meeting of the Society for Historical Archaeology, Denver, January.

Bassett, Everett
1994   "We Took Care of Each Other Like Families Were Meant To": Gender, Social Organization, and Wage Labor among the Apache at Roosevelt. In *"Those of Little Note": Gender, Race and Class in Historical Archaeology.* E. M. Scott, ed. Pp. 55–81. Tucson: University of Arizona Press.

Battle, Whitney
2004   A Space of Our Own: Redefining the Enslaved Household at Andrew Jackson's Hermitage Plantation. In *Household Chores and Household Choices: Theorizing the Domestic Sphere in Historical Archaeology.* Kerri S. Barile and Jamie C. Brandon, eds. Pp. 33–51. Tuscaloosa: University of Alabama Press.

Baugher, Sherene, and Judith Baragli
1987   *The Archaeological Investigation at the Matron's Cottage, Snug Harbor Cultural Center, Staten Island, New York.* New York: New York City Landmarks Preservation Commission.

Beaudry, Mary C.
1993   Public Aesthetics versus Personal Experience: Worker Health and Well-Being in 19th-Century Lowell, Massachusetts. *Historical Archaeology* 27(2):90–106.

Beaudry, Mary C., and Stephen A. Mrozowski
2004   Cultural Space and Worker Identity in the Company Town: Lowell, Massachusetts. In *The Archaeology of Urban Landscapes: Explorations in Slumland.* Alan Mayne and Tim Murray, eds. Pp. 118–32. Cambridge: Cambridge University Press.

Beecher, Catharine E., and Harriet Beecher Stowe
   [1869] 1975   *The American Woman's Home, or Principles of Domestic Science.* Reprint, with
                 an introduction by Joseph Van Why. Hartford, CT: Stowe-Day Foundation.
Bell, Alison
   2001   "The Strong Prejudice of Propinquity": Inheritance Patterns and Women's
          Empowerment in 19th Century Virginia. Paper presented at a 2001 Society
          for Historical Archaeology symposium, Long Beach, CA, January 12.
Bescherer Metheny, Karen, Judson Kratzer, Anne Elizabeth Yentsch, and Conrad M.
Goodwin
   1996   Method in Landscape Archaeology: Research Strategies in a Historic New
          Jersey Garden. In *Landscape Archaeology: Reading and Interpreting the American Histori-
          cal Landscape.* R. Yamin and K. Bescherer Metheny, eds. Pp. 6–32. Knoxville:
          University of Tennessee Press.
Bickford, Anne
   1987   *Calthorpe's House: A Museum Guide.* Canberra: Australian Government Publishing
          Service.
   1993   Women's Historic Sites. In *Women in Archaeology: A Feminist Critique.* Hilary du
          Cros and Laurajane Smith, eds. Pp. 195–205. Canberra: Australian National
          University.
Binford, Lewis R.
   1962   Archaeology as Anthropology. *American Antiquity* 28(2):217–25.
   1983   *Working at Archaeology.* New York: Academic Press.
Birmingham, Judy
   1993   Engenderdynamics: Women in the Archaeological Record at Wybalenna,
          Flinders Island 1835–1840. In *Women in Archaeology: A Feminist Critique.* Hilary
          du Cros and Laurajane Smith, eds. Pp. 121–28. Canberra: Australian
          National University.
Bonine, Mindy
   2004   Analysis of Household and Family at a Spanish Colonial Rancho along the
          Rio Grande. In *Household Chores and Household Choices: Theorizing the Domestic Sphere
          in Historical Archaeology.* Kerri S. Barile and Jamie C. Brandon, eds. Pp. 15–33.
          Tuscaloosa: University of Alabama Press.
Boorstin, Daniel J., and Ruth F. Boorstin
   1989   *Hidden History: Our Secret Past.* New York: Vintage Books.
Brandon, Jamie C.
   2004   Reconstructing Domesticity and Segregating Households: The Intersections
          of Gender and Race in the Postbellum South. In *Household Chores and Household
          Choices: Theorizing the Domestic Sphere in Historical Archaeology.* Kerri S. Barile and
          Jamie C. Brandon, eds. Pp. 197–210. Tuscaloosa: University of Alabama
          Press.

Brashler, Janet G.
   1991   When Daddy Was a Shanty Boy: The Role of Gender in the Organization
            of the Logging Industry in Highland West Virginia. *Historical Archaeology*
            25(4):54–68.
Brighton, Stephen A.
   2001   Prices That Suit the Times: Shopping for Ceramics at the Five Points. *Histori-
            cal Archaeology* 35(3):16–31.
Bunch, Charlotte
   1987   *Passionate Politics: Essays 1968–1986—Feminist Theory in Action.* New York: St.
            Martin's Press.
Casey, Mary
   1999   Local Pottery and Dairying at the DMR Site, Brickfields, Sydney, NSW.
            Australasian Historical Archaeology 17:3–38.
   2002   Remaking the Government Domain, 1788–1821: Landscape, Archaeology
            and Meaning. Ph.D. dissertation, University of Sydney.
Chambers-Schiller, Lee Virginia
   1984   *Liberty a Better Husband. Single Women in America: The Generations of 1780–1840.*
            New Haven, CT: Yale University Press.
Clements, Joyce M.
   1993   The Cultural Creation of the Feminine Gender: An Example from 19th Cen-
            tury Military Households at Fort Independence, Boston. *Historical Archaeology*
            27(4):39–64.
   2005   ". . . A Winding Sheet for Deborah George . . ." Searching for the Women
            of Ponkapoag. Ph.D. dissertation, York University.
Cogan, Frances B.
   1989   *All-American Girl: The Ideal of Real Womanhood in Mid-Nineteenth-Century America.*
            Athens: University of Georgia Press.
Conkey, Margaret W., and Joan M. Gero
   1991   Tensions, Pluralities, and Engendering Archaeology: An Introduction to
            Women and Prehistory. In *Engendering Archaeology: Women and Prehistory.* J. M.
            Gero and M. W. Conkey, eds. Pp. 3–30. Oxford: Basil Blackwell.
Conkey, Margaret W., and Janet D. Spector
   1984   Archaeology and the Study of Gender. *Advances in Archaeological Method and Theory*
            7:1–38.
Cook, Lauren J.
   1997   "Promiscuous Smoking": Interpreting Gender and Tobacco Use in the
            Archaeological Record. *Northeast Historical Archaeology* 26:23–38.
   1998   "Kathrine Nanny, Alias Naylor": A Life in Puritan Boston. *Historical
            Archaeology* 32(1):15–20.
Costello, Julia G.
   2000   Red Light Voices: An Archaeological Drama of Late Nineteenth-Century

Prostitution. In *Archaeologies of Sexuality*. Peter A. Schmidt and Barbara L. Voss, eds. Pp. 160–79. London: Routledge.

Crass, David C., Bruce R. Penner, and Tammery R. Forehand
   1999   Gentility and Material Culture on the Carolina Frontier. *Historical Archaeology* 33(3):14–31.

Davidson, James M.
   2004   "Living Symbols of Their Lifelong Struggles": In Search of the Home and Household in the Heart of Freedman's Town, Dallas, Texas. In *Household Chores and Household Choices: Theorizing the Domestic Sphere in Historical Archaeology*. Kerri S. Barile and Jamie C. Brandon, eds. Pp. 75–108. Tuscaloosa: University of Alabama Press.

Deagan, Kathleen A.
   1983   *Spanish St. Augustine: The Archaeology of a Colonial Creole Community*. New York: Academic Press.

De Cunzo, Lu Ann
   1995   Reform, Respite, Ritual: An Archaeology of Institutions; the Magdalen Society of Philadelphia, 1800–1850. *Historical Archaeology* 29(3).
   2001   On Reforming the "Fallen" and Beyond: Transforming Continuity at the Magdalen Society of Philadelphia, 1845–1916. *International Journal of Historical Archaeology* 5(1):19–45.

Deetz, James F.
   1977   *In Small Things Forgotten*. Garden City, NY: Anchor Press/Doubleday.
   1988   Material Culture and Worldview in Colonial Anglo-America. In *The Recovery of Meaning: Historical Archaeology in the Eastern United States*. Mark P. Leone and Parker B. Potter Jr., eds. Pp. 219–34. Washington, DC: Smithsonian Institution Press.

Delle, James A.
   2000   Gender, Power, and Space: Negotiating Social Relations under Slavery on Coffee Plantations in Jamaica 1790–1834. In *Lines That Divide: Historical Archaeologies of Race, Class, and Gender*. J. A. Delle, S. A. Mrozowski, and R. Paynter, eds. Pp. 168–205. Knoxville: University of Tennessee Press.

Delphy, Christine
   1984   *Close to Home: A Materialist Analysis of Women's Oppression*. Diana Leonard, trans. and ed. Amherst: University of Massachusetts Press.

Devens, Carol
   1991   Gender and Colonization in Native Canadian Communities: Examining the Historical Record. In *The Archaeology of Gender*. Proceedings of the 22nd Annual Chacmool Conference. Dale Walde and Noreen D. Willows, eds. Pp. 510–14. Calgary: Department of Archaeology.

Donovan, Josephine
   2001   *Feminist Theory: The Intellectual Traditions*. 3rd ed. New York. Continuum.

Elliott, Suzanne W.
  1977   Historical Archaeology and the National Market: A Vermont Perspective, 1795–1920. Ph.D. dissertation, University of Massachusetts, Amherst.
Englestad, Erica
  1991   Feminist Theory and Post-Processual Archaeology. In *The Archaeology of Gender*. Proceedings of the 22nd Annual Chacmool Conference. Dale Walde and Noreen D. Willows, eds. Pp. 116–20. Calgary: Department of Archaeology, University of Calgary.
Feister, Lois M.
  1991   The Orphanage at Schuyler Mansion. *Northeast Historical Archaeology* 20:27–36.
  2003   Archaeology at a 19th-Century Orphanage: Why Toys? Paper presented at the 36th Annual Conference on Historical and Underwater Archaeology, Providence, RI, January 14–18.
Fitts, Robert K.
  1999   The Archaeology of Middle-Class Domesticity and Gentility in Victorian Brooklyn. *Historical Archaeology* 33(1):39–63.
  2001   The Rhetoric of Reform: The Five Points Missions and the Cult of Domesticity. *Historical Archaeology* 35(3):115–33.
Franklin, Maria
  2001   Black Feminist-Inspired Archaeology? *Journal of Social Archaeology* 1(1):108–25.
Frink, Lisa
  2005   Gender and the Hide Production Process in Colonial Western Alaska. In *Gender and Hide Production*. Lisa Frink and Kathryn Weedman, eds. Pp. 89–105. Walnut Creek, CA: AltaMira Press.
Garrow, Patrick H.
  1987   The Use of Converging Lines of Evidence for Determining Socioeconomic Status. In *Consumer Choice in Historical Archaeology*. Suzanne M. Spencer-Wood, ed. Pp. 217–33. New York: Plenum.
Gero, Joan M.
  1991   Genderlithics: Women's Roles in Stone Tool Production. In *Engendering Archaeology: Women and Prehistory*. Joan M. Gero and Margaret W. Conkey, eds. Pp. 163–94. Oxford: Basil Blackwell.
Gibb, James G., and Julia A. King
  1991   Gender, Activity Areas, and Homelots in the 19th Century Chesapeake Region. *Historical Archaeology* 25(4):109–31.
Gibb, James G., and Lee Preston
  2003   Patapsco Female Institute (1837–1890): A Light upon a Hill Relit. Paper presented at the 36th Annual Conference on Historical and Underwater Archaeology, Providence, RI, January 14–18.
Glassie, Henry
  1975   *Folk Housing in Middle Virginia*. Knoxville: University of Tennessee Press.

Goodwin, Lorinda B. R.
   1999   *An Archaeology of Manners: The Polite World of the Merchant Elite of Colonial Massachu-setts.* New York: Kluwer Academic/Plenum.
Griggs, Heather J.
   2001   "By Virtue of Reason and Nature": Competition and Economic Strategy in the Needletrades at New York's Five Points, 1855–1880. *Historical Archaeology* 35(3):76–89.
Guettel, Charnie
   1974   *Marxism and Feminism.* Toronto: Women's Educational Press.
Hardesty, Donald L.
   1989   Gender Roles on the American Mining Frontier: Documentary Models and Archaeological Strategies. Paper presented at the 22nd Annual Chacmool Conference, Calgary, November.
   1994   Class, Gender Strategies, and Material Culture in the Mining West. In *"Those of Little Note": Gender, Race and Class in Historical Archaeology.* Elizabeth M. Scott, ed. Pp. 129–49. Tucson: University of Arizona Press.
Harding, Sandra
   1987   Conclusion: Epistemological Questions. In *Feminism and Methodology.* Sandra Harding, ed. Pp. 181–90. Bloomington: Indiana University Press.
   1993   Rethinking Standpoint Epistemology: "What Is Strong Objectivity"? In *Feminist Epistemologies.* Linda Alcoff and Elizabeth Potter, eds. Pp. 49–83. New York: Routledge.
Hartsock, Nancy C. M.
   1983   *Money, Sex and Power: Toward a Feminist Historical Materialism.* New York: Longman.
Hautaniemi, Susan
   1994   Race, Gender, and Health at the W. E. B. DuBois Boyhood Homesite. *Bulletin of the Massachusetts Archaeological Society* 55(1):1–7.
Hautaniemi, Susan I., and Deborah L. Rotman
   2003   To the Hogs or to the House? Municipal Water and Gender Relations at the Moors Site in Deerfield, Massachusetts. In *Shared Spaces and Divided Places: Material Dimensions of Gender Relations and the American Historical Landscape.* Deborah L. Rotman and Ellen-Rose Savulis, eds. Pp. 135–60. Knoxville: University of Tennessee Press.
Heck, Dana B., and Joseph F. Balicki
   1998   Katherine Naylor's "Home of Office": A Seventeenth-Century Privy. *Historical Archaeology* 32(3):24–38.
Henretta, J. A.
   1971   Economic Development and Social Structure in Colonial Boston. In *The Reinterpretation of American Economic History.* R. W. Fogel and S. W. Engerman, eds. Pp. 54–63. New York: Harper and Row.

Hodder, Ian, and Scott Hutson
  2003   *Reading the Past: Current Approaches to Interpretation in Archaeology.* 3rd ed. Cambridge: Cambridge University Press.
Hodder, I.
  1991a. Gender Representation and Social Reality. In *The Archaeology of Gender.* Proceedings of the 22nd Annual Chacmool Conference. Dale Walde and Noreen D. Willows, eds. Pp. 11–17. Calgary: Department of Archaeology, University of Calgary.
  1991b. Postprocessual Archaeology and the Current Debate. In *Processual and Postprocessual Archaeologies: Multiple Ways of Knowing the Past.* Robert W. Preucel, ed. Pp. 30–41. Occasional Paper 10. Carbondale: Center for Archaeological Investigations, Southern Illinois University.
Hollimon, Sandra E.
  2005   Hideworking and Changes in Women's Status among the Arikara 1700–1862. In *Gender and Hide Production.* Lisa Frink and Kathryn Weedman, eds. Pp. 77–89. Walnut Creek, CA: AltaMira Press.
Jackson, Louise M.
  1994   Cloth, Clothing and Related Paraphernalia: A Key to Gender Visibility in the Archaeological Record of Russian America. In *"Those of Little Note": Gender, Race and Class in Historical Archaeology.* E. M. Scott, ed. Pp. 27–55. Tucson: University of Arizona Press.
Jamieson, Ross W.
  2000   Doña Luisa and Her Two Houses. In *Lines That Divide: Historical Archaeologies of Race, Class, and Gender.* J. A. Delle, S. A. Mrozowski, and R. Paynter, eds. Pp. 142–68. Knoxville: University of Tennessee Press.
Karskens, Grace
  2003   Revisiting the Worldview: The Archaeology of Convict Households in Sydney's Rocks Neighborhood. *Historical Archaeology* 37(1):34–55.
Kennedy, Margaret
  1989   Houses with Red Lights: The Nature of Female Households in the Sporting Subculture Community. In *Households and Communities.* Proceedings of the 21st Annual Chacmool Conference. Scott MacEachern, David J. W. Archer, and Richard D. Garvin, eds. Pp. 93–101. Calgary: Department of Archaeology, University of Calgary.
Knapp, Bernard
  1998   Boys Will Be Boys: Masculinist Approaches to a Gendered Archaeology. In *Reader in Gender Archaeology.* Kelley Hays-Gilpin and David S. Whitley, eds. Pp. 365–74. London: Routledge.
Kruczek-Aaron, Hadley
  2002   Choice Flowers and Well-Ordered Tables: Struggling over Gender in a Nineteenth-Century Household. *International Journal of Historical Archaeology* 6(3):173–87.

Kuhn, Annette, and Ann Marie Wolpe, eds.
   1978   *Feminism and Materialism: Women and Modes of Production*. Boston: Routledge and
         Kegan Paul.
Larsen, Eric L.
   1994   A Boardinghouse Madonna—Beyond the Aesthetics of a Portrait Created
         through Medicine Bottles. In *An Archaeology of Harpers Ferry's Commercial and
         Residential District*. Paul A. Shackle and Susan E. Winter, eds. *Historical Archaeol-
         ogy* 28(4):68–80.
Lawrence, Susan
   1999   Towards a Feminist Archaeology of Households: Gender and Household
         Structure on the Australian Goldfields. In *The Archaeology of Household Activities:
         Gender Ideologies, Domestic Spaces and Material Culture*. Penelope M. Allison, ed. Pp.
         121–42. London: Routledge.
Lawrence-Cheney, Susan
   1991   Women and Alcohol: Female Influence on Recreational Patterns in the West
         1880–1890. In *The Archaeology of Gender*. Proceedings of the 22nd Annual
         Chacmool Conference. Dale Walden and Noreen D. Willows, eds. Pp. 479–
         89. Calgary: Department of Archaeology, University of Calgary.
   1993   Gender on Colonial Peripheries. In *Women in Archaeology: A Feminist Critique*.
         Hilary du Cros and Laurajane Smith, eds. Pp. 134–37. Canberra: Australian
         National University.
Leedecker, Charles H., Terry H. Klein, Cheryl A. Holt, and Amy Friedlander
   1987   Nineteenth-Century Households and Consumer Behavior in Wilmington,
         Delaware. In *Consumer Choice in Historical Archaeology*. Suzanne M. Spencer-
         Wood, ed. Pp. 233–61. New York: Plenum.
Lewis, Kenneth E.
   2003   The Tin Worker's Widow: Gender and the Formation of the Archaeological
         Record in the South Carolina Backcountry. In *Shared Spaces and Divided Places:
         Material Dimensions of Gender Relations and the American Historical Landscape*. Deborah
         L. Rotman and Ellen-Rose Savulis, eds. Pp. 86–104. Knoxville: University
         of Tennessee Press.
Little, Barbara J.
   1994   "She Was . . . an Example to Her Sex": Possibilities for a Feminist Historical
         Archaeology. In *Historical Archaeology of the Chesapeake*. Paul A. Shackel and Bar-
         bara J. Little, eds. Pp. 189–201. Washington, DC: Smithsonian Institution
         Press.
Longino, Helen
   1989   Can There Be a Feminist Science? In *Feminism and Science*. Nancy Tuana, ed.
         Pp. 45–58. Bloomington: Indiana University Press.
Longino, Helen, and Ruth Doell
   1983   Body, Bias and Behavior: A Comparative Analysis of Reasoning in Two Areas
         of Biological Science. *Signs: Journal of Women in Culture and Society* 9(2):206–27.

Lorber, Judith
    2001   *Gender Inequality: Feminist Theories and Politics.* 2nd ed. Los Angeles: Roxbury.
Lucas, Michael T.
    1994   A la Russe, a la Pell-Mell, or a la Practicall: Ideology and Compromise in
            the Late Nineteenth-Century Dinner Table. In *An Archaeology of Harpers Ferry's
            Commercial and Residential District.* Paul A. Shackle and Susan E. Winter, eds.
            Historical Archaeology 28(4):80–94.
Lydon, Jane
    1993a. Archaeology in The Rocks, Sydney, 1979–1993: From Old Sydney Gaol to
            Mrs Lewis' Boarding House. *Australasian Historical Archaeology* 11:33–42.
    1993b   Task Differentiation in Historical Archaeology: Sewing as Material Culture.
            In *Women in Archaeology: A Feminist Critique.* Hilary du Cros and Laurajane
            Smith, eds. Pp. 129–33. Canberra: Australian National University.
    1995   Gender in Australian Historical Archaeology. In *Gendered Archaeology: The Second
            Australian Women in Archaeology Conference.* Jane Balme and Wendy Beck, eds. Pp.
            72–80. Canberra: ANH Publications, Research School of Pacific Studies,
            Australian National University.
McEwan, Bonnie G.
    1991   The Archaeology of Women in the Spanish New World. *Historical Archaeology*
            25(4):33–41.
McKee, Larry
    1996   The Archaeology of Rachel's Garden. In *Landscape Archaeology: Reading and Inter-
            preting the American Historical Landscape.* R. Yamin and K. Bescherer Metheny, eds.
            Pp. 70–91. Knoxville: University of Tennessee Press.
McMurray, Sally
    1987   Women and the Expansion of Dairying: The Cheesemaking Industry in
            Oneida County, New York, 1830–1860. Paper presented at the annual Berk-
            shire History Conference, Wellesley, MA, June.
Millett, Kate
    1970   *Sexual Politics: A Surprising Examination of Society's Most Arbitrary Folly.* Garden City,
            NY: Doubleday.
Morenon, E. Pierre
    2003   Children at Play: Archaeological Studies of Toys, Buildings and Institutions.
            Paper presented at the 36th Annual Conference on Historical and Underwa-
            ter Archaeology, Providence, RI.
Mrozowski, Stephen A.
    2000   The Growth of Managerial Capitalism and the Subtleties of Class Analysis
            in Historical Archaeology. In *Lines That Divide: Historical Archaeologies of Race,
            Class, and Gender.* J. A. Delle, S. A. Mrozowski, and R. Paynter, eds. Pp. 276–
            307. Knoxville: University of Tennessee Press.
Mrozowski, Stephen A., James A. Delle, and Robert Paynter
    2000   Introduction. In *Lines That Divide: Historical Archaeologies of Race, Class, and Gender.*

J. A. Delle, S. A. Mrozowski, and R. Paynter, eds. Pp. xi–xxxi. Knoxville: University of Tennessee Press.

Muller, Nancy Ladd
1994   The House of the Black Burghardts: An Investigation of Gender, Race and Class at the W. E. B. DuBois Boyhood Homesite. In *"Those of Little Note": Gender, Race and Class in Historical Archaeology*. E. M. Scott, ed. Pp. 81–97. Tucson: University of Arizona Press.

Mullins, Paul R.
1999   *Race and Affluence: An Archaeology of African America and Consumer Culture*. New York: Kluwer Academic/Plenum.

Nassaney, Michael S., D. L. Rotman, D. O. Sayers, and C. A. Nickolai
2001   The Southwest Michigan Historic Landscape Project: Exploring Class, Gender, and Ethnicity from the Ground Up. *International Journal of Historical Archaeology* 5(3):219–61.
2002   Gender in Archaeology: The Professional Is Political. Paper presented at the 2002 centennial meetings of the American Anthropological Association, New Orleans.
2003   *Ancient Queens: Archaeological Explorations*. Walnut Creek, CA: AltaMira Press.

Nickolai, Carol A.
2003   Class and Gender in Nineteenth-Century Rural Michigan: The Merriman-Sharp Hillside Farm. *Historical Archaeology* 37(4):69–83.

Ortner, Sherry B.
1974   Is Female to Male as Nature Is to Culture? In *Woman, Culture and Society*. Michelle Z. Rosaldo and Louise Lamphere, eds. Pp. 67–88. Stanford, CA: Stanford University Press.

Piddock, Susan
2001   "An Irregular and Inconvenient Pile of Buildings": The Destitute Asylum of Adelaide, South Australia and the English Workhouse. *International Journal of Historical Archaeology* 5(1):73–97.

Praetzellis, Adrian, and Mary Praetzellis, eds.
1998   *Archaeologists as Storytellers. Historical Archaeology* 32(1).

Purser, Margaret
1991   "Several Paradise Ladies Are Visiting in Town": Gender Strategies in the Early Industrial West. *Historical Archaeology* 25(4):6–16.

Rosaldo, Michele Zimbalist
1974   Woman, Culture, and Society: A Theoretical Overview. In *Woman, Culture and Society*. Michelle Z. Rosaldo and Louise Lamphere, eds. Pp. 17–42. Stanford, CA: Stanford University Press.
1980   The Use and Abuse of Anthropology: Reflections on Feminism and Cross-Cultural Understanding. *Signs* 5(3):389–417.

Rosaldo, Michele Z., and Louise Lamphere
1974   Introduction. In *Woman, Culture and Society*. Michelle Z. Rosaldo and Louise Lamphere, eds. Pp. 1–16. Stanford, CA: Stanford University Press.

Rotman, Deborah L., and Michael S. Nassaney
   1997   Class, Gender and the Built Environment: Deriving Social Relations from
           Cultural Landscapes in Southwest Michigan. *Historical Archaeology*
           331(2):42–62.
Russell, Penny
   1993   In Search of Woman's Place: An Historical Survey of Gender and Space in
           Nineteenth-Century Australia. *Australasian Historical Archaeology* 11:28–32.
Ryan, Mary P.
   1990   *Women in Public: Between Banners and Ballots, 1825–1880.* Baltimore: The Johns
           Hopkins University Press.
Savulis, Ellen-Rose
   2003   Zion's Zeal: Negotiating Identity in Shaker Communities. In *Shared Spaces and
           Divided Places: Material Dimensions of Gender Relations and the American Historical Land-
           scape.* Deborah L. Rotman and Ellen-Rose Savulis, eds. Pp. 160–90. Knox-
           ville: University of Tennessee Press.
Sayers, D. O., and Michael S. Nassaney
   1999   Antebellum Landscapes and Agrarian Political Economies: Modeling Pro-
           gressive Farmsteads in Southwest Michigan. *The Michigan Archaeologist*
           45(3):74–117.
Schuyler, Robert L., ed.
   1980   *Archaeological Perspectives on Ethnicity in America: Afro-American and Asian American
           Culture History.* Farmingdale, NY: Baywood.
Scott, Elizabeth M.
   1991a   A Feminist Approach to Historical Archaeology: Eighteenth-Century Fur
           Trade Society at Michilimackinac. *Historical Archaeology* 25(4):82–109.
   1991b   Gender in Complex Colonial Society: The Material Goods of Everyday Life
           in a Late Eighteenth Century Fur Trading Community. In *The Archaeology of
           Gender.* Proceedings of the 22nd Annual Chacmool Conference. Dale Walde
           and Noreen D. Willows, eds. Pp. 270–79. Calgary: Department of Archaeol-
           ogy, University of Calgary.
   1994   Through the Lens of Gender: Archaeology, Inequality and "Those of Little
           Note." In *"Those of Little Note": Gender, Race and Class in Historical Archaeology.*
           E. M. Scott, ed. Pp. 3–27. Tucson: University of Arizona Press.
Seifert, Donna J.
   1991a   Introduction. In *Gender in Historical Archaeology.* D. J. Seifert, ed. *Historical Archae-
           ology* 25(4):1–5.
   1991b   Within Sight of the White House: The Archaeology of Working Women.
           Historical Archaeology 25(4):82–108.
   1994   Mrs. Starr's Profession. In *"Those of Little Note": Gender, Race and Class in Historical
           Archaeology.* E. M. Scott, ed. Pp. 149–74. Tucson: University of Arizona Press.
Singleton, Theresa L.
   1990   The Archaeology of the Plantation South: A Review of Approaches and
           Goals. *Historical Archaeology* 24(4):70–78.

Sipe, Amy E. S.
 2003   Understanding Gender, Reform, and Social Change in 19th Century Central
         New York. Paper presented at the Society for Historical Archaeology 36th
         Annual Conference on Historical and Underwater Archaeology, Providence,
         RI, January.
Slocum, Sally
 1975   Woman the Gatherer: Male Bias in Anthropology. In *Towards an Anthropology
         of Women*. Rayna R. Reiter, ed. Pp. 36–51. New York: Monthly Review Press.
Smith, Sheli O.
 1989   Women and Seafaring. Paper presented at the 22nd Annual Chacmool Con-
         ference, Calgary, November 11.
South, Stanley
 1977   *Method and Theory in Historical Archaeology*. New York: Academic Press.
Spector, Janet D.
 1983   Male/Female Task Differentiation among the Hidatsa: Toward the Develop-
         ment of an Archaeological Approach to the Study of Gender. In *The Hidden
         Half: Studies of Plains Indian Women*. P. Albers and B. Medicine, eds. Pp. 77–99.
         Washington, DC: University Press of America.
 1993   *What This Awl Means: Feminist Archaeology at a Wahpeton Dakota Village*. St. Paul:
         Minnesota Historical Society Press.
Spencer-Wood, Suzanne M. A.
 1987a   A Survey of Domestic Reform Movement Sites in Boston and Cambridge,
         ca. 1865–1905. *Historical Archaeology* 21(2):7–36.
 1987b   Miller's Indices and Consumer Choice Profiles: Status-Related Behaviors and
         White Ceramics. In *Consumer Choice in Historical Archaeology*. Suzanne Spencer-
         Wood, ed. Pp. 321–58. New York: Plenum.
 1989a   The Community as Household: Domestic Reform, Mid-Range Theory and
         the Domestication of Public Space. In *Household and Communities*. Proceedings
         of the 21st Annual Chacmool Conference. S. MacEachern, D. J. W. Archer,
         and R. D. Garvin, eds. Pp. 113–22. Calgary: Department of Archaeology,
         University of Calgary.
 1989b   Feminist Historical Archaeology. Symposium organized for the 22nd Annual
         Chacmool Conference, Calgary, November.
 1989c   Making Women Visible through Historical Archaeology. Symposium orga-
         nized at the First Joint Archaeological Congress, Baltimore, January 8.
 1991a   Feminist Empiricism: A More Holistic Theoretical Approach. Paper pre-
         sented at the Conference on Historical and Underwater Archaeology, Rich-
         mond, VA, January.
 1991b   Toward an Historical Archaeology of Domestic Reform. In *The Archaeology of
         Inequality*. R. McGuire and R. Paynter, eds. Pp. 231–86. Oxford: Basil Black-
         well.
 1991c   Towards a Feminist Historical Archaeology of the Construction of Gender.

In *The Archaeology of Gender*. Proceedings of the 22nd Chacmool Conference. Dale Walde and Noreen D. Willows, eds. Pp. 234–44. Calgary: Department of Archaeology, University of Calgary.

1992   A Feminist Program for a Non-Sexist Archaeology. In *Quandaries and Quests: Visions of Archaeology's Future*. LuAnn Wandsnider, ed. Pp. 98–113. Occasional Paper 20. Carbondale: Center for Archaeological Investigations, Southern Illinois University.

1993   Review of "The Recovery of Meaning: Historical Archaeology in the Eastern United States," by Mark P. Leone and Parker B. Potter. *Bulletin of the History of Archaeology* 3(1):27–35.

1994a   Diversity in 19th Century Domestic Reform: Relationships among Classes and Ethnic Groups. In *"Those of Little Note": Gender, Race and Class in Historical Archaeology*. Elizabeth Scott, ed. Tucson: University of Arizona Press.

1994b   Turn of the Century Women's Organizations, Urban Design, and the Origin of the American Playground Movement. *Landscape Journal* 13(2, fall):125–38.

1995   Toward the Further Development of Feminist Historical Archaeology. *World Archaeological Bulletin* 7:118–36.

1996   Feminist Historical Archaeology and the Transformation of American Culture by Domestic Reform Movements, 1840–1925. In *Historical Archaeology and the Study of American Culture*. L. A. De Cunzo and B. L. Herman, eds. Pp. 397–46. Knoxville: Winterthur Museum and University of Tennessee Press.

1997a   Feminist Inclusive Theory: Crossing Boundaries in Theory and Practice. Paper invited for the Fourth Australian Women in Archaeology Conference, Cairns, Australia, July 3–5.

1997b   Pragmatism and Feminism. Paper invited for an American Anthropological Association symposium, Washington, DC, November 19–23.

1999a   Archaeology and the Gendering of American Historical Landscapes: A Brief Overview. Paper presented at the Fifth Australian Women in Archaeology Conference, Sydney, Australia, July 2–4.

1999b   The Formation of Ethnic-American Identities: Jewish Communities in Boston. In *Historical Archaeology: Back from the Edge*. Pedro Paulo A. Funari, Martin Hall, and Sîan Jones, eds. Pp. 284–307. London: Routledge.

1999c   Gendering Power. In *Manifesting Power: Gender and the Interpretation of Power in Archaeology*. Tracy L. Sweely, ed. Pp. 175–83. London: Routledge.

1999d   The World Their Household: Changing Meanings of the Domestic Sphere in the Nineteenth Century. In *The Archaeology of Household Activities*. Penelope M. Allison, ed. Pp. 162–89. London: Routledge.

2000   Strange Attractors: Non-Linear Systems Theory and Feminist Theory. In *Exploring Social Theory in Archaeology*. Michael B. Schiffer, ed. Pp. 112–26. Salt Lake City: University of Utah Press.

2001a   Introduction. In *The Archaeology of Seventeenth and Eighteenth Century Almshouses*.

Sherene Baugher and S. M. Spencer-Wood, eds. *International Journal of Historical Archaeology* 5(2):115–22.

2001b   What Difference Does Feminist Theory Make? In *The Archaeology of Nineteenth Century Institutions for Reform*. Suzanne M. Spencer-Wood and Sherene Baugher, eds. *International Journal of Historical Archaeology* 5(1):97–114.

2002a   Feminist Theory. Entry invited for the *Encyclopedia of Historical Archaeology*. Charles E. Orser, ed. Pp. 205–9. London: Routledge.

2002b   Utopian Visions and Architectural Designs of Turn-of-the-Century Social Settlements. In *Embodied Utopias: Gender, Social Change and the Modern Metropolis*. Amy Bingaman, Lise Shapiro, and Rebecca Zorach, eds. Pp. 116–32. London: Routledge.

2003   Gendering the Creation of Green Urban Landscapes in America at the Turn of the Century. In *Shared Spaces and Divided Places: Material Dimensions of Gender Relations and the American Historical Landscape*. Deborah L. Rotman and Ellen-Rose Savulis, eds. Pp. 24–62. Knoxville: University of Tennessee Press.

2004   A Historic Pay-for-Housework Community Household: The Cambridge Cooperative Housekeeping Society. In *Household Chores and Household Choices: Theorizing the Domestic Sphere in Historical Archaeology*. Kerri Barrile and Jamie Brandon, eds. Pp. 138–58. Tuscaloosa: University of Alabama Press.

2005   Feminist Boundary Crossings: Challenging Androcentric Assumptions and Stereotypes about Hideworking. Invited commentary chapter in *Gender and Hide Production*. Lisa Frink and Kathryn Weedman, eds. Pp. 197–215. Walnut Creek, CA: AltaMira Press.

2006   A Feminist Theoretical Approach to the Historical Archaeology of Utopian Communities. *Historical Archaeology* 40(1): 152–85.

Spencer-Wood, Suzanne M., and Sherene Baugher

2001   Introduction. In *The Archaeology of Nineteenth Century Institutions for Reform*. Suzanne M. Spencer-Wood and Sherene Baugher, eds. *International Journal of Historical Archaeology* 5(1):3–17.

Spude, Cathy H.

1999   Predicting Gender in Archaeological Assemblages: A Klondike Example. In *Restoring Women's History through Historic Preservation*. Gail Dubrow and J. Goodman, eds. Baltimore: The Johns Hopkins University Press.

Stansell, Christine

1986   *City of Women: Sex and Class in New York 1789–1860*. New York: Alfred A. Knopf.

Starbuck, David R.

1994   The Identification of Gender at Northern Military Sites of the Late Eighteenth Century. In *"Those of Little Note": Gender, Race and Class in Historical Archaeology*. E. M. Scott, ed. Pp. 115–29. Tucson: University of Arizona Press.

Stewart-Abernathy, Leslie C.

2004   Separate Kitchens and Intimate Archaeology: Constructing Urban Slavery on the Antebellum Cotton Frontier in Washington, Arkansas. In *Household Chores and Household Choices: Theorizing the Domestic Sphere in Historical Archaeology*. Kerri S. Barile and Jamie C. Brandon, eds. Pp. 51–75. Tuscaloosa: University of Alabama Press.

Valian, Virginia
1998   *Why so Slow? The Advancement of Women*. Cambridge, MA: MIT Press.

Wall, Diana di Zerega
1991   Sacred Dinners and Secular Teas: Constructing Domesticity in Mid-19th-Century New York. *Historical Archaeology* 25(4):69–81.

1994   *The Archaeology of Gender: Separating the Spheres in Urban America*. New York: Plenum.

2000   Family Meals and Evening Parties: Constructing Domesticity in Nineteenth-Century Middle-Class New York. In *Lines That Divide: Historical Archaeologies of Race, Class, and Gender*. J. A. Delle, S. A. Mrozowski, and R. Paynter, eds. Pp. 109–42. Knoxville: University of Tennessee Press.

Weber, Carmen A.
1991   The Genius of the Orangery: Women and Eighteenth Century Chesapeake Gardens. In *The Archaeology of Gender*. Proceedings of the 22nd Annual Chacmool Conference. Dale Walde and Noreen D. Willows, eds. Pp. 263–69. Calgary: Department of Archaeology.

1996   The Greenhouse Effect: Gender-Related Traditions in Eighteenth-Century Gardening. In *Landscape Archaeology: Reading and Interpreting the American Historical Landscape*. R. Yamin and K. Bescherer Metheny, eds. Pp. 32–52. Knoxville: University of Tennessee Press.

Welter, Barbara
1966   The Cult of True Womanhood: 1820–1860. *American Quarterly* 18:151–74.

Wertheimer, Barbara M.
1977   *We Were There: The Story of Working Women in America*. New York: Pantheon Books/Random House.

Wheeler, Kathleen L.
2000   Using archaeology to debunk the myth of the "poor widow." Paper presented at the 99th annual meeting of the American Anthropological Association, San Francisco, November 22.

2001   Women, Architecture and Artifact. Paper presented at a 2001 Society for Historical Archaeology conference symposium, Long Beach, CA, January 12.

Whelan, Mary K.
1991   Gender and Historical Archaeology: Eastern Dakota Patterns in the 19th Century. *Historical Archaeology* 25(4):17–32.

Wilkie, Laurie A.
1996   Medicinal Teas and Patent Medicines: African American Women's Consumer Choices and Ethnomedical Traditions at a Louisiana Plantation. *Southeastern Archaeology* 14(2):136–48.

2000   Not Merely Child's Play: Creating a Historical Archaeology of Children and Childhood. In *Children and Material Culture.* Joanna S. Derevenski, ed. Pp. 100–115. London: Routledge.

2003   *The Archaeology of Mothering: An African-American Midwife's Tale.* Berkeley: University of California Press.

Wood, Margaret C.

2004   Working-Class Households as Sites of Social Change. In *Household Chores and Household Choices: Theorizing the Domestic Sphere in Historical Archaeology.* Kerri S. Barile and Jamie C. Brandon, eds. Pp. 210–35. Tuscaloosa: University of Alabama Press.

Woodhouse-Beyer, K.

1999   Artels and Identities: Gender, Power and Russian America. In *Manifesting Power: Gender and the Interpretation of Power in Archaeology.* Tracy L. Sweely, ed. Pp. 129–55. London: Routledge.

Woodruff, Janet

2005   African Spiritual Practices in the Diaspora: A Preliminary Look at Connecticut. Paper presented at the 38th Annual Conference on Historical and Underwater Archaeology, York.

Wylie, Alison

1991a   Feminist Critiques and Archaeological Challenges. In *The Archaeology of Gender.* Proceedings of the 22nd Annual Chacmool Conference. Dale Walde and Noreen D. Willows, eds. Pp. 17–23. Calgary: Department of Archaeology, University of Calgary.

1991b   Gender Theory and the Archaeological Record: Why Is There No Archaeology of Gender? In *Engendering Archaeology: Women and Prehistory.* J. M. Gero and M. W. Conkey, eds. Pp. 31–54. Oxford: Basil Blackwell.

1992   The Interplay of Evidential Constraints and Political Interests: Recent Archaeological Research on Gender. *American Antiquity* 57:15–35.

Yamin, Rebecca

2004   Alternative Narratives: Respectability at New York's Five Points. In *The Archaeology of Urban Landscapes: Explorations in Slumland.* Alan Mayne and Tim Murray, eds. Pp. 154–71. Cambridge: Cambridge University Press.

Yamin, Rebecca, and Sarah T. Bridges

2002   Children's Strikes, Parents' Rights: Paterson and Five Points. *International Journal of Historical Archaeology* 6(2):113–27.

Yentsch, Anne E.

1991a   Access and Space, Symbolic and Material, in Historical Archaeology. In *The Archaeology of Gender.* Proceedings of the 22nd Chacmool Conference. Dale Walde and Noreen D. Willows, eds. Pp. 252–63. Calgary: Department of Archaeology, University of Calgary.

1991b   Engendering Visible and Invisible Ceramic Artifacts, Especially Dairy Vessels. *Historical Archaeology* 25(4):17–32.

1991c   The Symbolic Divisions of Pottery: Sex-Related Attributes of English and Anglo-American Household Pots. In *The Archaeology of Inequality*. R. H. McGuire and R. Paynter, eds. Pp. 192–230. Cambridge: Basil Blackwell.

1994   *A Chesapeake Family and Their Slaves: A Study in Historical Archaeology*. Cambridge: Cambridge University Press.

Young, Amy

2003   Gender and Landscape: A View from the Plantation Slave Community. In *Shared Spaces and Divided Places: Material Dimensions of Gender Relations and the American Historical Landscape*. Deborah L. Rotman and Ellen-Rose Savulis, eds. Pp. 104–35. Knoxville: University of Tennessee Press.

Young, Linda

2003   *Middle-Class Culture in the Nineteenth Century: America, Australia and Britain*. New York: Palgrave Macmillan.

Zeising, Grace H.

1989   Analysis of Personal Effects from the Excavations of the Boott Mills Boardinghouse Backlots in Lowell, Massachusetts. In *Interdisciplinary Investigations of the Boott Mills, Lowell, Massachusetts. Vol. 3: The Boardinghouse System as a Way of Life*. Boston: National Park Service, North Atlantic Regional Office.

Gender, Things, and Material Culture 3

MARIE LOUISE STIG SØRENSEN

THE ASPECT OF GENDER that archaeology can investigate with the greatest expertise is the way in which gender construction and the living of gendered lives involve and are affected by material culture. Material culture is not, however, merely things. Rather, it is an extremely interesting and flexible medium that is used both to create notions of traditions, the maintenance of conventions, and normative behavior and as a means of defiance against and disrupting these same norms. Material culture is therefore not just a source for the finding of representations of gender; rather, it is in itself implicated in the construction of gender at different levels. Conceptualizing the meaning of things should therefore be thought of as a dynamic rather than a decoding process (Kirkham and Attfield 1996:11, n. 2). We should think of material culture as a place of creation as well as resistance, and both qualities come into play in the construction and experience of gender. One of the distinct achievements of gender research has therefore been its explicit attention to this intricate relationship between material culture and social and psychological ideas about and categories of gender. In the history of gender archaeology, we can accordingly identify a distinct line of argument concerned with analyzing and utilizing the connections between gender (as both a social construction and a personal experience) and the external physical means through which such constructions and experiences are formulated. We have seen the debate move quickly from a position in the 1970s to 1980s in which objects were approached as the reflections, symbols, or signs of gender without in themselves adding any dynamic to the situations studied to the current one in which different theoretical positions are used to explore material culture as a medium intimately involved in the construction of meaning. During this development, a number of key concerns have been raised, and substantially different perceptions of gender have become apparent, all of which contribute to the current self-critical and explorative stage in the development of gender archaeology. In particular, these discussions manage to show archaeological data in a new light, they outline complex and potentially contradictory understandings of gender, and they provide challenges to and links with developments in other disciplines, such as design history, material culture study, and history—in other words, they add to our means of exploring how people and communities construct gendered worlds around themselves.

The following discussion of material culture and gender begins by outlining some of the main changes in our understanding and analyses of this relationship since the first explicit discussions of gender in archaeology. Thereafter, two main thematic foci will be used to provide exemplars that outline some of the arguments of recent developments. One theme is the relationship between the learning and acquiring of gender identity and the use of objects to fabricate differences in people's appearances. The other theme is the manner in which gender ideology can be manifest in the construction of space and the development of routines or *habitus* that this encourages. Finally, some reflections on the advances currently taking place and the emergence of a new range of arguments will be given. The overall aim throughout is to illuminate the explicit yet intricate relationship between different dimensions of gender and the production, circulation, and consumption of material culture and to give some insights into with what strength and thoughtfulness archaeology has been exploring this relationship to the benefit of the study of gender, the discipline, and material culture studies more generally.

On the Changing Role of Material Culture in Gender Studies

Material Objects as Reflection of Gender

The first explicit studies of gender and material culture were motivated by a strong desire to find women's past, to locate their roles and contribution in society, and to find evidence of their importance. Epistemologically, this work was guided by an understanding of material culture that saw it as passive and its role to be the representation of social relations. The analyses were also often influenced by an expectation that association with wealth of various kinds would evidence the importance of women; studies were accordingly formulated within an analytical framework that focused on general patterns, repetition, and various quantitative measures. This led in particular to studies looking for evidence of women's rank and wealth in mortuary data. These studies were theoretically influenced by approaches to mortuary studies that equated objects found in a person's grave (in particular, their amount and rarity) with the importance of that person; they searched for "correlations." An early example of this kind of approach is found in Dommasnes's investigation of Norwegian Iron Age graves in which she aimed to answer why some women obtain rank seemingly equal to men in a society that written testimony shows was male dominated (Dommasnes 1987:69). Her initial analysis is based on a simple proposition, very similar to others used in mortuary studies at the time, as she states, "The ratio of male/ female graves is here used as a measure of the general status of women within an area" (Dommasnes 1987:71). The analysis of the number of graves is, however, supplemented by further analysis of possible socioeconomic factors, such as affinity to good agricultural land and differentiation between locations in terms of their access to wider trade networks (Dommasnes 1987:72). Through these additional analyses, Dommasnes was able to answer her question by proposing that "women achieved high rank when they took over male tasks and responsibilities. In the period in question this happened because men invested their energy in other fields than farming [e.g., expedition of war and trade]" (Dommasnes 1987:76).

Another clear emphasis arose from the desire to show women's importance in past societies. This often took the form of reassigning value to what was considered to be undervalued or downgraded elements of women's material culture, such as domestic utensils or weaving equipments (e.g., Bevan 1997; Brumfiel 1991; Wright 1996; see also the discussion in Nelson 1997:85–111), or, alternatively, studies aimed to insert women as participants into what had typically been considered male spheres of activities. The former often took the form of arguing that the resources or activities represented by these objects were central to the sustenance and reproduction of society, and in this light objects associated with gathering or cooking were highlighted. The latter emphasis was often formed around theoretical propositions, such as the idea of gendered division of labor (e.g., Wright 1991), or it took the form of a challenge to existing interpretations, as in the case of the debate around women's contribution to hunting in the Palaeolithic (e.g., papers in Balme and Beck 1993; Hager 1997). Where historical sources were available, this interest in identifying women doing what was traditionally seen as men's work is even more obvious with examples ranging from discussions of women in the coal mining industry (Preece 1996) to analyses of the involvement of women in various crafts and guilds, such as women working as smiths (Weinstein 1996). Regardless of these differences, these early attempts at finding women's past share an understanding of the relationship between gender and material culture in which the latter is thought of as essentially passive.

The attempts at looking for women's past outside the sphere of mortuary practices largely had to develop their own interpretative framework for the analysis of domestic activities and the material remains of production since existing ones provided little guidance beyond economic analysis. These restraints caused a lack of subtleties in the interpretations put forward, but this phase was nonetheless significant for further developments, as it brought attention to neglected aspects of past societies and also increasingly raised questions about how we assess the social significance of objects. It became, for example, apparent that some artifacts were difficult to rank without using our own value judgment regarding the activities they represent. In particular, mundane artifacts, such as the spindle whorl, provided interesting challenges insofar as they at one level were clearly not very valuable while at another level might be seen as expressing women's relationship to and control over certain products and thus as a sign of their specific social roles and therefore also their economic significance. As part of domestic production, these objects were typically associated with women as well as with low value and rank, and there was a clear need for reconsidering how we analyze such artifacts and understand their incorporation in different contexts.

These early gender studies used material culture as an essentially passive component of gender construction, seeing objects as the outward sign or representation of gender roles rather than as partners to the production of gendered meaning. Material culture was still perceived primarily as a fossil record of chronology, as an expression of material and stylistic variation, as evidence of craft and technologies, as a means of investigating trade and exchange relationships, and as a value in and of itself. These aspects of objects are still being pursued, but we have added to them an interest in understanding the involvement that material culture has with its context of production and consumption: how is material culture partner to the maintenance as well as the transformation of social and cultural conditions, including the conditions of gender?

From Things to Contexts

There were different responses to the challenges emerging from the first flow of studies that had aimed to return to women (in the past and the present) their history and their material culture. One important reaction was to reconsider the meaning of objects and to foreground the question of to whom this meaning "belongs." Another was to make the relationship between objects and people personal and intimate, part of the life histories of both (e.g., Tringham 1991). For these budding ideas, Spector's work in the 1990s was seminal, as it provided an innovative way of framing and responding to such needs. As her device, she focused on an awl found during the excavation of a nineteenth-century Wahpeton Dakota village in Minnesota and used it to connect to and construct a narrative of events in the life of an individual woman known to have lived on the site (Spector 1991, 1993).

A somewhat different solution to the problem of how objects were valued and therefore how women's work was considered was provided by Conkey (1991). Reinterpreting the assemblage from the Palaeolithic rock-shelter site at Cuerto de la Mina, Spain, her solution was to sensitize our research questions to how objects are embedded within contexts of action and therefore that they cannot be interpreted in isolation. Rather than demonstrating the presence of women, her concern was to explore how the material culture revealed a range of different activities and contexts that were likely to have involved gender. This study is one of the earliest and clearest advocates of an approach where "engendering" is dependent not on the physical identification of women but rather on a different way of investigating the material culture. As an example, Conkey used the worked bone and antler from the site to argue that extensive bone and antler industry took place on the site, and on this basis she made inferences about supplementary activities, such as the making and use of cord, string, line, and, by extension, perhaps even weaving (Conkey 1991:76). The objects were interpreted as relating to contexts of action, and using this as an interpretative device, a dense and interconnected range of activities were demonstrated to have taken place on and close to the site. It was also clearly demonstrated how the performance of these activities would have involved social differentiation of different kinds and at different scales (Conkey 1991:77f.). On this basis, an argument about women's active engagement with several levels of productive activities could be made (Conkey 1991:78). Conkey also suggested that these technologies are simultaneously partitioned by the occupants and generate such partitioning and that such divisions give rise to both social order and tension inasmuch as the different tasks have to be scheduled and may be dependent on each other (Conkey 1991:80).

Others used the classic concern with women's seclusion in the domestic sphere as their starting point. Tools used in textile production, especially spindle whorls and loom weights, were often singled out, and interesting arguments about ways of interpreting them were made. Gräslund (2001:96–97), for instance, making the simple point that "in earlier times, one of women's main tasks was to produce textiles needed on the farm, which was absolutely crucial work," was able to use this to show how the discipline was now ready to work from such propositions and to use them to reinterpret complex social and economic relations. Gräslund also used studies showing that for southern German Merovingian women, social differentiation based on grave goods generally corresponded with differences in what tools they had to remind us that potentially complex relations may exist between women within many domestic contexts (i.e., all women are not necessarily equal) (96–97). Furthermore, she used her review of evidence for the tasks and roles associated with Viking women to show that even when woman's place was inside, within the domestic sphere, this does not necessarily mean she had no value; on the contrary, being the head of the domestic sphere could be the basis of powerful positions (99).

Another focus that developed was concerned with how material culture, as various kinds of resources, is central to and entrenched in the negotiation over and legitimization of power. It was recognized that material culture becomes absorbed into the political economy and therefore that gender can become one of the structures through which power relations seep into the very fabric of communities. This intrinsic relationship was clearly outlined in a case study by Hastorf (1991). She showed how the expansion of the Inca Empire influenced local gender relations in the intermontane Mantaro Valley in Peru. Using palaeo-ethnobotanical data from two different Sausa compounds, one from the later pre-Hispanic period just before the Inca expansion (Wanka II, A.D. 1300–1460) and the other from during the period of Inca control (Wanka III, A.D. 1460–1532), Hastorf made a comparison between the two phases in terms of the distribution of equipments and residues related to food processing and consumption. These data were further supplemented by isotope analysis of human bones. It was well known that communities such as that of Wanka III were transformed and incorporated into the Inca state through imperial conquest, but Hastorf's study demonstrated how during this transformation local gender relations were affected. In particular, she used the changing distribution of equipment and food residues to suggest that the period saw increased circumscription of certain, presumably female, activities associated with food preparation (Hastorf 1991:148), while the isotope analysis showed that entry into the Inca state locally resulted in differential access to certain types of food and in particular beer, which was consumed by selected males as part of ritual, political, and social meetings (Hastorf 1991:150–52).

Brumfiel's various studies of textile and weaving activities in Aztec societies similarly provide a challenging connection between the distribution of apparently mundane weaving equipment, such as spindle whorl, and the complexity of economic strategies and dependencies that they were part of. The written record states that women were the weavers; but using the numbers and size of spindle whorls from different sites in the Valley of Mexico, Brumfiel (1991) was able to argue that weaving played different economic roles on different sites. The implication of this analysis is that women's participation in different kinds of work varied between sites, and their contribution to the market economy varied accordingly. It was through studies like these, which were finding new ways of identifying women as producers and partners in complex production strategies, that new approaches to how women's contribution to society could be reclaimed were being formulated.

One may also see Dommasnes's (1987) arguments, outlined previously, about the effect that Late Iron Age raids had on the domestic power relations of those left behind as bringing together the political economy, material culture, and gender, while Stalsberg's (2001) study of Varangian women (the Scandinavians in Old Russia during the Viking period) in Russia illustrates another dimension of the relationship between gender and the economy. In her work, the common occurrence of weighing equipment in women's graves is used to mount a strong argument for women taking part in the trading of the family (Stalsberg 1991, 2001:73) and for seeing men and women not as equals but both as "indispensable members of their economic micro-unit (i.e. their family), but with sharply separated tasks" (Stalsberg 2001:75).

The subtleties of such studies come from their concerns with gender as part of wider social and economic relations and as shaped around the opportunities and restrictions arising from particular historical conditions. They did, however, in the main continue to approach material culture in a limited fashion in which remains were seen as symbols of positions and roles, as representing certain value, and as means of empowerment but not yet as dynamically involved in the processes through which meanings and understandings of the world and of ways of acting in it are formed.

During this phase, mortuary studies continued to be an area of gender analysis, as graves often provide the least ambiguous evidence about gender roles and ideologies. Gradually, however, the focus of such studies shifted from being about establishing women's positions in past societies to a concern with identifying key aspects of gender as part of social relations more widely (e.g., papers in Arnold and Wicker 2001; Moore and Scott 1997). The examples vary, covering the whole time period of archaeology and various regions and including detailed comparison between communities or investigating specific conditions within them, such as food allocation.

The latter is exemplified by Rega's (1997) study of an Early Bronze Age cemetery in the former Yugoslavia. She used isotope analysis (to establish the proportion of meat and plant food in a diet) in combination with dental caries rates and attrition (as an indirect indication of dietary carbohydrate consumption) to investigate differences in diet. For this population, the analysis showed that males and females had similar diets, while, on the other hand, differences in food consumption were observed between groups within the cemetery interpreted as representing family or residence groups (Rega 1997:238–39). The Early Bronze Age is a period of considerable change in material culture partly because of the rapid development and elaboration of bronze metallurgy and extensive exchange systems. So far, it has been common to suggest that the social impact of these changes resulted in growing asymmetries between men and women, as it is assumed that men became the metalworkers and were the ones engaged in and controlling exchange (Shennan 1993). Rega's analysis, although based on only one cemetery, may suggest that social responses to these changes were more complex and less divided along gender lines than we have assumed. Another example of dietary variance that is interpreted as resulting from social differences comes from Early Iron Age temperate Europe. Here skeletal differences were used to argue that the people buried in some of the richest graves, in contrast to the rest of the population, "came from a privileged background on several generations of good food" (Oliver 1992:57). Central to this kind of study is the question of how differences within communities affect resource allocations and in turn may consolidate and legitimize difference.

From these attempts at engaging with ways of contextualizing how objects were used and of recognizing their diverse meanings arose an interest in theoretical approaches that not only granted objects an active role in society but also explicitly aimed to discuss the nature and quality of objects. Prominent among the influences behind this shift were arguments, such as that by Appadurai (1986), about the "social life of things" that led to increased interest in the life history or bibliography of objects. Bourdieu (1977) was another central influence. His concept of *habitus*, with its focus on the enactment of everyday life, its opening up of new ways of understanding the social impact of routine action, and its valorization of practical logic, introduced new avenues of thought. It also brought intellectual legitimacy to the study of "the small things" and to domesticity. It is furthermore of significance that such arguments reinserted the social into the relationship between things and people, readdressing the risk of treating things as if their meanings and impacts were totally separate from human actions and perceptions.

From Contexts to Materiality, Norms, and Subversion

Arising out of these arguments, the focus of gender archaeology has recently shifted further, and its early preoccupation with the presence and status of gender has in general been replaced with an interest in how gender is constructed and negotiated. Our approaches to and exploration of material culture have changed accordingly. Following on critiques that argued that gender is neither static nor stable and an emphasis on gender as made and not given, the media through which gender is constructed and experienced have come into sharper focus. This has fueled further attention to the characteristics of material culture as objects, including discussions of "what they do" (e.g., Fisher and Loren 2003; Sørensen 2000). Moving beyond the recognition that material culture arguably is central to discourses about identity and power as well as a basic medium for the performance and staging of social categorization, investigation and arguments about how these processes unfold have come into the foreground. This has included arguments by Joyce (2002), based on Butler (1990), who sees material culture as providing a means of reiteration through citation and quotations. For Butler, "Gendered identity is created through the repetition of postures, gestures, dress language and so on, performed as the repeated citation of a gendered norm" (Gilchrist 1999:82).

The proposition that material culture can be understood as a medium of performance has also been explored, and this has provided new ways of approaching and of deconstructing the significant metaphors and messages in, for example, elaborate burial contexts (e.g., Arwill-Nordbladh 1998; Sørensen 2004). In short, the call for gender studies to focus on the discursive construction of gender has in itself given rise to a need to deconstruct how such discourses are shaped. Along the way, substantial and methodologically innovative studies have been conducted, and our insight into the relationship between gender and material culture has been formed through a range of case studies as well as theoretical debate.

One approach emerging from this emphasis has been concerned with the explicit materiality of gender and how this affects its perception and the practices of gendered life. It is argued that objects and action make gender "real" and give it material consequences and impact (Sørensen 2000). In other words, it is emphasized that it is through objects and their associated activities that gender is enacted and becomes an effective dimension of both personal and social life. Objects simultaneously represent and affect gender, and it is essential that our analyses encompass both qualities. Such arguments have changed the outlook of gender archaeology from a perspective that saw objects as mere things reflecting or representing norms, values, and roles to one that approaches objects as dynamic and actively involved with the construction of contexts and meaning to the current concern with the very nature of material culture as a medium of or partner to social discourse.

Another focus has been formulated around the concern with maintaining embodiment as our central focus, as "it is the experience of the body in the landscape, constituted through material culture in daily praxis and situated in the discourse of bodily representation, that frame the lived experience of the body and that informs us about constructions of identity. . . . And it is this process that we are just coming to grips with in archaeological inquiry" (Fisher and Loren

2003:227). In this emphasis, the articulation of embodiment becomes key to understanding the use of material culture in the formation of different identities (Fisher and Loren 2003:228).

In response to these developments, it has been argued that the tangible physical character as well as the affective properties of objects give them particular qualities in social discourses (Sørensen 2000). They are the material and substantive form of meaning and understandings as well as a media of repetition of association, and they are therefore one of the means through which meaning shifts from the individual to become part of social corporate spheres of meaning making. It is further argued that objects are made and used within contexts of meaning; that they are produced with intentions and shaped according to assumptions about how, when, and who may be using them; and that in their use they reinforce or alter such expectations. At the same time, objects exist beyond such intentions, and their potentials are not preset. Many different areas of study have now begun to recognize and respond to these qualities, as when Smart Martin, working in material culture studies, states that "material objects matter because they are complex, symbolic bundles of social, cultural and individual meanings fused onto something we can touch, see and own. That very quality is the reason that social value can so quickly penetrate into and evaporate out of common objects" (Taylor 2002:72). It is because of such qualities that material culture and gender are so intricately linked. Gender gains material reality and affects individuals and groups as it becomes acted out and experienced through material culture (Sørensen 2000). In the process of "learning" how to act in the material world, including learning the use and meaning of material culture, people built up an understanding of the self in its relationship to other—an understanding that sits at the heart of acquiring and transforming one's gender identity through life (Sofaer 2006).

Moreover, the use of objects always involves negotiation, and material culture is always involved in social processes. It is, for example, partner to processes and actions through which differently constituted groups (such as develop around kin, age set, gender, ethnicity, or rank) participate in social dialogues about identity and associated distribution of demands and responsibilities. There are significant and interesting consequences of this connectedness between material culture, social discourse, and experience. For instance, ornaments are never just emblems of status or wealth but are also in themselves involved with the creation of such qualities. And following on from this, the same objects do not mean the same regardless of contexts: a sword does not necessarily signify the same in a grave, in a hoard, or as part of a depiction, although it brings the quality of "sword-ness" to each of these contexts. Such arguments identify social actions and intentions as the context of meaning while not necessarily the sole arbiter of meaning-content. This strongly suggests that analyses of gender should always aim to identify its context as well as its discursive qualities.

Such contextualized use of objects in the construction and performance of gender is by now demonstrated by a range of examples from different branches of archaeology and neighboring disciplines. They show how material culture is incorporated into and used as a medium for the construction of gender (including its very meaning) as well as in the negotiation and transformation of existing gender arrangements. Kirkham and Attfield (1996:10) have labeled this "people-object relations," arguing that objects lend meaning to people's lives and that people construct their identities through these relations.

Gilchrist's (1999:50) arguments about the relationship between gender and textile production may be seen as an example of this concern with the dynamic of gender. She argues that female labor can be a crucial means of the construction of femininity and a basis for the definition of gender roles as ideological constructions. She illustrates this complex relationship by showing how changes in the technology of weaving by the eleventh century A.D. affected the value, visibility, and social significance of textile production in England. As textile production was moved out of its domestic context, "female labour was not automatically accorded lower prestige, although there were attempts to confine it to a non-professional, domestic context, and to limit its financial reward" (Gilchrist 1999:50–51), while at the same time textile production as such became the affair of guilds and in the control predominantly of men. Another point about textile production has been pursued by Arwill-Nordbladh (1998:204–6), who argues that textile production, just like many other activities, within itself contains the possibility of differentiation between its practitioners as well as contact and dependency with other spheres, as the production is constituted by many different stages that may involve different skills. Spinning (and thus the spindle whorl) is particularly interesting in this regard; it is easily learned and can be done in combination with other activities, as known from ethnographic and historical sources. This means that spinning, which so consistently is assumed to have been done by women in the past, is in fact a fluid practice that can be fitted in between other activities and can potentially be done by anyone and at anytime. The fluidity of such practices opens interesting questions about how they are made gendered. It also makes it clear how easily categorizations may become blurred and therefore that social "instruments" are needed to maintain differentiation.

Mortuary studies have also become influenced by these concerns, and their focus has recently turned in particular to the interconnection between gender and the life cycle (e.g., papers in Struwe et al. 2004). Studies have been carried out that focus on how material objects or material practices (such as head shaping [Lorentz 2005]) may be used to mark life cycle changes; they argue for the inter-twining of life, objects, and practices. Theoretical arguments as well as case stud-ies have also been used to argue that "gender is not static throughout the life course, but must be constantly negotiated in the light of increased gendered knowledge and changes in social situations. The acquisition of gender knowledge is time dependent" (Sofaer-Derevenski 1997:487). In these studies, material cul-ture is often assigned a role as the mediator of gender relations.

This means that mortuary studies, in addition to identifying the presence and roles of different members of society, are increasingly also being seen as a way of accessing how social understandings and articulation of difference are variously constructed by societies. The question of how differences between people's bodies (including apparent perceptions held about such bodies) were explored in the construction of ideals and ideas about the social person has therefore become a major trend within this part of gender archaeology (e.g., Sofaer-Derevenski and Sørensen 2002). Crucial to these approaches is the recognition that "these dimen-sions [gender and age] of our identities are both individual characteristics and fluid social potentials that will be shaped and reinforced as part of specific social discourses. Gender . . . while emerging from universal characteristics of the human body are nonetheless also always cultural and relational" (Sørensen 2004).

The materialization and performance of gender are in many societies particu-larly clearly articulated during burial rituals. It has been suggested (Sørensen 2004) that in order to elucidate the insertion of gender into the social discourse that burials constitute, it is helpful to recognize that these events were composed of distinct stages and that each of these may have provided an opportunity for gender negotiation and performance. In particular, the preparation of the body for the funeral (i.e., how it was dressed and what happened around it) and the burial itself are two obvious contexts of action in which gender may have been emphasized and distinctions performed. For instance, during the late third millen-nium B.C., a burial practice developed throughout most of central and western Europe (the Bell Beaker culture and the Earliest Bronze Age) that rigidly empha-sized people as belonging in one of two categories. What is interesting here, how-ever, is how these categories become expressed during the burial rituals as the bodies are placed differently in the grave (i.e., the orientation and/or positioning of the body) depending on their biological sex. Thus, the burial would have expressed and been designed around a social understanding of what kind of body was being buried, including its similarities with and differences from other bodies, and a normative understanding of the appropriate position of such bodies. Fur-ther analysis of the objects found with the bodies confirms that these categories were also emphasized during the stage when the body was dressed for the funeral. In particular, differential use of dress accessories depending on biological sex was commonly maintained (Sørensen 2004).

This focus on gender as part of the processes through which society maintains and regulates itself and how it creates traditions and norms makes gender archaeology a partner to the larger projects and concerns about the relationship between the individual and society that are currently being put forward by the humanities. Our special role in this debate must be the analysis of how difference was conceptualized and materialized by communities living lives that were distinctly different from ours.

Appearance: The Construction of the Social Person

Dress or items of dress are significant elements of material culture and associated practices. This importance of dress is vividly illustrated by contemporary discussions of the use of Muslim head coverings and the veil in western Europe. Such discussions show how both the objects per se and the act of using them can become embroiled in symbolic and political discourses. This is not a new phenomenon, however. The veil, for example, as discussed by Yeğenoğlu (1998), has a complex history of involvement with politics, and it has often been used as a central object-partner in complex identity constructions. With reference to the political struggle between Islamism and secular/Western nationalism in Turkey during the late nineteenth and early twentieth centuries, Yeğenoğlu (1998:126) argues that "it is the veil which becomes one of the most effective and convenient instruments of this battle. The visible cultural effects one can induce by veiling or unveiling women makes it a convenient signifier for the contending parties to fight out their differences through manipulating this highly charged symbol." The political and cultural-symbolic dimensions of dress are also well illustrated by the many instances of sumptuary laws that through time have been used to dictate how different social groups could be dressed. Schama's (1988) study of sumptuary laws in the Netherlands during the sixteenth to seventeenth century is a classic case, but similar directives and measures aimed at social control over the means of appearance are widespread (e.g., Gilchrist 1999:114; Roach and Eicher 1979:12). Hall (2000:70–71), for instance, in his study of the colonial world, discusses the emphasis on cultural display—the use of dress to make it known that one matters. He exemplifies this by showing how in the Cape the colonial administration used sumptuary laws to enforce a tight connection between status and its material signifiers, including dictates for the clothes to be worn by slaves

(Hall 2000:72–73). The Romans (Harlow 2004) formulated similar laws encoding social rules about dress. In fact, social restrictions and regulations of appearance are probably common features of complex societies and in particular early states even if they do not all take the same legalistic form.

This explicit social and political significance of dress has recently guided many different disciplines to more focused investigation of the practices and objects used to construct our outward appearances. This has led to associated questions about how the manipulation of the surface of the body affects the experience of being in the body as well as questions about how societies perceive, use, and make restrictions on the dressed body. Arising from an earlier interest in the body's signal, where clothing was seen as costumes and as a system of communication, the interest has recently become more broadly based and now embraces questions such as how dress is part of social learning (including the acquiring of gender identity) and a means of constructing dialogues between the self and society. The recent development of the distinct field of dress history and the approaches and aims it has come to entail over the past two decades outline the transformation of this general area of study very well (e.g., Taylor 2002). Prior to the 1980s, textile was investigated primarily as part of economic history; it was recognized as a significant commodity and as an important area of production and employment. Textile was therefore part of the history of the transformation of labor organization, of technological advances, and of economic transformative processes. During the 1980s to 1990s, we see a seminal shift, as the focus became dress rather than textiles and textile/dress became a subject of social history and more particular consumption studies (Taylor 2002:69f.). This shift was followed by explicit theoretical work on dimensions such as fashion, use, style, communication, and identity with gender playing a central role in the latter. Attention has also moved to the cultural processes surrounding the exploitation of dress in the construction of identities, be it gender, race, or class, and the formation of subculture or counterculture dress codes. It has been pointed out, however, that in this shift of interest from the object of dress to the practice of dressing, the actuality of objects risk becoming marginalized again (Taylor 2002:83); this is similar to the concerns recently expressed by Olsen (2003) with regard to archaeology. If, however, our analysis of dress can combine both objects and practice, then the study of clothing can indeed be seen, as suggested by Crane, as "a strategic site for studying changes in meanings of cultural goods in relation to changes in social structures, in the character of cultural organisations and in other forms of culture" (Taylor 2002:84).

Through this and parallel developments within other academic fields, the study of clothing has become an area fueled by curiosity about how differences, such as masculinity and femininity, are made and understood. Inspired by such debates and challenged by its own data, gender archaeology has turned the tradition of the archaeological study of textiles and ornaments into a study of how the construction of the external appearance of the person is part of social dialogues about identity and membership. Moreover, the effectiveness of visual representation of the categorization of people is being recognized and drawn into our analyses. The challenge remains, however, to understand more fully (and through more case studies, especially from nonliterate societies) how objects mediate between the self and social ideals and to recognize the distinction between discourse about identity and actual lived identity experiences (Fisher and Loren 2003:225–26).

Archaeological examples of intricate uses and rules governing dress and the use of accessories in prehistoric as well as historic societies have become abundant over recent years. For instance, mortuary data have been used to show how during the Middle Bronze Age in central Europe the arrangement of dress accessories (such as pins, rings for different parts of the body, and belts) in every region and regardless of local typological differences follows one of two set schema in their composition on the body. This differentiation seemed to have separated biological women into two groups: one with ornament sets mainly arranged on the chest and one with the ornaments placed around the waist (Sørensen 1997). In contrast, analyses of the Bell Beaker culture and the Early Bronze Age from central Europe show remarkable widespread consistency in the association of certain type of dress accessories, in particular, items used on the head and around the neck, with only either men or women without any obvious further visual distinctions in the appearance of members of these groups. Furthermore, detailed analyses of Early Bronze Age cemeteries have also begun to show how the acquiring of gender identity in these communities was tied in with the life cycle. For some communities, for instance, it can be argued that separate gender identities are first fully emerging among subadults, as male and female children, while treated differently in their positions in the graves, are nonetheless associated with the same range of objects, a similarity that is in contrast to what we see among adults (e.g., Neugebauer 1991). In other areas, apparently similar communities seem to emphasize difference and act on people in terms of separate gender categories from a young age (e.g., Sofaer-Derevenski 1997).

The social significance of dress codes is by now widely demonstrated not only by studies based on textual evidence but also increasingly through archaeological sources. Attitudes to dress in the Roman world have, for example, been extensively discussed. Harlow (2004) has most recently used a combination of pictorial and literary representations to study change in the dress of the elite man in order to investigate changing expressions of gender in the later Roman world. She showed how the traditional Roman dress of tunic and toga was transformed by the inclusion of new elements and concluded, "When the earlier Roman fought to obscure outside influences, later Roman man embraced them and, in so doing, accepted a transformation both in the individuals who held power and in the way they expressed that power in dress code" (Harlow 2004: 69).

Studies of one of the largest groups of artifacts from later prehistory in Europe, namely, the fibulae and brooches, have witnessed similar shifts (e.g., Effros 2004). Such dress accessories were commonly elements of the costume. They were meant to be seen, and they were often affected by regulation about how and where they were worn (Jundi and Hill 1997:125). Such details of dress often play a role in commenting on the identity of the wearer, and the political and social dimensions of these comments are demonstrated by change in dress styles and fashions during periods of rapid political change. For instance, in Britain, brooches changed during the first century A.D., the conquest period, and Jundi and Hill (1997:134) interpret the appearance of the visually distinct dragonesque brooches at this time as a way of "asserting a new, and possible non-military, non-Roman identity in the years following conquest."

To advance the archaeological study of the gendered aspects of appearance, it is, however, crucial to appreciate the specific qualities that come with dress and dressing. Two distinct set of practices are involved with dress. One is the putting together of the dress, the "getting dressed" part, where decisions are made about how elements are composed, while the other arises from being dressed. This difference gives dress and dressing some distinct temporal qualities that are different from, for example, those associated with the experience of architecture discussed later in this chapter. It is, therefore, analytically helpful to separate the composition of a dress from the act of wearing it. The composition of a dress is about decisions and the negotiation of possibilities within available resources, while the wearing of it involves primarily performance of the body and social communication rather than further manipulation of the material possibilities. Therefore, while gender is a decisive influence at both stages, different aspects of gender may come into play at each. The archaeology of gender can with great benefit aim to investigate both the distinct elements used and the choices made in the composition of dress in different contexts and the social implications of the dresses worn by different people within particular societies, but it will also benefit from recognizing these as separate practices.

The Material Culture of Space

The other main theme, one that will be used to exemplify current development, is that of the relationship between space and the performance of gender, with particular attention to space in the form of the built environment and architecture. This theme arises from increased attention to the intersection of gendered ideals and practices with material culture and how spatial constructions provide an arena for the performance and experience of gender. This in turn is based on the recognition that spatial constructions encourage routine; they are a means of repetition, and within them are embodied separations, privileges, and emphasis, qualities that bring an explicit awareness of the lived practices of gendered lives to our interpretative engagement with the past.

The intersection is the main point here, as space otherwise would become reduced to a place in which gender is enacted. This, however, can also be seen as involving, on the one hand, the material building and, on the other, both ways of doing things and their timing. Space is then "not a prior condition of something else ('place'), but rather the outcome, the product of an activity, and so it necessarily has a temporal dimension" (Morris 1992:3). This emphasis on the timing of action in space, on temporarily and embodied movement, shows clear similarities to some of the arguments put forward when phenomenology is used in archaeological studies of the landscape (e.g., Tilley 1994). It seems, however, that phenomenology tends to lessen the significance of gender, as it sees it as just one of the formative aspects of the experiencing subject, and it does not provide a clear basis for analyzing both gender and space as simultaneously social constructs and materialities. There are, therefore, other layers of meaning and representation affecting the intersection of gender and space that need to be detailed and explored beyond recognizing how they are produced in the action. Colomina (1992a) makes these points clear when, commenting on the relationship between sexuality and space, she reminds us, "It is not a question of looking at how sexuality acts itself out in space, but rather to ask: How is the question of space already inscribed in the question of sexuality? This formulation required that we abandon the traditional thought of architecture as object, a bounded entity addressed by an independent subject and experienced by a body. Instead, architecture must be thought of as a system of representation. . . . Likewise, the body has to be understood as a political structure, a product of such systems of representation rather than the means by which we encounter them." Later, she also points out that "architecture is not simply a platform that accommodates the viewing subject. It is a viewing mechanism that produces the subject. It precedes and frames its occupant" (Colomina 1992b:83).

To explore these arguments further in terms of their relevance to our analysis of the built environments of past communities, we now look at some of the main propositions used in archaeology when attempting to interpret the relationship between social relations and architecture in terms of value and meaning. One of these is the argument that power relations commonly are embedded within spatial relations and that gender, as part of power relations, therefore will be reflected as well as reproduced in spatial constructions. This has been most vividly argued in studies of households, ranging from analyses of the British prehistoric round-houses (e.g., Parker Pearson and Richards 1994) to domestic settings (Allison 2002) to Greek houses from the Iron Age (e.g., Nevett 2001) to historical archaeology (Kinchin 1996; Wall 1994). Such studies become especially power-ful when they simultaneously analyze the particular historical manifestation of this relationship and explore the mechanisms through which space affects or allows specific understandings and performances of gender and other social iden-tities.

Different analytical approaches have also been explored (see also the discus-sion in Gilchrist 1999:111–13). Among these, the spatial syntax model, devel-oped by Hillier and Hansen (1984), represents an interesting early approach, as it proposes a method for evaluating the social significance and value of the differ-ent parts of an architectural construction. It is also an early example of critical awareness of the significance of movement for understanding architectural space. Focusing on two axes of significance, one being spatial depth and the other the degrees of connectedness between different parts of a structure, the model pro-poses that the different rooms, passages, and courtyards that may make up a building can be analyzed in terms of their degree of hierarchy. The model also makes it possible to characterize differences between spaces in value terms and includes among these seclusion and access. In architecture, this model and related approaches have been used to characterize, for example, the social changes expressed in vernacular architecture and their grammar (Glassie 1975) and in his-torical studies of the institutional architecture of the modern city (Hillier and Hansen 1984). In archaeology, the method on its own has been used mainly to track changes in social organization, such as the emergence of social elites (e.g., Foster's [1989] comparison of Early and Later Iron Age brochs on Orkney). The general approach can be criticized for its mechanical and ahistorical dissection of spatial construction, but it nonetheless injected a helpful concern with the differ-ential value and composite nature of such constructions, and the echoes of this concern are found in some of the most interesting and influential archaeological investigations of gender and architecture (e.g., Gilchrist 1994, 1997, 1999). Approaches like the spatial syntax model can be obviously strengthened if com-bined with historical or ethnographic evidence that help discriminate between different social scenarios. Brusasco's (2004) comparison of houses from Ur with, on the one hand, houses from the patrilineal and patrilocal society of modern Iraq and, on the other, houses from the Ashanti, who live in a matrilineal and matrilocal society, is a case in point. In this case, the richness of the ethnographic data provides the insights needed to connect the spatial pattern with the differential use of the various elements of the architecture. Lacking such data, another response would be to explore in greater depth how and why such architectural qualities are valued and responded to in social strategies. Among such analyses, Gilchrist's as well as Nevett's studies are excellent examples of how gender archaeology has explored and further developed these kinds of arguments with specific regard to the phenomenon of seclusion and the subversion of spatial constraints. Nevett's (1994, 2001) work has focused on the architectural structures of the house in ancient Greece. It is known from other sources that women were secluded within the house during this period, but Nevett's (1994) study showed the greater subtleties of what this seclusion was about. She investigated the routes of access and lines of vision that characterize the interior space of the house and its connection to the world outside, and on this basis she demonstrated that the space was not constructed to create absolute segregation between men and women within the household, as previously argued, but rather functioned to seclude women from contact with strangers. Seclusion and segregation have also been a central concern in Gilchrist's (1994, 1999, 2000) work. She has investigated the relationship between the materiality of space and gender ideologies with particular reference to medieval buildings. She has, for example, identified some of the specific ways in which the overall architectural plan of nunneries as well as details in their construction were used both to segregate the nuns from other communities and to provide access for men representing the religious hierarchy. She further showed how the enclosure of women, both through architectural mechanisms, such as interior enclosing walls, and through observances was particularly strict as the women were perceived as in need of particularly rigid seclusion because of their untamed sexuality (Gilchrist 2000:94). Her analyses show how churches, when shared by a nunnery and the parish congregation, often became divided along distinct lines by the addition of architectural elements, such as gallery-choirs, screened aisles, or a separation between choir and nave (Gilchrist 2000:95–96). Gilchrist (2000:89) also proposes that the coupling of such strict physical enclosures with an emphasis on sexual denials meant that the sexuality of medieval religious women "was turned inside out: sexuality became an interior space, a place of elevated senses and ecstatic states of consciousness." Gilchrist's (1999) work has expanded to include analysis of the later medieval castle and the seclusion of the high-ranking women within them. Throughout Gilchrist's work on the link between space and the embodiment of gender, the underlying argument has been that "such embodiment is perceived materially through the concrete, everyday world, and the physical processes of the life cycle" (Gilchrist

1999:109). This means that the gendered constructs and relations within, for example, the castle can be studied through "the contrasting locales, concerns and textures surrounding its men and women" (Gilchrist 1999:110).

Another distinct influence has been to analyze architecture and in particular houses as symbolic signifiers of the body or the world inhabited. A particular approach has been to explore binary oppositions as the basic structuring principles affecting the layout and the use of a house. Hingley (1990), for instance, used this as a means of investigating the organization of activities within the different rooms of the Romano-British aisled house, while Parker Pearson (1996, 1999) linked the significance of cosmologies and binary oppositions in his analysis of the British Iron Age roundhouse, demonstrating the consistency in the division of activities within the houses.

The study of gender and the built environment has also moved in another direction explicitly concerned with the concept of domesticity and with the social dynamic embedded within the organization of households. In such approaches, the house is understood as a social and semantic "stage" as well as an arena of routine practices. Differences in architectural plans, such as entranceways and internal divisions, are emphasized as influential for how ideas such as home, house, and households are conceptualized and materialized and how these differences would have impacted life in and around the domestic center in various ways. The architectural form affects the organization and flow of a wide range of practices performed within and in relationship to the house, including the engendering of labor divisions and collaborations of various kinds. Simply put, domestic life is always affected by and structured in response to the different physical and logistic constraints as well as the allowances provided by the space in which it takes place. Historical archaeology has provided some extremely useful case studies of these relationships and their historical contingency. Wall's (1994) analysis of the developing middle-class New York in the period from 1790 to 1840 shows how architecture and space was becoming gendered as well as class based. Her analysis shows a growing distinction of male versus female spheres, and it tracks how this was expressed and manufactured through an increasing range of minor as well as more noteworthy means of differentiations, such as etiquettes at mealtimes, architectural details, and increased physical and social distance between people. The male sphere became one of the public life of commerce, while women's was the private one of domesticity. Kitchen's (1996:12) study of the nineteenth-century interior space of the English middle-class home shows a similar scenario but adds to it the further gendered division within the house, as rooms were often designed as explicitly masculine or feminine. The emergence of literature guiding women on household taste further shows the extent to which these views were codified and the deliberate use of architecture to assign strikingly different ideological roles to men and to women. Colomina's (1992b) discussion of the expression of sexuality within houses built by Adolf Loo and by Le Corbusier shows how these central structures are transformed yet repeated even in architecture that is more recent. The tension between the interior and exterior is, for instance, also here responding to the difference between private and public spheres (Colomina 1992b:85–94), while architectural depth and seclusions are associated with female spaces (Colomina 1992b:81). Such case studies enforce views that see the body as a political construct rather than as solely a means of experience (e.g., Colomina 1992a).

When we consider these various points and reflect on the methods used and the arguments made by the archaeological case studies that have added most to current understanding of gender and space, a few proposals may be put forward. First, the various arguments that stress that the gendering of space involves temporality and movement make important points. It is, however, equally crucial that we do not stop there but make the connection between this and practice—the act of doing things. It is in the living within built structures, responding to their qualities and differences and to their existing gender templates and ideologies, that space and people connect. The archaeological investigation of gender and space therefore needs a dual focus on the material construction and the doing of things within them. Second, built structures are composed of different kinds of spaces and therefore also of points of connections and transitions. It is around these points that practices are most poignantly revealing meanings and change in meaning. An obvious example of this is the transition from the nunnery part of a medieval church to the part used by the congregation and the need to construct discontinuity of meaning within the continuity of the building. In practice, the solution is often different types of physical segregation, such as screens (as discussed by Gilchrist 2000). Archaeological investigation of spatial control of meanings should therefore pay particular attention to such pivotal points in the architecture and how they are embellished or in other ways accentuated and made to direct the meaning of the spatial encounter or how they may allow change in meaning. This means that the meeting points of different rooms or kinds of spaces, the liminal areas that may be neutral or in-between spaces, are places that may reveal some of the dialogues about identity that are performed through routine practices in the house. Thresholds, entrances, doorways, corridors, and boundaries and the remains and traces accumulated there are therefore archaeologically important parts of buildings (Gilchrist 1999:112; Sørensen 2000).

Recent Developments

Within current arguments and the enlarged scope of gender studies in archaeology, one can outline a number of central trajectories for the further exploration of the relationship between gender and material culture. One of these is the continuous investigation of the nature and qualities of material culture and its role or incorporation into social discourse (e.g., Olsen 2003). It is interesting here to note how earlier propositions that in various ways tried to comprehend material culture through its similarities to other cultural products or practices, such as the analogy drawn between material culture and text (e.g., Hodder 1986, 1989), are generally being abandoned in favor of approaches that focus on the material qualities of objects.

One approach has been to emphasize the thing-ness of material culture (e.g., Olsen 2003; Sørensen 2000) in reaction to the emerging inclination to present things entirely and only as social discourse (Olsen 2003:88). Olsen (2003:88), expanding on Schiffer's criticism of the current tendency to marginalize the thing and how this treats people–artifact interaction as secondary to processes of culture, has argued for a different way of seeing material culture as "things, all those physical entities we refer to as material culture, are beings in the world alongside other beings, such as humans, plants and animals. All these beings are kindred, sharing substances ('flesh') and memberships in a dwelt-in-world. . . . [Through time] humans have extended their social relations to non-human agents with whom they have swapped properties and formed collectives."

One response that is in line with arguments made in other disciplines is to move attention to how we can investigate the effects of objects, including the significance of their evocative and affective qualities. For some time, archaeologists have been investigating material culture as active, but to this is now added a language that animates it and places it centrally in social understanding. The material culture we are trying to explore is now seen by some as never neutral but rather as contaminated and affected by intentions (Joyce 2002; Riegel 1996:99–100). This position is producing a perspective in which the object becomes social and directly involved with notions of difference. This approach to material culture has already been explored for some time by prominent feminist museologists (e.g., Porter 1991, 1996; Sandahl 1995), and it provides new interpretative potentials for understanding, for example, the gender dimension of complex material situations like the adaptation of technological innovations (e.g., Sofaer-Derenvenski and Sørensen 2002). This kind of reflection is also providing a different background for mortuary studies insofar as it gives us a means of discriminating interpretatively between different objects in terms of what meanings they may bring to the specific burial construction. Arwill-Nordbladh's (1998) study of the rich Viking-period grave at Oseberg, Norway, is an interesting example of this approach. Her focus is not the objects per se but rather how they are incorporated into the grave, the choreography of their inclusion, and the meanings and associations they draw with them into the construction. Arwill-Nordbladh uses the concept of "contexts of actions" (based on Conkey 1991) to group the objects used in the funerary setting in terms of what spheres of actions, social relations, and interests they represent and bring with them into the grave construction. This approach shows that in the construction of this grave, objects are used to make references to four main contexts of actions: the productive activities of a farm, textile production, communication and movement, and rituals. She further proposes that these contexts of actions in the construction of the burial may be perceived as preunderstandings attached to the objects and that it is within this that the essence of their significance can be found. Arwill-Nordbladh (1998:257) states, "The act of bringing the objects from their different preunderstandings on board the ship, could be read as the creation of a material metaphor. . . . In this way a completely new meaning is created. This meaning is expressed by the artefacts, and can only be expressed in this particular way."

Another distinct development has emerged in reaction to the separation usually made between the body and material culture. Recognizing that the body is a malleable cultural material, various authors have been linking the construction of gender with various types of technologies of the body. Some of these studies follow arguments made by Foucault (1978) and others about the body being the product of discourse (e.g., Treherne 1995), while Sofaer in particular has taken this argument further to argue that the body can be approached not just as material manifestation but as material culture itself. In her most recent work, Sofaer (2006) has advanced from her earlier studies of gender and the life cycle to even more fundamental questions about the nature of bodies. She aims to problematize the tendency to draw a distinction between the material body and the materialized body that has evolved in the wake of embodiment theories. In response to arguments that see the enactment of cultural practices as leading to the materiality of the body, she proposes that "the material qualities of the human body are key to its materiality" (Sofaer 2006). She bases this argument on the very physicality of the body, the recognition that it is materially constituted and that embodiment is about acting within and on the material possibilities and restraints imposed by the body through its life cycle. She therefore also argues that the materiality of the body is the product of social relations in that the traditions, values, and skills of the living may be expressed as a result of the plasticity of the body, but that it is not produced in a purely discursive manner. The body exists in a very real way where actions have the potential for often predictable material consequences (Sofaer 2006). This proposition, furthermore, is not merely a rhetorical shift in position but rather a fundamental change in orientation in which the body is seen to have specific material qualities that go beyond the meanings they may have in social discourse or how they may be used as signifiers.

There are interesting resonances between the points made by Sofaer and those of Olsen (2003) about the nature of material culture referred to earlier. While their starting points seem to be at opposite ends, one discussing the body and the other the things, both argue for the necessity of dissolving the perceived dichotomy between persons and things.

A different trajectory is outlined by Joyce (2002:141), who suggests that material remains in archaeological sites can be viewed as utterances by people in the past who made and used them. She makes it clear that this is neither a return to a simple textual analogy nor a concern with recovering past communicative intentions. Based on self-critical reflection about her own earlier analyses and publications of the burials at Tlatilco (a central Mexican pre-Classic site, for which the interpretation has undergone several changes from being focused on spatial patterns as evidence of the habitual practices of social groups to a concern with the effects of life cycle changes), she traces how she came to this position (2002:138–142). In her words, viewing objects as utterances "is to say that the object created was expressive, that it is a representation of, at the very least, a social engagement with the past world in which the people of Tlatilco lived. It is to say that objects recovered archaeologically are comparable to each other because they were manufactured by people engaged in dialogically seeking responses from those around them" (Joyce 2002:142). She further suggests that "the evidence of the dialogic communication of utterances is present in the chain of their reproduction" and that our task "is at least partly to respond to the objects produced in terms of their existence as unique entries in a dialogue, responses to prior material utterances" (Joyce 2002:142).

In various ways, these most recent developments emerge from and react to long-standing concerns within any historical analysis of social relations, including archaeology's. For instance, they are responding critically and self-reflexively to archaeology's classic angst about the nature of its knowledge claims, and they show strong affinities to its traditional concern with investigating change as well as continuity. These concerns are, however, shown in a new light because of the emphasis on self-reflection and the concern with investigating the conditions of real people who lived at another time and on the psychical as well as cultural qualities of objects. The commitment to analyses that aim to investigate gender as simultaneously integrated within society and in the process of becoming also ensure depth to our studies. A core view of many of these recent arguments is therefore that the meaning of gender is never fixed but is part of ongoing dialogues about and between people and material culture.

Conclusion

Gender archaeology has changed in its theoretical position toward material culture and the ways in which it has seen this as a means of identifying women or as a way of exploring the construction and experiences of gender. Rather than growing toward a collective view and a shared understanding of what material culture is and how we can best harness it to our research questions, this development has spawned a number of positions, differences, and debates. Despite these differences, there is a common interest in what gender may be, how it is experienced and expressed, and how this was part of the conditions and possibilities affecting the lives of individuals and groups in past societies. Regardless of period and area, material culture can be used to focus analysis on how society needs and constructs meaning around and attitudes toward fundamental differences between people. This can then be followed up by exploration of how these understandings became expressed in ideologies and its prescribed practices and regulative mechanisms, and that gets us back to people.

References

Allison, Penelope M.
    2002   *The Archaeology of Household Activities.* London: Routledge.
Appadurai, Arjun
    1986   *The Social Life of Things: Commodities in Cultural Perspective.* Cambridge: Cambridge University Press.
Arnold, Bettina, and Nancy L. Wicker, eds.
    2001   *Gender and the Archaeology of Death.* Walnut Creek, CA: AltaMira Press.
Arwill-Nordbladh, Elisabeth
    1998   *Genuskonstruktioner i Nordisk Vikingatid: Förr och nu.* Gothenburg: Gothenburg University.
Balme, Jane, and Wendy Beck, eds.
    1993   *Gendered Archaeology: The Second Australian Women in Archaeology Conference.* Research Papers in Archaeology and Natural History 26. Canberra: Australian National University.
Bevan, Lynn
    1997   Skin Scrapers and Pottery Makers? "Invisible" Women in Prehistory. In *Invisible People and Processes: Writing Gender and Childhood into European Archaeology.* Jenny

Moore and Eleanor Scott, eds. Pp. 81–87. London: Leicester University Press.

Bourdieu, Pierre
1977   *Outline of a Theory of Practice.* Cambridge: Cambridge University Press.

Brumfiel, Elizabeth M.
1991   Weaving and Cooking: Women's Production in Aztec Mexico. In *Engendering Archaeology: Women and Prehistory.* Joan W. Gero and Margaret W. Conkey, eds. Pp. 224–54. Oxford : Blackwell.

Brusasco, Paolo
2004   Theory and Practice in the Study of Mesopotamian Domestic Space. *Antiquity* 78(299, March 2004):142–57.

Butler, Judith
1990   *Gender Trouble: Feminism and the Subversion of Identity.* London: Routledge.

Colomina, Beatriz
1992a   Introduction. In *Sexuality and Space.* Beatriz Colomina, ed. New York: Princeton Architectural Press.
1992b   The Split Wall: Domestic Voyeurism. In *Sexuality and Space.* Beatriz Colomina, ed. Pp. 73–128. New York: Princeton Architectural Press.

Conkey, Margaret W.
1991   Contexts of Action, Contexts for Power: Material Culture and Gender in the Magdalenian. In *Engendering Archaeology: Women and Prehistory.* Joan W. Gero and Margaret W. Conkey, eds. Pp. 57–92. Oxford: Blackwell.

Dommasness, Liv Helga
1987   Male/Female Roles and Ranks in Late Iron Age Norway. In *Were They All Men? An Examination of Sex Roles in Prehistoric Society.* Acts from a workshop held in Utstein Kloster, Rogaland, November 2–4, 1979. Reidar Bertelsen, Arnvid Lillehammer, and Jenny-Rita Næss, eds. Pp. 65–77. Stavanger: Arkeologisk Museum i Stavanger.

Effros, Bonnie
2004   Dressing Conservatively: Women's Brooches as Markers of Ethnic Identity? In *Gender in the Medieval World: East and West, 300–900.* Leslie Brubaker and Julia M. H. Smith, eds. Pp. 165–84. Cambridge: Cambridge University Press.

Fisher, Genevieve, and Diana DiPaolo Loren
2003   Introduction. Special Section: Embodying Identity in Archaeology. *Cambridge Archaeological Journal* 13(2, October 2003):225–30.

Foster, Sally M.
1989   Analysis of Spatial Patterns in Buildings (Access Analysis) as an Insight into Social Structure: Example from the Scottish Atlantic Iron Age. *Antiquity* 63(238, March 1989):40–50.

Foucault, Michel
1978   *The History of Sexuality.* Harmondsworth: Penguin.

Gilchrist, Roberta

1994   *Gender and Material Culture: The Archaeology of Religious Women.* London: Routledge.

1997   Gender and Medieval Women. In *Invisible People and Processes: Writing Gender and Childhood into European Archaeology.* Jenny Moore and Eleanor Scott, eds. Pp. 42–58. London: Leicester University Press.

1999   *Gender and Archaeology: Contesting the Past.* London: Routledge.

2000   Unsexing the Body: The Interior Sexuality of Medieval Religious Women. In *Archaeologies of Sexuality.* Robert A. Schmidt and Barbara L. Voss, eds. Pp. 89–103. London: Routledge.

Glassie, Henry H.

1975   *Folk Housing in Middle Virginia: A Structural Analysis of Historic Artefacts.* Knoxville: University of Tennessee Press.

Gräslund, Anne-Sofia

2001   The Position of Iron Age Scandinavian Women: Evidence from Graves and Rune Stones. In *Gender and the Archaeology of Death.* Bettina Arnold and Nancy L. Wicker, eds. Pp. 81–102. Walnut Creek, CA: AltaMira Press.

Hager, Lori D., ed.

1997   *Women in Human Origins.* London: Routledge.

Hall, Martin

2000   *Archaeology and the Modern World: Colonial Transcripts in South Africa and the Chesapeake.* London: Routledge.

Harlow, Mary

2004   Clothes Maketh the Man: Power Dressing and Elite Masculinity in the Later Roman World. *In Gender in the Medieval World: East and West, 300–900.* Leslie Brubaker and Julia M. H. Smith, eds. Pp. 44–69. Cambridge: Cambridge University Press.

Hastorf, Christine A.

1991   Gender, Space, and Food in Prehistory. In *Engendering Archaeology: Women and Prehistory.* Joan W. Gero and Margaret W. Conkey, eds. Pp. 132–59. Oxford: Blackwell.

Hillier, Bill, and Julienne Hansen

1984   *The Social Logic of Space.* Cambridge: Cambridge University Press.

Hingley, Richard

1990   Domestic Organisation and Gender Relations in Iron Age and Romano-British Households. In *The Social Archaeology of Houses.* Ross Samson, ed. Pp. 125–47. Edinburgh: Edinburgh University Press.

Hodder, Ian

1986   *Reading the Past.* Cambridge: Cambridge University Press.

1989   This Is Not an Article about Material Culture as Text. *Journal of Anthropological Archaeology* 8:250–69.

Joyce, Rosemary A.

2002   *The Languages of Archaeology.* Oxford: Blackwell.

Jundi, Sophia, and J. D. Hill
    1997   Brooches and Identities in First Century AD Britain: More Than Meets the Eye? In *TRAC 97, Proceedings of the Seventh Annual Theoretical Roman Archaeology Conference Nottingham 1997.* Colin Forcey, John Hawthorne, and Robert Witcher, eds. Pp. 125–37. Oxford: Oxbow.

Kinchin, Juliet
    1996   Interiors: Nineteenth-Century Essays on the "Masculine" and the "Feminine" Room. In *The Gendered Object.* Pat Kirkham, ed. Pp. 12–29. Manchester: Manchester University Press.

Kirkham, Pat, and Judy Attfield
    1996   Introduction. In *The Gendered Object.* Pat Kirkham, ed. Pp. 1–11. Manchester: Manchester University Press.

Lorentz, K. O.
    In press   The Malleable Body: Headshaping in Greece and the Surrounding Regions. In *New Directions in the Skeletal Biology of Greece.* S. C. Fox, C. Bourbou, and L. Schepartz, eds. Athens: Wiener Laboratory, American School of Classical Studies in Athens.

Moore, Jenny, and Eleanor Scott, eds.
    1997   *Invisible People and Processes: Writing Gender and Childhood into European Archaeology.* London: Leicester University Press.

Morris, Meaghan
    1992   Great Moments in Social Climbing: King Kong and the Human Fly. In *Sexuality and Space.* Beatriz Colomina, ed. Pp. 1–51. New York: Princeton Architectural Press.

Nelson, Sarah Milledge
    1997   Gender in Archaeology: Analyzing Power and Prestige. Walnut Creek, CA: AltaMira Press.

Neugebauer, J.-W.
    1991   *Die Nekropole F Von Gemeinlebarn, Niederösterreich: Untersuchungen zu den Bestattungssitten und zum Grabraub in der ausgehenden Frühbronzezeit in Niederösterreich südlich der Alten Donau zwischen Enns und Wienerwald.* Römisch-Germanische Forschungen 49. Mainz: Philipp Von Zabern.

Nevett, Lisa C.
    1994   Separation or Seclusion? Towards an Archaeological Approach to Investigating Women in the Greek Household in the Fifth to Third Centuries BC. In *Architecture and Order: Approaches to Social Space.* Mike Parker Pearson and Colin Richards, eds. Pp. 98–112. London: Routledge.
    2001   *House and Society in the Ancient Greek World.* Cambridge: Cambridge University Press.

Oliver, Laurent
    1992   The Tomb of Hochdorf. *Archaeological Review from Cambridge* 11(1):51–63.

Olsen, Bjørnar
   2003   Material Culture after Text: Re-membering Things. *Norwegian Archaeological Review* 36(2):87–104.
Parker Pearson, Mike
   1996   Food, Fertility and Front Doors: Houses in the First Millennium BC. In *The Iron Age in Britain and Ireland: Recent Trends*. In Timothy Champion and John Collis, eds. Pp. 117–32. Sheffield: J. R. Collis Publications.
   1999   Food, Sex and Death: Cosmologies in the British Iron Age with Particular Reference to East Yorkshire. *Cambridge Archaeological Journal* 9(1):43–69.
Parker Pearson, Mike, and Colin Richards, eds.
   1994   *Architecture and Order: Approaches to Social Space*. London: Routledge.
Porter, Gaby
   1991   Partial Truths. In *Museum Languages: Objects and Texts*. Gaynor Kavanagh, ed. Pp. 103–17. Leicester: Leicester University Press.
   1996   Seeing through Solidity: A Feminist Perspective on Museums. In *Theorizing Museums*. Sharon Macdonald and Gordon Fyfe, eds. Pp. 105–26. Oxford: Blackwell.
Preece, Rosemary
   1996   "Equal to Half a Man": Women in the Coalmining Industry. In *Women in Industry and Technology: From Prehistory to the Present Day*. Amanda Devonshire and Barbara Wood, eds. Pp. 155–61. London: Museum of London.
Rega, Elizabeth
   1997   Age, Gender and Biological Reality in the Early Bronze Age Cemetery at Mokrin. In *Invisible People and Processes*. Jenny Moore and Eleanor Scott, eds. Pp. 229–47. London: Leicester University Press.
Riegel, Henrietta
   1996   Into the Heart of Irony: Ethnographic Exhibitions and the Politics of Difference. In *Theorizing Museums*. Sharon Macdonald and Gordon Fyfe, eds. Pp. 83–104. Oxford: Blackwell.
Roach, M. E., and J. B. Eicher
   1979   The Language of Personal Adornment. In *The Fabrics of Culture*. Justine M. Cordwell and Ronald A. Schwarz, eds. Pp. 7–21. New York: Mouton.
Sandahl, Jette
   1995   Proper Objects among Other Things. *Nordisk Museologi* 1995(2):97–106.
Schama, Simon
   1988   *The Embarrassment of Riches: An Interpretation of Dutch Culture in the Golden Age*. Berkeley: University of California Press.
Shennan, Stephen J.
   1993   Commodities, Transactions and Growth in the Central-European Early Bronze Age. *Journal of European Archaeology* 1(2):59–72.
Sofaer, Joanna
   2006   *The Body as Material Culture*. Cambridge: Cambridge University Press.

Sofaer-Derevenski, Joanna
    1997   Linking Age and Gender as Social Variables. *Ethnographisch-Archäologische Zeitschrift* 38(3–4):485–93.

Sofaer-Derevenski, Joanna, and Marie Louise Stig Sørensen
    2002   Becoming Cultural: Society and the Incorporation of Bronze. In *Metals and Society*. Barbara Ottoway and Emma C. Wager, eds. Pp. 117–21. Bar International Series 1061. Oxford: Bar International.

Sørensen, Marie Louise Stig
    1997   Reading Dress: The Construction of Social Categories and Identities in Bronze Age Europe. *Journal of European Archaeology* 5(1):93–114.
    2000   *Gender Archaeology*. Cambridge: Polity Press.
    2004   Stating Identities: The Use of Objects in Rich Bronze Age Graves. In *Explaining Social Change: Studies in Honour of Colin Renfrew*. John Cherry, Chris Scarre, and Stephen Shennan, eds. Pp. 167–76. Cambridge: McDonald Institute.
    2004   The Interconnection of Age and Gender: A Bronze Age Perspective. In *Von der Geburt bis zum Tode: Individuelle und gesellschaftliche Dimensionen von Alter und Geschlecht in der Urgeschichte*. Ruth Struwe and Linda Owen, eds. Pp. 327–338. *Ethnographisch-Archäologische Zeitschrift* 45, 2004, Heft 2.

Spector, Janet
    1991   What This Awl Means: Towards a Feminist Archaeology. In *Engendering Archaeology: Women and Prehistory*. Joan W. Gero and Margaret W. Conkey, eds. Pp. 388–406. Oxford: Blackwell.
    1993   *What This Awl Means: Feminist Archaeology at a Wahpeton Dakota Village*. St. Paul: Minnesota Historical Society Press.

Stalsberg, Anne
    1991   Women as Actors in North European Viking Trade. In *Social Approaches to Viking Studies*. Ross Samson, ed. Pp. 75–83. Glasgow: Cruithne Press.
    2001   Visible Women Made Invisible: Interpreting Varangian Women in Old Russia. In *Gender and the Archaeology of Death*. Bettina Arnold and Nancy L. Wicker, eds. Pp. 65–79. Walnut Creek, CA: AltaMira Press.

Struwe, Ruth and Linda Owen, eds.
    2004   *Von der Geburt bis zum Tode: Individuelle und gesellschaftliche Dimensionen von Alter und Geschlecht in der Urgeschichte. Ethnographisch-Archäologische Zeitschrift* 45, 2004, Heft 2.

Taylor, Lou
    2002   *The Study of Dress History*. Manchester: Manchester University Press.

Tilley, Christopher
    1994   *A Phenomenology of Landscape: Places, Paths and Monuments*. London: Berg.

Treherne, Paul
    1995   The Warrior's Beauty: The Masculine Body and Self-Identity in Bronze Age Europe. *Journal of European Archaeology* 3(1):105–44.

Tringham, Ruth
    1991   Households with Faces: The Challenge of Gender in Prehistoric Architectural

Remains. In *Engendering Archaeology: Women and Prehistory*. Joan W. Gero and Margaret W. Conkey, eds. Pp. 93–131. Oxford: Blackwell.

Wall, Diana diZerega
   1994   *The Archaeology of Gender: Separating the Spheres in Urban America*. New York: Plenum.

Weinstein, Rosemary
   1996   Women Pewterers of London 1500–1800. In *Women in Industry and Technology: From Prehistory to the Present Day*. Amanda Devonshire and Barbara Wood, eds. Pp. 125–29. London: Museum of London.

Wright, Rita P.
   1991   Women's Labor and Pottery Production in Prehistory. In *Engendering Archaeology: Women and Prehistory*. Joan W. Gero and Margaret W. Conkey, eds. Pp. 194–223. Oxford: Blackwell.

   1996   Technology, Gender, and Class: Worlds of Difference in Ur III Mesopotamia. In *Gender and Archaeology*. Rita P. Wright, ed. Pp. 79–110. Philadelphia: University of Pennsylvania Press.

Yeğenoğlu, Meyda
   1998   *Colonial Fantasies: Towards a Feminist Reading of Orientalism*. Cambridge: Cambridge University Press.

Gender and Archaeological Mortuary Analysis

4

BETTINA ARNOLD

IDEALIZED SOCIAL RELATIONSHIPS are concretized in burial ritual in many ethnographically as well as archaeologically documented societies (Bahn 2003:4). Gender, as a virtually universal form of social categorization, is one of the most frequently encountered forms of mortuary differentiation and can be expressed in a wide range of ways, from burial location through the orientation of the body to specific sets of grave goods associated with a particular gender. Just as gender has increasingly become an integral part of archaeological analysis in general, archaeology continues to inform gender studies, particularly in terms of understanding the materiality of gender (Sørensen 2000:72). In the case of funerary archaeology, which has been described as "a crucial element of any research into past gender categorizations" (Parker Pearson 2000:96), this dialectic is especially important. The relationship between the representation of gender in the mortuary record and in the living population is not a straightforward one, however. "In particular, the mortuary context tells us that the individual seen by archaeologists represents not only a woman [or man], as constructed by the gender ideologies of her [or his] time, but specifically a *dead* woman [or man], going to her [or his] grave. Thus, the artifacts accompanying her [him] are not just associated with the idea of femininity [masculinity], but are the objects appropriate to her [his] transition from the living to the dead" (Tarlow 1999:178). Death as a transitional process not only separates the individual from her or his community but to some degree also confounds the ability of archaeologists to draw inferences between the burial record and the living society. At the same time, burial evidence remains one of the most evocative sources of information regarding past gender configurations available to us, and the inferential difficulty inherent in all mortuary analysis should not preclude its use in the interpretation of social systems in the past.

Brief History of Gender and Mortuary Archaeology

Some of the earliest explicit attempts to engender archaeological mortuary analysis were initiated in Scandinavia (Arnold and Wicker 2001:viii). The 1979 conference in Bergen titled "Were They All Men?" was certainly one of the first to articulate a growing sense of dissatisfaction with the state of archaeological interpretation from a gendered perspective. This was followed by several Anglo-American publications, notably the article by Conkey and Spector (1984) and the 1988 *Archaeological Review* issue dedicated entirely to gender (Lucy 1997:153).

Medieval archaeologists, particularly in Britain (Härke 1990, 1992; Lucy 1995, 1997; Pader 1982; Stoodley 1999), have also been engaged in engendered mortuary analysis for some time, but their publications are rarely referenced by prehistoric archaeologists, and not all the applications developed in this text-aided subfield are relevant for prehistorians. Nevertheless, several of the medieval studies are potentially of great interest to archaeologists working in earlier periods, and I will discuss some of them here and later in this chapter. Ellen Jane Pader (1982:129) was one of the first Anglo-Saxon scholars to develop an approach to mortuary analysis that included a consideration of gender configurations "from a structural perspective, concluding that sex-based relations could be seen to be articulated by constraints placed on the distribution of artifact classes, artifacts and skeletal positioning, and that these relations differed between cemeteries" (Lucy 1997:152). For some reason, archaeologists working in prehistoric and Roman Britain have been relatively unaffected by these developments in medieval archaeology and the archaeology of Roman Britain (with some exceptions, notably Parker Pearson), and there have been relatively few attempts at engendered mortuary analyses. "Feminist critique, which had developed in social anthropology and other social sciences since the 1970s, has, until now, had very little impact on the agendas of Anglo-Saxon archaeology. In contrast, studies of the Scandinavian Iron Age, the chronologically equivalent period on the other side of the North Sea, have been in the forefront of the development of feminist and gender archaeologies" (Lucy 1997:150; Dommasnes 1982, 1987, 1991; Gibbs 1987; Hjørungdal 1991, 1994; Høgestøl 1986; Stalsberg 1984, 1987a, 1987b).

A significant problem is the fact that there is little or no overlap or information exchange between archaeological subfields, which leads to much duplication of effort and tends to block the transfer of potentially valuable data between these different areas of research. Researchers working on mortuary ritual in early medieval England or continental Europe rarely interact directly with scholars investigating mortuary ritual in prehistoric Europe or the British Isles, and the gap is even wider between North American scholars and their counterparts in the

Old World (Arnold 2002c:417–20; Sørensen 2000:16–17). Classical archaeologists tend to focus on their own citation circles and only infrequently venture into the wilds of the prehistoric mortuary literature. Naturally there are some exceptions, but these are usually scholars who have migrated temporally, geographically, or in terms of discipline (sometimes all three) in the course of their careers, and while the bibliographies of their publications do serve as bridges between subfields, in general this has not tended to have much of an impact on the state of inquiry in general.

For example, Classical and Near Eastern archaeologists concerned with gender have tended to focus primarily on the analysis of texts and imagery; there are very few studies that attempt to engender mortuary analysis on the basis of bioarchaeological data or grave good analyses (but see Bolger and Serwint 2002; Keswani 2004; Strömberg 1993). One of the few exceptions is the volume edited by Ruth D. Whitehouse (1998), which includes several chapters that engage in engendered mortuary analysis (Brown 1998). In her introduction to the volume, Whitehouse indicates the extent of this divide: "Although the title of the volume employs the inclusive term 'Italian Archaeology,' the majority of the papers deal with prehistory or protohistory and none are concerned with anything later than early Classical Archaeology. This was not my choice: I included classical and medieval archaeologists in my mailings, for both the seminar and the publication, but received offers mainly from prehistorians" (Brown 1998:1). She attributes this mainly to the fact that "in later periods work on gender has tended to focus on textual sources and on art, with few explicitly archaeological studies" (Brown 1998:1). She makes another point in this introduction that is worth pondering: she was unable at the time the volume was being organized to find any Italian archaeologists working on any aspect of gender archaeology (Brown 1998:2; Vida 1998) and expresses the hope "that this will be the last volume on the topic to depend solely on Anglo-American contributions" (Whitehouse 1998:2).

A review article by Carol Meyers (2003) outlines the history of gender studies in Syro-Palestinian archaeology and discusses some of the reasons why this area of study has lagged behind other temporal and geographic areas (but see Wright 1996:79–110). She confirms that "for the most part the practice of excavation in the eastern Mediterranean and the nature of the interpretation of excavated remains have barely been touched by the paradigm shift in the academy that has brought gender into the mainstream of scholarly discourse in most humanities and social science disciplines" (Meyers 2003:185). She argues that this neglect is due in part to the fact that the agenda for fieldwork and interpretation in Near Eastern archaeology has been set by the agenda of the textual sources, which tend to be male generated and male dominated in this part of the world (Meyers

2003:187), and concludes as follows: "Clearly the traditional research goals of Syro-Palestinian archaeology have not been congenial to the recovery of data that can contribute to the identification of gendered forms of behavior and thus to the social dynamics of human beings inhabiting the ancient sites" (Meyers 2003:187). Significantly, however, Meyers focuses mainly on settlement data in her discussion, which underscores the relative neglect of burial evidence, apart from elite interments, in this part of the world.

Sarah Nelson (2002:73) describes gender as a "relatively new topic in Asian archaeology" as well, and while much of her own research has dealt with mortuary analysis in Korea and China (Nelson 1993, 1997) and there have been other engendered analyses of Asian mortuary data (Higham 2002; Jiao 2001; Linduff 2002), the great potential of this region to contribute to the development of theoretical and methodological approaches to gender and mortuary studies has yet to be fully realized. It is no coincidence that a geographic shift toward eastern Europe and central Asia is currently under way in Anglo-American archaeology or that there is an increasing number of research projects in those regions focusing on mortuary analysis (Hanks, Smith, Alcock and Cherry, and so on). East will soon meet West, at least in archaeological terms, and mortuary analysis is one area that should flourish as a result.

North American archaeologists have been actively involved in engendering archaeological practice since at least the late 1980s, but even here there have been relatively few attempts to develop approaches specific to mortuary analysis (Arnold and Wicker 2001:ix). Gender configurations are implicitly addressed by a number of North American researchers who are known especially for their mortuary research (Buikstra et al. 1986; Carr 1995; Charles 1995; Charles and Buikstra 1983, 2002; Goldstein 1995; among others), but in general explicit analyses of gender in the mortuary context are conspicuous by their absence. Several chapters published in *Gender and the Archaeology of Death* (Crass 2001; Doucette 2001; Hamlin 2001; Hollimon 2001; O'Gorman 2001) demonstrate the potential of such studies. The situation in Central America is similar, with most of the emphasis placed on engendered analysis of iconography or systems of production (Joyce 1996, 1998; but see Joyce 1999; see also Brumfiel 1991; but see McCafferty and McCafferty 1994).

Gender Is a Verb

Gender as both category and practice is constructed as well as lived (Sørensen 2000:65). The frequent invocation of performance theory and agency in publications dedicated to gender studies in various disciplines (Feree et al. 1998; Joyce

1998; McNay 2000; Moore and Scott 1997; Nelson and Rosen-Ayalon 2002; Ortner 1996; Sørensen 2000; Sweely 1999), including engendered archaeological mortuary analysis (Arnold 2001, 2002b; Cannon 2005; Chapman 2000; Effros 2003; Härke 2000; among others), is an indication of the fluidity of the concept of gender and its social expression. As Marie Louise Stig Sørensen (2000:70–71) has suggested, "Gender is a process, a set of behavioral expectations or an effect, but it is not a thing."

A number of researchers have productively applied the work of Judith Butler (1990, 1993) to their investigations of gender as a performance as well as a process. This approach has been particularly fruitful in the interpretation of representations of the human form (see, e.g., Joyce 1996; Wicker and Arnold 1999:5–74). The body in the mortuary context can be viewed as a particular form of representation, distinguishable from wall paintings or sculpture mainly by the organic nature of many of the elements of the gender coding arranged in the burial and by the partial or complete decay of the body itself, simultaneously a literal sedimentation and disintegration of bodily practice (Joyce 1996). The *chaîne opératoire* concept, originally generated in the context of lithic analysis, has also been applied to mortuary ritual, implicitly invoking the concept of this aspect of social interaction as "a set of connected practices that produces a deliberate meaningful space that can be compared to narration" (Sørensen 2000:88; see Olivier 1992:59–60).

In addition to the "gender as process/performance" concept, there is also the problem of social identity as palimpsest. Since layers of meaning make up individual identity, with the various layers interacting differently at different stages of the life cycle and in different contexts, age, status, and individual versus group identity are all potentially enmeshed with gender in ways that make attempts to isolate it for analysis neither possible nor desirable. Ultimately, it is the way in which these variables interact with one another that should be the primary focus of any social analysis of mortuary practices.

Walking the Talk: Approaches to Engendered Mortuary Analysis

Sørensen makes the point that it is the materiality of gender in the archaeological record that makes it a potentially productive form of inquiry into the construction and evolution of past gender configurations. She suggests that mortuary ritual is perhaps ideally suited as an arena of investigation of the ontogeny of gender as a social construction precisely because in death various forms of social categorization, including gender, are idealized in concrete form, what she calls the "visualization and ideological reproduction of gender systems" (Sørensen 2000:85). A complicating factor in the application of such concepts is the problem of analytical scale. There are several scales of analysis in engendered mortuary analysis, as is also true for mortuary analysis in general:

Level 1: Cemetery landscape
Level 2: Cemetery
Level 3: Form of disposal
Level 4: Position/orientation of body/remains
Level 5: Spatial distribution of objects in graves
Level 6: Type/number/material of grave goods

At any one of these levels, gender distinctions may or may not be expressed and, if present, may be expressed to varying degrees. As Sørensen (2000:92) correctly points out, "Burials, since these are situations in which many societies most strongly and explicitly reflect upon and renegotiate identities and relationships, necessarily involve a response to gender (even if the burial appears to ignore gender this in itself constitutes a particular interpretation of gender)."

Although archaeologists tend to create an artificial distinction between settlement and mortuary remains, in fact whether or not such a division exists is culturally specific. In many past cultures, there are close connections between the house and death and between domestic structures and mortuary structures, from Bronze Age European house urns (Sørensen 2000:156ff.) and Sarmatian burial chambers (Härke 2000:184–85) to the Oneota burials associated with longhouses in the midcontinent of North America (O'Gorman 2001) and the multichambered burial compounds of Sicán in Peru (Shimada et al. 2004). Human skeletal remains are frequently found in domestic contexts, often disarticulated and incomplete but nevertheless crossing that line between the world of the dead and the living. These associations are complex and may reflect geographic as well as kin-based spatial relationships between individuals, distinctions that often include gender as a distinguishing variable. Temporal and geographic variables affect all six of the levels of analysis outlined previously. As Cannon (2005:41) has argued, "Burial treatments are known to vary among individuals and to change over time . . . but these sources of variability are more often controlled for in the process of interpretation than viewed as both the source of structural variation and a focus of interpretation in their own right."

The differential preservation of bone in archaeological contexts has tended to result in most gender assignments being made on the basis of grave goods rather than skeletal material in any case. That this is potentially problematic, leading to circular reasoning at best and a complete misinterpretation of the evidence at worst, has been pointed out by several researchers working with cultures in which gender was weakly differentiated or gender distinctions were not marked in mortuary ritual (Crass 2001; Weglian 2001). Text-aided archaeological interpretation seems particularly prone to privileging grave goods over physical remains in assigning gender to burials. As Lucy (1997:154) has pointed out for Anglo-Saxon burial archaeology, "A determination of gender based on associated grave goods is almost always preferred over biological sexing of the skeleton," particularly since so much of the sexing data tends to be based on nineteenth- or early twentieth-century determinations of material since discarded and not available for reanalysis. Under those circumstances, it seems best to avoid the term "sex" when describing mortuary contexts where preservation or identification are dubious while bearing in mind that although gender may manifest itself as a primarily dichotomous system in prehistoric contexts, the possibility of multiple permutations must be considered as well (Arnold 2002b). In a sense, the body itself is perhaps best viewed mainly as a particular form of grave good whose relationship (male bodied or female bodied) may or may not coincide with the gender code(s) represented by the other elements of the burial assemblage. As Sørensen (2000:132; emphasis added) puts it, "If with a particular society swords are a masculine and masculating item, then the contexts within which swords were deposited can be interpreted as related to or commenting upon masculinity independently of the sex (and sexuality) of the person with whom the object was associated and also *irrespective of whether the remains of a person are in fact present.*"

The ongoing debate about whether sex and gender should be treated as distinct categories differently constituted (i.e., one is phenotypic while the other is socioculturally determined) or whether this distinction can be made at all (Hubbard 1990; Kessler 1998; Walker and Cook 1998; among others) creates an additional layer of interpretive complexity. One solution is to acknowledge the contingent nature of both sex and gender since even biological sex (traditionally viewed as strictly dichotomous) should be considered a continuum rather than a binary category set (Arnold 2002b:239–40).

Ultimately, skeletal morphology must be considered in any mortuary analysis if bone preservation allows this. Sexing skeletal remains is dependent on a number of variables, not all of which can be controlled for by archaeologists (Lucy 2000:65–74). These include the following:

1. Preservation
2. Age of the individual at death
3. Degree of sexual dimorphism in a given population
4. Degree of bias inherent in the analysis

Poor preservation is far more typical than well-preserved skeletal remains, and infants and children remain difficult to sex, even though some progress has been made in refining the standards of sexing children and neonates (see, e.g., Loth and Henneberg 2001). Since sex determination is based on a series of morphological markers and the range of variation within and between the sexes can be considerable with regard to most of them, individuals who fall into the zone between the "male" and "female" ends of the spectrum have always been a problem (Henderson 1989). In a much-cited study, Kenneth Weiss (1972) was able to demonstrate that in cases where sex identification was ambiguous, there was a 12 percent bias in favor of classifying such individuals as male. This problem can to some degree be mitigated by double-blind studies in which the identification is made by at least two independent specialists without prior knowledge of the mortuary assemblage. Sex identification through the analysis of nuclear DNA may be an option in a small number of cases, but this approach is complicated by preservation as well as contamination issues. Moreover, genetic analyses are expensive and time consuming and in spite of their early promise have yet to replace more conventional methods of determining sex.

When sex can be identified on the basis of skeletal remains with some degree of certainty (in cemeteries with good adult skeletal preservation, the accuracy rate can be as high as 97 percent [Molleson and Cox 1993:91]), it should be compared to the gender categories identified on the basis of grave goods. If more than two genders existed in a prehistoric society, this should be reflected in the correlation between phenotypically identifiable sex and gender if the latter is represented in mortuary ritual. The presence of multiple genders, then, can be archaeologically recognized only under relatively ideal conditions. Unfortunately, in a large number of burials—sometimes 50 percent or more of the graves in a given cemetery population in prehistoric European contexts (the Anglo-Saxon cemetery sample analyzed by Lucy [1997: 157] is fairly typical, but see also Burmeister [2000] for an Iron Age population in Germany in which gender was strongly marked in mortuary contexts)—the grave goods may not be indicative of gender, or there may be no grave goods preserved at all. The Iron Age cemeteries of Las Cogotas and La Osera in Iberia are a good example. More than 50 percent of the graves in both cemeteries contained no grave goods at all, and of those that did contain grave goods, the majority did not contain gender-specific items (Lorrio and Zapatero 2005:fig. 29).

In such cases, other variables, including orientation or body position, may provide clues as to a range of social distinctions, including gender. However, societies in which gender is not reflected in mortuary ritual are known ethnographically, and it can be assumed that gender configurations existed in past societies that are not represented in the ethnographic record today, so the goal must be to identify the range of patterns present in each context, at the level of the cemetery, the region, and the time period, before attempting to interpret the gender configurations represented in the mortuary record. As Lucy (1997:155) has argued, "The relationship between grave goods, gender and sex must be investigated, not assumed."

A good example of the complexities of engendering mortuary analysis is the "female warrior" phenomenon. Although the best-known manifestation is probably the so-called Amazons of Ukraine and the Caucasus, who first appear in the accounts of Hippocrates and Herodotus of armed female warriors, there are New World versions as well (Fraser 1988; Hollimon 2001; Parker Pearson 2000:99–101; Taylor 1996:199–205). While the Iron Age "warrior women" of Scythia and Sauromatia are by now well documented by extensive weapons sets that include armor, spears, arrows, and shields (not, however, swords) in conjunction with skeletal evidence for trauma and stress markers from repetitive activity like riding and archery (Davis Kimball 2002; Rolle 1989; Rolle et al. 1991; Taylor 1996:201–2), this can be a tricky interpretive category for several reasons. One of the main problems is distinguishing between injuries sustained as a noncombatant and those received in battle. As the fictional character Éowyn, "shield-maiden of Rohan," says in the recent film version of J. R. R. Tolkien's epic *The Two Towers*, "The women of Rohan learned long ago that those who do not wear swords can still die upon them."

Traumatic injuries inflicted by sword, spear, ax, or arrow do not necessarily constitute evidence that the individual who suffered those injuries sustained them while engaging actively in warfare. Raiding and similar small-scale violent interactions were common in many prehistoric (and historic) societies, and a single individual could survive a number of sequential injuries simply by being in the wrong place at the wrong time. To claim that a category of "female warrior" existed in a prehistoric society, several lines of evidence should ideally be present in the female burial population (a large sample size is also useful):

1. Evidence in more than one or two cases of traumatic injury forensically consistent with battle. Examples include injuries sustained while on horseback or a preponderance of injuries (some healed premortem) to the front of the body.
2. Evidence for repetitive stress markers consistent with the use of weapons (archery, horseback riding, and swordplay would all leave distinctive signatures if engaged in for a sufficient amount of time).
3. Grave goods marking warrior status, including weapons and possibly other material culture associated with "maleness."

4. Ethnographic or contemporary written records describing such a phenomenon. If all these lines of evidence are present, a strong case can be made
for a category of "female warrior" in the society in question. If not, caution
is indicated.

Multiple burials are an example of another problematic mortuary category.
Defined as graves containing the remains of more than one individual (not including mass, collective, or communal burials, which belong to a different category of
interment, usually containing the remains of more than ten persons), multiple
burials are frequently interpreted in an unconsidered and stereotypical fashion.
For example, graves containing the remains of a woman and a subadult are usually
interpreted as mother and child, while burials with an adult male and an adult
female are typically described as husband and wife. In the latter case, the assumption is usually made that the male individual represents the primary interment,
while the female is merely an accompanying "object" much like the other grave
goods. There have been relatively few attempts to analyze this category of burial
in a systematic fashion (but see Keswani 2004; Lucy 2000:82; Oeftiger 1984),
which is unfortunate since it clearly has the potential to be an extremely informative source on prehistoric social configurations, including gender.

The ideal situation—one in which skeletal remains are well preserved and
analyzed independently by several specialists, isotope and genetic analysis can be
carried out, the number of systematically excavated burials is large, grave goods
are part of an elaborate mortuary display, and there is iconographic and textual
evidence of gender configurations—is unfortunately very rare. One of very few
examples where at least some of these criteria are present is a project involving
the analysis of a recently excavated complex of 1,000-year-old Middle Sicán shaft
tombs on the northern coast of Peru (Shimada et al. 2003), which integrates
analyses of mitochondrial DNA, odontological analysis (an approach often combined with genetic data [Alt 1997; Alt et al. 1995; Scott and Turner 1997]),
developmental health, diet, placement of interred individuals, and associated grave
goods to provide a window into the social organization of this particular complex
society. However, even when not all of these sources of evidence are available, it
is possible to engage in engendered mortuary analysis, as I hope to show in the
case study presented later in this chapter.

Related to but distinct from mortuary ritual is the testimony of the body
itself, or what remains after the disposal ceremony is carried out and various
taphonomic processes have acted on the skeletal material (Grauer and Stuart-
Macadam 1998). The bones themselves contain a record of what was consumed
(in terms of both food and drink) by the individual in life, making a range of

determinations possible: where the person grew up (Budd et al. 2004; Lucy 2004), what kinds of foods the person had regular access to (Parkington 1991; Richards 2000; Sobolik 1994), the reproductive role of the individual (Bentley 1996; Buikstra et al. 1986), and whether the person experienced dietary stress, disease, or injury during his or her lifetime (Roberts and Manchester 1995; Wood et al. 1992). If bone preservation is good enough, these are specific facts about the deceased that can be definitively determined without the need for reference to ethnographic analogy. On the other hand, once the scale of the inquiry shifts from the determination of an individual's life history to the subsistence patterns represented by the skeletal remains of a population, moving beyond the simple description of those patterns requires recourse to some kind of societal model. The fact that women in a given cemetery apparently ate less meat than men, for example, can be observed and described, but not interpreted, solely on the basis of the skeletal remains (Arnold, in press).

Many of the activities engaged in or suffered by individuals are inscribed on the skeletal remains themselves. Examples include the following:

1. Evidence for differential pathologies (Cohen and Bennett 1998). For example, at certain times and places in European prehistory, women exhibit greater number of parry fractures to the lower arm, which suggests high levels of domestic abuse, while men tend to exhibit weapon-induced injuries to a greater degree than women.

2. Evidence for differential repetitive stress markers with respect to type and degree of bone deformation. In many ethnographically documented preindustrial societies, women or men are engaged in more labor tasks, fewer labor tasks for longer periods, or only certain kinds of tasks. In precontact Mesoamerica and in the Neolithic Near East, for example, women exhibit characteristic deformation of the knees and shoulders consistent with hours spent grinding corn on stone mortars, while the right arm and upper body of a male blacksmith buried with his tools in Iron Age Britain was twice the size of the left arm and side. Recent publications like Jane Peterson's (2002) study of musculoskeletal stress markers, tooth wear, dental trauma, and caries in Natufian populations illustrate what such evidence can tell us about "gender and labor at the dawn of agriculture."

3. Evidence for differential nutritional stress (Cohen and Bennett 1998). In some societies, women or men had access to certain foods in greater quantities at certain periods during their lives, and the chemical signatures of the foods they consumed can be recovered from their skeletal remains. In some Mesoamerican and South American skeletal populations, for exam-

ple, men seem to have had access to more meat in their diets than women, suggesting (in conjunction with other evidence) that they may have enjoyed a higher status in society (Hastorf and Johannessen 1993). Differential wear and differential presence of caries can also provide insights into possibly gender-based dietary patterns (Lillie 1997).

4. Evidence for differential demographic representation in the burial record. In a demographically normal population, women should be represented in slightly higher numbers than men. If an archaeological burial population deviates from the expected pattern, some sort of cultural, preselection behavior must be the cause. Examples include selective infanticide (Scott 2001; Wicker 1998) or disposal of some or all members of one gender in a way that is not represented in the mortuary record. The segregated burial of suicides, unbaptized infants, and other individuals viewed as deviant in Christian communities is an obvious example, but another relatively common phenomenon ethnographically speaking is the special treatment of women who have died in childbirth (Baum 1999:105–6; Schwidetzky 1965:231). This may be represented by the absence of such individuals in the "normative" cemetery population or by their special deposition in anomalous contexts, such as caves or other locations. On the other hand, as Baum (1999:106) points out, at some point, so-called anomalous burials should be considered simply another form of normative deposition, given a sufficient number of individuals, as in the case of the numerous skeletal remains in caves and rock shelters dating to the European Iron Age.

   Cemeteries may also be segregated by gender or profession, among other criteria. For example, female burials marked by brooches, needles, and curved utility knives and male burials containing swords, spears, shields, and long knives are concentrated in separate sections of first-century B.C. to first-century A.D. Iron Age cremation cemeteries in northern Germany and southern Jutland (Parker Pearson 2000:12).

5. Evidence for differential care (Cohen and Bennett 1998). This includes the differential healing of fractures, a higher incidence of disease, or a higher incidence of certain preventable diseases that indicate that little or no care is available for some groups while others have access to it, occasionally based on gender (Czarnetzki 1996).

6. Evidence that allows us to reconstruct fertility in the archaeological record, in turn allowing inferences to be drawn regarding women's reproductive roles in past societies (Buikstra et al. 1986). Gillian Bentley's (1996:24) research on the relationship between reproduction, production, and social

roles in prehistoric societies, especially foraging groups, makes it clear that female social roles, including contributions to production, are often linked to reproduction in ethnographic contexts and must therefore be considered in the interpretation of societies that are accessible to us only through archaeological evidence. She draws on the field of reproductive ecology, which investigates ecological factors that affect fertility, including disease, nutritional status, and workloads (Bentley 1996:25). Osteological markers related to fertility include the occurrence of sexually transmitted diseases that affect fertility, the mean ages for the onset of menarche and menopause, the length of birth intervals and/or lactation, diachronic changes in women's nutritional status related to pregnancy and lactation, age at weaning of infants, and so on (Bentley 1996:30–35). Bentley acknowledges that her results are drawn mainly from hunting and gathering societies and suggests that similar studies might be productively applied for complex, food producing societies as well (Bentley 1996:26).

7. Evidence for the movement of people, whether at the level of the individual or the group (Alt 1997; Alt et al. 1995; Anthony 1990; Arnold, in press; Konigsberg and Buikstra 1995:194–201; among others). Genetic studies have only recently begun to take into consideration the possibility that male and female mobility patterns might have been different enough consistently enough through time to have had an effect on the patterns seen in mtDNA and Y chromosome data (Arnold, in press; Gibbons 2000). Differences in the migration rate of males and females would be expected to influence the geographic patterns and relative level of diversity on the Y chromosome, autosomes, and mtDNA (Seielstad et al. 1998:278). Most of the discrepancy between Y chromosome and mtDNA and autosomal variation can be explained by a higher female than male migration rate due to patrilocality and the tendency for a wife to move into her husband's natal household (Seielstad et al. 1998:278). If, therefore, smaller numbers of men in prehistory moved longer distances (macromovement) while larger numbers of women moved shorter distances (micromovement) on a regular enough basis, this should produce different patterns of genetic variation for males and females (Alt et al. 1995; Konigsberg and Buikstra 1995:194). Isotope analysis also promises to provide new directions for research in this area. This form of analysis is based on the principle that what individuals ingest in the form of food or drink, including water, leaves chemical traces in the bones and teeth that can provide clues regarding everything from diet to the place in which an individual spent his or her formative years. Dietary isotope analysis can reveal the

relative proportions of protein derived from meat as compared to plant food (Hastorf 1991), seafood as compared to terrestrial protein sources, and so on. The carbon and strontium isotope ratios found in teeth, on the other hand, have been used to determine whether some individuals in cemeteries might not be local, patterns that could reveal gender distinctions that might in turn be used to generate models of residence or other social configurations (Lucy 2004). In most cases, such studies also reveal the complex interplay between status and gender (Rega 1997:238–39; Sørensen 2000:121).

The analysis of gender-specific mobility on the basis of archaeologically recoverable material culture patterns rests on a number of assumptions, among them the possibility of identifying "regional" patterns in the material marking of other social categories (including age, marital status, and occupation)—which could be interpreted as mapping ethnic distinctions (Reinhold 2003)—as well as gender differences in mortuary practices and the material culture associated with such differences (MacBeth 1993). For example, one would expect to see greater variability in female mortuary assemblages than in male assemblages in patrilocal societies in which gender was strongly marked in life as well as in death and where regional differences were reflected in costume and personal ornament, assuming that the newly married woman was permitted or required to retain the costume of her natal community.

Whether women retained the material culture markers of their natal community or reproduced them in their husband's community (e.g., in the form of pottery or textiles) would affect the archaeological visibility of such movement, and the patterns should vary depending on whether female mobility was restricted to certain social strata. The degree to which mortuary costume mirrored the costume of the living is also a factor (Brandt 1998:277). Archaeologists must develop methods of distinguishing these various forms of material culture marking from one another to avoid conflating the different archaeologically documented forms of intercommunity contact (Olausson 1988:19; Schier 1998:510).

In addition to the question of scale (including temporal and geographic variation), an engendered mortuary analysis must also take into consideration the interconnectedness of gender and a number of other variables related to social identity, notably age and status (Burmeister 1997; 2000; Hamlin and Redfern 2004; Müller 1994a, 1994b, 1994c; Rega 1997; Sofaer-Derevenski 1997; Stavish 2004). Too often, gender is analyzed and presented as independent of other social categories, resulting in a seriously skewed representation of the ways in which such identities are constituted and expressed in material form. For example, gender and power are inextricably linked in contemporary societies, yet archaeologists have only recently begun to recognize that this was also the case in the past, a realization that has led to the development of much more complex theoretical and methodological approaches to gender in archaeological interpretation (Clark 2000; Hays-Gilpin and Whitley 1998; Kästner 1997; Kehoe 1999; Moore and Scott 1997; Nelson 2002; Silverblatt 1991; Sullivan 2001; Sweely 1999). The interpretive difficulties archaeologists face are due primarily to the fact that when gender and power are combined with additional social and ideological variables, they may morph in ways that have no contemporary analogues. Archaeology poses special challenges to interpretation in the area of gender studies in part because gender and power are inextricably linked, and as a result gender can be understood only if viewed through the lens of power relationships. How power is constituted may vary considerably, however, and it should not be automatically assumed that the primary basis for such distinctions was economic, that is, based on wealth. In fact, there is good evidence to suggest that at least in western, central, and eastern Europe following the advent of metal technology, age and age-associated rites of passage such as marriage and parenthood may have played a more important role than wealth with respect to the material marking of difference in the form of costume (Arnold 2004; Burmeister 2000; Lucy 2000:87–90; Reinhold 2003:29).

Archaeologists interested in mapping gender and power relations have several sources available to them, and each of these sources can be evaluated for the degree to which gender relations are tied to the expression of power relationships. In archaeological terms, this association manifests itself in terms of visibility, both intentional (who is represented in the archaeological record and in what ways) and taphonomical (certain sources of information are more likely to be preserved than others). For example, the consistent archaeological invisibility of certain groups of people (including but not limited to nonpersons, such as slaves; children, especially infants; and, to varying degrees, women) has recently become the focus of systematic study in the archaeological literature (Moore and Scott 1997; Nelson 1999).

Ultimately, it is gender ideology (Spector and Whelan 1991) that is expressed in prehistoric European burial contexts more frequently than gender roles, in the sense that relatively few individuals are buried with implements or tools, while in the majority of complex societies in prehistoric Europe, masculinity was signaled by weapons and femininity by specific combinations of personal ornament. Weapons can, of course, be considered tools, but they are a problematic category since their symbolic significance appears to override their functional meaning in mortuary contexts in many societies—that is, they tend to communicate masculinity without necessarily representing the functional category "warrior" (Härke 1990:33; Stoodley 1999:77–78; Strömberg 1993:108).

Another confounding phenomenon is the so-called neutral burial category, that is, graves whose contents (especially when skeletal remains are not preserved and sexing is not an option) do not communicate a particular gender association (Parker Pearson 2000:97). Several researchers have noted that individuals in this category often account for more than half the burials in a given cemetery population (Arnold, in press; Brush 1988; Burmeister 2000; Lorrio and Zapatero 2005:fig. 29; Lucy 1997; Stoodley 1999:76)), which means that inferences regarding gender configurations are often being made without reference to a significant segment of the population. The assumption is that burials in which gender is not visibly marked in mortuary contexts differ with respect to some other variable or set of variables: age, status, social role, ethnicity, or a combination of these. However, considering how common this "neutral" subset of burial populations seems to be, it is significant that thus far as a category such graves have tended to be ignored—they are present in the graphs and tables of archaeological publications but are deemphasized or rationalized in the discussion and interpretation.

The differential archaeological visibility of a particular gender category compared to others is another problem since not all elements of costume, personal ornament, or mortuary assemblages are imperishable. This may result in an overrepresentation of one group compared to others that might have been present but are not archaeologically identifiable. Associating greater visibility in contemporary archaeological contexts with greater importance in past social contexts is not uncommon in the interpretation of the mortuary record, and this can lead to some egregious distortions of social configurations. For example, in the Iron Age of west-central Europe, weapon-bearing (usually adult) men (buried with bronze or iron swords, dagger, spears, or axes as well as defensive equipment) and adult women or girls with metal (bronze or iron), amber, jet, coral, glass, or other imperishable personal ornament are overrepresented in the archaeological record compared to boys, adult males not buried with weapons, or adult females or girls not buried with imperishable grave goods (Arnold 2004, in press).

Case Study: Iron Age Europe

By 600 B.C., Iron Age Europe was characterized by hierarchically organized societies in which the basis of social power was agrarian and also based to varying degrees on pastoral wealth, especially in the form of cattle. Status differences appear to have been marked mainly in the form of costume, including personal ornament and weaponry. Archaeologically less visible features such as hairstyle, body ornamentation (e.g., tattooing), and status-specific textile colors and patterns can be assumed to have been in use as well. The few systematic attempts to outline gender and power configurations have thus far all been in the realm of mortuary studies, partly because Iron Age societies evidently chose to demarcate such distinctions on their own bodies rather than expressing them in the form of settlement structures (Arnold 2004). Although there is disagreement as to the precise nature of their political structure—were they complex chiefdoms or early states?—most archaeologists would agree that age, gender roles, and status differences were both recognized and marked in these Iron Age societies. As Sofaer-Derevenski (1997:196) has pointed out, "Material culture influences gender development since it acts as a reflector of gender and is associated with culturally defined gender stereotypes from a very early age."

Some of these distinctions were marked in very consistent ways through space and time. For example, infants, especially neonates, are not represented in formal burial contexts during the Iron Age, suggesting that the definition of personhood was age dependent to some extent and that before a certain age individuals were not considered fully human. Typically their remains are found in informal contexts in settlements, including rubbish pits, abandoned structures, and ditches. While children are occasionally found buried in west-central European Iron Age mounds, the grave goods found in these burials are typically of above-average quality and quantity. Infants are found very rarely, and then always newborns in association with an adult female of childbearing age, suggesting that the deaths were simultaneous.

Gender distinctions were tied to costume in consistent ways as well, although the individual elements of the costume varied through time and space. Where large samples with good skeletal preservation are available, such as at the sites of Hallstatt (Hodson 1990; Kromer 1959), Münsingen-Rain (Müller 1998), or Wederath-Belginum (Haffner 1989), grave good assemblages can be correlated with the anthropological identification of sex, providing a basis for comparison with burial contexts in which physical anthropological analysis is not possible because of poor preservation or complete calcination of cremated bone.

The association between maleness and weapons, particularly swords, daggers, and spears, in the West Hallstatt zone (Burmeister 2000), and defensive armor, including helmets and breastplates as well as axes, in the East Hallstatt zone (Potrebica 2001) is clearly represented in the archaeological as well as the documentary record, even though there are regional and temporal variations in the vocabulary of maleness. Male personal ornament also tends to be distributed asymmetrically, so that when ring jewelry is present (bracelets, hair rings, or earrings) in biologically male graves, it tends to be found on only one side of the body (i.e., only left wrist, left upper arm, or, depending on handedness, right wrist and right upper arm and left or right ear or side of the head) (Arnold 2002a). In male burials, the wheels tend to remain on the vehicle, and the body is placed either on or under the wagon or chariot. Regularly patterned "female" costume elements include ankle rings, more than one earring, symmetrically distributed ring ornaments (especially bracelets) as well as hair, bonnet, or veil ornaments and, if a wagon is present, the separation of the wheels from the vehicle body. Also significant is the higher frequency of beads of glass, amber, jet, and other materials as well as various amulets, including unworked natural objects, in female burials. Even though male graves do contain such items, they occur in fewer male graves and in smaller numbers than in female burials. Interestingly, children's burials also frequently contain amulets and unmodified natural items (Pauli 1975), suggesting that women, probably mainly those of childbearing age, and children were seen as being more vulnerable and requiring greater protection than men. Whether this interpretation can be extrapolated to the realm of gender ideology to argue that women were viewed on a par with children and therefore inferior to men appears doubtful. Nevertheless, apart from Ludwig Pauli (1972, 1975), very few researchers have attempted a systematic study of the amulet category and its distribution in the mortuary context, and given the much larger database available now, the topic should be revisited. Obviously, regional and temporal variations exist with regard to all these gender-specific grave good categories, but it is possible to claim that gender in the European Iron Age was marked through personal ornament and weaponry as well as the regularized placement of certain categories of objects within burials (Arnold 2001, 2004, in press).

This gender "vocabulary" intersects with the vocabulary of status in the sense that elites in the uppermost tier contain the entire suite of high-status markers, such as gold neckings, Mediterranean imports (including metal drinking vessels), wheeled vehicles, and/or horse trappings (a four-wheeled wagon in the late Hallstatt period and a two-wheeled chariot in the La Tène), regardless of gender. The same elements mark paramount status whether the deceased individual was male or female. This is interesting because it suggests that even though there are smaller numbers of female paramount elites, the material culture correlates of their social personae do not differ qualitatively from their male counterparts, and it can be postulated that they had similar rights and responsibilities.

In addition, the presence of individuals whose anthropologically determined sex does not correspond to the gender assigned to their grave good assemblage suggests that more than two institutionalized gender categories existed in Iron

Age Europe (Arnold 2002b). Both biologically female individuals with "male" gendered grave goods and biologically male individuals with "female" gendered grave goods are known, but whether they constitute separate gender categories or represent a single "gender transforming" category is unknown. Stoodley's (1999:76) discussion of this phenomenon in Anglo-Saxon burials in Britain is relevant here:

> The interpretation of these individuals though is problematic. Were they fully accepted members of the gender category signaled by their assemblages? Moreover, did their communities allow the burial of individuals with assemblages that were contrary to their sex? If this were the case, then these burials were blurring the gender boundaries through their possession of a kit usually confined to the opposite sex. Or did they constitute a recognized separate, perhaps special group of people, who were permitted to transcend social boundaries? Contravening social rules by adopting the kit of the opposite gender to their sex would have made a clear statement concerning their special role/status. This would be an example of a third gender. The problem will by now be clear: as the same medium is used for both a blurred and a third gender, how can we know which is in evidence?

Significantly, although the numbers of such ambiguous burials are never very high (e.g., Stoodley estimates that masculine females represent 0.37 percent of his sample and feminine males 2.08 percent), they are represented in virtually every prehistoric and early historic European burial tradition (Breitsprecher 1987:tables 1 and 2; Knüsel and Ripley 2000). To clarify this phenomenon, significantly more would have to be known about gender configurations and about Iron Age social structure more generally. More recent studies are just beginning to systematically investigate the topic on a regional basis (Burmeister 1997, 2000), building on and responding to the pioneering efforts of researchers like Ludwig Pauli (1972, 1975) and a handful of others.

New Directions

A significant problem is the tendency of many researchers to either shoehorn all burials into one of two dichotomous sex/gender categories, ignoring or minimizing ambiguous mortuary assemblages that suggest the presence of a suprabinary gender system (Arnold 1991, 2002b; Lucy 1997:161; Stoodley 1999:76), or, conversely, the tendency to reject the presence of dichotomous binary gender systems in the past while emphasizing individual agency to a degree that comes dangerously close to temporal ethnocentrism (Sørensen 2000:55–56, 65). The richly varied forms of gender expression represented in the archaeological record tend to be obscured by various forms of contemporary preconceptions regarding gender configurations that are conceived of either as immutable and universal or as endlessly negotiated and ambiguous. As Moira Gatens (1996:35) has pointed out, "The privileged relation which each individual has to her or his own body does *not* include a privilege over its construction." Sørensen (2000:50) summarizes Gatens's perspective as follows: "This means that bodies are sexed, and that society recognizes 'its' bodies as differently sexed. She [Gatens] also shows that it is significant to accept that societies, despite transgressionary practices and contrary to personal experiences, in general see bodies as variations upon male and female." I have discussed the construction of chronocentrist limitations in the interpretation of past gender configurations:

> Prehistoric peoples constructed sex and gender on the basis of observed morphological or behavioral features. They could not have distinguished between individuals on the basis of chromosomal features if those features had no phenotypical or behavioral manifestations, for example. At least as important, our 20th-century [now 21st-century] political agendas and concerns were not theirs. (Arnold 2002:240)

To paraphrase Liam de Paor (1986:12), nobody lived, loved, or died in prehistory to prove a point about the present.

A related point is that as archaeologists we are dependent on the recognition of patterns and must be careful when arguing from exceptional examples to general social conventions. At the same time, the fact that a binary system of gender categorization is the dominant pattern in a given cemetery population should not blind us to the possibility that other categories existed as well. The same can be said for the so-called biological imperative that is rejected by many feminists as an explanation for the widespread presence of patriarchal social systems. As Sørensen (2000:67) correctly points out, "Universals do not imply that there will be no exceptions, merely that something is found worldwide in many different contexts and that in all of these the particular phenomenon is common. That women can give birth to children is thus a universal phenomenon despite some women being unable [or choosing not] to do so." In much the same way, as Sørensen (2000:91) also argues, wholesale rejection of traditional ideas about gendered objects, such as swords being male and personal ornament being female, is not the answer; "rather it is the recognition of their contextual genesis that is called for."

Just as problematic, in my opinion, are more recent attempts to identify individual sexual identity on the basis of archaeological evidence, one of the main themes of the 2004 Chacmool Conference titled "Qu(e)erying Archaeology." It is no coincidence that eleven of the fourteen case studies in Schmidt and Voss's (2000) *Archaeologies of Sexuality* are drawn from text-aided contexts, and only one makes use of prehistoric burial evidence (Schmidt 2003:224–25). Apart from the fact that the question of the extent to which agency can be archaeologically identified remains unresolved (Arnold 2001; Dobres and Robb 2000), not all social systems rely on sexual identity or the choice of sexual partner in characterizing gender (Arnold 2002b:247). Ironically, traditional, androcentric interpretations have tended to invoke sexual identity when attempting to reconcile "anomalous" sex/gender associations. The interpretation of the Early Iron Age high-status burial of Vix as a "transvestite priest" (Arnold 1991) or the characterization of an Anglo-Saxon "double weapon burial as evidence for homosexuality, rather than accepting the sexing of one of the skeletons as possibly female" (Lucy 1997:161) are just two examples. While it can be assumed that a small percentage of individuals in any prehistoric population may have exhibited biologically indeterminate or ambiguous sexual characteristics, they would not have been sufficiently numerous to constitute a normative category of sex identification (Parker Pearson 2000:96; Rega 1997:242). On the other hand, because the way in which different cultures treat such individuals can vary considerably, from selective infanticide to the creation of positions of social importance, the visibility in the mortuary context of sex/gender disjunction can be revealing in and of itself.

One of the primary ongoing goals of engendered mortuary analysis should be to ensure that past gender configurations are allowed to speak to us through the archaeological record as unencumbered as possible by the concerns and agendas of today. Physical anthropologist Linda Hurcombe (1995:96) makes this point in her discussion of the pedagogical challenges of teaching students about the evolution of the division of labor by sex and why the available evidence suggests that most men were probably hunters: "To say that such ideas are sexist is to miss the point of sexual dimorphism as an evolutionary strategy and to be biased by our own cultural experience of the *status* of activities. The female students wanted women to be seen as hunters because this was the task *they* valued more." While projecting current perspectives regarding the construction of gender onto past social systems in archaeological interpretation is clearly inevitable to some degree and while all archaeological data are potentially subject to various forms of manipulation, both conscious and unconscious, the tremendous variety of past gender configurations and the varied degree to which these are expressed in mortuary ritual dictate caution. We should try to avoid speaking for the archaeological record, even when what it has to say may not reflect contemporary attitudes toward the role of the individual in constructing identities, including gender.

Only in this way can mortuary archaeology contribute fully to the continuing exploration and discussion of gender and its material expression in past as well as present societies.

References

Alt, Kurt
   1997   *Odontologische Verwandtschaftsanalyse: Individuelle Charakteristika der Zähne in Ihrer Bedeutung für Anthropologie, Archäologie und Rechtsmedizin.* Stuttgart: Gustav Fischer.
Alt, Kurt, Martina Munz, and Werner Vach
   1995   Hallstattzeitliche Grabhügel im Spiegel ihrer biologischen und sozialen Strukturen am Beispiel des Hügelgräberfeldes von Dattingen, Kr. Breisgau-Hochschwarzwald. *Germania* 73(2):281–316.
Anthony, David
   1990   Migration in Archaeology: The Baby and the Bathwater. *American Anthropologist* 92:895–914.
Arnold, Bettina
   1991   The Deposed Princess of Vix: The Need for an Engendered European Prehistory. In *The Archaeology of Gender.* Proceedings of the 22nd Annual Chacmool Conference. D. Walde and N.D. Willows, eds. Pp. 366–74. Calgary: Department of Archaeology, University of Calgary.
   2001   The Limits of Agency in the Analysis of Elite Celtic Iron Age Burials. *Journal of Social Archaeology* 1(2):211–23.
   2002a   A Landscape of Ancestors: The Space and Place of Death in Iron Age West-Central Europe. In *The Space and Place of Death.* H. Silverman and D. B. Small, eds. Pp. 129–44. Archaeological Papers of the American Anthropological Association 11. Washington, DC: American Anthropological Association.
   2002b   "Sein und Werden": Gender as Process in Mortuary Ritual. In *In Pursuit of Gender: Worldwide Archaeological Approaches.* Sarah Nelson and Myriam Rosen-Ayalon, eds. Pp. 239–56. Walnut Creek, CA: AltaMira Press.
   2002c   A Transatlantic Perspective on German Archaeology. In *Archaeology, Ideology and Society: the German Experience.* 2nd ed. Heinrich Härke, ed. Pp. 401–25. Frankfurt: Peter Lang.
   2004   Machtbeziehungen und Geschlechterdifferenz in der vorgeschichtlichen Eisenzeit Europas. In *Machtbeziehungen, Geschlechterdifferenz und Religion.* Bernhard Heininger, Stephanie Böhm, and Ulrike Sals, eds. Pp. 9–34. Münster: LIT Verlag.
   2005   Mobile Men, Sedentary Women? Material Culture as a Marker of Regional and Supra-Regional Interaction in Early Iron Age Southwest Germany. In *Celts on the Margin: Studies in European Cultural Interaction 7th c. BC–1st c. AD.* Essays in Honor of Zenon Wozniak. Halina Dobrzanska, J. V. S. Megaw, and Pau-

lina Poleska, eds. Pp. 17–26. Krakow: Institute of Archaeology and Ethnology of the Polish Academy of the Sciences.

In press   Fieldwork in the Country of Death: Mortuary Variability and Archaeological Inference. In *Archaeological Concepts for the Study of the Cultural Past*. Alan Sullivan, ed. Salt Lake City: University of Utah Press.

Arnold, Bettina, and Nancy L. Wicker, eds.

2001   *Gender and the Archaeology of Death*. Walnut Creek, CA: AltaMira Press.

Bahn, Paul, ed.

2003   *Written in Bones: How Human Remains Unlock the Secrets of the Dead*. Toronto: Firefly.

Baum, Norbert

1999   Die Dietersberghöhle bei Egloffstein, Kr. Forchheim—von der Opferhöhle zum Bestattungsplatz. *Prähistorische Zeitschrift* 74(1):79–121.

Bentley, Gillian R.

1996   How Did Prehistoric Women Bear "Man the Hunter"? Reconstructing Fertility from the Archaeological Record. In *Gender and Archaeology*. Rita P. Wright, ed. Pp. 23–51. Philadelphia: University of Pennsylvania Press.

Bolger, Diana R., and Nancy J. Serwint, eds.

2002   *Engendering Aphrodite: Women and Society in Ancient Cyprus*. Boston: American Society for Oriental Research.

Brandt, Helga

1998   Frauen in der keltischen Eisenzeit. In: *Frauen—Zeiten—Spuren*. Bärbel Auffermann and Gerd-Christian Weniger, eds. Pp. 271–301. Mettmann: Neandertal Museum.

Breitsprecher, Ute

1987   Zum Problem der geschlechtsspezifischen Bestattungen in der römischen Kaiserzeit: Ein Beitrag zur Forschungsgeschichte und Methode. BAR International Series 376. Oxford: British Archaeological Reports.

Brown, Keri A.

1998   Gender and Sex: Distinguishing the Difference with Ancient DNA. In *Gender and Italian Archaeology: Challenging Stereotypes*. Ruth D. Whitehouse, ed. Pp. 35–44. London: Accordia Research Institute/University College London.

Brumfiel, Elizabeth M.

1991   Weaving and Cooking: Women's Production in Aztec Mexico. In *Engendering Archaeology: Women and Prehistory*. Joan Gero and Margaret Conkey, eds. Pp. 224–51. Cambridge: Blackwell.

Brush, Karen

1988   Gender and Mortuary Analysis in Pagan Anglo-Saxon Archaeology. *Archaeological Review from Cambridge* 7:76–89.

Budd, Paul, Andrew Millard, Carolyn Chenery, Sam Lucy, and Charlotte Roberts

2004   Investigating Population Movement by Stable Isotope Analysis: A Report from Britain. *Antiquity* 78(299):127–41.

Buikstra, Jane, Lyle Konigsberg, and Jill Bullington

1986   Fertility and the Development of Agriculture in the Prehistoric Midwest. *American Antiquity* 51:528–46.

Burmeister, Stefan

1997   Zum sozialen Gebrauch von Tracht: Aussagemöglichkeiten hinsichtlich des Nachweises von Migrationen. *Ethnologisch-Archäologische Zeitschrift* 38:177–203.

2000   *Geschlecht, Alter und Herrschaft in der Späthallstattzeit Württembergs.* Tübinger Schriften zur Ur- und Frühgeschichtlichen Archäologie Band 4. New York: Waxmann Münster.

Butler, Judith

1990   *Gender Trouble: Feminism and the Subversion of Identity.* New York: Routledge.

1993   *Bodies That Matter: On the Discursive Limits of "Sex."* New York: Routledge.

Cannon, Aubrey

2005   Gender, Agency, and Mortuary Fashion. In *Interacting with the Dead: Perspectives on Mortuary Archaeology for the New Millennium.* Gordon F. M. Rakita, Jane E. Buikstra, Lane A. Beck, and Sloan R. Williams, eds. Pp. 41–65. Gainesville: University Press of Florida.

Carr, Christopher

1995   Mortuary Practices: Their Social, Philosophical-Religious, Circumstantial and Physical Determinants. *Journal of Archaeological Method and Theory* 2(2):105–200.

Chapman, John

2000   Tensions at Funerals: Social Practice and the Subversion of Community Structure in Later Hungarian Prehistory. In *Agency in Archaeology.* Marcia-Ann Dobres and John E. Robb, eds. Pp. 169–95. London: Routledge.

Charles, Douglas K.

1995   Diachronic Regional Social Dynamics: Mortuary Sites in the Illinois Valley/ American Bottom Region. In *Regional Approaches to Mortuary Analysis.* Lane A. Beck, ed. Pp. 77–100. New York: Plenum.

Charles, Douglas K., and Jane E. Buikstra

1983   Archaic Mortuary Sites in the Central Mississippi Drainage: Distribution, Structure, and Behavioral Implications. In *Archaic Hunters and Gatherers in the American Midwest.* James L. Phillips and James A. Brown, eds. Pp. 117–45. New York: Academic Press.

2002   Siting, Sighting and Citing the Dead. In *The Space and Place of Death.* Helaine Silverman and David B. Small, eds. Pp. 13–25. Arlington, VA: Archaeological Papers of the American Anthropological Association.

Clark, John E.

2000   Towards a Better Explanation of Hereditary Inequality: A Critical Assessment of Natural and Historic Human Agents. In *Agency in Archaeology.* Marcia-Anne Dobres and John Robb, eds. Pp. 92–112. London: Routledge.

Cohen, M. N., and S. Bennett
    1998   Skeletal Evidence for Sex Roles and Gender Hierarchies in Prehistory. In
            Reader in Gender Archaeology. Kelley Hays-Gilpin und David S. Whitely, eds. Pp.
            297–318. London: Routledge.
Conkey, Margaret W., and Janet Spector
    1984   Archaeology and the Study of Gender. *Archaeological Advances in Method and Theory*
            7:1–38.
Crass, Barbara A.
    2001   Gender and Mortuary Analysis: What Can Grave Goods Really Tell Us? In
            Gender and the Archaeology of Death. Bettina Arnold and Nancy L. Wicker, eds.
            Pp. 105–18. Walnut Creek, CA: AltaMira Press.
Czarnetzki, Alfred
    1996   *Stumme Zeugen ihrer Leiden: Paläpathologische Befunde*. Tübingen: Attempto Verlag.
Davis Kimball, Jeanine
    2002   *Warrior Women: An Archaeologist's Search for History's Hidden Heroines*. New York:
            Warner Books.
de Paor, Liam
    1986   *The Peoples of Ireland: From Prehistory to Modern Times*. London: Hutchinson and
            Co.
Dobres, Marcia-Ann, and John E. Robb, eds.
    2000   *Agency in Archaeology*. London: Routledge.
Dommasnes, L. H.
    1982   Late Iron Age in Western Norway: Female Roles and Ranks as Deduced
            from an Analysis of Burial Customs. *Norwegian Archaeological Review* 15:1–2,
            70–84.
    1987   Male/Female Roles and Ranks in Late Iron Age Norway. In *Were They All
            Men? An Examination of Sex Roles in Prehistoric Societies*. R. Bertelsen, A. Lilleham-
            mer, and J.-R. Naess, eds. Pp. 65–78. Stavanger: Arkeologisk Museum i Sta-
            vanger.
    1991   Women, Kinship and the Basis of Power in the Norwegian Viking Age. In
            Social Approaches to Viking Studies. Ross Samson, ed. Pp. 65–73. Glasgow: Cru-
            ithne Press.
Doucette, Dianna L.
    2001   Decoding the Gender Bias: Inferences of Atlatls in Female Mortuary Con-
            texts. In *Gender and the Archaeology of Death*. Bettina Arnold and Nancy L.
            Wicker, eds. Pp. 159–78. Walnut Creek, CA: AltaMira Press.
Effros, Bonnie
    2003   *Merovingian Mortuary Archaeology and the Making of the Middle Ages*. Berkeley: Univer-
            sity of California Press.
Ferree, Myra Marx, Judith Lorbeer, and Beth B. Hess, eds.
    1998   *Revisioning Gender*. Thousand Oaks, CA: Sage.

Fraser, Antonia
  1988   *The Warrior Queens*. New York: Vintage Books.
Gatens, Moira
  1996   *Imaginary Bodies: Ethics, Power, and Corporeality*. London: Routledge.
Gibbons, A.
  2000   Europeans Trace Ancestry to Paleolithic People. *Science* 290 (November 10):1080–81.
Gibbs, L.
  1987   Identifying Gender Representation in the Archaeological Record: A Contextual Study. In *The Archaeology of Contextual Meanings*. Ian Hodder, ed. Pp. 79–89. Cambridge: Cambridge University Press.
Goldstein, Lynne
  1995   Landscapes and Mortuary Practices: A Case for Regional Perspectives. In *Regional Approaches to Mortuary Analysis*. Lane A. Beck, ed. Pp. 101–24. New York: Plenum.
Grauer, Anne L., and Patricia Stuart-Macadam, eds.
  1998   *Sex and Gender in Paleopathological Perspective*. Cambridge: Cambridge University Press.
Haffner, Alfred
  1989   *Gräber—Spiegel des Lebens: Totenbrauchtum der Kelten und Römer*. Mainz: Philipp von Zabern Verlag.
Hamlin, Christine
  2001   Sharing the Load: Gender and Task Division at the Windover Site. In *Gender and the Archaeology of Death*. Bettina Arnold and Nancy L. Wicker, eds. Pp. 119–36. Walnut Creek, CA: AltaMira Press.
Hamlin, Christine, and Rebecca Redfern
  2004   The Dead of Dorset: Potentials and Problems with Engendered Mortuary Analysis. Paper presented at the 15th Anniversary Gender Conference, Chacmool 2004, University of Calgary, Calgary, November 11–14.
Härke, Heinrich
  1990   "Warrior Graves"? The Background of the Anglo-Saxon Weapon Burial Rite. *Past and Present* 126:22–43.
  1992   Changing Symbols in a Changing Society: The Anglo-Saxon Weapon Burial Rite in the Seventh Century. In *The Age of Sutton Hoo: The Seventh Century in North-Western Europe*. Martin Carver, ed. Pp. 149–62. Woodbridge: Boydell.
  2000   Die Darstellung von Geschlechtergrenzen im frühmittelalterlichen Grabritual: Normalität oder Problem? In *Grenze und Differenz im Frühen Mittelalter*. Walter Pohl and Helmut Reimitz, eds. Pp. 181–96. Wien: Verlag der Österreichischen Akademie der Wissenschaften.
Hastorf, Christine A.
  1991   Gender, Space and Food in Prehistory. In *Engendering Archaeology: Women and*

Prehistory. Joan M. Gero and Margaret W. Conkey, eds. Pp. 132–62. Oxford: Basil Blackwell.

Hastorf, Christine A., and Sissell Johannessen

1993   Pre-Hispanic Political Change and the Role of Maize in the Central Andes of Peru. *American Anthropologist* 95:115–38.

Hayes-Gilpin, Kelley, and David S. Whitely, eds.

1998   *Reader in Gender Archaeology.* London: Routledge.

Henderson, J.

1989   Pagan Saxon Cemeteries: A Study of the Problems of Sexing by Grave Goods and Bones. In *Burial Archaeology: Current Research, Methods and Development.* Charlotte A. Roberts and Frances Lee and John Bintliff, eds. Pp. 77–83. BAR British Series 211. Oxford: British Archaeological Reports.

Higham, Charles F. W.

2002   Women in the Prehistory of Mainland Southeast Asia. In *In Pursuit of Gender: Worldwide Archaeological Approaches.* Sarah M. Nelson and Myriam Rosen-Ayalon, eds. Pp. 207–24. Walnut Creek, CA: AltaMira Press.

Hjørungsdal, T.

1991   Det skjulte kjønn: Patriarkal tradisjon og feministic visjon i arkeologien belyst med focus på en jernalderkontekst. *Acta Archaeologica Ludensia Series in 8* 19:1–188.

1994   Poles Apart: Have There Been Any Male or Female Graves? *Current Swedish Archaeology* 2:141–49.

Hodson, Frank

1990   *Hallstatt—The Ramsauer Graves: Quantification and Analysis.* Bonn: Rudolf Habelt Verlag.

Høgestøl, M.

1986   Endringer i sosial posisjon hos jernalders kvinner. *Kvinner i Arkeologi i Norge* 3:49–58.

Hollimon, Sandra

2001   Warfare and Gender in the Northern Plains: Osteological Evidence of Trauma Reconsidered. In *Gender and the Archaeology of Death.* Bettina Arnold and Nancy L. Wicker, eds. Pp. 179–94. Walnut Creek, CA: AltaMira Press.

Hubbard, Ruth

1990   *The Politics of Women's Biology.* New Brunswick, NJ: Rutgers University Press.

Hurcombe, Linda

1995   Our Own Engendered Species. *Antiquity* 69:87–100.

Jiao, Tianlong

2001   Gender Studies in Chinese Neolithic Archaeology. In *Gender and the Archaeology of Death.* Bettina Arnold and Nancy L. Wicker, eds. Pp. 51–64. Walnut Creek, CA: AltaMira Press.

Joyce, Rosemary A.

1996   The Construction of Gender in Classic Mayan Monuments. In *Gender and*

Archaeology. Rita P. Wright, ed. Pp. 167–95. Philadelphia: University of Pennsylvania Press.

1998   Performing the Body in Pre-Hispanic Central America. *Res* 33:147–65.

1999   Social Dimensions of Preclassic Burials. In *Ritual Behavior, Social Identity and Cosmology in Pre-Classic Mesoamerica.* David C. Grove and Rosemary A. Joyce, eds. Pp. 15–47. Washington, DC: Dumbarton Oaks.

Kästner, Sibylle

1997   Rund ums Geschlecht: Ein Überblick zu feministischen Geschlechtertheorien und deren Anwendung auf die archäologische Forschung. In *Vom Knochenmann zur Menschenfrau: Feministische Theorie und archäologische Praxis.* Sigrun M. Karlisch and Sibylle Kästner, eds. Pp. 13–35. Münster: Agenda Verlag.

Kehoe, Alice

1999   A Resort to Subtler Contrivances. In *Manifesting Power: Gender and the Interpretation of Power in Archaeology.* Tracy L. Sweely, ed. Pp. 17–29. London: Routledge.

Kessler, Suzanne

1998   *Lessons from the Intersexed.* New Brunswick, NJ: Rutgers University Press.

Keswani, Priscilla

2004   *Mortuary Ritual and Society in Bronze Age Cyprus.* London: Equinox.

Knüsel, Christopher, and Kathryn Ripley

2000   The *Berdache* or Man-Woman in Anglo-Saxon England and Early Medieval Europe. In *Social Identity in Early Medieval Britain.* William O. Frazer and Andrew Tyrrell, eds. Pp. 157–91. London: Leicester University Press.

Konigsberg, Lyle W., and Jane E. Buikstra

1995   Regional Approaches to the Investigation of Past Human Biocultural Structure. In *Regional Approaches to Mortuary Analysis.* Lane A. Beck, ed. Pp. 191–219. New York: Plenum.

Kromer, Karl

1959   *Das Gräberfeld von Hallstatt.* Firenze: Sansoni.

Lillie, Malcolm C.

1997   Women and Children in Prehistory: Resource Sharing and Social Stratification at the Mesolithic-Neolithic Transition in Ukraine. In *Invisible People and Processes: Writing Gender and Childhood into European Archaeology.* Jenny Moore and Eleanor Scott, eds. Pp. 213–28. London: Leicester University Press.

Linduff, Kathy

2002   Women's Lives Memorialized in Burial in Ancient China at Anyang. In *In Pursuit of Gender: Worldwide Archaeological Approaches.* Sarah M. Nelson and Myriam Rosen-Ayalon, eds. Pp. 257–88. Walnut Creek, CA: AltaMira Press.

Lorrio, Alberto J., and Gonzalo Ruiz Zapatero

2005   The Celts in Iberia: An Overview. *E-Keltoi* 6:167–254.

Loth, Susan R., and Maciej Henneberg

2001   Sexually Dimorphic Mandibular Morphology in the First Few Years of Life. *American Journal of Physical Anthropology* 115(2):179–86.

Lucy, Sam J.
 1995   The Anglo-Saxon Cemeteries of East Yorkshire. Ph.D. diss., Cambridge Uni-
        versity.
 1997   Housewives, Warriors and Slaves? Sex and Gender in Anglo-Saxon Burials.
        In *Invisible People and Processes: Writing Gender and Childhood into European Archaeology*.
        Jenny Moore and Eleanor Scott, eds. Pp. 150–68. London: Leicester Univer-
        sity Press.
 2000   *The Anglo-Saxon Way of Death: Burial Rites in Early England*. Stroud: Sutton.
 2004   Gender and Identity in Medieval Britain. Paper presented at the 15th Anni-
        versary Gender Conference, Chacmool 2004, University of Calgary, Calgary,
        November 11–14.
Macbeth, H.
 1993   Ethnicity and Human Biology. In *Social and Biological Aspects of Ethnicity*. M.
        Chapman, ed. Pp. 47–91. Oxford: Oxford University Press.
McCafferty, Sharisse, and Geoffrey McCafferty
 1994   Engendering Tomb 7 at Monte Alban. *Current Anthropology* 35(2):143–66.
McNay, Lois
 2000   *Gender and Agency*. Cambridge: Polity Press.
Meyers, Carol
 2003   Engendering Syro-Palestinian Archaeology: Reasons and Resources. *Near
        Eastern Archaeology* 66(4):185–97.
Molleson, T., and M. Cox
 1993   *The Spitalfields Project. Volume II: The Anthropology: The Middling Sort*. CBA Research
        Report 86. York: Council for British Archaeology.
Moore, Jenny, and Eleanor Scott
 1997   *Invisible People and Processes: Writing Gender and Childhood into European Archaeology*.
        London: Leicester University Press.
Müller, Felix, ed.
 1998   Münsingen-Rain, ein Markstein der keltischen Archäologie: Funde, Befunde
        und Methoden im Vergleich. Bern: Bernisches Historisches Museum.
Müller, Johannes
 1994a Altersorganisation und Westhallstatt: Ein Versuch. *Ethnographisch-Archäologische
        Zeitschrift* 35:220–40.
 1994b Bestattungsformen als Spiegel dualer Organisation in prähistorischen Gesell-
        schaften? *Mitteilungen Berliner Gesellschaft Anthropologie, Ethnologie, Urgeschichte*
        15:81–88.
 1994c Zur sozialen Gliederung der Nachbestattungsgemeinschaft vom Magdalen-
        enberg bei Villingen. *Prähistorische Zeitschrift* 1994(2):122–75.
Nelson, Sarah M.
 1993   Gender Hierarchy and the Queens of Silla. In *Sex and Gender Hierarchies*. Bar-
        bara Diane Miller, ed. Pp. 297–315. Cambridge: Cambridge University
        Press.

1997   *Gender in Archaeology: Analyzing Power and Prestige.* Walnut Creek, CA: AltaMira Press.

2002   Ideology, Power and Gender: Emergent Complex Society in Northeastern China. In *In Pursuit of Gender: Worldwide Archaeological Approaches.* Sarah M. Nelson and Myriam Rosen-Ayalon, eds. Pp. 73–80. Walnut Creek, CA: AltaMira Press.

Nelson, Sarah M., and Myriam Rosen-Ayalon, eds.

2002   *In Pursuit of Gender: Worldwide Archaeological Approaches.* Walnut Creek, CA: AltaMira Press.

Oeftiger, Claus

1984   *Mehrfachbestattungen im Westhallstattkreis: Zum Problem der Totenfolge.* Bonn: Antiquitas.

O'Gorman, Jodie A.

2001   Life, Death and the Longhouse: A Gendered View of Oneota Social Organization. In *Gender and the Archaeology of Death.* Bettina Arnold and Nancy L. Wicker, eds. Pp. 23–50. Walnut Creek, CA: AltaMira Press.

Olausson, D.

1988   Dots on a Map: Thoughts about the Way Archaeologists Study Prehistoric Trade and Exchange. In *Trade and Exchange in Prehistory: Studies in Honor of Berta Stjernquist.* Birgitta Hårdh, L. Larsson, D. Olausson, and R. Petré, eds. Pp. 15–24. Lund: Lunds Universitets Historiska Museum.

Olivier, Laurent

1992   The Tomb of Hochdorf. *Archaeological Review from Cambridge* 11(1):51–63.

Ortner, Sherry

1996   *Making Gender: The Politics and Erotics of Culture.* Boston: Beacon Press.

Pader, Ellen Jane

1982   *Symbolism, Social Relations and the Interpretation of Mortuary Remains.* BAR British Series 130. Oxford: British Archaeological Reports.

Parker Pearson, Michael

2000   *The Archaeology of Death and Burial.* College Station: Texas A&M University Press.

Parkington, John E.

1991   Approaches to Dietary Reconstruction in the Western Cape: Are You What You Have Eaten? *Journal of Archaeological Science* 18:331–42.

Pauli, Ludwig

1972   Untersuchungen zur Späthallstattkultur in Nordwürttemberg: Analyse eins Kleinraumes im Grenzbereich zweier Kulturen. *Hamburger Beiträge zur Archäologie* 2(1):1–166.

1975   *Keltischer Volksglaube: Amulette und Sonderbestattungen am Dürrnberg bei Hallein und im eisenzeitlichen Europa.* Munich: C. H. Beck'sche Verlagsbuchhandlung.

Peterson, Jane

2002   *Sexual Revolutions: Gender and Labor at the Dawn of Agriculture.* Walnut Creek, CA: AltaMira Press.

Potrebica, Hrvoje
  2001   Some Aspects of the Warrior Concept in the Eastern Hallstatt Circle. *Prehistoria 2000* I(I):62–81.

Rega, Elizabeth
  1997   Age, Gender and Biological Reality in the Early Bronze Age Cemetery at Mokrin. In *Invisible People and Processes: Writing Gender and Childhood into European Archaeology.* Jenny Moore and Eleanor Scott, eds. Pp. 229–47. London: Leicester University Press.

Reinhold, Sabine
  2003   Traditions in Transition: Thoughts on Late Bronze Age and Early Iron Age Burial Costumes from the Northern Caucasus. *European Journal of Archaeology* 6(I):25–54.

Richards, Michael P.
  2000   Human Consumption of Plant Foods in the British Neolithic: Direct Evidence from Bone Stable Isotopes. In *Plants in Neolithic Britain and Beyond.* Andrew S. Fairbairn, ed. Pp. 123–35. Oxford: Oxbow Monograph.

Roberts, Charlotte A., and Keith Manchester
  1995   *The Archaeology of Disease.* 2nd ed. Stroud: Sutton.

Rolle, Renate
  1989   *The World of the Scythians.* London: Batsford.

Rolle, Renate, Michael Müller-Wille, and Kurt Schietzel, eds.
  1991   *Das Gold der Steppe: Archäologie der Ukraine.* Neumünster: Karl Wachholtz Verlag.

Sangmeister, Eduard
  1994   Einige Gedanken zur Sozialstruktur im Westhallstattgebiet. *Marburger Studien zur Vor- und Frühgeschichte* 16:523–34.

Schier, Wolfram
  1998   Fürsten, Herren, Händler? Bemerkungen zu Wirtschaft und Gesellschaft der westlichen Hallstattkultur. In *Archäologische Forschungen in urgeschichtlichen Siedlungslandschaften: Festschrift für Georg Kossack zum 75. Geburtstag.* Hans-Jörg Küster, Amei Lang, and Peter Schauer, eds. Pp. 493–514. Regensburg: Universitätsverlag Regensburg.

Schmidt, Robert A.
  2003   Shamans and Northern Cosmology: The Direct Historical Approach to Mesolithic Sexuality. In *Archaeologies of Sexuality.* Robert A. Schmidt and Barbara L. Voss, eds. Pp. 220–35. London: Routledge.

Schmidt, Robert A., and Barbara L. Voss
  2003   *Archaeologies of Sexuality.* London: Routledge.

Schwidetzky, I.
  1965   Sonderbestattungen und ihre paläodemographische Bedeutung. *Homo* 16:230–47.

Scott, Eleanor
  2001   Killing the Female? Archaeological Narratives of Infanticide. In *Gender and the*

Archaeology of Death. Bettina Arnold and Nancy L. Wicker, eds. Pp. 1–22. Walnut Creek, CA: AltaMira Press.

Scott, G. Richard, and Christy G. Turner II

1997   *The Anthropology of Modern Human Teeth*. Cambridge: Cambridge University Press.

Seielstad, M. T., E. Minch, and Luigi Cavalli-Sforza

1998   Genetic Evidence for a Higher Female Migration Rate in Humans. *Nature Genetics* 20(November):278–80.

Shimada, Izumi, Ken-ichi Shinoda, Julie Farnum, Robert Corrucini, and Hirokatsu Watanabe

2004   An Integrated Analysis of Pre-Hispanic Mortuary Practices: A Middle Sicán Case Study. *Current Anthropology* 45(3):369–402.

Silverblatt, Irene

1991   Interpreting Women in States: New Feminist Ethnohistories. In *Gender at the Crossroads of Knowledge: Feminist Anthropology in the Postmodern Era*. Micaela di Leonardo, ed. Pp. 140–71. Berkeley: University of California Press.

Sobolik, Kristin D., ed.

1994   *Paleonutrition: The Diet and Health of Prehistoric Americans*. Center for Archaeological Investigations Occasional Paper 22. Carbondale: Southern Illinois University Press.

Sofaer-Derevenski, Joanna

1997   Linking Age and Gender as Social Variables. *Ethnologisch-Archäologische Zeitschrift* 38:485–93.

Sørensen, Marie Louise Stig

2000   *Gender Archaeology*. Cambridge: Polity Press.

Spector, Janet, and Mary Whelan

1991   Incorporating Gender into Archaeology Courses. In *Gender and Anthropology: Critical Reviews for Research and Teaching*. Sandra Morgan, ed. Pp. 65–94. Washington, DC: American Anthropological Association.

Stalsberg, Anne

1984   Skandinaviske Vikingtidsfunn fra Russland med saerlig vekt påkvinnefunnere: Et bidrag til kvinne-arkeologien. *Unitekst fagskrift* 6:68–102.

1987a   The Implications of the Women's Finds for the Understanding of the Activities of the Scandinavians in Russia during the Viking Age. *Kvinner i Arkeologi i Norge* 5:33–49.

1987b   The Interpretation of Women's Objects of Scandinavian Origin from the Viking Period Found in Russia. In *Were They All Men? An Examination of Sex Roles in Prehistoric Societies*. R. Bertelsen, A. Lillehammer, and J.-R. Naess, eds. Pp. 89–101. Stavanger: Arkeologisk Museum i Stavanger.

Stavish, Patricia

2004   "Women and Children First": The Distribution of Grave Goods in the La Tène Cemetery at Münsingen-Rain, Switzerland. Paper presented at the 15th Anniversary Gender Conference, Chacmool 2004, University of Calgary, Calgary, November 11–14.

Stoodley, Nick
   1999   *The Spindle and the Spear: A Critical Enquiry in the Construction and Meaning of Gender in the Early Anglo-Saxon Burial Rite.* BAR British Series 288. Oxford: Archaeopress.
Strömberg, Agneta
   1993   *Male or Female? A Methodological Study of Grave Gifts as Sex-Indicators in Iron Age Burials from Athens.* Jonsered: Paul Åströms Förlag.
Sullivan, Lynn P.
   2001   Those Men in the Mounds: Gender, Politics and Mortuary Practices in Late Prehistoric Eastern Tennessee. In *Archaeological Studies of Gender in the Southeastern United States.* Jane M. Eastman und Christopher B. Rodning, eds. Pp. 101–26. Gainesville: University Press of Florida.
Sweely, Tracy L., ed.
   1999   *Manifesting Power: Gender and the Interpretation of Power in Archaeology.* London: Routledge.
Tarlow, Sarah
   1999   *Bereavement and Commemoration: An Archaeology of Mortality.* Oxford: Blackwell.
Taylor, Timothy
   1996   *The Prehistory of Sex.* New York: Bantam Books.
Vida, M. Carmen
   1998   The Italian Scene: Approaches to the Study of Gender. In *Gender and Italian Archaeology: Challenging Stereotypes.* Ruth D. Whitehouse, ed. Pp. 15–22. London: Accordia Research Institute/University College London.
Walker, Phillip L., and Della Collins Cook
   1998   Gender and Sex: Vive la Difference! *American Journal of Physical Anthropology* 106:255–59.
Weglian, Emily
   2001   Grave Goods Do Not a Gender Make: A Case Study from Singen am Hohentwiel, Germany. In *Gender and the Archaeology of Death.* Bettina Arnold and Nancy L. Wicker, eds. Pp. 137–58. Walnut Creek, CA: AltaMira Press.
Weiss, Kenneth M.
   1992   On Systematic Bias in Skeletal Sexing. *American Journal of Physical Anthropology* 37:239–50.
Whitehouse, Ruth D., ed.
   1998   *Gender and Italian Archaeology: Challenging Stereotypes.* London: Accordia Research Institute/University College London.
Wicker, Nancy L.
   1998   Selective Female Infanticide as Partial Explanation for the Dearth of Women in Viking Age Scandinavia. In *Violence and Society in the Early Medieval West.* Guy Hallsall, ed. Pp. 205–21. Woodbridge: Boydell.
Wicker, Nancy L., and Bettina Arnold
   1999   *From the Ground Up: Beyond Gender Theory in Archaeology.* Proceedings of the Fifth

Gender and Archaeology Conference. BAR International Series 812. Oxford: Archaeopress.

Wood, J. W., George R. Milner, H. C. Harpending, and K. M. Weiss
1992   The Osteological Paradox: Problems of Inferring Prehistoric Health from Skeletal Samples. *Current Anthropology* 33:343–70.

Wright, Rita P.
1996   Technology, Gender and Class: Worlds of Difference in Ur III, Mesopotamia. In *Gender and Archaeology*. Rita P. Wright, ed. Pp. 79–110. Philadelphia: University of Pennsylvania Press.

The Engendered Household   5

JULIA A. HENDON

THE STUDY OF BOTH GENDER and households became integral to archaeological research in the 1980s. Although the household has been an important focus of gender research, not all household archaeology has adopted an engendered perspective. Thus, studies of gender in a household context and studies of the household form overlapping but not identical bodies of research. Archaeological research on the household intersects with the archaeological study of gender for four reasons. First is the household's association with the domestic group. The domestic group has responsibilities for economic production and social reproduction in many societies. The household becomes an institution through which people of different genders and ages interact on a regular basis. Second is the connection to a particular spatial locus—called for convenience the *dwelling area* (intended as a shorthand for residential space where people live on a more or less permanent basis and that may take many forms, including buildings and open spaces). Dwelling areas provide an identifiable location often used over long periods of time. Third is the scale of the social formation. This allows for finer-grained analyses of action and identity that may be contrasted with large-scale political and social structures. And finally is opportunity for comparison across classes, status groups, wealth differences, ethnicity, or other aspects of social relations and structure created by the existence of multiple households within society. In this chapter, I discuss how and why the household is a useful social formation and scale of analysis for archaeologists interested in gender. Investigation of women's and men's socially meaningful action in a domestic context has led to a richer and more nuanced understanding of issues relating to status, identity, and role.

Defining Gender in Studies of the Household

In most household-based research that also considers gender, gender is defined as a social construct that differs from biological sex, and discussion focuses on socially defined men and women. Although consideration of women's activities, role, and status figures prominently in this body of scholarship in order to rectify the lack of attention paid to women in previous scholarship (Joyce and Claassen 1997), it has also taken up the challenge of multiple social actors, such as men and women, adults and children, and the effects of differences in class, social status, wealth, or ethnicity on households (see, e.g., Allison 2003; Axelsson 1999; Bertelsen et al. 1987; Crown 2000b; Lightfoot et al. 1998; Malan 1997; Mro-zowski et al. 2000; Robin 2002b; Tringham 1994; Wood 2002; Woolf 1997). The multiethnic nineteenth-century settlement of Fort Ross in California has been studied by Kent Lightfoot, Antoinette Martinez, and Ann Schiff (Lightfoot et al. 1998) to determine how daily practices informed by gender, ethnicity, and class differences become the basis for the negotiation of intimate and larger-scale social relations and identities. It should be pointed out that household archaeolo-gists not interested in gender have not in fact focused only on men's activities; instead, they have generally not discussed people at all, preferring to treat the household as a single entity or irreducible unit of behavioral analysis. Gender archaeologists' insistence on women has thus had the welcome effect of making their studies of the household more "enpeopled" and of demonstrating the value of studying the day-to-day lives of people, with positive consequences for our understanding of social dynamics at multiple social scales (Hendon 2004).

Social relations among household members, who would be of different gen-ders, ages, and seniority; their role in economic production; and the implications of the often unequal relationship between households or between households and the larger community or the state have proved to be productive ways of investigat-ing the roles, status, and power of different social actors within society. A recogni-tion of the value of studying ancient societies at different social scales or levels of analysis has also contributed to archaeological interest in day-to-day life as mani-fested in the activities and interactions of men and women in a household setting. These developments have grown in tandem with larger shifts in theoretical orien-tation in the discipline away from ecological, functionalist, or other deterministic paradigms. Among the multiplicity of perspectives that have emerged, those based on some version of practice theory "in which human intentionality matters" (Ortner 2001:272) and political economy or the study of "the organization of production and exchange that underlies and supports a system of power" (Brum-fiel 2001:58) have been productive (see Brumfiel 1992; Cowgill 1993; Hendon 1996, 2004; Pauketat 2001). Crucial to these engendered household studies has been a focus on households as groups of people, not just economic or social cooperative units, or "households with faces" in Ruth Tringham's (1991) evoca-tive phrase. The idea of collectivity inherent in social science approaches to the household must be balanced with the focus on individuals or types of social actors common to studies of gender, as must the degree to which gender is a matter of difference or inequality (Morgan 1999).

The Household from a Social Science Perspective: Definitions and Debates

Standard social science definitions of the household emphasize economic cooperation, coresidence, and responsibility for domestic tasks (Abercrombie et al. 2000; Guyer 1981, 1997; Johnson 2000; Netting et al. 1984; Yanagisako 1979). Household members are economically interdependent through their participation in activities related to production and consumption. They are involved in decision making about the allocation of their own and other members' time, skills, and resources. Household members are coresident because they share a dwelling or some sort of living space; in more general terms, households are marked by residential propinquity (Bender 1967). Residential propinquity does not mean that all members must live "under one roof" or all occupy one structure that we would identify as a house. Residential propinquity may result from functionally differentiated structures, such as kitchens or storage buildings, or from several multipurpose buildings ("houses") arranged in such a way as to form a spatially related area. Features of the built or used environment, such as barriers, orientation of structures, location of shrines, or paths, may be used to define the social framework. The most basic obligations of household members are domestic and, at a minimum, entail a significant responsibility for social reproduction, which may include child rearing, and for food preparation and consumption. In short, the term "household" is often used to refer primarily to an economic entity or, more precisely, a social entity with important economic functions. This may be only one way of approaching the household (Beaudry 1984; Svensson 1998), but it is the one that archaeologists have found most congenial. The household has even been associated with a mode of production, the domestic or household mode of production, and its ability to generate surplus evaluated in the context of evolutionary models of social and political change (Costin 1991; Saitta 1984).

Archaeology's long-standing interest in economic processes and its focus on material remains, among which dwellings often figure prominently, provided the original impetus behind household archaeology (Wilk and Rathje 1982a, 1982b). Household archaeology has become a prolific area of investigation applied to ancient, past, and historical societies in many world areas. The bulk of this household-related research has been carried out by North American–trained archaeologists writing in English, with some research by European and Latin

American scholars also evident (see Allison 1999; Ashmore and Wilk 1988; Haugen 1987; Hendon 1996, 2004; MacEachern et al. 1989; Manzanilla 1990; Robin 2003; Santley and Hirth 1993; Smith 1993; Svensson 1998).

The household's rise to prominence may be traced in part to increasing dissatisfaction with attempts to identify patterns of descent, postmarital residence, and other staples of kinship analysis archaeologically. Its rise relates to the move away from kinship studies and the questioning of commonly used definitions of the family in anthropology (Netting et al. 1984; Yanagisako 1979). These critiques did not eliminate the need to study the economic and social relations and activities of small-scale groups, but they demonstrated convincingly that anthropologists could not assume these people formed a family and would not be able to answer their research questions by focusing only on descent, genealogy, and kinship (Bender 1967; Carter 1984).

The lower level of interest by archaeologists trained outside the North American tradition in applying the term "household" or in identifying their work as household archaeology does not mean that they ignore dwellings or are uninterested in questions of domestic relations and activities, including those connected to gender. Archaeologists have discussed dwellings, *unidades domesticas* or *habitacionales, la maisonnée,* or the *oikos* without worrying so much about the need to distinguish between families and households that has affected British and American sociologists or cultural anthropologists (Forest 1997; Goldberg 1999; Hingley 1990; Manzanilla 1986, 1990; Nevett 1999; Svensson 1998; Uruñuela and Plunket Nagoda 1998).

Debated Elements of the Definition of the Household

Coresidence

As might be expected when social scientists attempt to turn a folk concept dominant in their own social and cultural milieu into a systematic and widely applicable analytical concept, these elements of economic interdependence, coresidence, and domesticity have been debated and disputed. Cultural anthropologists have given a great deal of attention to the question of coresidence. Anthropology's commitment to making visible the variety of social arrangements across cultures makes it less comfortable with standard sociological definitions of the household as "one or more people who share common living circumstances, especially in sharing a dwelling and/or facilities for preparing food" (Johnson 2000:145) or "a single person or group sharing living accommodation" (Abercrombie et al. 2000:166). According to Jane Guyer (1997:245),

> "Household" derives from the English version of feudalism, where each "holding" (of land) was identified with a house and its inhabitants, which was geographically fixed and had some social permanence. . . . Although most societies have domestic groups of some kind, only some have this particular institution, and the English term "household" translates poorly [into other languages].

In some societies, people sharing residential space may not constitute an economic unit or share responsibility for domestic tasks. Economic and social connections and responsibilities may be organized in ways that link together people living not only apart from one another but at some distance as well (Guyer 1981; Netting et al. 1984; Yanagisako 1979). Two possible solutions to the problems of definition and generalizability have been proposed. One is to accept that the term "household" must be defined using some other criteria than residence (Carter 1984; Netting et al. 1984; Wilk and Rathje 1982b). The other is to suggest that the definition of "household" be restricted to "economic units based on common residence" (Guyer 1997:245). These solutions clearly have different consequences. The first approach retains the household as a universal type of social formation or institution but requires that the details of residential organization be specified for each situation. The second affirms the association between the social institution and a particular spatial location but rejects the assumption that the household may be seen as a universal as well as fundamental social formation present in every society. The household becomes historically contingent rather than an ideal type.

In an early discussion of the usefulness of the household to archaeologists, Richard Wilk and William Rathje (1982b) viewed the household as universal but cautioned against assuming coresidence—although they noted the connection often does pertain. Most archaeologists engaged in household archaeology have adopted this viewpoint while ignoring the caution. At best, they acknowledge the issue but set it aside because they do not see how they would study a social group in the absence of some identifiable spatial locus. Guyer's definition provides an effective alternative perspective that moves archaeology's focus on residential space or propinquity beyond mere expediency. If the household is historical and cultural, not ontological or universal, then the archaeologist must evaluate the probability of the existence of a household society (or a society with households) by asking whether the group living in the dwelling or residential space constitutes an economic unit (Hendon 2004).

Domesticity, Public/Private, and Household Relations

The economic role of the household is generally defined in terms of production, consumption, and allocation of resources (Guyer 1981). Its status as a unit implies that household members do not act solely on the basis of their individual wants or desires. Instead, they cooperate with one another in order to benefit the group through mechanisms of sharing and by making decisions that put the group first. While economists are generally content to subsume all this under the rubric of economic behavior, it is clear to anthropologists that we are really talking about a set of social relations and structures through which economic tasks and relations are enacted and justified. Household economics are not merely a set of behaviors. "While a household can be defined by the activities it performs and by its shape and size, it can also be defined as a symbolic entity" (Netting et al. 1984:xxix). Anthony Carter (1984:47) has referred to these activities as "culturally recognized tasks," those shared economic and social activities that are culturally recognized as the province of the coresidential domestic group. Responsibility for the enactment of these tasks becomes central to why people define themselves as a group that we would label households.

An important part of the economic and social purpose of the household are domestic tasks and responsibilities, making the household the locus of domestic labor. Like household, domestic is a folk or "commonsense" category that social scientists have taken over for analytical purposes (Wilk and Netting 1984). In the process, specification of the meaning of domestic tasks has been debated in much the same way as the definition of household. As noted previously, social reproduction, including childbearing and child rearing, and food preparation on behalf of all household members are often taken as the minimal elements of domestic tasks (Yanagisako 1979). Both sociologists and anthropologists have pointed out that responsibilities for raising children may be organized in other ways involving people who do not live together and who do not form an economic unit. Some households may in fact not contain children at all and may never have done so. People who are coresident may not have share food together or expect that someone is responsible for preparing food for all to share. Once again, the expectation that it should be possible to create a clearly defined ideal type that does not overlap with other types of social institutions or groups is confounded by the realities of the historical and cultural variety documented by anthropology, sociology, and social history. On the other hand, as with economic production more generally, food production and consumption are activities that archaeologists can identify through the material record.

A more serious problem with the concept of the domestic has been raised by feminist scholars in several disciplines. Because domestic activities in capitalist economies are subsumed under the term "housekeeping," are "stereotyped as non-productive" (Wilk and Netting 1984:6–7), and are unremunerated, they are often assumed to be irrelevant to an understanding of larger-scale social or politi-cal structures or developments. They may even be seen as an uninteresting aspect of the household's economic function. Bender (1967:498–99) notes that "as a folk concept, our term 'domestic' refers to those activities associated with the household or the home. Furthermore, it connotes female activities more than male activities." If this folk concept is not examined critically, the household risks becoming "an analytical heading that tends to submerge women and their work within undifferentiated, closed household organizational systems" (Netting et al. 1984:xxv).

This assumption has also been propped up by the adoption by anthropolo-gists of another folk concept, one that has its roots in nineteenth-century middle-class Euro-American values. It has been used to create an analytical division of society into separate domains, the domestic and the political or politico-jural, or private and public spheres of activity:

> Underlying the politico-jural domain are jural norms guaranteed by "external" or "public" sanctions which may ultimately entail force. In con-trast, the domestic . . . domain is constrained by "private" affective and moral norms, at the root of which is the fundamental axiom of prescrip-tive altruism. (Yanagisako 1979:187)

Early work by feminist anthropologists accepted this division and used women's restriction to the domestic sphere and their symbolic association with hearth, home, and reproduction to explain women's universal subordination (e.g., Ortner 1974; Rosaldo 1974). The work by Sherry Ortner and Michelle Rosaldo sparked a great deal of research by feminist scholars, resulting in the realization that these ideas can be situated in a particular historical and cultural context out of which much anthropological and historical research has come but that does not neces-sarily apply to the societies being studied (Marti 1993; Ortner 1996; Reverby and Helly 1992; Rosaldo 1980; Silverblatt 1995; Wylie 1992). Once again, a set of contingent ideas was generalized into a universal contrast: "women everywhere dominated by men [and] everywhere inhabiting a separate social domain" (di Leonardo 1991:229).

These issues have created something of a quandary for feminist scholars and those interested in gender. By using the household as the focus of research on women, is one merely reinforcing existing stereotypes on women's place in society or perpetuating the naive extension of Victorian ideals about womanhood and female nature that have found their way into analytical models of society? At the same time, it is clear that people's involvement in household relations and activities can form an important part of their daily life and play a role in how they give meaning to their lived experience. Thus, any interest in the study of what people did a lot of the time requires some consideration of household-level action and interaction. Furthermore, practice-based approaches to the study of society suggest that all action is meaningful, not just what takes place in particular social contexts or spatial settings (Bourdieu 1977).

Moreover, the ability to define households in part through a particular spatial setting has proved enormously productive for the project of engendering and enpeopling the past. Thus, like most archaeologists, those focused on the study of gender have continued to endorse a framework that views society as made up of different arenas of social action that are often associated with distinctive areas of the built environment or the landscape. These areas provide a setting in which people interact; although the associations between kind of setting and kinds of interactions are to some degree fluid and variable, it is nevertheless the case that particular configurations may be established (see Tringham 1994, 1995). Focusing on one such area or social formation, such as the dwelling area or the household, does not imply that households are best studied in isolation from the larger society of which they are a part (Beaudry 1984; Haugen 1987; Hendon 2002). Such a focus does indicate that something worthwhile may be learned by considering the particular social scale and set of relationships. The issue is not so much the labels employed but the meanings connected with those labels that impede understanding. While studying households could do no more than result in a conservative reification of women's apolitical status (e.g., Hayden 1992), gendered research has in fact for the most part worked against this point of view by asking, What is the nature of the relations among members of these culturally defined task groups?

Social Action and Interaction at the Household Level

Gender Attribution

Research focused on practice and political economy insists on a close engagement with the material record and its meaning. The cultural logic of households may be carried out through the study of the "mutually constituting" (Birdwell-Pheasant and Lawrence-Zúñiga 1999:4) relationship between houses, people, action, material culture, and meaning, or practice. In what ways does gender organize production and give meaning to social action as part of a process that produces not only material goods but also social relations and identities? This question was first approached by focusing on gender attribution, or the identification of activities associated with women carried out in a household setting.

A division of labor by gender (and age) is a common organizational mechanism for households, but what is actually done varies. Central to an identification of "women's work" is an understanding of how cultural expectations about gender make salient or emphasize certain forms of action as gendered. Like any archaeologist attempting to address interpretive questions, gender-focused archaeologists have used those mainstays of the discipline, specific and general analogy. Multiple lines of evidence for particular societies or time periods, including written sources, visual imagery, and burial practices, have been employed to determine what kinds of activities were women expected to engage in and with which they were associated (Allison 2003; Axelsson 1999; Costin 1996; Dommasnes 1987; Goldberg 1999; Hegmon et al. 2000; Hendon 1997; Malan 1997; Mills 2000; Nevett 1999; VanDerwarker and Detweiler 2002; Wall 2000; Wood 2002). Such lines of evidence are not always available, of course, but when they are, they have proved extremely helpful in identifying some range of activities that were given significance as female work. Research on preconquest Mesoamerican societies, for example, has noted the insistent association between female gender and cloth production in indigenous and European writings and in a variety of large- and small-scale forms of visual representation (Brumfiel 1991, 1996; Hendon 1997; Joyce 1993, 2000a). Such associations do not preclude variation based on social status or assume that all women did was weave. In fact, a range of activities and occupations are attested for women (Hendon 1999), and practices such as farming required the participation of all household members in patterned ways (Robin 2002a). These associations do create a cultural expectation that has implications for what socially defined women did in the course of their daily lives.

The identification of weaving as a gendered process does not even mandate that only individuals who we would recognize as biologically female engaged in these activities. Spindle whorls, taken as a marker of involvement in cloth production and female gender, have been found in some burials in Mesoamerica containing skeletons sexed as biologically male. Elizabeth Brumfiel (2001) has suggested that such burials at the site of Cholula reflect the impact of a historical process, the increasing tribute demands of the Aztec state that required households or communities to bring more people into the production system. Since gender is a social construct, it does not necessarily equate with biological sex (itself not as independent of cultural expectations as often assumed), and participation by biological males does not by itself call into question the association of female gender and textile production. While the participation by males may masculinize a formerly feminine technology, it is equally possible that the participants may become feminized through their adoption of a particular productive role or that the gender associations may be unaffected; it all depends on the cultural, social, and historical context (see Lerman et al. 2003).

Gender attribution research has also looked to the possibility of more general associations between women and domestic tasks as a way to augment or substitute for culturally or historically specific information. The search for such associations is fraught with the potential for reification of our own assumptions about women and folk notions about domesticity discussed earlier. However, cross-cultural comparison has provided strong support for an association between women and certain kinds of food preparation (for fuller discussion, see Crown 2000c; Mills 2000). In reviewing research on gender and the household, what does emerge is a high degree of self-awareness on the part of the researchers about the importance of supporting claims for gendered work or activities through a careful process of analogy and analysis.

Gender and Space

An important consequence of efforts to identify material correlates of women's and men's activities has been to seriously call into question notions of male and female space. The idea that certain parts of a dwelling area or the social landscape more generally may have strong symbolic associations with gender is not in itself problematic (Low and Lawrence-Zúñiga 2003). However, application of this possibility has generally been informed by an unreflexive structuralism that assumes the existence of binary opposition between male and female space that does not take into account how meaning is created through practice in a dynamic and often spatialized process. Static assumptions about gendered space have also led to simplistic notions of how such space would be used, notions contradicted by studies of spatial associations. Lisa Nevett's (1999) analysis of the distribution of female-associated artifacts in houses at Olynthos, Greece, combined with a study of other sources of information such as vase paintings, has led her to take issue with the standard interpretation of written sources. She argues that female members of the *oikos*, or household, were not confined to one section of the house, nor did men and women occupy separate quarters while at home:

Women were present throughout the house as their activities required, and . . . there was no need for a specific room to be set aside for them. This does not exclude the possibility that certain areas would have been more frequented by the female members of the household than others. . . . There is, however, a conceptual difference between suggesting that an area was specifically set aside for the use of women, and that it was habitually used by them. (Nevett 1999:71)

Marilyn Goldberg's (1999) examination of the Athenian house and household agrees with Nevett's conclusions. Goldberg's analysis also raises the issue of who controls the attempt to propagate certain kinds of behaviors or attitudes as societal norms. She notes that the written sources tell us about power relations between men and women and about the attitudes of elite, educated men in Athenian society as they do about the use of space. Archaeological evidence, however, indicates that these attitudes and relations did not result in women living in seclusion. Studying space as a dynamic arena in which concepts of gender are negotiated and defined through practice, as opposed to representing some fixed deep structure, allows archaeologists to consider questions of power and multiple meanings (Moore 1996).

The use of domestic space has also been addressed for the pre-Columbian Maya through the study of dwelling areas of high-status elites and farmers. In a study of the distribution of weaving tools and food preparation activities, especially corn grinding, in an elite residential area at Copan, Honduras, I found that

women ground maize, cooked, wove, or spun in close proximity to those people, male or female, who manufactured obsidian tools, shell ornaments, or bone items, and carried out rituals. . . . Such differences cannot be used to define a symbolically meaningful segregated "women's space." . . . In other words, the gendering of space achieves cultural significance only in certain contexts. . . . During the Classic period, it is public space under the control of the ruler which is most visibly gendered. (Hendon 1997:42–44)

Work on the location of women's activities at the farming hamlet of Ceren, El Salvador, by Tracy Sweely (1999a) argues for some separation of activities by function that may in turn have led to members of the same gender interacting frequently as when women gathered to grind corn. Distribution of spinning and weaving tools and materials between houses at the site also suggests that some households may have been specializing in the production of certain kinds of thread or cloth (Beaudry-Corbett and McCafferty 2002). Both studies, however, show no patterns of spatial exclusion or restriction by gender. Research on another Maya farming community, Chan Noohol in Belize, confirms the lack of restriction or exclusion by gender. Based on artifact and ecofact associations and soil chemistry analysis, Cynthia Robin (2002a, 2002b) has identified open-air work areas near houses and agricultural areas:

> People who were making tools and people who were preparing food were doing these activities in the same space, regardless of whether or not they were the same or different people or whether they were working there simultaneously or sequentially. . . . People who were involved in agriculture were able to see, talk, or call to people who were preparing food and making stone tools. (Robin 2002a:29)

Engendering Production and Consumption

While gender attribution studies have been fundamental to the development of an engendered household, they represent only one part of the process. The fact that we cannot divvy up all possible tasks by gender has led some to assume that we cannot discuss gender in the absence of unequivocal attributions. If activities do not fall neatly into a male or female sphere of operation or if a supposedly female activity is performed by men under some circumstances or if the archaeological data are ambiguous, this naive perspective assumes that all is lost. But this perspective also assumes that the only goal is to identify what specific women did at specific points in time in specific places.

If, however, we attempt to consider issues of time, labor, and scale of production in order to understand how gender, as a set of ideas, can be a fundamental organizing principle, we move beyond the identification of who did what to modeling the consequences of household-level choices or needs for its members of all genders. Economic production by household members when it occurs at home often involves other members. Rita Wright's (1991) study of pottery production in South Asia demonstrates how certain household members, in this case adult males, may be seen as "the potters"; that is to say, making pottery is their occupation. At the same time, others (here adult females and children) carry out crucial roles in the production process on a regular basis. Similar assistance by Aztec men and children in home-based cloth production made them integral to the process but did not make them weavers (Hicks 1994). Barbara Mills (2000:306) argues that "the probability that more members of the household participated in the production activity can be scaled according to increasing intensity of production." She suggests that changes in the scale or location of production may be used to argue for more or less gendered organization. Such changes may carry important implications for the allocation of people's time, skill, and energy. The development of pottery vessels and their adoption as the main food-processing and storage containers in the American Southwest meant that women's workloads increased as they took on responsibility for the preparation of different kinds of foods or different preparation techniques as well as the production of the containers themselves (Crown 2000c; Crown and Wills 1995). Brumfiel (1991) has noted how food habits changed in Mexico under Aztec rule during a time of increased tribute demands on households. The shift to meals based on corn tortillas rather than stews or porridge made more work for women even as they had to increase their weaving output. But the use of tortillas made for foods that were more transportable and allowed at least some household members to work away from home as part of their tribute obligations.

Identifying and interpreting actions relating to production and consumption by household members thus becomes crucial to an understanding of how household members interacted with one another, negotiated their identities, and formed part of larger spatial, social, and political groups. In many societies, past and present, the dwelling area is frequently also the place of work. While industrialization may have created a disjunction between home and work, some forms of production continue to be associated with the home even under global capitalism. The presence of items not manufactured by the household itself in association with the dwelling has been crucial to studies of how households interacted with the larger community or other societies. Political economy models typically focus on specialized production or production for exchange and emphasize the production of what are variously known as nonutilitarian, prestige, wealth, status, or luxury goods (Brumfiel 1987; Brumfiel and Earle 1987; Costin 1991, 1993, 1996). Practice-based approaches are more likely to find relevance in the production of items of daily use, including food, as well as in the ways that production for exchange is organized (Allison 2003; Lightfoot et al. 1998; Meadows 1999; Silliman 2001). The production, exchange, and use of "ordinary goods" (Smith 1999) can be equally significant in the creation and maintenance of multiple group identities and affiliations. Historical archaeologists have focused on how the household becomes a primary locus of consumption as capitalism develops in nineteenth-century North America. Diana Wall (2000) has demonstrated how class-based issues of taste and decorum encouraged the development of consumption practices that are early forms of consumerism among women in nineteenth-century New York City even at the height of the dominance of the separate-spheres, women-as-angels-of-the-hearth ideology.

Households and Identity

An intensive focus on what people, especially women, do in a household setting undermines the assumption that the household is best approached as a unit rather than as a set of people. Central to this approach is the assumption that someone functions as a head of household who not only serves as the representative of all household members in the public sphere but also has the greatest ability to make decisions. Differences in decision-making ability, in the ability to allocate the time and labor of others, and to otherwise enforce prescriptive altruism have long been assumed to connect to differences in age, gender, and seniority within the household. Such differences may be seen as one of the most fundamental forms of inequality in society (Blanton 1995); they certainly represent a common source of disagreement and negotiation by household members (McKie et al. 1999). Feminist economists and anthropologists have asked, What is the best way to model household relations? Are they best viewed as a form of moral economy, characterized by reciprocity and altruism, or as a kind of political economy, marked by self-interest and power struggles (Cheal 1989)? The agendas and interests of people differentiated by age, gender, role, and the ability to impose their wishes do not always coincide (Collier 1974; Hart 1992; Moore 1992). Although recognizing the interdependence of household members, this scholarship has argued that cooperation may result from differences in power or may mask ways in which household members work against or counter to others. This scholarship has also questioned whether decisions are always made at the level of the household as a whole (with the implication that there is one member whose decisions carry the greatest weight).

Archaeologists have joined other social scientists in approaching the domestic group as made up of social actors differentiated by age, gender, role, and power whose agendas and interests do not always coincide (Hart 1992; Hendon 1996; Moore 1992; Wilk 1989). Hadley Kruczek-Aaron (2002) places the material remains of a nineteenth-century New York household in the context of documented disagreements between father and daughter and between family and servants. Her analysis demonstrates the degree to which household members viewed their interactions and material practices in very different ways. Households may differ in terms of how decisions are made and how much weight is put on the contributions of various members (Svensson 1998; Wilk 1989). From this perspective, the household as a collective social formation becomes something that must be actively reproduced through practice. Dwelling areas and the domestic setting are not merely neutral locations or containers for useful activities. They become a space in which and through which certain kinds of social relations and identities are defined and given prominence through meaningful action that draws on ideas about gender, age, and other variables, such as class, into socially constructed identities that were sometimes reinforced by the cultural hegemonies of the state. The effort of producing cloth by Aztec and Maya women was legitimated through an ideology that posited a complementary relationship between social identities important to the political economy of the Aztec state and Maya polities. These identities seem to balance the male gendered role of warrior with the female one of weaver. These identities were enacted through practice (including state-mandated military training and taxation), validated through periodic ritual, and idealized through visual representation.

It must be recognized that research on dwellings (as broadly defined here) provides insight into only some aspects of household activities and interactions (Fish 2000; Hendon 1997). One way that archaeologists have made creative use of this is by using the consistent material correlate provided by the dwelling area as a useful point of reference against which to contrast the meaning of the same activities occurring in different spatial contexts. Food preparation, for example, takes on a different social significance when performed away from the dwelling and has been interpreted as evidence for women's involvement in larger-scale social, religious, or political events or relationships (Hastorf 1991; Hegmon et al. 2000; Mobley-Tanaka 1997; VanDerwarker and Detwiler 2002). Analysis of plant remains from trash pits at the Coweeta Creek site, a prehistoric and proto-historic Cherokee town in North Carolina, suggests to Amber VanDerwarker and Kandace Detwiler (2002) that women prepared food in two different locations: in association with domestic structures and near the townhouse, a structure used for ritual, social, and political interactions among members of the community. Their results suggest a greater female presence in this more "public" space than might be expected given the townhouse's frequent association with male political leaders.

Historical archaeologists have shown how class and ethnic variation in the United States affected not only household composition and activities but also the values associated with these differences, with direct implications for acceptable female behavior (Spencer-Wood 1999; Wood 2002). Moreover, middle-class stereotypes (which often approached the level of racist fantasy) about how working-class and immigrant households deviated from proper forms of organization and gender roles served as one way to maintain class and ethnic (or racial) divides that had implications for employment as well as more general social attitudes. Margaret Wood's study of the mining community of Berwind, Colorado, shows that the CF & I coal company's decision to provide housing for married workers and company-supervised boardinghouses for single male employees was part of a strategy to inculcate a set of middle-class values about individualism, loyalty to the company, capitalism, and domesticity that would discourage collective action and strikes on the work front. In the process, women who had earlier contributed to household support through taking in boarders lost a vital source of income.

Prestige and Power

Underlying much of the research discussed so far has been a concern with women's status in the household and society. This concern often takes the form of a focus on prestige and power. Both of these terms are broad and subject to a range of meanings, both folk and analytical (Crown 2000a; Hendon 1999; Lamphere 2000; Ortner 1996). Rather than construe power as something certain people have or as a particular capacity, practice or political economy perspectives start from the premise that "power is an effect of the operation of social relations" (Moore 1996:205). Studying power, therefore, needs to take a multiscalar approach (O'Donovan 2002; Sweely 1999b). The household represents one level of social relations and interaction where differences in relations of power are enacted not only through the control of such tangible factors as material resources or labor (Blanton 1995) but also through the identities that are defined and inscribed through routinized quotidian and periodic action, much of which occurs as part of household daily practice (Joyce 2000a, 2000b; Kokkinidou and Nikolaidou 1997; Robin 2002b; Tringham 1994).

Considering power dynamics within the household or at the scale of the household may yield insights into how households or certain household members acquired or reproduced social status or economic wealth in the larger context of their community or society. Feasting has become a focus of archaeological theorizing on these issues because it provides a mechanism for creating enduring social obligations between individuals or groups that involve the transfer of material resources. Such transfers and obligations raise the possibility of accumulation or control of surplus. Control may in turn lead to more permanent forms of inequality (Bray 2003; Dietler and Hayden 2001). Successful feasts require the ability to mobilize the labor of many people, both men and women. The gender dynamics of these occasions have begun to be an important area of study and offer the possibility of deepening our understanding of household relations (Fung 1995; Gero 1991; Hendon 2003).

Discussion of power frequently considers not just what people were able to do but also how social roles, action, or identities were accorded greater value or significance. As with power, consideration of prestige has moved from assuming a single form of evaluation or ranking to a perspective that sees prestige structures as multiple and based on a variety of forms of social evaluation (Hendon 1999). Gender is a frequent factor in such systems of evaluation although not the only one. It is not unusual for certain forms of prestige to be hegemonic and given more visibility with society as a whole; at the same time, counterhegemonic structures may develop in the same society that resist the hegemonic ones (Lamphere 2000). Patricia Crown and Suzanne Fish (1996) postulate that Hohokam women's status changed over time based in part on the enclosure of patios and houses, making these day-to-day activities less visible. Under these circumstances, houses and the domestic setting become not just a neutral location for activities but also a space within which certain kinds of social relations and identities are defined, created, and emphasized through meaningful action. The connection between visibility and status in southwestern Native American societies is further developed by Michelle Hegmon, Scott Ortman, and Jeannette Mobley-Tanaka (Hegmon et al. 2000) in a discussion of how gendered differences in status and prestige may be reflected in and created by the location and spatial setting of various activities or events. Their analysis attempts to assess autonomy, prestige, and power, and they find that women's autonomy seems to decrease as social hierarchies become more entrenched; thus, some women were of high status but had relatively less autonomy. Although, as the authors acknowledge, the apparent negative relationship between autonomy and prestige may be in part an artifact of how they have defined these terms, their study shows a careful attention to how the complexities of social status may be reflected in daily practice.

Participation in ritual events or exclusion from ritual spaces has emerged as one aspect of social life that archaeologists focus on when considering status. Of particular interest has been whether women were excluded from "public" ritual occasions or nondomestic ritual spaces, such as the Cherokee townhouse mentioned previously. Sweely's (1999a) Ceren data lead her to conclude that women were not excluded from ritual structures. Hegmon et al. (2000) note the association between kivas, subterranean ritual structures, and corn-grinding areas or rooms as suggestive of women's involvement in ritual life (see also Mobley-Tanaka 1997).

Concluding Thoughts

Out of this body of research and debate, it is possible to extract an archaeologically useful and empirically valid definition of the household: a coresident domestic group that functions as an economic unit in that the relations and interactions of its members provide a way to organize production, allocate resources, and structure consumption. These activities sustain household members by providing them access to resources. Production and consumption refers to something as basic as alimentation but does not stop there. Furthermore, the kinds of productive and consumptive activities may vary among households in the same society since other factors may affect household size, composition, and responsibilities. Households are, after all, only one kind of social formation, and membership in a household does not represent the only group to which its members may belong or associate themselves with. Household size and composition within a society may be affected by social status, wealth, class, occupation, seasonal cycles, or other factors.

In reviewing recent scholarship on the household and gender for this chapter, four themes emerge as central. One theme is the identification, meaning, and significance, both socially and economically, of women's activities. Another is the debate over the very existence of a division into public and private spheres of society and, if such a division reflects some social reality, what is its meaning. A third theme is the study of the economic and social implications of women's participation in production and consumption of goods and resources. The final theme considers the factors affecting or contributing to women's prestige, status, or power in society. These four themes are overlapping and interdependent. All are ultimately concerned with the social (and political) implications of economic activities. All assume a connection between social identity, action, and the location of that action. All take as a starting assumption that women's social position is likely to be different from that of men, but all are interested in complicating and disrupting facile claims of universal female subordination. And all share a conviction in the value of studying actions and interactions formerly considered too small in scale, too common in occurrence, and too intimate in psychological affect to contribute to models of social evolution or the explanation of culture change.

References

Abercrombie, Nicholas, Stephen Hill, and Bryan S. Turner
    2000   *The Penguin Dictionary of Sociology*. 4th ed. London: Penguin.
Allison, Penelope M., ed.
    1999   *The Archaeology of Household Activities*. London: Routledge.
Allison, Penelope M.
    2003   The Old Kinchega Homestead: Doing Household Archaeology in Outback New South Wales, Australia. *International Journal of Historical Archaeology* 7:161–94.
Ashmore, Wendy, and Richard R. Wilk
    1988   Household and Community in the Mesoamerican Past. In *Household and Com-*

munity in the Mesoamerican Past. Richard R. Wilk and Wendy Ashmore, eds. Pp. 1–27. Albuquerque: University of New Mexico Press.

Axelsson, Susanne
    1999   "Peopling" the Farm: Engendering Life at a Swedish Iron Age Settlement. In *From the Ground Up: Beyond Gender Theory in Archaeology.* Nancy L. Wicker and Bettina Arnold, eds. Pp. 93–102. BAR International Series 812. Oxford: Archaeopress.

Beaudry, Mary C.
    1984   Archaeology and the Historical Household. *Man in the Northeast* 28:27–38.

Beaudry-Corbett, Marilyn, and Sharisse McCafferty
    2002   Spindle Whorls: Household Specialization at Ceren. In *Ancient Maya Women.* Traci Ardren, ed. Pp. 52–67. Walnut Creek, CA: AltaMira Press.

Bender, Donald R.
    1967   A Refinement of the Concept of Household: Families, Co-Residence, and Domestic Function. *American Anthropologist* 69:493–504.

Bertelsen, Reidar, Arnvid Lillehammer, and Jenny-Rita Næss, eds.
    1987   *Were They All Men? An Examination of Sex Roles in Prehistoric Society.* Stavanger: Arkeologisk Museum.

Birdwell-Pheasant, Donna, and Denise Lawrence-Zúñiga
    1999   Introduction: Houses and Families in Europe. In *House Life: Space, Place and Family in Europe.* Donna Birdwell-Pheasant and Denise Lawrence-Zúñiga, eds. Pp. 1–35. Oxford: Berg.

Blanton, Richard E.
    1995   The Cultural Foundations of Inequality in Households. In *Foundations of Social Inequality.* T. Douglas Price and Gary M. Feinman, eds. Pp. 105–27. New York: Plenum.

Bourdieu, Pierre
    1977   *Outline of a Theory of Practice.* Richard Nice, trans. Cambridge: Cambridge University Press.

Bray, Tamara L., ed.
    2003   *The Archaeology and Politics of Food and Feasting in Early States and Empires.* New York: Kluwer Academic/Plenum.

Brumfiel, Elizabeth M.
    1987   Consumption and Politics at Aztec Huexotla. *American Anthropologist* 89:676–86.
    1991   Weaving and Cooking: Women's Production in Aztec Mexico. In *Engendering Archaeology: Women and Prehistory.* Joan M. Gero and Margaret W. Conkey, eds. Pp. 224–51. Oxford: Basil Blackwell.
    1992   Breaking and Entering the Ecosystem—Gender, Class, and Faction Steal the Show. *American Anthropologist* 94:551–67.
    1996   Figurines and the Aztec State: Testing the Effectiveness of Ideological Domi-

nation. In *Gender and Archaeology*. Rita P. Wright, ed. Pp. 143–66. Philadelphia: University of Pennsylvania Press.

2001   Asking about Aztec Gender: The Historical and Archaeological Evidence. In *Gender in Pre-Hispanic America*. Cecelia F. Klein, ed. Pp. 57–85. Washington, DC: Dumbarton Oaks.

Brumfiel, Elizabeth M., and Timothy K. Earle
1987   Specialization, Exchange, and Complex Societies: An Introduction. In *Specialization, Exchange, and Complex Societies*. Elizabeth M. Brumfiel and Timothy K. Earle, eds. Pp. 1–9. Cambridge: Cambridge University Press.

Carter, Anthony T.
1984   Household Histories. In *Households: Comparative and Historical Studies of the Domestic Group*. Robert M. Netting, Richard M. Wilk, and Eric J. Arnould, eds. Pp. 44-83. Berkeley: University of California Press.

Cheal, David
1989   Strategies of Resource Management in Household Economies: Moral Economy or Political Economy? In *The Household Economy: Reconsidering the Domestic Mode of Production*. Richard R. Wilk, ed. Pp. 11–22. Boulder, CO: Westview.

Collier, Jane F.
1974   Women in Politics. In *Woman, Culture, and Society*. Michelle Z. Rosaldo and Louise Lamphere, eds. Pp. 89–96. Palo Alto, CA: Stanford University Press.

Costin, Cathy L.
1991   Craft Specialization: Issues in Defining, Documenting, and Explaining the Organization of Production. *Archaeological Method and Theory* 3:1–56.

1993   Textiles, Women, and Political Economy in Late Prehispanic Peru. *Research in Economic Anthropology* 14:3–28.

1996   Exploring the Relationship between Gender and Craft in Complex Societies: Methodological and Theoretical Issues of Gender Attribution. In *Gender and Archaeology*. Rita P. Wright, ed. Pp. 111–40. Philadelphia: University of Pennsylvania Press.

Cowgill, George L.
1993   Beyond Criticizing New Archeology. *American Anthropologist* 95:551–73.

Crown, Patricia L.
2000a   Gendered Tasks, Power, and Prestige in the Prehispanic American Southwest. In *Women and Men in the Prehispanic Southwest: Labor, Power, and Prestige*. Patricia L. Crown, ed. Pp. 3–41. Santa Fe, NM: School of American Research Press.

Crown, Patricia L., ed.
2000b   *Women and Men in the Prehispanic Southwest: Labor, Power, and Prestige*. Santa Fe, NM: School of American Research Press.

Crown, Patricia L.
2000c   Women's Role in Changing Cuisine. In *Women and Men in the Prehispanic Southwest: Labor, Power, and Prestige*. Patricia L. Crown, ed. Pp. 221–66. Santa Fe, NM: School of American Research Press.

Crown, Patricia L., and Suzanne K. Fish
1996   Gender and Status in the Hohokam Pre-Classic to Classic Tradition. *American Anthropologist* 98:803–17.
Crown, Patricia L., and W. H. Wills
1995   The Origins of Southwestern Ceramic Containers: Women's Time Allocation and Economic Intensification. *Journal of Anthropological Research* 51:173–86.
Dietler, Michael, and Brian Hayden, eds.
2001   *Feasts.* Washington, DC: Smithsonian Institution Press.
di Leonardo, Micaela
1991   Women's Culture and Its Discontents. In *The Politics of Culture.* Brett Williams, ed. Pp. 219–42. Washington, DC: Smithsonian Institution Press.
Dommasnes, Liv Helga
1987   Male/Female Roles and Ranks in Late Iron Age Norway. In *Were They All Men? An Examination of Sex Roles in Prehistoric Society.* Reidar Bertelsen, Arnvid Lillehammer, and Jenny-Rita Næss, eds. Pp. 65–77. Stavanger: Arkeologisk Museum.
Fish, Suzanne K.
2000   Farming, Foraging, and Gender. In *Women and Men in the Prehispanic Southwest: Labor, Power, and Prestige.* Patricia L. Crown, ed. Pp. 169–96. Santa Fe, NM: School of American Research Press.
Forest, Jean Daniel
1997   Maison, maisonnée et structure sociale en Mésopotamie préhistorique (6è–4è millénaire). *al-Rafidan* 18:81–91.
Fung, Christopher D.
1995   Domestic Labor, Gender and Power on the Mesoamerican Frontier. In *Debating Complexity.* Proceedings of the 26th Annual Chacmool Conference. D. Meyer, P. Dawson, and D. Hanna, eds. Pp. 65–75. Calgary: Chacmool Archaeological Association.
Gero, Joan M.
1991   Who Experienced What in Prehistory? A Narrative Explanation from Queyash, Peru. In *Processual and Postprocessual Archaeologies: Multiple Ways of Knowing the Past.* Robert W. Preucel, ed. Pp. 126–39. Occasional Paper 10. Carbondale: Center for Archaeological Investigations, Southern Illinois University.
Goldberg, Marilyn Y.
1999   Spatial and Behavioural Negotiation in Classical Athenian City Houses. In *The Archaeology of Household Activities.* Penelope M. Allison, ed. Pp. 142–61. London: Routledge.
Guyer, Jane I.
1981   Household and Community in African Studies. *African Studies Review* 24(2/3):87–137.
1997   Households. In *The Dictionary of Anthropology.* Thomas Barfield, ed. Pp. 245–46. Oxford: Blackwell.

Hart, Gillian
   1992   Imagined Unities: Constructions of "the Household" in Economic Theory.
           In *Understanding Economic Processes*. Sutti Ortiz and Susan Lees, eds. Pp. 111–29.
           Monograph in Economic Anthropology 10. Lanham, MD: University Press
           of America.
Hastorf, Christine A.
   1991   Gender, Space, and Food in Prehistory. In *Engendering Archaeology: Women and
           Prehistory*. Joan M. Gero and Margaret W. Conkey, eds. Pp. 132–59. Oxford:
           Basil Blackwell.
Haugen, Inger
   1987   Concentrating on Women: Introduction to a Debate in Social Anthropology.
           In *Were They All Men? An Examination of Sex Roles in Prehistoric Society*. Reidar
           Bertelsen, Arnvid Lillehammer, and Jenny-Rita Næss, eds. Pp. 15–21. Sta-
           vanger: Arkeologisk Museum.
Hayden, Brian
   1992   Observing Prehistoric Women. In *Exploring Gender through Archaeology: Selected
           Papers from the 1991 Boone Conference*. Cheryl Claassen, ed. Pp. 33–47. Mono-
           graphs in World Prehistory 11. Madison, WI: Prehistory Press.
Hegmon, Michelle, Scott G. Ortman, and Jeannette L. Mobley-Tanaka
   2000   Women, Men, and the Organization of Space. In *Women and Men in the Prehis-
           panic Southwest: Labor, Power, and Prestige*. Patricia L. Crown, ed. Pp. 43–90.
           Santa Fe, NM: School of American Research Press.
Hendon, Julia A.
   1996   Archaeological Approaches to the Organization of Domestic Labor: House-
           hold Practice and Domestic Relations. *Annual Review of Anthropology* 25:45–61.
   1997   Women's Work, Women's Space and Women's Status among the Classic
           Period Maya Elite of the Copan Valley, Honduras. In *Women in Prehistory:
           North America and Mesoamerica*. Cheryl Claassen and Rosemary A. Joyce, eds. Pp.
           33–46. Philadelphia: University of Pennsylvania Press.
   1999   Multiple Sources of Prestige and the Social Evaluation of Women in Prehis-
           panic Mesoamerica. In *Material Symbols: Culture and Economy in Prehistory*. John
           E. Robb, ed. Pp. 257–76. Occasional Paper 26. Carbondale: Center for
           Archaeological Investigations, Southern Illinois University.
   2002   Social Relations and Collective Identities: Household and Community in
           Ancient Mesoamerica. In *The Dynamics of Power*. Maria O'Donovan, ed. Pp.
           273–300. Occasional Paper 30. Carbondale: Center for Archaeological
           Investigations, Southern Illinois University.
   2003   Feasting at Home: Community and House Solidarity among the Maya of
           Southeastern Mesoamerica. In *The Archaeology and Politics of Food and Feasting in
           Early States and Empires*. Tamara L. Bray, ed. Pp. 203–33. New York: Kluwer
           Academic/Plenum.
   2004   Living and Working at Home: The Social Archaeology of Household Pro-

duction and Social Relations. In *A Companion to Social Archaeology*. Lynn Meskell and Robert W. Preucel, eds. Pp. 272–86. Malden, MA: Blackwell.

Hicks, Frederic
1994   Cloth in the Political Economy of the Aztec State. In *Economies and Polities in the Aztec Realm*. Mary G. Hodge and Michael E. Smith, eds. Pp. 89–111. Albany: Institute for Mesoamerican Studies, State University of New York.

Hingley, Richard
1990   Domestic Organisation and Gender Relations in Iron Age and Roman-British Households. In *The Social Archaeology of Houses*. Ross Samson, ed. Pp. 125–47. Edinburgh: Edinburgh University Press.

Johnson, Allan G.
2000   *The Blackwell Dictionary of Sociology*. 2nd ed. Malden, MA: Blackwell.

Joyce, Rosemary A.
1993   Women's Work: Images of Production and Reproduction in Pre-Hispanic Southern Central America. *Current Anthropology* 34:255–74.
2000a   *Gender and Power in Prehispanic Mesoamerica*. Austin: University of Texas Press.
2000b   Girling the Girl and Boying the Boy: The Production of Adulthood in Ancient Mesoamerica. *World Archaeology* 31:473–83.

Joyce, Rosemary A., and Cheryl Claassen
1997   Women in the Ancient Americas: Archaeologists, Gender, and the Making of Prehistory. In *Women in Prehistory: North American and Mesoamerica*. Cheryl Claassen and Rosemary A. Joyce, eds. Pp. 1–14. Philadelphia: University of Pennsylvania Press.

Kokkinidou, Dimitra, and Marianna Nikolaidou
1997   Body Imagery in the Aegean Neolithic: Ideological Implications of Anthropomorphic Figurines. In *Invisible People and Processes: Writing Gender and Childhood into European Archaeology*. Jenny Moore and Eleanor Scott, eds. Pp. 88–112. London: Leicester University Press.

Kruczek-Aaron, Hadley
2002   Choice Flowers and Well-Ordered Tables: Struggling over Gender in a Nineteenth-Century Household. *International Journal of Historical Archaeology* 6:173–85.

Lamphere, Louise
2000   Gender Models in the Southwest: A Sociocultural Perspective. In *Women and Men in the Prehispanic Southwest: Labor, Power, and Prestige*. Patricia L. Crown, ed. Pp. 379–401. Santa Fe, NM: School of American Research Press.

Lerman, Nina E., Ruth Oldenziel, and Arwen P. Mohun
2003   Introduction: Interrogating Boundaries. In *Gender and Technology*. Nina E. Lerman, Ruth Oldenziel, and Arwen P. Mohun, eds. Pp. 1–9. Baltimore: The Johns Hopkins University Press.

Lightfoot, Kent, Antoinette Martinez, and Ann M. Schiff
1998   Daily Practice and Material Culture in Pluralistic Social Settings: An Archae-

ological Study of Culture Change and Persistence from Fort Ross, California. *American Antiquity* 63:199–222.

Low, Setha M., and Denise Lawrence-Zúñiga

2003   Locating Culture. In *The Anthropology of Space and Place: Locating Culture.* Setha M. Low and Denise Lawrence-Zúñiga, eds. Pp. 1–47. Malden, MA: Blackwell.

MacEachern, Scott, D. J. W. Archer, and R. D. Garvin, eds.

1989   *Households and Communities.* Proceedings of the 21st Annual Chacmool Conference. Calgary: Department of Archaeology, University of Calgary.

Malan, Antonia

1997   The Material World of Family and Household. In *Our Gendered Past: Archaeological Studies of Gender in Southern Africa.* Lyn Wadley, ed. Pp. 273–301. Johannesburg: Witwatersrand University Press.

Manzanilla, Linda, ed.

1986   *Unidades habitacionales mesoamericanas y sus áreas de actividad.* Mexico City: Instituto de Investigaciones Antropológicas, UNAM.

Manzanilla, Linda

1990   Niveles de análisis en el estudio de unidades habitacionales. *Revista Española de Antropología Americana* 20:9–18.

Marti, Judith

1993   Introduction. In *The Other Fifty Percent: Multicultural Perspectives on Gender Relations.* Mari Womack and Judith Marti, eds. Pp. 179–83. Prospect Heights, IL: Waveland.

McKie, Linda, Sophia Bowlby, and Susan Gregory

1999   Connecting Gender, Power, and the Household. In *Gender, Power and the Household.* Linda McKie, Sophia Bowlby, and Susan Gregory, eds. Pp. 3–21. New York: St. Martin's Press.

Meadows, Karen

1999   The Appetites of Households in Early Roman Britain. In *The Archaeology of Household Activities.* Penelope M. Allison, ed. Pp. 101–20. London: Routledge.

Mills, Barbara J.

2000   Gender, Craft Production, and Inequality. In *Women and Men in the Prehispanic Southwest: Labor, Power, and Prestige.* Patricia L. Crown, ed. Pp. 301–43. Santa Fe, NM: School of American Research Press.

Mobley-Tanaka, Jeannette L.

1997   Gender and Ritual Space during the Pithouse to Pueblo Transition: Subterranean Mealing Rooms in the North American Southwest. *American Antiquity* 62:437–48.

Moore, Henrietta

1992   Households and Gender Relations: The Modeling of the Economy. In *Understanding Economic Processes.* Sutti Ortiz and Susan Lees, eds. Pp. 131–48. Monograph in Economic Anthropology 10. Lanham, MD: University Press of America.

1996   *Space, Text, and Gender: An Anthropological Study of the Marakwet of Kenya*. New York: Guilford Press.

Morgan, David
1999   Gendering the Household: Some Theoretical Considerations. In *Gender, Power and the Household*. Linda McKie, Sophia Bowlby, and Susan Gregory, eds. Pp. 22–40. New York: St. Martin's Press.

Mrozowski, Stephen A., James A. Delle, and Robert Paynter
2000   Introduction. In *Lines That Divide: Historical Archaeologies of Race, Class, and Gender*. James A. Delle, Stephen A. Mrozowski, and Robert Paynter, eds. Pp. xi–xxxi. Knoxville: University of Tennessee Press.

Netting, Robert M., Richard M. Wilk, and Eric J. Arnould
1984   Introduction. In *Households: Comparative and Historical Studies of the Domestic Group*. Robert M. Netting, Richard M. Wilk, and Eric J. Arnould, eds. Pp. xiii–xxxviii. Berkeley: University of California Press.

Nevett, Lisa C.
1999   *House and Society in the Ancient Greek World*. Cambridge: Cambridge University Press.

O'Donovan, Maria
2002   Grasping Power: A Question of Relations and Scales. In *The Dynamics of Power*. Maria O'Donovan, ed. Pp. 19–34. Occasional Paper 30. Carbondale: Center for Archaeological Investigations, Southern Illinois University.

Ortner, Sherry B.
1974   Is Female to Male as Nature Is to Culture? In *Women, Culture, and Society*. Michelle Z. Rosaldo and Louise Lamphere, eds. Pp. 67–88. Palo Alto, CA: Stanford University Press.
1996   *Making Gender: The Politics and Erotics of Culture*. Boston: Beacon Press.
2001   Commentary: Practice, Power and the Past. *Journal of Social Archaeology* 1:271–80.

Pauketat, Timothy R.
2001   Practice and History in Archaeology: An Emerging Paradigm. *Anthropological Theory* 1:73–98.

Reverby, Susan M., and Dorothy O. Helly
1992   Introduction: Converging on History. In *Gendered Domains: Rethinking Public and Private in Women's History*. Dorothy O. Helly and Susan M. Reverby, eds. Pp. 1–24. Ithaca, NY: Cornell University Press.

Robin, Cynthia
2002a   Gender and Maya Farming: Chan Noohol, Belize. In *Ancient Maya Women*. Traci Ardren, ed. Pp. 12–30. Walnut Creek, CA: AltaMira Press.
2002b   Outside of Houses: The Practices of Everyday Life at Chan Noohol, Belize. *Journal of Social Archaeology* 2:245–68.
2003   New Directions in Classic Maya Household Archaeology. *Journal of Archaeological Research* 11(4):279–356.

Rosaldo, Michelle

1974   Women, Culture, and Society: A Theoretical Overview. In *Women, Culture, and Society*. Michelle Z. Rosaldo and Louise Lamphere, eds. Pp. 17–42. Palo Alto, CA: Stanford University Press.

1980   The Use and Abuse of Anthropology: Reflections on Cross-Cultural Understandings. *Signs* 5:389–417.

Saitta, Dean J.

1984   The Archaeology of Households: Alternative Approaches. *Man in the Northeast* 28:1–8.

Santley, Robert S., and Kenneth G. Hirth

1993   Household Studies in Western Mesoamerica. In *Prehispanic Domestic Units in Western Mesoamerica: Studies of the Household, Compound, and Residence*. Robert S. Santley and Kenneth G. Hirth, eds. Pp. 3–17. Boca Raton, FL: CRC Press.

Silliman, Stephen

2001   Agency, Practical Politics and the Archaeology of Culture Contact. *Journal of Social Archaeology* 1:190–209.

Silverblatt, Irene

1995   Lessons of Gender and Ethnohistory in Mesoamerica. *Ethnohistory* 42:639–50.

Smith, Michael E.

1993   New World Complex Societies: Recent Economic, Social, and Political Studies. *Journal of Archaeological Research* 1:5–41.

Smith, Monica L.

1999   The Role of Ordinary Goods in Premodern Exchange. *Journal of Archaeological Method and Theory* 6:109–35.

Spencer-Wood, Suzanne M.

1999   The World of the Household: Changing Meanings of the Domestic Sphere in the Nineteenth Century. In *The Archaeology of Household Activities*. Penelope M. Allison, ed. Pp. 162–89. London: Routledge.

Svensson, Eva

1998   Expanding the Household. *Lund Archaeological Review* 4:85–100.

Sweely, Tracy L.

1999a   Gender, Space, People and Power at Ceren, El Salvador. In *Manifesting Power: Gender and the Interpretation of Power in Archaeology*. Tracy L. Sweely, ed. Pp. 153–71. London: Routledge.

1999b   Introduction. In *Manifesting Power: Gender and the Interpretation of Power in Archaeology*. Tracy L. Sweely, ed. Pp. 1–14. London: Routledge.

Tringham, Ruth

1991   Households with Faces: The Challenge of Gender in Prehistoric Architectural Remains. In *Engendering Archaeology: Women and Prehistory*. Joan M. Gero and Margaret W. Conkey, eds. Pp. 93–131. Oxford: Basil Blackwell.

1994   Engendered Places in Prehistory. *Gender, Place and Culture* 1:169–203.

1995   Archaeological Houses, Households, Housework and the Home. In *The Home:*

Words, Interpretations, Meanings, and Environments. David N. Benjamin, ed. Pp. 79–107. Aldershot: Avebury.

Uruñuela Ladrón de Guevara, Gabriela, and Patricia Plunket Nagoda
   1998   Áreas de actividad en unidades domésticas del Formativo terminal en Tetimpa, Puebla. *Arqueología* 20:3–19.

VanDerwarker, Amber M., and Kandace R. Detwiler
   2002   Gendered Practice in Cherokee Foodways: A Spatial Analysis of Plant Remains from the Coweeta Creek Site. *Southeastern Archaeology* 21:21–28.

Wall, Diana diZerega
   2000   Family Meals and Evening Parties: Constructing Domesticity in Nineteenth-Century Middle-Class New York. In *Lines That Divide: Historical Archaeologies of Race, Class, and Gender.* James A. Delle, Stephen A. Mrozowski, and Robert Paynter, eds. Pp. 109–41. Knoxville: University of Tennessee Press.

Wilk, Richard M.
   1989   Decision Making and Resource Flows within the Household: Beyond the Black Box. In *The Household Economy: Reconsidering the Domestic Mode of Production.* Richard R. Wilk, ed. Pp. 23–52. Boulder, CO: Westview.

Wilk, Richard M., and Robert M. Netting
   1984   Households: Changing Forms and Functions. In *Households: Comparative and Historical Studies of the Domestic Group.* Robert M. Netting, Richard M. Wilk, and Eric J. Arnould, eds. Pp. 1–28. Berkeley: University of California Press.

Wilk, Richard M., and William L. Rathje, eds.
   1982a   *Archaeology of the Household: Building a Prehistory of Domestic Life.* Special issue of *American Behavioral Scientist* 25:617–39.

Wilk, Richard M., and William L. Rathje
   1982b   Household Archaeology. In *Archaeology of the Household: Building a Prehistory of Domestic Life.* Richard R. Wilk and William L. Rathje, eds. Special issue of *American Behavioral Scientist* 25:617–39.

Wood, Margaret C.
   2002   Women's Work and Class Conflict in a Working-Class Coal-Mining Community. In *The Dynamics of Power.* Maria O'Donovan, ed. Pp. 66–87. Occasional Paper 30. Carbondale: Center for Archaeological Investigations, Southern Illinois University.

Woolf, Alex
   1997   At Home in the Long Iron-Age: A Dialogue between Households and Individuals in Cultural Reproduction. In *Invisible People and Processes: Writing Gender and Childhood into European Archaeology.* Jenny Moore and Eleanor Scott, eds. Pp. 68–74. London: Leicester University Press.

Wright, Rita
   1991   Women's Labor and Pottery Production in Prehistory. In *Engendering Archaeology: Women and Prehistory.* Joan M. Gero and Margaret W. Conkey, eds. Pp. 31–54. Oxford: Blackwell.

Wylie, Alison
    1992   Feminist Theories of Social Power: Some Implications for a Processual
        Archaeology. *Norwegian Archaeological Review* 25:51–68.
Yanagisako, Sylvia J.
    1979   Family and Household: The Analysis of Domestic Groups. *Annual Review of
        Anthropology* 8:161–205.

Gender and Landscapes

6

WENDY ASHMORE

> *We can ponder an empowering and often gendered landscape, while recognizing that the gendering of the elements will surely vary across cultures, and meanings will shift and change depending on context, and on people's variable knowledge.*

(BENDER 1998:44–45)

TAKING A CUE FROM Bender's comment, I suggest that archaeological landscapes are commonly if not universally gendered. If so, then, the question is not whether they are but rather under what circumstances, in what ways, and by whom.

Substantive responses to the refocused questions first require defining what a landscape is. In archaeology and other fields, the concept can be described simultaneously as slippery, contentious, and absolutely fundamental. Gosden and Head (1994:114–15) insightfully characterized the term as usefully ambiguous. The focus of inquiry may vary, highlighting economy and land use, social ordering, ritual and belief, or some combination of the foregoing. Paraphrasing Wilson and David (2002:5–6), the proliferation of recent work defines landscape in three principal ways: (1) as a measurable, physical world independent of human signification; (2) as a painterly representation of the world; and (3) as meaningful, socially constructed places involving bodily and cognitive experience.

What differs most among perspectives and definitions are positivist as compared with humanist stances and, by extension, the range of topics thereby deemed appropriate for consideration in landscape study (e.g., Anschuetz et al. 2001; Ashmore 2004; Bender 1993; Fisher and Thurston 1999; Knapp and Ashmore 1999; Layton and Ucko 1999). Recognition of gender in landscapes emerges most often in more humanistic treatments, of Wilson and David's third kind.

The landscapes with and among which people interact include topographic features in both earth and water forms as well as subterranean zones and the overarching sky. Wind and weather also figure in landscape experience. Although this kind of inclusiveness is necessary conceptually for the fullest understanding, not all components are equally accessible to archaeologists' investigation. And with regard to recognizing gender, inference is never direct. It does, however, draw on a range of cues and clues, some tangible in the archaeological record, others nonmaterial evidence from oral histories, ethnohistories, ethnographies, and social theory.

The sections that follow identify aspects of landscape gendering for closer consideration. These are intended as provisional responses to questions phrased at the outset—the who, how, and when of landscape gendering. The categories are no more than working analytical constructs, however, and, as will quickly become clear, expressions in each category overlap with those in others.

Landscapes from a Gendered Gaze

An initial answer to who genders landscape is that Western analysts do. That is, scholars have called attention repeatedly to the whole notion of landscape as a product of the rise of capitalism and its attendant social inequities, especially in class and gender (e.g., Bender 1999; Cosgrove 1984; Olwig 1993; Thomas 2001). Through the advent of landscape painting and the linear perspective that permitted such imagery, wealthy landowners could commission portraits of their holdings. Not only did this distinctly "Western gaze" objectify the surrounding world, distancing and removing it from direct experience, the vantage also marked possession and feminization of landscape by the men who contracted for the works. "Just as western painting defines men as the active producers and viewers of images, while women are passive objects of visual pleasure, so landscape is feminized" (Thomas 2001:169, citing S. Ford). In other words, the mere concept of landscape is loaded with connotations both of control and of hierarchical gender relations. That this may not be exclusively a Western perspective is noteworthy (e.g., Faust 2003, concerning Aztec imagery) but does not remove concern for acknowledging and seeking to neutralize the effective hold of Western intellectual traditions on landscape thinking.

As fundamentally, the Cartesian heritage in the "gaze" customarily constrains us to recognize only two sexes and two genders, female and male, and in archaeological writing about embodied sex and gender, it is women and women's bodies that are singled out for scrutiny (Faust 2003; Joyce 2004; Meskell 1996:4–5). Just as feminist archaeology and the archaeology of gender are not "just about women," so must study of gendering in landscapes continue to move beyond seeking female and male elements—and only those. Third genders and androgyny are among alternatives that may have been recognized by the societies we seek to understand, as are gender identities that change during the life cycle or with social circumstance (e.g., Fausto-Sterling 1992; Joyce 2004; Moore 1993; Talalay 2005; Yates 1993).

A further testament to the strength of Cartesian thinking, structuralist approaches figure frequently in inquiries on gender, including treatments of landscape. Although not all such works follow Lévi-Strauss in seeking timeless, universal binary oppositions, reduction of analytic categories to female and male nonetheless can appear to simplify a search for patterns—and thereby to facilitate recognizing structure. This fact should not obviate using structuralist analyses, but they might best be treated as "first forays" in search of meaning (e.g., Conkey 2001; see also Ashmore 2002).

Despite some attempts to move beyond dichotomies, then, many analysts still focus unsurprisingly on one or both of two genders. Moreover, findings seem most often to imply either competition or complementarity between female and male roles, whether the implication is intended or only apparent (compare Hays-Gilpin 2004:150). Commonplace assertions, these analytical categorizations constitute another legacy of Cartesian thinking and belie the constant negotiations more plausibly shaping socially constructed gender relations in ancient society as today (e.g., Ashmore 2002; Joyce 2004; Pyburn 2004).

Gendered Embodiment of Landscape

Inasmuch as the first entity a human experiences is her or his own body, it is hardly surprising that landscapes are embodied in human and gendered terms. Allusions to "Mother Earth" and "Mother Nature" are widespread cross-culturally and often said to tap primeval ideas about a gendered universe. Certainly, for the Greeks, Earth, or Gaia (or Gê) was female (e.g., Cole 2004:23). Some strands of the modern "Goddess movement" promote belief in a primordial gynocentric world, as do a number of current writers about feminist spirituality. Drawing in part on the archaeological record (especially but far from solely from the writings of Marija Gimbutas), multiple authors describe a "Great Cosmic Mother" as constituting the original "religion of the earth" (e.g., Gadon 1989; Plaskow and Christ 1989; Sjöö and Mor 1991). From this vantage, women's bodies and bodily functions model and are models for the seasonal round, lunar cycles, and the earth's fertility. Other authors, however, vigorously decry what they see as unfounded arguments, uncritical appropriation of archaeological data; they argue instead that it is far more complicated to interpret the often ambiguous and subtle evidence for ancient beliefs gendering landscape and the earth (e.g., Anthony 1995; Goodison and Morris 1998; Meskell 1995, 1998).

If not primordial, however, a concept of "Mother Earth" certainly emerges frequently in beliefs among more recent societies that are attested archaeologically, notably in the Americas. Even there, some have cautioned that gendering landscape as embodied deities is more intricate than simply a division between female, male, or other genders. For example, Hays-Gilpin (2000) points to the complexity of gendered embodiments among Acoma, Navajo, and other Native American deities and to the possibility that some of the specific ideas crystallized in their current forms as recently as the past few centuries. Nevertheless, among the Inca half a millennium ago, histories and oral accounts indicate that Pachamama was emphatically and unambiguously Earth Mother, whose reproductive potentials were realized by actions of her male counterpart, Illapa, the god of thunder or lightning (Silverblatt 1987). Her "daughters were emblems of the specifics of highland [Andean] bounty—maize, . . . potatoes, . . . coca, . . . even metals . . . and clay (Silverblatt 1987:25). Mamacocha, a descendant of the moon, was "Mother Sea" and the source of all water, whether manifest as rivers, springs, rain clouds, or irrigation (Silverblatt 1987:48). As always, the crucial point is critical evaluation of evidence for the impact of gender, not simply presuming from overgeneral analogies, Freudian (or other social) theory, or what seems "common sense."

Other societies gendered landscapes in contrasting ways. Indeed, Roth calls attention to quite different gendering of fertility, fecundity, sexuality, and their expressions in the landscape. In specific grounds for her argument, ancient Egyptian texts credit males with creativity in reproduction; after receiving the male seed, females served simply as receptacles, making no creative contributions to the child. Material representations of Egyptian fecundity were usually identified as male, depicted with male genitalia, but also with breasts and bellies suggestive of pregnancy. According to Roth (2000:195), the reason for such portrayal relates directly to landscape along the Nile

and is rooted in the nature of its resulting agricultural cycle. In most parts of the world, the earth is made fertile by rain from the sky. By analogy with human reproduction, the sky is viewed as an active male deity, from which comes the rain that penetrates the passive and female mother earth and causes her to bring forth new life. The rain is crucial, but the creative power resides in the earth. The sky is thus gendered male and the mother earth, female.

In Egypt, by contrast, the earth was fertilized by the annual flood of the Nile. . . . The water and silt, which renewed the land and made the drops grow, came not from the sky but from the earth. Grammatically, both the earth and the floodwaters were regarded as males, and the deities that personified them . . . were also male.

The Egyptian sky was female, however, her nude body arching across the recumbent earth, stimulating his erection and thereby his acts of procreation and creation (Roth 2000:195). The two landscape forces were complementary but not equal; again, situated evidence is the key to implicating gender-related distinctions.

Elsewhere as well, celestial bodies and the sky itself were commonly gendered, as indicated in text and imagery. Sun, moon, Venus, other stars, and whole constellations were ascribed gendered identities. Sun and moon do often form a male and female pair, usually interpreted as reflecting culture-specific (if not more generalized) ideas of male potency and women's menstrual cycle resembling lunar cycles. And the same astral body can have different genders under different conditions, as when the usually female Maya moon assumes a dual-sexed identity (Taube 1992:64–68) or "becomes male at the time of the full moon" (Milbrath 1999:32). And where Western views identify lunar topography as depicting a "man in the moon," the Maya recognize a rabbit, companion to the Moon Goddess, in pre-Columbian imagery more than a millennium ago as well as today (e.g., Milbrath 1999:32, 119–20; Schele and Miller 1983). And among the Aztec, the tribal origin story pits the sun against the moon and stars, all in a context of gendered siblings. As Huitzilopochtli, the Aztec patron deity, lies in his mother's womb, his sister and "400" (i.e., countless) brothers plot to prevent his birth. Overhearing their conspiracy, he leaps, full grown, from the womb, slaying and dismembering his sister, Coyolxauhqui, and sending his brothers fleeing his wrath. The story is frequently glossed as the birth of the sun (Huitzilopochtli), whose brightness and heat cause the death of the moon (his sister) and of the stars (the brothers). It is a tale embodied materially in the Aztec Templo Mayor, where the bodies of those whose hearts were extracted, to feed and sustain the sun with their blood, were thrown down the temple steps toward the sculpture depicting the dismembered Coyolxauhqui. As Faust (2003) argues, this is one aspect of gendering in the Aztec celestial landscape, in which women are portrayed as dangerous and threatening and must be controlled or even destroyed to safeguard the continuity of the world (see also Brumfiel 1996).

Writing of "sexual cosmology," Olwig (1993:316) captures the larger situation concisely: "It is readily apparent to any farmer that there is something going on between the sky and the earth which is critical to the fertility of the land."

What remains to archaeologists interested in gender is to determine, insofar as possible, what it was that ancient people, farmers and otherwise, inferred about what was going on in earth, sky, or both. Gender may be embodied in landscape, but its expression is not necessarily universal in presence and definitely not universalized in form. It is certainly the case that recognized instances of gendered landscape embodiment have been considered most often as tropes for human reproduction, expressing aspects of anatomy and social relations. But they are also cast in other terms that equate proper maintenance of gender relations as critical to the world's survival, let alone prosperity. Whatever the story told, analysts typically identify two sexes and two genders, if sometimes recognizing situated, changeable, or ambiguous categories. Rarely, however, are identities portrayed as negotiated social states; rather, they tend to be cast as expressions of idealized roles and relations, unchanging models for human emulation.

Gendered Activity Spaces on the Landscape

A more directly materialist approach designates areas within landscapes as domains of gendered activities. The inferences are based most often in ethnographic analogy and presumptions about division of labor in antiquity and, more specifically, the gendering of particular kinds of artifacts, features, and the activities they represent. Such inference is widely recognized as difficult at best. It not only risks presumptive gender ascriptions but also risks trivializing any such ascriptions as more mechanical than a reflection of negotiated roles in socially fluid contexts (e.g., see critiques by Robin 2002). Nevertheless, provisionally identifying gendered activity arenas in the landscape can suggest some of the lines along which roles were negotiated and how gender figured in social practices.

For example, in a structural analysis of Inuit belief and myth, McGhee (1977) describes the gendering of landscape and seasons such that women are linked to the sea, winter, and marine life, while land, summer, and terrestrial game are the world of men. Among artifacts in Thule archaeological assemblages of Inuit ancestors, most objects were made from bone and antler. Ivory, however, was less easily acquired and more difficult to work: that raw material was limited to very particular items—marine hunting weapons, implements for life on the winter ice, sewing kits, and personal ornaments. Based on information in Inuit ethnographies, McGhee links the ancient Thule ivory objects to women, even though some—especially for sea hunting—were used by men in modern times. Accounts from the Alaskan northern coast may shed light on the apparent inconsistency just noted in that Bodenhorn (1993) reports that a northern coast woman's ability to call sea mammals is deemed responsible for her husband's success in the hunt. In this sense, the material hunting implements are used by men but seem, in part, an extension of women's facilitating role and a sign of complementarity in fostering family and community well-being.

From ethnographic, ethnohistoric, and archaeological research in northwestern Tanzania, Schmidt (1983, 1997) paints a striking picture of gendered and sexualized landscapes of iron smelting in the seventeenth century A.D., perhaps extending back two millennia in time. Adjacent to archaeological discovery of an ancient smelting furnace of the mid-first millennium B.C., the region's most prominent shrine is today known as Kaiija, meaning "the place of the forge." Oral history and myth describe erection of an iron tower at that forge that had fallen long ago. Modern place-names there and in the vicinity for rivers, villages, and landforms are rich in punning allusions in their joint association with iron smelting, sexual reproduction, and gender relations. In local vocabulary independent of Freudian analysis, the iron tower is considered a phallus. Its collapse metaphorically and nominally stands for a particular stage in sexual intercourse wherein the phallus beats on a woman's genitalia and thereby elicits vaginal fluid. Apparently further reducing ambiguity about the symbolism, the name for this fluid is also the name of the river adjoining the iron tower site. Moving across the landscape, from the elevated location of the tower toward lower-lying swampland and lake, the place-names continue to evince sequential stages in sexual intercourse, especially involving movements of the phallus.

During ethnoarchaeological reenactments of smelting, the men eschewed sexual relations, and women, especially menstruating women, were prohibited from contact with the smelting site and furnace. The risks for violation of these self-imposed taboos were stated in terms that linked failed smelting with reproductive breakdown, from miscarriage to sterility. Schmidt (1997:214) summarizes that "the cosmic iron tower is a symbol of human and economic fecundity." It is also inferentially a statement of normative behavior between two genders. In this highly gendered landscape, men have the kind of procreative force noted earlier in ancient Egyptian views and iconography, and relations with women are distinctly hierarchical.

A different picture emerges among the Mono Indians of California, where Jackson (1991) identified bedrock mortars as women's acorn-processing stations and argued that the seasonal movement across the landscape was structured by returns to where the mortars had been created and remained available. Here women's work structured the annual round and thereby contributed to affirming the wider importance of women's roles in Mono society. Productivity was not the domain solely of women, but the gendered landscape is consistent with more egalitarian or "balanced" gender relations than those implied in other examples.

Gendered activity realms can also be identified in landscape imagery. Writing of the Minoan Bronze Age, for example, Rehak (1999) describes gendered landscape iconography in Thera frescoes. In multiple images within the same building, women of varied life stages are shown with animals and diverse plants, especially saffron crocus. Like the women, the crocus is illustrated at various life stages, as bud and blossom, singly and by the basketful. Yellow coloring of the women's hands, feet, and mouths, as well as the presence of crocus blossoms in their hair, all suggest participation in gathering the saffron as dyestuff and food. In contrast, men portrayed in adjacent rooms occupy quite different scenes, with few or no landscape elements. Intriguingly, the youngest boy shown is painted with eye and skin colors (blue-streaked and yellow-orange, respectively) suggestive of carotene deficiency. Because saffron is high in carotenes and vitamins A and B, Rehak (1999:13) proposes that the gendered distribution of motifs and colors as well as the inclusion with women of other potentially medicinal plants all imply that females had a "detailed knowledge of the medicinal properties of saffron." Such knowledge would have benefited at least them and their families, and the frescoes' prominence suggests material acknowledgment for women's contributions to health and economy in Minoan society. As with the Mono interpretation, landscape-related activities implicate ideals of gender complementarity, with gender ranking relegated to background or unstated expression (e.g., perhaps in differential access to the frescoed chambers as well as manifestations in other venues and genres).

For Greek society in the time of Hesiod, text analyses point to strong gendering of landscape in which women's activities contributed to unifying society in political and ritual terms. As one instance, while the most important sanctuaries of Artemis, the goddess of the wilderness and of fertility, were located in the countryside, their replicas in cities "protected the city by creating a unity between the center and its borderlands" (Cole 2004:196). That is, processions of women ritually crossed the expanse from rural to urban realms; in so doing, the "females who walked unmolested . . . tested with their own bodies the security of the whole population [and] expressed the confidence and security of a community safe from incursion and confident in its own future" (Cole 2004:228). Although the ancient processions have little material trace, the sanctuaries remain, with their social and political significance clarified by textual records.

In many instances, however, recognizing gendered activities in archaeological landscapes is somewhere between challenging and impossible. The risk of presumptive gender attribution seems too great, unless there is demonstrable or strongly inferable continuity with more thoroughly documented societies and practices. Drawing on such continuities and specific accounts from California and the Great Basin, for example, Whitley (1998:18) finds that "rock-art sites were feminine-gendered places, even though they were primarily (if not exclusively) used by male shamans." The terms used to describe these shamans' portals were strongly feminine: *choishishiu*, female dog, signifying a spirit helper; *pachki*, the color red, associated in particular with menstrual blood; and *taiwan*, "basketry gambling tray, made by women and used by them in the women's walnut dice game" (Whitley 1998:18–19). Moreover, many of the rock-art images and the forms of the sites themselves are said to be vaginas. Whitley and others interpret some of the imagery as male shamans' acts to control dangerous or unruly forces, including those pertaining to women. Inversion of gender associations is acknowledged in other circumstances as a means of manipulating social relations and identities.

The gendering of the region's landscape itself offers a more encompassing explanation for associating male-gendered actors with feminine forms and words through which to act: "When the [ethnographically documented] masculine symbolism of mountain peaks is . . . matched against the [likewise, ethnographically documented] feminine symbolism of rock-art sites, the symbolic logic of rock-art site *distribution* becomes apparent. Rock-art sites as feminine places only logically fit within the feminine-gendered portions of the supernatural landscape: rock outcrops and caves, and water sources, found at relatively lower elevations" (Whitley 1998:23; emphasis added). In other words, gender is identified as a structuring principle operating in multiple social spheres in this region, most of whose recognition relies wholly on the strength of ethnographic records.

Marking Gender on Landscape

Gender marks landscapes in many ways. Landscapes are rich in meanings conveyed orally through stories, poems, songs, and other genres (e.g., Basso 1984, 1996). Of themselves, however, these do not leave material traces and are quite elusive for archaeological inquiry. The Mono bedrock mortars are one instance of material marking; the western North American rock art is another. Indeed, the best-known forms of material signs in the landscape are rock art and architecture or other monuments.

Rock-art research has exploded in quantity and sophistication in recent years. As a genre, rock art comprises human-made marks on nonportable stone surfaces, including pictographs applied onto rock and petroglyphs cut into rock (Taçon and Chippindale 1998:6). Gendered imagery has been noted virtually worldwide, from Australia and southern Africa to Europe and the Americas. Mural imagery of Paleolithic European caves is widely known if not always well understood; its study has been somewhat of a bellwether for inquiry elsewhere, and gender and sexuality were early themes in its interpretation (e.g., Bahn 1986; Conkey 2001). The most concerted consideration of gender in rock art to date is Hays-Gilpin's (2004) aptly named volume *Ambiguous Images*. As the title implies, rock art may offer what some observers see as clear and "obvious" depictions, while to others the same imagery is opaque—or simply ambiguous.

Monuments on the landscape have suggested gendered meanings in both pre-historic and historical contexts. Neolithic monuments on landscapes of southern England and the island of Malta have attracted particular attention from scholars and the wider public. Some have viewed the tombs and temples of Malta as embodiments of the Great Goddess, as her habitations, and as places for celebrat-ing feminine principles (e.g., Biaggi 1994; but see alternatives and critiques by Malone et al. 1993; Stoddart et al. 1993). The buildings' plans are said to outline women's bodies, emphasizing the womb and other anatomical elements associated with female fecundity. Parallel interpretations have been made for monuments and landscapes at Silbury and Avebury in southern England (Dames 1976, 1977). Too often, however, these interpretations seem to place more interpretive weight on the evidence than it can be expected to bear.

In a more complicated set of arguments about landscapes of Neolithic Europe, Hodder (1984, 1990) has interpreted spatial bounding as, in part, reflective of gender relations. Arguing not for a primeval conceptualization of the world, he attends specifically to the advent of sedentary, food-producing societies and separation of tamed domestic shelter from untamed and dangerous spaces beyond. Houses and burial sites are the monuments that mark bounding of the landscape. Initially, Hodder (1984:62) argued explicitly that the internal arrange-ment of the longhouses and their furnishings placed women's activities deep inside, farthest away from the entry—and, by extension, from others. In the same essay, he asserted that elongated trapezoidal houses were models for the forms of long megalithic tombs, monuments frequently viewed as constituting claims to land tenure. The transformation in construction emphasis he linked to shifts in social strategies and implicated gender relations as fundamental:

> In the first phase the domestic context is the central focus of competing claims to reproductive resources. Material culture is used to form a world in which women are to be emphasised, celebrated but controlled as repro-ducers of the lineage, and in which women and extra-lineage ties have a central importance. In the second phase the domestic context is with-drawn from its central focus by changes in material culture, and these changes are part of the developing social control of productive resources.

Competing claims to the inheritance of those resources, whether land or livestock, are restricted by de-emphasising and devaluing the domestic context, the role of women as reproducers and the extra-lineage ties. (1984:66)

In a subsequent, more comprehensive study, the argument shifted emphasis, and gender receded as a factor directly mediating structure, especially at the scale of landscapes. Although maintaining "that early Neolithic material symbolism is involved in the celebration and control of the wild, and that the control relates to social power through the representation of male and female and through the organization of domestic space" (Hodder 1990:10–11), he recognized greater ambiguity and variability in the roles that gender identities and relations contributed to the mix (Hodder 1990:9–10, 68, 308; see also Bradley 1998; Hamilton 2000). Changes in inference in this one instance are emblematic, in many ways, of the shifts to more fluid and complex theorizing that has emerged in the interim. The same shifts are consistent with growing suspicion of inferences about gendered space that hint at replicating modern ideas, assigning men to the outdoors and women to the house (e.g., critique by Talalay 2005). Such statements apply to understanding gender and social identities more generally as well as treatments of rock art and monuments on the landscape.

Landscapes of Gendered Cosmology and History

People come to know landscapes by living within and moving across them. Landscapes become vested with history and social identity of its inhabitants, often embodying understandings of social origins and cosmology (e.g., Ingold 1973; Knapp and Ashmore 1999; Tilley 1994). Prominent features of topography come to signify episodes and actors in the deep social past as well as from more recent times. Dreaming Tracks of Australia are perhaps the most widely recognized specific manifestations linking present and past through landscape (e.g., Taçon 1999). Parallel evidence or strong inference that history and cosmology were mapped on the land is virtually worldwide in occurrence, often but not always marked materially with rock art or monuments (e.g., Bradley 1993, 1997, 1998; Graham-Campbell 1994; Hays-Gilpin 2004; Richards 1996; van de Guchte 1999). Taçon (1999:37) notes that visually dramatic kinds of places tend to attract attention in the landscape:

Often these are places where concepts of an upper world, a lower world and the earth plain come together visually in a striking manner. These are places where the center of the world may be experienced, where an *axis mundi* is located.

With or without material marking, landscapes sometimes implicate gender references in cosmology and history. For example, near the site of Vingen, in southern Norway, Mandt suggests imaginatively that

> the entire layout of the Vingen landscape may have characterized the site as something different from the profane world. When approaching the outlet of the tiny fjord, one gets the impression of passing through a "gate," of being let into a secluded, almost secret, and even a little awe-inspiring, space. The whole scenario could be construed as a hierophany, as nature's representation of the female body: the fjord is the narrow birth canal between the woman's thighs—that is the hillsides—and the water of life is streaming from above—from the very habitat of the red deer. And in clear view from the enclosed Vingen space is Hornelen, its peak—almost like a phallus—reaching right into the firmament. (quoted by Hays-Gilpin 2004:159)

Unfortunately, as Hays-Gilpin notes, little or no independent evidence can be cited to support or refute this specific interpretation. As attractive as it is in light of comments like Taçon's, the account falters by seeming to reify what must remain only one plausible scenario.

In other instances, however, oral or written histories can be invoked to understand landscape meanings and gendered beliefs. In indigenous societies of Mesoamerica, for example, the universe is "perceived, at least by some, as formed during the creation with pliant cords stretched out as on a giant loom" (Klein 1982:4). Acts of creation in daily life are microcosmic reenactments of primordial creation, and whether building a house, laying out a cornfield, or setting up a loom, proper completion or performance of the action situates the people in an orderly universe. Weaving on the back-strap loom of the Maya and their neighbors is traditionally women's work. According to the *Popol Vuh*, the seventeenth-century document recording Quiché Maya creation, a

> textile itself, like the skyearth [universe], the milpa [cornfield], and the house, has four sides and four corners. The backstrap loom, unlike the European treadle loom, permits selvages on all four sides, since the warp threads pass continuously back and forth between one loom bar and the other without being cut. . . . Further, it should be noted that the process of weaving (-*quem*-), as distinct from plaiting, netting, or lacing (all -*jitz'o*-),

involves the intersection of two distinct systems of threads, just as the measuring out of the skyearth involves two distinct systems of solar movements. (Tedlock and Tedlock 1985:128)

In other words, because weaving and textiles are viewed as means by which the cosmos and the order and continuity of social life are ritually and materially reproduced, women (i.e., as weavers) are on a par with men (i.e., as creators of milpa space) and with the primordial gods of creation (Ashmore 2002:240; Morris 1986). With regard to Maya landscapes, then, gender structures the creation and perpetual recreation of the properly constituted world.

Just as cosmic and historical actors are gendered, so then can landscapes incorporate gender expressions, integral to the record of society's heritage recorded in the earth, water, and sky. Once again, the challenge for archaeologists is to draw from a strong array of evidence, situated as salient for the particular landscapes under study. As Ingold (1993:172) phrases this in a different but relevant context, "Meaning is there to be *discovered* in the landscape, if only we know how to attend to it. Every feature . . . is a potential clue, a key to meaning rather than a vehicle for carrying it."

Concluding Thoughts

At the outset of this chapter, I asserted that archaeological landscapes were commonly gendered and suggested that it would be more productive to ascertain under what circumstances, in what ways, and by whom aspects of gender were ascribed. The foregoing review offers initial assessment of how archaeologists have approached these questions. Discussions of landscape and gender are relatively dispersed and their authors theoretically diverse.

With regard to who genders landscapes, archaeologists have acknowledged that while considerable attribution seems to have occurred in antiquity, intellectual and political traditions have socialized Western scholars to a pervasive "gendering" gaze at the outset of analysis. Some have sought to break free of this perspective, but it remains a matter for concern.

With regard to how landscapes have been gendered in the past, the four overlapping ways recognized in the literature are embodiment of sex and gender in landscape forms, differentiating landscape space by gender-linked activities, physically marking landscapes with gender-related images and monuments, and constituting gendered aspects of cosmology and history in the landscape.

Finally, with regard to the circumstances under which gender is expressed in archaeological landscapes, the situations are perhaps most commonly portrayed as normative statements of status quo, idealizations of proper human gender identities, roles, and relations. Some manifestations, such as Jackson's analysis of Mono bedrock mortars, seem principally to acknowledge what gendered individuals do in society, without either moral exhortation or direct indications of either equal or hierarchical relations. In others, gendered roles are relatively explicitly identified and accorded public recognition with variable degrees of what appear to be alternately appreciation or threat of dire consequences. When there is danger, women are commonly the named source, as in Aztec cosmology and East African iron-smelting landscapes. Negotiation of gender identities and roles is recognized infrequently, Whitley's discussion of far-western North American rock-art landscapes being perhaps the closest approximation in the materials reviewed here. Authors who are most explicit about the subtleties and fluidity of gender have not generally tackled issues of gender and landscape, with the notable exception of rock-art research (e.g., Hays-Gilpin 2004; Yates 1993).

Although many investigators have boldly opened new ways of thinking about landscape and about gender and the authors cited in this chapter have made strongly productive and provocative contributions to understanding landscape and gender jointly, more concerted forays will surely repay efforts. There is certainly ample room for more of the pondering of which Bender writes in the epigraph to this chapter and for going beyond pondering to develop our concrete understanding.

Acknowledgments

I am grateful to Sarah Milledge Nelson for inviting me to participate in this volume and thank her and Mitch Allen for encouragement and understanding. Conversations with Chelsea Blackmore and Kata Faust have been invaluable in my thinking about landscapes in recent years and in formulating thoughts for this chapter. Thanks to Jane Buikstra for extended communication on this and other topics and for critical reading at critical times. As always, I am immensely grateful to Tom Patterson, for encouragement and gentle but consistently insightful critique and for being my rock of morale support.

References

Anschuetz, Kurt F., Richard H. Wilshusen, and Cherie L. Scheick
    2001   An Archaeology of Landscapes: Perspectives and Directions. *Journal of Archaeological Research* 9:157–211.
Anthony, David
    1995   Nazi and Eco-Feminist Prehistories: Ideology and Empiricism in Indo-Euro-

pean Archaeology. In *Nationalism, Politics, and the Practice of Archaeology*. Philip L. Kohl and Clare Fawcett, eds. Pp. 82–96. Cambridge: Cambridge University Press.

Ashmore, Wendy
  2002   Encountering Maya Women. In *Ancient Maya Women*. Traci Ardren, ed. Pp. 229–45. Walnut Creek, CA: AltaMira Press.
  2004   Social Archaeologies of Landscape. In *A Companion to Social Archaeology*. Lynn Meskell and Robert W. Preucel, eds. Pp. 255–71. Oxford: Blackwell.

Bahn, Paul G.
  1986   No Sex, Please, We're Aurignacians. *Rock Art Research* 3:99–105.

Basso, Keith H.
  1984   "Stalking with Stories": Names, Places, and Moral Narratives among the Western Apache. In *Text, Play, and Story: The Construction and Reconstruction of Self and Society*. Stuart Plattner and Edward M. Bruner, eds. Pp. 19–55. Washington, DC: American Ethnological Society.
  1996   *Wisdom Sits in Places: Landscape and Language among the Western Apache*. Albuquerque: University of New Mexico Press.

Bender, Barbara, ed.
  1993   *Landscape: Politics and Perspectives*. Oxford: Berg.

Bender, Barbara
  1998   *Stonehenge: Making Space*. Oxford: Berg.
  1999   Subverting the Western Gaze: Mapping Alternative Worlds. In *The Archaeology and Anthropology of Landscape: Shaping Your Landscape*. Peter J. Ucko and Robert Layton, eds. Pp. 31–45. London: Routledge.

Biaggi, Christina
  1994   *Habitations of the Great Goddess*. Manchester, CT: Knowledge, Ideas and Trends.

Bodenhorn, Barbara
  1993   Gendered Spaces, Public Places: Public and Private Revisited on the North Slope of Alaska. In *Landscape: Politics and Perspectives*. Barbara Bender, ed. Pp. 169–203. Oxford: Berg.

Bradley, Richard
  1993   *Altering the Earth: The Origins of Monuments in Britain and Continental Europe*. The Rhind Lectures 1991–92. Monograph Series, no. 8. Edinburgh: Society of Antiquaries of Scotland.
  1997   *Rock Art and the Prehistory of Atlantic Europe: Signing the Land*. London: Routledge.
  1998   *The Significance of Monuments: On the Shaping of Human Experience in Neolithic and Bronze Age Europe*. London: Routledge.

Brumfiel, Elizabeth M.
  1996   Figurines and the Aztec State: Testing the Effectiveness of Ideological Domination. In *Gender and Archaeology*. Rita P. Wright, ed. Pp. 143–66. Philadelphia: University of Pennsylvania Press.

Cole, Susan Guettel
    2004   *Landscapes, Gender, and Ritual Space: The Ancient Greek Experience.* Berkeley: University of California Press.
Conkey, Margaret W.
    2001   Structural and Semiotic Approaches. In *Handbook of Rock Art Research.* David S. Whitley, ed. Pp. 273–310. Walnut Creek, CA: AltaMira Press.
Cosgrove, Denis E.
    1984   *Social Formation and Symbolic Landscape.* London: Croom Helm.
Dames, Michael
    1976   *The Silbury Treasure: The Great Goddess Rediscovered.* London: Thames and Hudson.
    1977   *The Avebury Cycle.* London: Thames and Hudson.
Faust, Katherine A.
    2003   Body-Landscape Metaphors: The Coyolxauhqui Relief as an Index of Human and Environmental Connectivity. Paper presented at the 102nd annual meeting of the American Anthropological Association, Chicago.
Fausto-Sterling, Anne
    1992   *Myths of Gender: Biological Theories about Women and Men.* Rev. ed. New York: Basic Books.
Fisher, Christopher T., and Tina L. Thurston, eds.
    1999   Special Section: Dynamic Landscapes and Socio-Political Process: The Topography of Anthropogenic Environments in Global Perspective. *Antiquity* 73:630–88.
Gadon, Elinor W.
    1989   *The Once and Future Goddess.* New York: HarperSanFrancisco.
Goodison, Lucy, and Christine Morris, eds.
    1998   *Ancient Goddesses: The Myths and the Evidence.* London: British Museum Press.
Gosden, Chris, and Lesley Head
    1994   Landscape—A Usefully Ambiguous Concept. *Archaeology in Oceania* 29:113–16.
Graham-Campbell, James, ed.
    1994   Archaeology of Pilgrimage. *World Archaeology* 26(1) (whole issue).
Hamilton, Naomi
    2000   The Conceptual Archive and the Challenge of Gender. In *Towards Reflexive Method in Archaeology: The Example at Çatalhöyük.* Ian Hodder, ed. Pp. 95–99. Cambridge: McDonald Institute for Archaeological Research.
Hays-Gilpin, Kelley A.
    2000   Beyond Mother Earth and Father Sky: Sex and Gender in Ancient Southwestern Visual Arts. In *Reading the Body: Representations and Remains in the Archaeological Record.* Alison E. Rautman, ed. Pp. 165–86. Philadelphia: University of Pennsylvania Press.
    2004   *Ambiguous Images: Gender and Rock Art.* Walnut Creek, CA: AltaMira Press.

Hodder, Ian

    1984   Burials, Houses, Women and Men in the European Neolithic. In *Ideology, Power and Prehistory*. Daniel Miller and Christopher Tilley, eds. Pp. 51–68. Cambridge: Cambridge University Press.

    1990   *The Domestication of Europe: Structure and Contingency in Neolithic Societies*. Oxford: Blackwell.

Ingold, Tim

    1993   The Temporality of the Landscape. *World Archaeology* 25:152–74.

Jackson, Thomas L.

    1991   Pounding Acorn: Women's Production as Social and Economic Focus. In *Engendering Archaeology: Women and Prehistory*. Joan M. Gero and Margaret W. Conkey, eds. Pp. 301–25. Oxford: Blackwell.

Joyce, Rosemary A.

    2004   Embodied Subjectivity: Gender, Femininity, Masculinity, Sexuality. In *A Companion to Social Archaeology*. Lynn Meskell and Robert W. Preucel, eds. Pp. 82–95. Oxford: Blackwell.

Klein, Cecilia

    1982   Woven Heaven, Tangled Earth: A Weaver's Paradigm of the Mesoamerican Cosmos. In *Ethnoastronomy and Archaeoastronomy in the American Tropics*. Anthony F. Aveni and Gary Urton, eds. *Annals of the New York Academy of Sciences* 385:1–35.

Knapp, A. Bernard, and Wendy Ashmore

    1999   Archaeological Landscapes: Constructed, Conceptualized, Ideational. In *Archaeologies of Landscape: Contemporary Perspectives*. Wendy Ashmore and A. Bernard Knapp, eds. Pp. 1–30. Oxford: Blackwell.

Layton, Robert, and Peter J. Ucko

    1999   Introduction: Gazing on the Landscape and Encountering the Environment. In *The Archaeology and Anthropology of Landscape: Shaping Your Landscape*. Peter J. Ucko and Robert Layton, eds. Pp. 1–20. London: Routledge.

Malone, Caroline, Anthony Bonanno, Tancred Gouder, Simon Stoddart, and David Trump

    1993   The Death Cults of Prehistoric Malta. *Scientific American* 269(6):110–17.

McGhee, Robert

    1977   Ivory for the Sea Woman: The Symbolic Attributes of a Prehistoric Technology. *Canadian Journal of Archaeology* 1:141–49.

Meskell, Lynn

    1995   Goddesses, Gimbutas and *New Age* Archaeology. *Antiquity* 69:74–86.

    1996   The Somatization of Archaeology: Discourses, Institutions, Corporeality. *Norwegian Archaeological Review* 29:1–16.

    1998   Oh My Goddess! *Archaeological Dialogues* 5:126–42.

Milbrath, Susan

    1999   *Star Gods of the Maya: Astronomy in Art, Folklore, and Calendars*. Austin: University of Texas Press.

Moore, Henrietta L.
   1993   The Differences Within and the Differences Between. In *Gendered Anthropology*. Teresa del Valle, ed. Pp. 193–204. London: Routledge.
Morris, Walter F.
   1986   Maya Time Warps. *Archaeology* 39(3):52–59.
Olwig, K. R.
   1993   Sexual Cosmology: Nation and Landscape at the Conceptual Interstices of Nature and Culture; or, What Does Landscape Really Mean? In *Landscape: Politics and Perspectives*. Barbara Bender, ed. Pp. 307–43. Oxford: Berg.
Plaskow, Judith, and Carol P. Christ, eds.
   1989   *Weaving the Visions: New Patterns in Feminist Spirituality*. New York: HarperCollins.
Pyburn, K. Anne
   2004   Rethinking Complex Society. In *Ungendering Civilization*. K. Anne Pyburn, ed. Pp. 1–46. London: Routledge.
Rehak, Paul
   1999   The Aegean Landscape and the Body: A New Interpretation of the Thera Frescoes. In *From the Ground Up: Beyond Gender Theory in Archaeology*. Nancy L. Wicker and Bettina Arnold, eds. Pp. 11–22. BAR International Series 812. Oxford: Archaeopress.
Richards, Colin
   1996   Henges and Water: Towards an Elemental Understanding of Monumentality and Landscape in Late Neolithic Britain. *Journal of Material Culture* 1:313–36.
Robin, Cynthia
   2002   Gender and Maya Farming: Chan Nòohol, Belize. In *Ancient Maya Women*. Traci Ardren, ed. Pp. 12–30. Walnut Creek, CA: AltaMira Press.
Roth, Ann Mary
   2000   Father Earth, Mother Sky: Ancient Egyptian Beliefs about Conception and Fertility. In *Reading the Body: Representations and Remains in the Archaeological Record*. Alison E. Rautman, ed. Pp. 187–201. Philadelphia: University of Pennsylvania Press.
Schele, Linda, and Jeffrey H. Miller
   1983   *The Mirror, the Rabbit, and the Bundle: "Accession" Expressions from the Classic Maya Inscriptions*. Studies in Pre-Columbian Art and Archaeology, 25. Washington, DC: Dumbarton Oaks.
Schmidt, Peter R.
   1983   An Alternative to a Strictly Materialist Perspective: A Review of Historical Archaeology, Ethnoarchaeology, and Symbolic Approaches in African Archaeology. *American Antiquity* 48:62–79.
   1997   *Iron Technology in East Africa: Symbolism, Science, and Archaeology*. Bloomington: Indiana University Press.

Silverblatt, Irene
   1987   *Moon, Sun, and Witches: Gender Ideologies and Class in Inca and Colonial Peru.* Princeton, NJ: Princeton University Press.

Sjöö, Monica, and Barbara Mor
   1991   *The Great Cosmic Mother: Rediscovering the Religion of the Earth.* 1987. Reprint, New York: HarperCollins.

Stoddart, Simon, Anthony Bonanno, Tancred Gouder, Caroline Malone, and David Trump
   1993   Cult in an Island Society: Prehistoric Malta in the Tarxien Period. *Cambridge Archaeological Journal* 3:3–19.

Taçon, Paul S. C.
   1999   Identifying Ancient Sacred Landscapes in Australia: From Physical to Social. In *Archaeologies of Landscape: Contemporary Perspectives.* Wendy Ashmore and A. Bernard Knapp, eds. Pp. 33–57. Oxford: Blackwell.

Taçon, Paul S. C., and Christopher Chippindale
   1998   An Archaeology of Rock-Art through Informed Methods and Formal Methods. In *The Archaeology of Rock-Art.* Christopher Chippindale and Paul S. C. Taçon, eds. Pp. 1–10. Cambridge: Cambridge University Press.

Talalay, Lauren E.
   2005   The Gendered Sea: Iconography, Gender, and Mediterranean Prehistory. In *The Archaeology of Mediterranean Prehistory.* Emma Blake and A. Bernard Knapp, eds. Pp. 130–55. Oxford: Blackwell.

Taube, Karl A.
   1992   *The Major Gods of Ancient Yucatan.* Studies in Pre-Columbian Art and Archaeology, 32. Washington, DC: Dumbarton Oaks.

Tedlock, Barbara, and Dennis Tedlock
   1985   Text and Textile: Language and Technology in the Arts of the Quiché Maya. *Journal of Anthropological Research* 41:121–46.

Thomas Julian
   2001   Archaeologies of Place and Landscape. In *Archaeological Theory Today.* Ian Hodder, ed. Pp. 165–86. Cambridge: Polity Press.

Tilley, Christopher
   1994   *A Phenomenology of Landscape: Places, Paths, and Monuments.* Oxford: Berg.

van de Guchte, Maarten
   1999   The Inca Cognition of Landscape: Archaeology, Ethnohistory, and the Aesthetic of Alterity. In *Archaeologies of Landscape: Contemporary Perspectives.* Wendy Ashmore and A. Bernard Knapp, eds. Pp. 149–68. Oxford: Blackwell.

Whitley, David S.
   1998   Finding Rain in the Desert: Landscape, Gender and Far Western North American Rock-Art. In *The Archaeology of Rock-Art.* Christopher Chippindale

and Paul S. C. Taçon, eds. Pp. 11–29. Cambridge: Cambridge University Press.

Wilson, Meredith, and Bruno David

2002   Introduction. In *Inscribed Landscapes: Marking and Making Place*. Bruno David and Meredith Wilson, eds. Pp. 1–9. Honolulu: University of Hawai'i Press.

Yates, T.

1993   Frameworks for an Archaeology of the Body. In *Interpretive Archaeology*. C. Tilley, ed. Pp. 31–72. Oxford: Berg.

Gender, Heterarchy, and Hierarchy

7

JANET E. LEVY

THE TERM "HETERARCHY" was introduced to archaeology by Carole L. Crumley in 1979 and expanded by her in later publications (Crumley 1979, 1995; Crumley and Marquardt 1987; and elsewhere). Crumley introduced the term as critique of evolutionary approaches to prehistoric social complexity. That perspective, according to Crumley, privileges the concepts of hierarchy and stratification and neglects other potential concepts of social complexity. It is striking that while the concept of heterarchy has been adopted by a variety of archaeologists, it has been little used in analyses of gender or gender relationships in the prehistoric world (but see Levy 1995, 1999a). As will become clear in this chapter, any examination of gender through the perspective of heterarchy also opens up discussion of the relationship of gender to hierarchy, ranking, and stratification. Concepts of heterarchy and gender together encourage a revision of our understanding of social complexity.

Background

Crumley (1987b:158) defines *heterarchy* as "structures are heterarchical when each element is either unranked relative to other elements or possesses the *potential* for being ranked in a number of different ways." She says further that *hierarchy* is a subset of *heterarchy* and that "the ultimate in complexity is not hierarchy but the play between hierarchy and heterarchy: across space, through time, and in the human mind" (163). Crumley cites the first use of the concept of heterarchy in the work of Warren McCulloch, a pioneer in artificial intelligence, who created the term in 1945 to describe the function of the human brain as "reasonably orderly . . . [but] not organized hierarchically" (157). From this arises Crumley's critique of many social evolutionary studies that, according to her, conflate complexity with structure, structure with order, and order with hierarchy: "This conflation of hierarchy with order makes it difficult to imagine, much less recognize and study, patterns of relations that are complex but not hierarchical" (Crumley 1995:3).

Crumley also links the concept of heterarchy to her discussion of scale: "the 'grain' of a unit of analysis relative to the matrix as a whole" (Marquardt and Crumley 1987:2). She and colleagues emphasize a multiscalar approach to analysis of landscape and social boundaries, pointing out that a region may be heterogeneous at one scale and homogeneous at another, hierarchical at one scale and heterarchical at another (5). Similarly, a location can be both an edge and a center, depending on the scale (15).

Outside of archaeology, the concept of heterarchy turns up in a surprising variety of scholarly contexts. A recent search for the term turned up references in periodicals as diverse as *Forest Policy and Economics, Journal of International Management, Computers in Industry, Netherlands Journal of Zoology, Journal of Common Market Studies, Memory,* and *Trends in Ecology and Evolution.* Within the field of international management, heterarchy has come to be seen as a new style of organization and management, potentially more effective in a globalized world than traditional hierarchical models. For example, "As a result, organizational design needs to be less hierarchical (and more heterarchical), with shifting positions and relationships, much more lateral sharing of knowledge, the development of shared vision across the organization, and more consensual forms of decision making" (Egelhoff 1999:22). Stark (2001:75, n. 9) states, "As a more general process heterarchy refers to a process in which a given element—a statement, a deal, an identity, an organizational building-block, or sequences of genetic, computer, or legal code—is simultaneously expressed in multiple cross-cutting networks. . . . [A]uthority is no longer delegated vertically but rather emerges laterally (77). . . . [H]eterarchies make assets of ambiguities" (78). Thus, understandings of heterarchy converge on a sense of entities, patterns, or institutions characterized by fluid but orderly complexity that may or may not be ranked in a linear fashion. The concept emphasizes cross-cutting, lateral patterns of relationships. It is linked to concepts of scale. Thus, it is a potentially powerful concept in analyses of gender, a social variable that may reinforce or cross-cut a variety of social relationships and may be salient at different scales of social organization (e.g., household, community, and polity).

Heterarchy in Anthropology and Archaeology

Crumley and others have applied heterarchy to specific archaeological data in the areas of landscape archaeology and settlement pattern. For example, Crumley and colleagues (Crumley 1994; Crumley and Marquardt 1987) analyze landscape, environment, and human adaptation in pre-Roman and Roman Iron Age France through the lens of heterarchy. Scarborough and colleagues (2003) use the concept in their book-long analysis of settlement pattern, environmental diversity, and economic specialization in the east-central Yucatán Peninsula, focusing on who controls/manages/manipulates key natural resources (Scarborough et al. 2003:xiii) within a pattern of dispersed settlement and land use but complex political economy (3).

Joyce and Hendon (2000) apply heterarchy to a detailed analysis of differing settlement patterns and community structures in Late Classic (ca. A.D. 300–900) Honduras. They note that "multiple scales of variation and multiple principles of settlement organization" (157) reflect the complexity of human choices within different social systems: "conscious actors using architecture to write different forms of community onto the landscape" (154).

In addition to landscape and settlement studies, archaeologists have applied the concept of heterarchy to prehistoric economic relationships (Potter and King 1995) and craft production (Ehrenreich 1995) as well as more directly to questions of social structure, social organization, and social change (McIntosh 1999; Mills 2000; Sastre 2002; White 1995). Sociocultural anthropologists have apparently paid little attention to the concept, although Bidney (1947) quoted McCulloch's article shortly after it was published. A volume by Znoj (2005) analyzes gender, kinship, and community in a matrilineal society in Sumatra through the lens of heterarchy.

A final point in this review is that a variety of authors propose similar perspectives without using the term "heterarchy." For example, Derevenski (2000:399) says, "The relationship between horizontal and vertical differentiation may therefore be more complex than has hitherto been realized within archaeology." And Crown (2000:18) argues, "First, status is highly context specific, so that an individual may have high status in one situation with one group of people and low status in another with another group of people." These perspectives and others suggest a widespread frustration with what McIntosh (1999:1) calls archaeology's "preoccupation with the development of vertical control hierarchies." Based on the bibliography consulted for McIntosh's paper, one might argue that the frustration is especially marked among female archaeologists, hinting at the interrelationship of heterarchy and gender.

Critiques of Heterarchy

Several critiques of heterarchy have been proposed. Brumfiel (1995) suggests that the term is useful and can expand perspectives on prehistoric social systems but that it is underspecified and not clearly defined (Brumfiel 1995:125); analyses of heterarchy would benefit from more precise attention to the structural contexts in which it develops (127). Similarly, Thomas (1994) suggests that the label of heterarchy is applied too loosely to be very helpful.

Another critique is found in the debate between Rautman (1998) and McGuire and Saitta (1996; Saitta and McGuire 1998) on western Pueblo social organization. In their original article, Saitta and McGuire propose a dialectical approach that demonstrates that both prehistoric and historic pueblo societies "embodied *both* consensual and hierarchical social relations" (McGuire and Saitta 1996:198) and that "tension between equality and hierarchy conditioned an internal dynamic that governed the aggregation and fissioning of communities in late pueblo prehistory" (209). Rautman (1998) points out that this kind of complexity sounds like heterarchy and, further, has implications for scale of analysis. In response, Saitta and McGuire (1998), while not rejecting the concept out of hand, declare that it is static and not helpful on issues of causality. They also state (1998:335) that the term does not "capture our interest in the 'lived experience' of ancestral pueblo people." The latter point would presumably be rejected by Brumfiel (1995:129), who suggests, "Certainly, heterarchy creates complexity in the lives of individuals." By integrating heterarchy and gender, I hope to respond to some of these critiques by showing how heterarchy can indeed illuminate the lives of individuals and how we can specify some of the archaeological correlates of heterarchy.

Gender and Heterarchy in Archaeology

The analytical strategy of heterarchy is relevant to a number of core topics in gender studies in archaeology: division of labor, gender diversity, ranking, social evolution, and, perhaps, organization of fieldwork. Heterarchy shares with gender analysis the quality of disruption: disrupting implicit assumptions about human social systems, social complexity, and social change. I will start by discussing the integration of gender and heterarchy within the topics of gender diversity, social agency, and division of labor.

Gender Diversity and Heterarchy

A key topic in most general discussions of gender in anthropology and archaeology is illumination of the range of diversity of gender (and sexual) identities beyond the modern Western dichotomous model of male and female. A dichotomous model lends itself too easily to conclusions of either gender hierarchy or gender complementarity (Gero and Scattolin 2002) because it is difficult to conceptualize two units or categories as anything other than either equal or not equal. The concept of heterarchy, in contrast, urges the consideration of greater diversity, including multiple categories of gender and sexual identity and multiple ways that individuals within these categories may interact. Thus, the focus on lateral differentiation and complexity, which is a core component of a heterarchical approach, is equally relevant to examination of diversity of gender and sexual identities within a prehistoric society. Indeed, one can argue that the implicit quality of disruption that is characteristic of heterarchy, as noted previously, is also explicitly characteristic of many discussions of gender diversity, especially from the perspective of queer archaeology (Dowson 2000).

Crumley's discussions of heterarchy, although not focused on gender, suggest several ways that heterarchy encourages an active examination of gender diversity. She (1995:2; 1987a) refers to shifting and cross-cutting boundaries—social, linguistic, climatic, administrative, and so on—that characterize different scales of human interaction. Here she is generally referring to landscape, but the boundaries of gender and sexual identities may also be conceptualized as shifting, cross-cutting, and salient at different scales (see also Gero and Scattolin 2002:170). On the one hand, this encourages the study of the intersection of age and status with gender (see the case study later in this chapter). On the other hand, it encourages the broader examination of third genders, fourth genders, "two-spirits," and diverse sexualities. In this context, Hollimon (2000, 2001) points out that gender is considered potentially temporary and flexible in some cultures, in part because of its links to age, spiritual practice, and labor activities. Thus, it may be that the age at death of an individual will influence the burial program not only as an independent variable but also as one that works together with biological sex and/or gender.

For example, while some prehistoric cultures practiced clearly differentiated ("bounded") burial scenarios for males and females, other cultures were more heterarchical, with body position, grave type, and accompanying goods (among other possible factors) varying on the basis of multiple, cross-cutting social factors (e.g., Derevenski 2002). The archaeological visibility of third-gender individuals may well vary, depending on the degree of differentiation or heterarchy in burial programs. Any specific archaeological case may represent a society where dichotomous gender identities were emphasized or one where there was more diversity in gender identities. Examples of the latter are proposed in a number of situations, including Mesolithic Scandinavia (R. Schmidt 2000), Early Bronze Age central Europe (Weglian 2001), central North America in the late prehistoric period (Emerson 2003), and elsewhere in North America in early historic periods

(Holliman 2000, 2001). However, there is no a priori reason to expect that third genders were universally recognized or memorialized.

In fact, Arnold (2002) has persuasively argued that a proposed identification of third-gender individuals (most frequently "berdache" or biological males in female gender roles) can be a way of ignoring or denying certain roles, especially leadership roles, to women. She discusses this regarding the well-known Iron Age burial from Vix in eastern France, which contains a skeleton identified as a biological female accompanied by some typical female-associated artifacts and several extraordinary artifacts associated with leadership positions in other so-called princely burials. Certain archaeologists have identified the buried individual as a male transvestite priest (Arnold 1991, 2002), but Arnold (2002: 252) points out, "We need to distinguish between patterned sex/gender disjunction in burial and the reluctance of a largely male archaeological establishment to accept the possibility that particular women as women may have achieved considerable social power under certain circumstances."

There is quite a lot of ethnographic and ethnohistoric evidence that third-gender individuals are often seen as controlling special ritual and supernatural powers (e.g., Emerson 2003; Price 2001). Thus, identification of such individuals and their role(s) in society may be strengthened in some cases by identification within graves of ritual objects, remains of psychoactive substances (and their paraphernalia, such as pipes), anomalous grave positions, and/or anomalous appearance, all of which might denote supernatural power. Knüsel (2002) suggests that the elite individual in the Iron Age Vix burial is indeed a female and indeed a leader; further, he argues that she is distinguished by a series of striking skeletal anomalies that would have impacted her ability to move around. He feels, on the basis of historic and ethnographic data, that this strengthens her identification as one whose leadership position is based on ritual power.

Shamanistic and other ritual practice are often associated with ideas of transformation in general, including from human to animal (or to bird) as well as from male to female (Price 2001; see also Emerson 2003). An archaeological example may be found in the late prehistoric images of "eagle dancers" or "hawk men" found in the central and southeastern United States. These humans, costumed or transformed to birds, are almost always identified as males; however, in some cases a costumed figure with breasts faces one without breasts (Brown 1982; see also Levy 1999a), suggesting complex intertwining themes of human/bird and male/female. Shamanism disrupts boundaries between human world and natural world and between natural world and supernatural world, as focus on gender diversity disrupts an entrenched dichotomous model and as heterarchy disrupts traditional culture evolutionary models.

Overall, then, the concept of heterarchy as a first step encourages the case-by-case examination of gender and sexual diversity and analysis of fluctuations in such identities as well as of the interconnections of these identities with other aspects of social organization.

Gender, Heterarchy, and Agency

Dobres and Robb (2000a) point out that there have been many definitions of *agency* in the context of archaeology. In any case, concepts of agency focus on the active involvement of individuals within a social system, differentially participating in, strengthening, challenging, and resisting the structural constraints of environment, values, and institutions: "people's practical engagement with the world" (Dobres and Robb 2000b:5). Concepts of agency entail attention to scale, as the saliency of individuals varies, depending on the scale of the phenomenon being examined (Dobres and Robb 2000b: 11; Gero and Scattolin 2002; Hodder 2000). Concepts of agency also suggest attention to performance (Robb 2001), which is relevant to both gender identity and status position.

Although the development of ideas about agency in anthropology are related, in part, to expanding feminist theory, it has been noted that gender in general and women in particular are frequently missing from agency-focused analyses (Gero 2000; Ortner 2001). The methodology for examining agency in the archaeological record must focus on detailed variability in material remains of the past but is underdeveloped (Brumfiel 2000; Robb 2001).

Even this simplified description of agency approaches in archaeology suggests links both to gender perspectives and to the concept of heterarchy. First, a focus on agency is congruent with examination of diversity in gender and sexual identities. Both emphasize the importance of variability among individuals, negotiation of identity and individual action in changing social circumstances, and the importance of performance and display in establishing individual identity and action. In this latter regard, agency links as well to archaeological studies of the body (Rautman 2000).

Further, as heterarchy is linked to and relevant to study of gender and sexual diversity, so it is congruent with agency as well. Smith (2001:167) points this out as he argues that to understand past human societies, we need to think about "multiple relationships among various structurally embedded social positions (e.g., elite institutions, grassroots social groups) and plurally sited individuals (that is, individuals located as profoundly in heterarchical roles as hierarchical ones)." That is, heterarchy—as does agency—encourages an examination of social variability, flexibility, and complexity at different scales (individual, community, and cross-community institution). Heterarchy also—as does agency, at least in principle—encourages an interest in lateral relationships as well as vertical ones. Heterarchy—as does agency—encourages a focus on active performance as a means of establishing and/or contesting a variety of salient social identities and relationships. Some relationships will be hierarchical in nature (e.g., a tribute payer and a tribute receiver), some will be balanced or lateral or collaborative (e.g., an independent craft worker in textiles and one in ceramics), and some will probably have elements of both patterns at different times (e.g., a parent and a child) or will be characterized by some other pattern I cannot at the moment imagine.

Finally, any of the variable social relationships that both heterarchy and agency encourage us to look at in detail may well have important gender components. Thus, I would disagree profoundly with Saitta and McGuire (1998: 335) when they say that heterarchy does not capture the lived experience of people's lives. The qualities of flexibility, fluctuation, and negotiation that are intrinsic to the concept of heterarchy are directly relevant to an individual's lived experience. In fact, heterarchy leads us to consider just how complex an individual's—a gendered and sexual individual's—lived experience may be.

Gender, Heterarchy, and Division of Labor

So far, the discussion of gender and heterarchy has been quite abstract. One way to make the discussion more concrete is to look at division of labor in the frame of gender and heterarchy. Just as interested archaeologists have struggled to move beyond dichotomous views of gender, we have also struggled to escape a tendency toward dichotomous views of the division of labor, such as that men hunt and women gather, men make lithics, women make pottery (but only in household craft situations), men trade, women cook, and so on. A heterarchical approach to division of labor will emphasize cross-cutting boundaries, lateral relationships as well as vertical ones, and multiple scales of analysis. That is, rather than assume a specific division of labor or specific trajectory of increasing specialization over time, we should consider evidence for variable organization of labor within family, community, and region. For example, Potter and King (1995:28) argue that ceramic and lithic production and distribution among the Classic period Maya are heterarchical: "To summarize, ceramic and lithic data suggest that Maya production and exchange occurred within two-cross-cutting systems," one of which was centrally controlled and one of which was not and both of which involved both categories of artifacts.

Mills (1995) makes several illuminating and relevant points about gendered division of labor on the basis of a study of Zuni pottery production and silver working in historic times. First, she makes a key point that there are often "hidden producers," where more than one person is involved in production of craft items (e.g., gathering clay, mixing clay, forming vessels, polishing, painting, gathering fuel, building kilns, and supervising firing); however, social authorship is focused on one individual, in fact, one gendered individual (Mills 1995:150). Mills also points out that as craft production becomes more central to household economies, more members of the family, presumably gendered members, participate in craft work (167). One of the counterintuitive implications of this pattern is that, at least in the Zuni case, more specialized craft production is *less* gendered. So with increasing commercial success through the twentieth century, Zuni pottery making, which had been originally part time and gendered female, became a more full-time craft practiced by both males and females. Furthermore, as silver work grew from a part-time to a full-time craft, it developed from a craft limited to a small number of males to one practiced by multiple members of families, including children.[1]

Finally, Mills points out that third-gender individuals may participate in both ostensibly male and ostensibly female activities; We'wha, the well-known Zuni third-gender person, was an accomplished potter at a time when most pottery was produced by women, produced weaving on both male- and female-style looms, and participated in male ritual activities (Mills 1995:151, summarizing from Roscoe 1991).

Mills's work encourages a heterarchical perspective on a gendered division of labor in archaeological cases: diverse participants in fluctuating and diverse relationships. It should be an open question whether craft work and other tasks were highly gendered, and it should be an open question whether specialization implies a single producer for each object or multiple, collaborative producers. In fact, there are very few craft production sequences that one can imagine that do *not* involve multiple contributors (certain kinds of lithic production might be one). Where we have evidence to suspect third-gender individuals, the association between craft production and gender is likely to be even more complex. Mills (1995:161) notes that in earlier stages of Zuni pottery and silver manufacture, when production was part time but highly gendered, the results look *more* specialized because there is less design variability. In later phases, when production is more full time and less gendered, there is more diversity of form and design. Thus, the interrelationships among specialization, production, and gender are clearly complex and flexible.

An archaeological example, although less well developed than Mills's work, can be drawn from metallurgy in Late Bronze Age Denmark (Levy 1991, 1995).

The archaeological evidence suggests at least three locales for production of bronze artifacts as well as variable production techniques, including casting in clay molds, casting in stone molds, and lost wax casting as well as hammering and engraving designs. Some types of bronze artifacts were produced in ordinary habitation sites, apparently in a household setting, as seen in the distribution of relevant finds. Other artifact types were apparently produced in another setting because almost all the stone molds are found outside of habitation sites; finally, there are certain, very elaborate artifacts for which we have no direct archaeological evidence for the locale of their manufacture. This suggests that they were produced in a third, specialized setting.

Metallurgical production not only included casting molten metal but must have included gathering and preparing fuel, producing clay and stone molds and wax models, hammering and polishing cast items, and engraving decoration on cast objects—all tasks that could be accomplished by household members of different genders and perhaps ages. I describe this pattern of craft work as heterarchical because the evidence suggests multiple contexts of production, lateral relationships between individuals at different stages of production, and different scales of distribution of bronze artifacts. The production of the most lavish artifacts may well have been controlled by an elite, while other bronze artifacts were widely produced and distributed; both the hierarchical pattern and the heterarchical pattern are real and important.

Despite Randsborg's (1986:148) claim that Danish metallurgy must have been male dominated, the full pattern of production of bronze objects probably included males, females, and perhaps third-gender individuals. He rests his argument on ethnographic evidence, but a careful examination of that evidence, most influentially in Africa, reveals the biases of both male observers and male metal workers (P. Schmidt 1998) that often hide women's contributions. While casting was a significant part of the technology, another significant phase of production must have been crafting the detailed, apparently symbolic, engraved designs on cast items; this is a task that requires an aesthetic sense, a steady hand, and perhaps special ritual knowledge but no obvious sex-linked qualities.

As Mills (1995) notes, it may be the Western cultural emphasis on autonomous artisanship that masks the likely complexity of production sequences in prehistory. Thus, the idea of increasing craft specialization is implicitly linked to increasing hierarchy of individuals, usually male individuals. But it should remain an open question whether objects are completely made and controlled by single individuals in any particular prehistoric case. Where production evidence turns up in household settings, the likelihood is that more than one household member was significantly involved in production. That is, as noted previously, the *scale* of a particular phenomenon is relevant to understanding the nature of its complexity.

Gender, Heterarchy, and Hierarchy

Finally, this interconnection of heterarchy, gender, and division of labor again turns attention to the common but usually implicit conflation of complexity with hierarchy. As noted earlier, Crumley's original goal in introducing the concept of heterarchy was to critique simplistic understandings of social complexity and, in particular, critique the conflation of complexity and hierarchy. While others have adopted this critique (e.g., McIntosh 1999; O'Reilly 2003; Sastre 2002), gender has rarely been incorporated into the critique. A volume edited by Pyburn (2004b) provides insight into a way to expand Crumley's critique through the incorporation of gender.

Pyburn and contributors originate their critique of cultural evolutionary studies of prehistoric and early historic complex societies with an analogy to Wolf's (1982) concept of "people without history." That is, all or almost all ethnographic observations of political systems, division of labor, and gendered social roles are tainted by the bias or lack of access of Western, Christian, male observers and/or by the sociocultural, political, and economic changes caused by contact with Western, Christian, patriarchal colonizers (for similar perspectives, see also Howell 1995; Kent 1998). Thus, first in early ethnographic accounts and later in archaeological utilizations of these accounts, women are "people without history" (Pyburn 2004a:6); that is, how they really lived, what they really did with much of their time, and how they participated in political structures are simply not known. Thus, most evolutionary studies of states either explicitly or implicitly give the impression that "the status of women, though clearly not uniform across time and space, is nevertheless thought to be uniformly subordinate throughout human history" (7). Often, this subordination is linked to women's child-rearing responsibilities (this is the commonly proposed reason why women do not participate in metallurgy), but Pyburn points out, on the basis of her own experience in a nonindustrialized Maya village, that "adults do not take care of small children. Infants are cared for by 8- to 10-year olds (both boys and girls)" (17). It has also been noted by a variety of other scholars that even if women do have extra child-rearing responsibilities, they are not raising children for their entire lives.

In terms of archaeological interpretation, these assumptions oversimplify the complexity of social roles, the cross-cutting of different social variables, and the potential for autonomous, powerful women: "it seems a likely possibility that the manner in which states are defined and identified archaeologically is based on sexist assumptions about what behavior counts as political, what organizations function as economic, and what material culture indicates either" (Pyburn 2004a:29). For example, standard interpretations of Viking graves suggests that when tools are found in men's graves, they indicate occupation of the deceased; however, when tools are found in women's graves, they are said to indicate the status or occupation of the *family* (Mortensen 2004). (This, by the way, is a convention I followed in earlier research [Levy 1982:79] where it was critiqued by Sørensen [1992].) Or, in analyses of early Sumerian states, secular power is a priori given higher status than ritual power. Thus, automatically, women—who could hold the highest ritual positions—are seen as subordinate in the political system: "Rather than considering the relations between different aspects of power . . . , archaeologists constantly separate these fields and rank them in terms of superiority and inferiority, as is done with the 'public' and the 'private'" (Al-Zubaidi 2004:128). Knüsel (2002) independently makes a similar point, suggesting that the separation of secular and ritual power is a recent development probably derived from competition between church and state in early modern Europe but is not an appropriate concept in most prehistoric cases.

By adopting the concept of heterarchy, an archaeologist is encouraged to look not at classifications (e.g., chiefdom/state or corporate/network, although these can be helpful concepts at times) but rather at cross-cutting variables of status, influence, and power and the fluctuations between and among them. These variables will include ritual influence, economic control, political power, age, lineage, and—most relevant to this discussion—gender. Analyses of chiefly societies often focus on the chiefs alone (e.g., Kristiansen 1991), but surely everyone else—90 percent or more of the population—was out and about, interacting, producing, worshiping, resisting, and contributing to the archaeological record. No chief could manage or even survive without the activities of all those other people. While the activities and roles of women will obviously vary from case to case, they must have been active agents at many levels of complex societies. By focusing on heterarchy rather than hierarchy, we are encouraged to consider the intertwining roles of women, men, and third and fourth genders in the establishment of influence, power, and inequality.

The key point here is to emphasize that complexity and fluctuation in social roles is probably more often the rule than the exception in human societies. While focusing on one or more "chiefs" or "craft specialists" or "ritual specialists" is a starting point, analysis must consider the cross-cutting and fluctuating roles that individuals play within the communities of different scale that they participate in. While being a female may be most relevant within the household, being a craft producer may be more relevant at the level of the local community and being a ritual specialist more relevant at the regional level.

A heterarchical perspective on questions of social change or social evolution in prehistoric societies improves our analysis. By emphasizing lateral social differentiation, we escape a conflation of complexity and "progress" with hierarchy. Such a conflation not only denies the complexity of daily lives in a variety of social systems but also, as implied by Pyburn (2004b) and colleagues, frequently eliminates women from interpretations of political life or even public life. Prehistoric Denmark can again provide an example.

Kristiansen (1984:85) says about Neolithic Denmark, "The system's evolutionary potential was not released until the introduction of bronze." Elsewhere (Kristiansen 1991:39), he says about Bronze Age Denmark, "The core components of Iron Age social organization were developed during the late Bronze Age, but their potential was constrained by the tribal rationality of Bronze Age society." The implication here is that societies that reach their potential (like good children) are those that develop more centralized and hierarchical political structures. But, we might ask, Potential for what or for whom? Further, in his discussion of Bronze Age Denmark, Kristiansen (1991:30–31, 38) labels the Late Bronze Age (ca. 1100–600 b.c.) as a period of "consolidation and decline" as opposed to an Early Bronze Age (ca. 1600–1100 b.c.) expansion phase. Notably, the earlier period is marked by the deposition of bronze wealth in the form of swords and other weapons in mostly male burials, while the later period is marked by the deposition of bronze wealth in the form of ornaments worn by women in hoards, not burials. The two periods are certainly *different*, but the latter period is a "decline" only if male competition and hierarchy alone count as complex and interesting.

Thus, with heterarchy, we are encouraged to always incorporate analyses of lateral social differentiation—including gender differentiation—and social relations into study of social change. In order to understand social change, it is essential to understand the life courses of diverse categories of people in a prehistoric society. Further, we are encouraged to examine explicitly the interactions of vertical and horizontal social relations. Increasing economic inequality, to suggest one example, may both derive from these complex interactions and influence their further development. Even in state societies, perhaps characterized by significantly hierarchical economic and political structures, lateral social relationships must impact daily lives, and daily lives must impact the development of nonegalitarian relationships and, of course, the creation of the archaeological record. Derevenski (2000) suggests that the first metallurgy developed in central Europe not just because of technological innovation but also to respond to social needs in a time of "exceptionally complex life course trajectories" (394): "Instead, the use of metal in the Copper Age was a socio-cultural response to perceptions of the life course and developments in the categorization of the person" (402).

A Small Case Study: Late Bronze Age Denmark

Bronze Age Denmark has been mentioned a number of times as demonstrating some themes within the study of heterarchy and gender. At this point, let me expand the case study. During the Late Bronze Age (ca. 1100–600 B.C.) in Denmark, all burials are cremations and the grave goods tend to be small and infrequent; there is almost no skeletal information available. However, during the same period, a large number of bronze and gold objects are deposited in hoards, that is, collections of artifacts purposefully deposited outside of graves or domestic settlements. The hoards are frequently deposited in bogs or other damp settings and include tools, weapons, and a large number of ornaments as well as special items, such as feasting equipment, military gear, horse gear, large musical horns (*lurs*), and other rare items (illustrations can be found in Coles and Harding 1979:491–532). The *lurs*, military items, and some of the feasting equipment are found in hoards without any other objects, and the horse gear and some of the cups and feasting equipment are found in hoards containing more "personal" items as well. There are good reasons to accept that many of these hoards were ritual deposits of some kind, and most of the artifacts show evidence of having been used in life.

Bronze Ornaments, Hierarchy, and Heterarchy

One can (and, in fact, I did [Levy 1982:59–67]) analyze these hoards as markers of hierarchy within a chiefdom with the chiefly class marked especially by the feasting equipment and military objects (such as bronze shields); it was implicit that the highest rank was assumed to be male (see also Kristiansen 1984, 1991; Randsborg 1986). However, a reappraisal of the material suggests that a perspective informed by both heterarchy and gender is more revealing. The largest sample comes from the chronological phase in the middle of the Late Bronze Age, when hoards are dominated by ornaments; 101 individual sets of ornaments are found in eighty-one hoards.[2] These range from a pair of neck rings or arm rings (i.e., a single artifact type) to sets of two artifact types (e.g., a necking and two arm rings) and up to five artifact types (necking, armoring, brooch, belt plate [attached to the front of the belt], and "hanging vessel" [attached to the back of the belt]). Table 7.1 shows the patterns.

First, it is clear that the ornament sets are organized in a roughly pyramidal

Table 7.1. Danish Late Bronze Age Ornament Sets

Sets of Bronze Ornaments[1]	No. of sets	No. of combinations	No. of possible combinations[2]
HV-BP-NR-AR-F (4)	4	1	1
HV-F-NR-AR (7) HV-BP-NR-AR (3) HV-BP-F-NR (1) HV-BP-F-AR (1)	12	4	5
HV-F-NR (3) HV-NR-AR (10) HV-BP-AR (6) HV-BP-NR (4)	23	4	20
F-AR (2) NR-AR (9) HV-F (2) HV-BP (5) BP-AR (1) HV-NR (4) HV-AR (4) BP-NR (1)	29	9	20
NR-NR (20) AR-AR (6) HV-HV (7)	33	3	5

[1] NR = neck ring; AR = arm ring; HV = "hanging vessel"; BP = "belt plate" (a belt ornament attached at the back); BP = "belt plate" (a belt ornament attached at the front); F = "fibula" (an elaborate brooch); (x) = number of examples known.

[2] $n!/r!(n - r)!$, where n = total number of artifact types (i.e., five) and r = number of artifact types in each set.

fashion, with more simple sets and fewer complex ones. Second, the table suggests that the combinations are nonrandom choices. At all levels where there are diverse options for combinations (i.e., all levels except the "top" one), not all the possible options have been utilized; further, some combinations are much more common than others. Indeed, there seem to be constraints on how the specific ornaments can be combined; for example, it is rare to find an ornament set containing a belt plate without a hanging vessel (two examples), but it is common to find the reverse, a hanging vessel without a belt plate (thirty examples, not including the seven sets that consist of hanging vessels alone). I have argued elsewhere (Levy 1982:69–74) that these sets represent sumptuary goods that indicate a variety of status positions.

There is certainly a degree of ranking demonstrated here, and the special items, such as feasting equipment, may denote one or more superordinate ranks. The ranking likely includes an economic aspect, as the objects are prestige goods of some kind made of relatively rare, imported resources. The ranking is also likely based on criteria other than economic, for the weight of some of the less complex sets is greater than that of some of the more complex ones. As metal weight can be a rough proxy of economic value here, complexity of display is not always positively correlated with economic value; both economic value and social value are being represented in complex ways. Thus, this set of archaeological data indicates at least two (and possibly several) axes of vertical differentiation.

There must also be several axes of horizontal differentiation, including sex and gender, demonstrated by the apparently nonrandom variability in artifact combinations across each level of complexity. For example, some of the variability in Bronze Age female costume has been attributed to marital status (Eskildsen and Lomborg 1976; Sørensen 1991:125). There is also limited evidence to assign different artifact types to males or females. That evidence suggests that the two kinds of belt ornaments were worn only by women. Evidence about the other three types is less clear; all three were certainly worn by women, but some were probably worn by men as well. There has not been any explicit examination of whether third- or fourth-gender individuals might also have participated in these displays.

Other material variables, such as associated artifacts, may reflect other social factors. Bronze sickles are found in some of these hoards, ornamental bronze horse gear in others, and cups or other feasting equipment in still others. Perhaps it was relevant how the objects were arranged, although these data are limited (most of the hoards were discovered by ordinary citizens, many in the nineteenth or early twentieth century, and there is no information about their arrangement); sometimes the metal objects are found within a large pottery vessel, while in other cases the objects were found in a careful pile without any container. In addition, while many of the hoards were found in wet places, there are differences in the locales of deposition. These differences may denote other social variables. Intensive analysis of the covariation of these factors may yield new patterns.

Discussion

Thus, patterns of material variability within this data set suggest that a variety of social variables were important enough to structure personal display in life and in ritual deposition. The variables of horizontal differentiation may include sex, gender, age, kinship status, ritual status, political role, work specialization, and so on. Although there is not space to analyze the variability in detail, I can suggest that the rarest ornament combinations, those that include a belt plate without a hanging vessel, might represent third-gender individuals; these individuals were wearing an object ordinarily affiliated with women only but in a rare combination—not with the other female ornament that is commonly associated with the belt plate but rather with an ornament that may be worn by both males and females. Other combinations may denote age groupings, kinship status, leadership position (e.g., personal items associated with feasting equipment or horse gear), and/or occupation.

The preliminary analysis given here was at a large scale, lumping data from all over Denmark. Another step in the analysis would be to focus the scale more narrowly. As a start, the distribution maps of these hoards and ornament sets demonstrate that they are not distributed evenly across Denmark (Levy 1982:72–74). In my original analysis, I said about this, "The ornament sets are not distributed evenly over Denmark, but at least three levels of ornament sets are found in each three relatively distinct areas (Zealand, Funen, northern Jutland). The organization of sumptuary sets differs in detail in each of these areas, but the inferred existence of several social ranks in each area is supported" (Levy 1982:74). Clearly, my interest was focused on hierarchy; further analysis might benefit from closely examining just how the organization of these ornament sets and associated artifacts does differ from region to region and the implications of those differences for understanding aspects of lateral or horizontal complexity, not just vertical differentiation.

Another perspective on these finds links heterarchy, gender, and agency. The ornament sets (as well as weapons and other objects) were worn by individuals. The objects represented not only economic resources and a variety of social statuses, but many probably also had symbolic significance. The symbolic or ritual significance could be communicated by color and sound as well as by engraved motifs (Levy 1999b). Both wearing these objects and depositing them in ritual contexts entailed performance at some level. Of course, it is social agents who create and participate in performances. But, to go further, it is heterarchical situations that encourage performance because individuals are manipulating the social resources available to them within a flexible and fluctuating social context. Perhaps this is especially true in those contexts, such as societies traditionally labeled as ranked, middle level, or chiefdoms, where ranking and stratification are evolving or changing and where status must be continually negotiated and asserted. Wolf (1990:593) reminds us that the cultural structures that establish some persons as more powerful than others must be repeatedly negotiated and actively maintained: "The cultural assertion that the world is shaped in this way and not in some other has to be repeated and enacted, lest it be questioned and denied."

Joyce (2000) and Derevenski (2000) provide other archaeological examples (Mesoamerica and central Europe, respectively) of variability in archaeologically recovered dress and ornament that identify cross-cutting and interacting age, gender, and status positions. Joyce's subtitle is "the *production* of adulthood in ancient Mesoamerica" (emphasis added). This production is clearly through dress, appearance, and performance, as it seems to be in Bronze Age Denmark as well.

The Danish hoards can be (and have been [Levy 1982:79; see also Randsborg 1986]) accepted as markers of family status and/or as markers of a general hierarchical social model. But this falls into the trap noted by Mortensen (2004) previously: men's objects are seen as marking their own status, while women's objects are seen as marking family or community status. By utilizing a heterarchical perspective, the significance of social factors beyond simply ranking—including gender—are emphasized. Women displayed and controlled significant economic and ritual resources in the objects found in the hoards, apparently including feasting equipment and horse gear. This suggests significant influence and rank; if we credit this rank simply to women's families, we implicitly impose an androcentric perspective and a passivity on women without providing well-thought-out justifications. Males also controlled a variety of economic and ritual resources, and it is certainly possible that third-gender individuals did as well. The challenge now is to seek further evidence in the archaeological record and analyze further how these variables of social role, rank, and influence interacted.

This rich set of finds from one period of the Danish Bronze Age demonstrates the advantage of a heterarchical perspective, especially when this analysis is integrated with examination of other parts of the archaeological record, such as the evidence of metalworking discussed previously. First, both the vertical and the lateral axes of social variability are considered. There is evidence of hierarchy, and this is real, but the lateral differentiation is real as well and had a daily life significance that must be considered. Second, because multiple axes of social variability are emphasized, sex and gender become important foci of research, as they must have been significant parameters of Bronze Age daily life. Where both rank and gender are considered, we are encouraged to develop a more nuanced understanding of status and rank that does not implicitly privilege males as the only active participants in high rank. Third, a multiscalar approach is encouraged; for example, one should ask how the subregions within a quite homogeneous cultural area, such as Bronze Age Denmark, differed in construction and expression of social differentiation. Given that there seems to have been communication between all the subregions (e.g., based on similar design motifs across the whole area), how might the internal social differences influence interaction and social change?

The Future

There are a number of challenges for continuing research into heterarchy and gender. First, there has been progress in specifying how heterarchy appears in the archaeological record. For example, Joyce and Hendon (2000) discuss certain landscape signatures of heterarchy. I have suggested here some ways to look at artifact data in a heterarchical perspective, examining variability that is both vertical in quality (e.g., number, size, or weight) and horizontal in quality (e.g., alternate decoration or combination). Derevenski (2002:206) provides another example, looking at the variable grave patterns of the Beaker period (ca. 2600–2000 B.C.) in southern England: "The construction of gender through the contrasting intersections between sex and other forms of difference is inherently volatile since it does not merely reflect other relations of power but is constantly contested and transformed."

Nevertheless, more work will improve our understanding of how heterarchy appears in the archaeological record in different cases. In the case of gender studies specifically, research will certainly utilize burial and habitation evidence and may benefit from ethnographic studies made richer and more critical by an understanding of the biases of current data (Pyburn 2004b). Data from biological anthropology may also contribute. For example, Peterson's (2002) work with musculoskeletal stress markers can contribute to a richer understanding of variability of occupation within a community. As she notes, these modifications of the human skeleton can provide data about labor activity that are independent of ethnographic analogy. For example, Peterson argues that activity patterns of men and women in the Levant are more similar in the early Neolithic than in the preceding Natufian (end of the period of foraging); this is due to more reorganization of male activities than female ones (Peterson 2002:73–74). In contrast, at the beginning of the Early Bronze Age, although populations overall were less robust than earlier, there appears to be more sex-based division of labor (145). There is clearly not a linear development here.

Other specialist analyses, such as compositional studies, may have a role to play. One can imagine a hierarchical situation where pots of one specific compositional pattern, perhaps from distant clays, are found in elite contexts and pots made of another, nearby clay are found in nonelite contexts. In contrast, Simon and Ravesloot (1995) suggest that the wide variability in composition of pots found in Salado (ca. A.D. 1250–1450 in Arizona) graves can be linked to a range of lateral social relationships participated in by the deceased; pots made of different clays come from dispersed individuals and groups related in a variety of ways to the deceased: "we have the potential to uncover the social framework by which Salado culture was woven together" (122), a nice metaphor for heterarchy.

Second, it may be informative to extend the notion of heterarchy to studies of gender and practice within the profession of archaeology. Conkey and Gero (1997) note the hierarchical—and often androcentric—structure of archaeological fieldwork and the impact of this structure on interpretation of the archaeological record. An explicitly heterarchical approach to fieldwork may yield very different results and provide more openings in archaeological practice for voices of women and others: "Instead, feminist practice might offer multiple interpretive judgments and evaluations at each nonreversible step of investigation, and coordinate multiple strategies and objectives of different co-investigators into the research of nonrenewable archaeological resources" (Conkey and Gero 1997:429). It remains an open question if this kind of approach, whether one calls it feminist, heterarchical, or postprocessual, can be pulled off in practice. One possible exemplar is the Çatalhöyük project in central Turkey, where multiple voices and fluid relations are explicitly encouraged: "One implication of this is that conclusions are always momentary, fluid and flexible as new relations are considered; being interactive in the sense of creating information that can be questioned and approached from different angles; being multivocal, plural, open or transparent so that a diversity of people can participate in the discourse about the archaeological process" (Hodder 1996).

Third, the concept of heterarchy can contribute to study of symbols and symbolism in the archaeological record. The focus in heterarchy on lateral differentiation and on multiscalar analysis links to Turner's (1969) concept of multivocal symbols. A single symbolic motif may have, in Turner's terms, exegetical, operational, and positional meanings, the interactions of which intensify the significance of the symbol. Hays-Gilpin (1995:134) suggests that iconography is "ambiguous by its very nature." Or, as sociologist Stark (2001:77) says in a rather different context, "Heterarchies make assets of ambiguities." This reference reminds us of the heterarchy of diverse gender identifications within different societies and the link of third- and fourth-gender individuals to ritual systems. Symbolism and ideology are significant aspects of archaeological gender studies; a heterarchical approach to symbols has the potential to enrich this topic.

Finally, there remains work to be done on applying a heterarchical perspective to analysis of culture change. Heterarchy is a rich and dense way to describe social complexity, and we can start by looking for evidence of interaction between lateral and vertical differentiation as an impetus for culture change. Certain situations may generate especially intense interaction between vertical and lateral; Crumley (1994:184) suggests that climatic conditions will have an effect here, as will times of economic stimulation (Crumley 1987b:418), perhaps including periods of new technologies and/or contact with previously unfamiliar populations.

Further, the heterarchical perspective allows a consideration of culture change that escapes the value-laden concepts of decline or collapse (Crumley 1995:4), concepts often fraught with ethnocentric and androcentric bias. Heterarchy alone does not cause culture change. Rather, a heterarchical perspective encourages investigators to focus on a broader set of social factors and gendered social players in examining culture change.

Conclusion

Because of heterarchy's emphasis on both lateral and vertical differentiation, it opens up analysis specifically to considerations of sex and gender. Thus, a heterarchical perspective discourages narratives about the past that focus on society as a whole, which usually privileges (implicitly or explicitly) the actions of only a small, usually male segment of the prehistoric population. Heterarchy requires that we keep several balls in the air at once, acknowledging fluctuations and flexibility within and interconnections among power, gender, agency, and social change.

Acknowledgments

Many thanks to Sarah Nelson for inviting me to join this project and continuing thanks to Carole Crumley, Patty Jo Watson, Joan Gero, Cheryl Claassen, Gregory Starrett, and others who have improved my research and writing on gender and other topics. My research in Denmark was supported by the American-Scandinavian Foundation, Washington University–St. Louis, and the University of North

Carolina at Charlotte. I have many debts, intellectual, practical, and personal, to a wide range of colleagues in Scandinavia.

Notes

1. Mills (1995:160) notes that while this change in labor organization did occur within a commercial context linked to capitalist markets, it happened without centralized control. Her research focused on independent, family-based producers, not the producers employed by jobbers located in the city of Gallup.

2. There were a total of 125 hoards from this period identified in 1975. The ornament sets are found both alone and combined with other objects in eighty-one hoards included in the analysis. In addition to these eighty-one hoards, four other hoards contain examples of these ornament types, but the objects cannot be easily divided into individual sets; while I believe that these four hoards do contain such sets, the objects from these four hoards are not included in the analysis. Some of the remaining hoards from this period contain bronze axes, swords, and/or spear points but no ornaments; others contain distinctive and unique items, such as shields or the *lurs* (trumpets). These clearly can and should be incorporated into a fuller analysis. The chronological period to which these objects are assigned (Montelius Period V) covers 150 to 200 years. Clearly, all the hoards cannot be contemporaneous; however, these objects cannot be dated to finer divisions within the period, so they are treated here as contemporary. For more information on the hoards in general, see Levy (1982). For general information on the Bronze Age in Denmark, see Coles and Harding (1979). Pictures are also available in Kristiansen (1984).

References

Al-Zubaidi, Layla
  2004   Tracing Women in Early Sumer. In *Ungendering Civilization*. K. Anne Pyburn,
          ed. Pp. 117–35. New York: Routledge.
Arnold, Bettina
  1991   The Deposed Princess of Vix: The Need for an Engendered European Pre-
          history. In *The Archaeology of Gender*. Proceedings of the 22nd Annual Chacmool
          Conference. Dale Walde and Noreen D. Willows, eds. Pp. 366–74. Calgary:
          Department of Archaeology, University of Calgary.
  2002   "Sein und Werden": Gender as Process in Mortuary Ritual. In *In Pursuit of
          Gender: Worldwide Archaeological Approaches*. Sarah Milledge Nelson and Myriam
          Rosen-Ayalon, eds. Pp. 239–56. Walnut Creek, CA: AltaMira Press.
Bidney, David
  1947   Human Nature and the Cultural Process. *American Anthropologist* 49:375–99.
Brown, Catherine
  1982   On the Gender of the Winged Being on Mississippian Period Copper Plates.
          Tennessee Anthropologist 7(1):1–8.

Brumfiel, Elizabeth M.
  1995   Heterarchy and the Analysis of Complex Societies: Comments. In *Heterarchy and the Analysis of Complex Societies*. Robert M. Ehrenreich, Carole L. Crumley, and Janet E. Levy, eds. Pp. 125–31. Archaeological Papers of the American Anthropological Association 6. Washington, DC: American Anthropological Association.
  2000   On the Archaeology of Choice: Agency Studies as a Research Stratagem. In *Agency in Archaeology*. Marcia-Anne Dobres and John E. Robb, eds. Pp. 249–55. New York: Routledge.
Coles, John, and Anthony F. Harding
  1979   *The Bronze Age in Europe*. London: Methuen.
Conkey, Margaret W., and Joan M. Gero
  1997   Programme to Practice: Gender and Feminism in Archaeology. *Annual Review of Anthropology* 26:411–37.
Crown, Patricia L.
  2000   Gendered Tasks, Power, and Prestige in the Prehispanic American Southwest. In *Women and Men in the Prehispanic Southwest*. Patricia L. Crown, ed. Pp. 3–42. Santa Fe, NM: School of American Research Press.
Crumley, Carole L.
  1979   Three Locational Models: An Epistemological Assessment of Anthropology and Archaeology. In *Advances in Archaeological Method and Theory*. Vol. 2. Michael B. Schiffer, ed. Pp. 141–73. New York: Academic Press.
  1987a   Celtic Settlement before the Conquest: The Dialectics of Landscape and Power. In *Regional Dynamics: Burgundian Landscapes in Historical Perspective*. Carole L. Crumley and William H. Marquardt, eds. Pp. 403–29. San Diego: Academic Press.
  1987b   A Dialectical Critique of Hierarchy. In *Power Relations and State Formation*. Thomas C. Patterson and Christine W. Gailey, eds. Pp. 155–69. Washington, DC: American Anthropological Association.
  1994   The Ecology of Conquest: Contrasting Agropastoral and Agricultural Societies' Adaptations to Climatic Change. In *Historical Ecology: Cultural Knowledge and Changing Landscapes*. Carole L. Crumley, ed. Pp. 183–202. Santa Fe, NM: School of American Research Press.
  1995   Heterarchy and the Analysis of Complex Societies. In *Heterarchy and the Analysis of Complex Societies*. Robert M. Ehrenreich, Carole L. Crumley, and Janet E. Levy, eds. Pp. 1–6. Archaeological Papers of the American Anthropological Association 6. Washington, DC: American Anthropological Association.
Crumley, Carole L., and William H. Marquardt, eds.
  1987   *Regional Dynamics: Burgundian Landscapes in Historical Perspective*. San Diego: Academic Press.
Derevenski, Joanna Sofaer
  2000   Rings of Life: The Role of Early Metalwork in Mediating the Gendered Life Course. *World Archaeology* 31:389–406.

2002   Engendering Context: Context as Gendered Practice in the Early Bronze Age of the Upper Thomas Valley, UK. *European Journal of Archaeology* 5:191–211.

Dobres, Marcia-Anne, and John E. Robb, eds.

2000a   *Agency in Archaeology.* New York: Routledge.

Dobres, Marcia-Anne, and John E. Robb

2000b   Agency in Archaeology: Paradigm or Platitude? In *Agency in Archaeology.* Marcia-Anne Dobres and John E. Robb, eds. Pp. 3–17. New York: Routledge.

Dowson, Thomas A.

2000   Why Queer Archaeology? An Introduction. *World Archaeology* 32:161–65.

Egelhoff, William G.

1999   Organizational Equilibrium and Organization Change: Two Different Perspectives on the Multinational Enterprise. *Journal of International Management* 5:15–33.

Ehrenreich, Robert M.

1995   Early Metalworking: A Heterarchical Analysis of Industrial Organization. In *Heterarchy and the Analysis of Complex Societies.* Robert M. Ehrenreich, Carole L. Crumley, and Janet E. Levy, eds. Pp. 33–40. Archaeological Papers of the American Anthropological Association 6. Washington, DC: American Anthropological Association.

Emerson, Thomas A.

2003   Materializing Cahokia Shamans. *Southeastern Archaeology* 22:135–54.

Eskildsen, L., and Ebbe Lomborg

1976   Giftetanker. *Skalk* 5:18–26.

Gero, Joan M.

2000   Troubled Travels in Agency and Feminism. In *Agency in Archaeology.* Marcia-Anne Dobres and John E. Robb, eds. Pp. 34–39. New York: Routledge.

Gero, Joan M., and M. Cristina Scattolin

2002   Beyond Complementarity and Hierarchy: New Definitions for Archaeological Gender Relations. In *In Pursuit of Gender: Worldwide Archaeological Approaches.* Sarah Milledge Nelson and Myriam Rosen-Ayalon, eds. Pp. 155–72. Walnut Creek, CA: AltaMira Press.

Hays-Gilpin, Kelley

1995   Gender Ideology and Ritual Activities. *Journal of Anthropological Research* 51:91–135.

Hodder, Ian

1996   Glocalising Catal: Towards Postprocessual Methodology. Paper presented at the Theoretical Archaeology Group, Liverpool. Electronic document, http://www.catalhoyuk.com/TAG_papers/ian.htm, accessed December 14, 2005.

2000   Agency and Individuals in Long-Term Processes. In *Agency in Archaeology.* Marcia-Anne Dobres and John E. Robb, eds. Pp. 21–33. New York: Routledge.

Hollimon, Sandra E.

2000   Archaeology of the '*Aqi*: Gender and Sexuality in Prehistoric Chumash Society. In *Archaeologies of Sexuality*. Robert A. Schmidt and Barbara L. Voss, eds. Pp. 179–96. London: Routledge.

2001   The Gendered Peopling of North America: Addressing the Antiquity of Systems of Multiple Genders. In *The Archaeology of Shamanism*. Neil S. Price, ed. Pp. 123–34. New York: Routledge.

Howell, Todd L.

1995   Tracking Zuni Gender and Leadership Roles across the Contact Period. *Journal of Anthropological Research* 51:125–47.

Joyce, Rosemary A.

2000   Girling the Girl and Boying the Boy: The Production of Adulthood in Ancient Mesoamerica. *World Archaeology* 31:473–83.

Joyce, Rosemary A., and Julia A. Hendon

2000   Heterarchy, History, and Material Reality: "Communities" in Late Classic Honduras. In *The Archaeology of Communities: A New World Perspective*. Marcello A. Canuto and Jason Yaeger, eds. Pp. 143–60. New York: Routledge.

Kent, Susan

1998   Gender and Prehistory in Africa. In *Gender in African Prehistory*. Susan Kent, ed. Pp. 9–21. Walnut Creek, CA: AltaMira Press/Sage.

Knüsel, Christopher J.

2002   More Circe Than Cassandra: The Princess of Vix in Ritualized Social Context. *European Journal of Archaeology* 5:275–308.

Kristiansen, Kristian

1984   Ideology and Material Culture: An Archaeological Perspective. In *Marxist Perspectives in Archaeology*. Matthew Spriggs, ed. Pp. 72–100. Cambridge: Cambridge University Press.

1991   Chiefdoms, States and Systems of Social Evolution. In *Chiefdoms: Economy, Power and Ideology*. Timothy Earle, ed. Pp. 16–43. Cambridge: Cambridge University Press.

Levy, Janet E.

1982   *Social and Religious Organization in Bronze Age Denmark*. BAR International Series 124. Oxford: British Archaeological Reports.

1991   Metalworking Technology and Craft Specialization in Bronze Age Denmark. *Archaeomaterials* 5:55–74.

1995   Heterarchy in Bronze Age Denmark: Settlement Pattern, Gender, and Ritual. In *Heterarchy and the Analysis of Complex Societies*. Robert M. Ehrenreich, Carole L. Crumley, and Janet E. Levy, eds. Pp. 41–54. Archaeological Papers of the American Anthropological Association 6. Washington, DC: American Anthropological Association.

1999a   Gender, Power, and Heterarchy in Middle-Level Societies. In *Manifesting Power: Gender and the Interpretation of Power in Archaeology*. Tracy Sweely, ed. Pp. 62–78. New York: Routledge.

1999b   Metals, Symbols, and Society in Bronze Age Denmark. In *Material Symbols:*

Culture and Economy in Prehistory. John Robb, ed. Pp. 205–23. Occasional Paper 26. Carbondale: Center for Archaeological Investigations, Southern Illinois University.

Marquardt, William H., and Carole L. Crumley
   1987   Theoretical Issues in the Analysis of Spatial Patterning. In *Regional Dynamics: Burgundian Landscapes in Historical Perspective.* Carole L. Crumley and William H. Marquardt, eds. Pp. 1–18. San Diego: Academic Press.

McGuire, Randall H., and Dean J. Saitta
   1996   Although They Have Petty Captains, They Obey Them Badly: The Dialectics of Prehispanic Western Pueblo Organization. *American Antiquity* 61:197–216.

McIntosh, Susan Keech
   1999   Pathways to Complexity: An African Perspective. In *Beyond Chiefdoms: Pathways to Complexity in Africa.* Susan Keech McIntosh, ed. Pp. 1–30. Cambridge: Cambridge University Press.

Mills, Barbara J.
   1995   Gender and the Reorganization of Historic Zuni Craft Production: Implications for Archaeological Interpretation. *Journal of Anthropological Research* 51:149–72.
   2000   Alternate Models, Alternate Strategies: Leadership in the Prehispanic Southwest. In *Alternative Leadership Strategies in the Prehispanic Southwest.* Barbara J. Mills, ed. Pp. 3–18. Tucson: University of Arizona Press.

Mortensen, Lena
   2004   The "Marauding Pagan Warrior" Woman. In *Ungendering Civilization.* K. Anne Pyburn, ed. Pp. 94–116. New York: Routledge.

O'Reilly, Dougald J. W.
   2003   Further Evidence of Heterarchy in Bronze Age Thailand. *Current Anthropology* 44:300–307.

Ortner, Sherry B.
   2001   Commentary: Practice, Power and the Past. *Journal of Social Archaeology* 1:271–78.

Peterson, Jane
   2002   *Sexual Revolutions: Gender and Labor at the Dawn of Agriculture.* Walnut Creek, CA: AltaMira Press.

Potter, Daniel R., and Eleanor M. King
   1995   A Heterarchical Approach to Lowland Maya Socioeconomics. In *Heterarchy and the Analysis of Complex Societies.* Robert M. Ehrenreich, Carole L. Crumley, and Janet E. Levy, eds. Pp. 17–32. Archaeological Papers of the American Anthropological Association 6. Washington, DC: American Anthropological Association.

Price, Neil S.
   2001   An Archaeology of Altered States: Shamanism and Material Culture Studies.

In *The Archaeology of Shamanism*. Neil S. Price, ed. Pp. 3–16. New York: Routledge.

Pyburn, K. Anne
   2004a   Introduction: Rethinking Complex Society. In *Ungendering Civilization*. K. Anne Pyburn, ed. Pp. 1–46. New York: Routledge.

Pyburn, K. Anne, ed.
   2004b   *Ungendering Civilization*. New York: Routledge.

Randsborg, Klavs
   1986   Women in Prehistory: The Danish Example. *Acta Archaeologica* 1984:143–54.

Rautman, Alison E.
   1998   Hierarchy and Heterarchy in the American Southwest: A Comment on McGuire and Saitta. *American Antiquity* 63:325–33.

Rautman, Alison E., ed.
   2000   *Reading the Body: Representations and Remains in the Archaeological Record*. Philadelphia: University of Pennsylvania Press.

Robb, John
   2001   Steps to an Archaeology of Agency. Paper presented at the Agency Workshop, November 2001, University College, London. Electronic document, http://www.arch.cam.ac.uk/~jer39/theory/agency2.html, accessed October 14, 2004.

Roscoe, Will
   1991   *The Zuni Man-Woman*. Albuquerque: University of New Mexico Press.

Saitta, Dean J., and Randall H. McGuire
   1998   Dialectics, Heterarchy, and Western Pueblo Social Organization. *American Antiquity* 63:334–36.

Sastre, Inés
   2002   Forms of Social Inequality in the Castro Culture of North-West Iberia. *European Journal of Archaeology* 5:213–48.

Scarborough, Vernon L., Fred Valdez Jr., and Nicholas Dunning, eds.
   2003   *Heterarchy, Political Economy, and the Ancient Maya: The Three Rivers Region of the East-Central Yucatán Peninsula*. Tucson: University of Arizona Press.

Schmidt, Peter
   1998   Reading Gender in the Ancient Iron Technology of Africa. In *Gender in African Prehistory*. Susan Kent, ed. Pp. 139–62. Walnut Creek, CA: AltaMira Press/ Sage.

Schmidt, Robert A.
   2000   Shamans and Northern Cosmology: The Direct Historical Approach to Mesolithic Sexuality. In *Archaeologies of Sexuality*. Robert A. Schmidt and Barbara L. Voss, eds. Pp. 220–35. London: Routledge.

Simon, Arleyn W., and John C. Ravesloot
   1995   Salado Ceramic Burial Offerings: A Consideration of Gender and Social Organization. *Journal of Anthropological Research* 51:103–24.

Smith, Adam T.
    2001   The Limitations of Doxa: Agency and Subjectivity from an Archaeological Point of View. *Journal of Social Archaeology* 1:155–71.

Sørensen, Marie-Louise Stig
    1991   The Construction of Gender through Appearance. In *The Archaeology of Gender.* Proceedings of the 22nd Annual Chacmool Conference. Dale Walde and Noreen D. Willows, eds. Pp. 121–29. Calgary: Department of Archaeology, University of Calgary.
    1992   Gender Archaeology and Scandinavian Bronze Age Studies. *Norwegian Archaeological Review* 25:31–49.

Stark, David
    2001   Ambiguous Assets for Uncertain Environments: Heterarchy in Postsocialist Firms. In *The Twenty-First-Century Firm: Changing Economic Organization in International Perspective.* Paul Di Maggio, ed. Pp. 69–104. Princeton, NJ: Princeton University Press.

Thomas, Julian
    1994   AAA Annual Meeting, Washington DC. *Anthropology Today* 10(1):21.

Turner, Victor
    1969   *The Ritual Process.* Chicago: Aldine.

Weglian, Emily
    2001   Grave Goods Do Not a Gender Make: A Case Study from Singen am Hohentwiel, Germany. In *Gender and the Archaeology of Death.* Bettina Arnold and Nancy L. Wicker, eds. Pp. 137–55. Walnut Creek, CA: AltaMira Press.

White, Joyce C.
    1995   Incorporating Heterarchy into Theory on Socio-Political Development: The Case for Southeast Asia. In *Heterarchy and the Analysis of Complex Societies.* Robert M. Ehrenreich, Carole L. Crumley, and Janet E. Levy, eds. Pp. 101–24. Archaeological Papers of the American Anthropological Association 6. Washington, DC: American Anthropological Association.

Wolf, Eric R.
    1982   *Europe and the People Without History.* Berkeley: University of California Press.
    1990   Distinguished Lecture: Facing Power—Old Insights, New Questions. *American Anthropologist* 92:586–96.

Znoj, Heinzpeter
    2005   *Heterarchy and Domination in Highland Jambi: The Contest for Community in a Matrilinear Society.* London: Kegan Paul.

Gender and Ethnoarchaeology   8

KATHRYN WEEDMAN

B ETWEEN 1960 AND 1966, Hanna and Barbera produced a cartoon series,
The Flintstones, which appropriately reveals Western gender ideologies and
the ease with which we transport them into the past. As a cartoon, *The
Flintstones* is a tool of enculturation; among other aspects of life, it demonstrates
to our youth our idealized gender roles. Wilma Flintstone and Betty Rubble (the
female leading roles) serve as archetypes by cooking, cleaning, gossiping, and caring for their children within their homes, but it is questionable whether they represent the Stone Age women they are supposed to portray. Their husbands, Fred
and Barney, leave every day to work in the stone quarry, and when they are not
"working," they are meandering out in the world taking risks and getting into
trouble. These gender roles clearly reflect those of Western industrialism, marked
by a period in which men were first called out of agricultural work in the household context to work in factories (Stone and McKee 1998:29–38). In the industrial age, manhood was achieved and measured against economic prosperity
gained through individualistic, competitive, and aggressive behavior. By default,
women were expected to care for the domestic sphere and to create a balance for
men by being social, noncompetitive, nonaggressive, and passive.

The *Flintstones* does not represent a reality in either the past or the present.
Obviously, people did not exist at the same time as dinosaurs, nor are telephones
made out of ram horns or sinks filled through elephant trunks. These are anachro-
nisms and mixings of domains: the present (realities and imaginations) and several
documented pasts. The mixing of the past and the present is obvious in the material culture and the text (i.e., the music and dialogue) of *The Flintstones* cartoon.
However, in many ways, *The Flintstones* represents a portrait of the past that is
often mimicked or perhaps encouraged by archaeological literature, illustrations,
and museum exhibits (Gifford-Gonzalez 1993b; Moser 1993; Weedman 2004).
As Gifford-Gonzalez (1993b:31) stated, "To those of us conversant with thirty
years' hunter-gatherer studies and with feminist critiques of 'Man the Hunter',

the cumulative perspective on women and men in the landscape bears a peculiarly Western, woman's-place-is-in-the-home, cultural stamp." When archaeologists ascribe names to artifacts and features, such as hunting spear and digging stick, they imply an unspoken meaning, including the gender of the producer. We describe the past as we see it in the present, reducing them to sameness (mixing two separate domains), which is a specific form of analogy called metonymy (Schmidt 1997:28–30). Since the day when objects were recognized as products of past human activities, we have been engaged in the process of metonymy; hence, both the past and the present have revolved around heavily Eurocentric and androcentric ideologies (Orme 1981:1–16; Schmidt 1997; Trigger 1989).

Archaeology is a tool of enculturation; we enter it to learn about ourselves, where we came from, and how we behaved, and we pass this knowledge on to our children through books, museum exhibits, and television shows. We search in the past for our humanity; thus, our past is filtered through our perceptions of how we live today, including our gender roles; if it were not, it is questionable whether we would still consider the past as relevant or even interesting in the present. In essence, our reconstructions of the past are a reflection of the present, and we can broaden our interpretations of the past only through studies of present-day people and their material culture (i.e., ethnoarchaeology). Ethnoarchaeology, as the study of living peoples and their relationship to their material culture to provide models for translating the past, offers an opportunity for ascertaining alternative gender identities and their reflection in material culture and use of space. Ethnoarchaeological studies have the potential to allow us to escape Eurocentric and androcentric interpretations and reconstructions of the past by focusing on emic perspectives (David 1992b; Schmidt 1997). The goals of this chapter are to explore how ethnoarchaeological studies of gender reflect the diversity of feminist theories and define gender, how ethnoarchaeologists methodologically study gender, how they view gender as reflected in the past, and to what extent ethnoarchaeology has served as a source for identifying alternative genders.

Feminism, Defining Gender, and Ethnoarchaeological Theories

Four decades ago, Ortner (1974) argued that gender roles are rooted in the essentials of reproduction, and since this time feminist anthropologists have sought worldwide examples that offer a distinction between gender and sex to "denaturalize gender asymmetry" (Morris 1995:568). Explanations for the status, role, and identity of women outlined in cultural anthropology (di Leonardo 1991) largely mirror those in other disciplines, such as biology and political science (Jaggar 1983; Rosser 1992), including liberal feminism, existential feminism, Marxist feminism, socialist feminism, essentialist feminism, and, more recently, postmodern queer theory and performance theory. For the most part, feminist cultural studies confirm that there is a universal male/female dichotomy, that gender correlates with biological sex, that gender is intertwined with cultural and racial power relations, and that men tend to disempower the feminine (Power and Watts 1997; Visweswaran 1997). In our androcentric culture, it is not surprising to find that most studies in gendered archaeology adopted a feminist approach that emphasized finding women in the archaeological record (Conkey and Gero 1997), which has resulted in correlating gender with biological sex (Voss 2000; but for exceptions, see Hollimon 1997; Matthews 2000). Voss (2000) argues that feminist archaeologists may remain conservative because of the fear that deconstructing sex and gender may destabilize archaeological reconstructions that rely on the naturalization of the dichotomy as an absolute truth rather than as symbolic ambiguity.

The earliest studies that discuss the possible visibility of differences in gender roles as reflected in space and material culture were written by cultural anthropologists (Beck 1978; Bourdieu 1973; Draper 1975; Dupire 1963). These studies of pastoral, forager, and agricultural societies emphasized symmetry, complementarity, and equality between the sexes and dissimilarity to Western gender ideologies but reinforced the concept of a binary male/female set. Furthermore, to some extent the female authors discussed the imposition of particular gender roles as a result of contact with the West emphasizing either change (Beck 1978; Draper 1975) or cultural retention (Dupire 1963). Dupire (1963) provided an explanation for gender through a study of Fulani language and practice. Bourdieu (1973) also emphasized that while there is a male/female dichotomy represented in the use and symbolic meaning of household space, it is a reversal of the order of the outside world that indicated a balance and symmetry and overlap of the sexes. These early studies exemplify an understanding of gender through ritual practice, serving as the forebears for gendered performance theory (Bourdieu 1977; Butler 1990; Foucault 1978, 1980).

Ethnoarchaeology, as the disciplinary slip between cultural and archaeological studies and the present and the past, should provide us with alternative worldviews concerning the relationship between sex and gender and a means for viewing gendered practices through material culture in the past. David and Kramer (2001:34) note that ethnoarchaeologists generally do not explicitly reveal their theoretical perspective, and this may be even more true in studies of gender, where early gendered studies were masked under titles related to activity areas (Kent 1984) and demographics (David 1971). This is not a criticism of the authors but simply reflects the resistance to gender-focused studies among archaeologists in the 1970s and early 1980s. However, even a review of current ethnoarchaeological studies fails to reveal research that either defines gender or outlines a particular feminist perspective (for exceptions, see Kent 1998; Lyons 1992; Moore 1986:166–73). Instead, ethnoarchaeological theoretical perspectives reflect the paradigmatic changes in anthropological and archaeological thought, and their understanding of gender becomes evident through the questions researchers ask and the answers. Before the 1970s, there were few attempts in archaeology to incorporate women into prehistory because the emphasis was on structural continuity and evolutionary development, and the past was basically a mirror of a non-Western society filtered through Western ideology. Reconstructions were exceptionally androcentric, and few if any contributions to societal change or progress were attributed to women (for a notable exception, see Murray 1949). For instance, although even the earliest documented ethnoarchaeological studies focused on women potters (Bunzel 1929; Colton 1953; Cushing 1886), there is no attempt to understand gender roles in particular cultural context, as the gender/sex of men and women is viewed as a given. In these studies, not only was the male/female division taken for granted, but it was assumed that because women make pots in the present, they must also have made them in the past, which marked these studies as clearly entrenched in the direct historical approach.

Since the early 1970s, archaeologists and ethnoarchaeologists have engaged in the general comparative, discontinuous or universal-core approach, which was a reaction against direct historical, evolutionary, and diffusionistic models that failed to appreciate the uniqueness of the past (Clark 1953; Cunningham 2003; Gould 1974, 1977; Willey 1953). The general comparative approaches were similar in that they shared a belief that there are prime movers or single regularities that drive culture and transcend time; however, which real things structured behavior is disputed, especially between processual, contextual/ideological, and evolutionary models (Cunningham 2003; Kosso 1991; Wylie 2000:228). In the processual ethnoarchaeological studies of the 1970s, there is a clear assumption that a gendered division of labor equaled a sexual division of labor (Binford 1978b, 1987; Hayden 1979; Yellen 1976, 1977). The goal of these early processual studies was to generate "objective" cross-cultural generalities and norms in the performance of forager activities, primarily hunting and stone-tool production and use, and to discern from these regularities the subsequent artifact form and distribution. Ironically, although the goal of ethnoarchaeology of that time was to create cross-cultural models for testing against the past rather than directly explaining the past, these early ethnoarchaeological studies continued to view gender roles as a stagnant representation of present-day Western gender. Women are mentioned in passing as adjunct to men in butchering, hunting, or fishing activities (Binford 1978b:152) and as gatherers (Yellen 1976, 1977) and stone-tool producers (Hayden 1979:183–86). However, the emphasis was not on deciphering how gendered division of labor affected the archaeological patterning but rather on how activities transcended time and space. Hence, there were no efforts to examine historical context or to understand indigenous ideology, especially concerning gender, because the ascription of gender roles to each sex was viewed as natural universal constants.

By the 1980s, almost a decade after cultural anthropologists began to focus on denaturalizing sex from gender, processual ethnoarchaeologists began to look at gender as a cultural construction. Janes's (1983, 1989) description of the overlap between activities and space between men and women suggested that gender was not biologically determined in Dene culture. Janes (1983:78) stated that the Dene greatly value the male hunter but that actual behavior does not reflect ideology because to do so would be "maladaptive in an environment where survival . . . is still contingent upon mastery of a wide range of practical skills." He also contended that ethnohistory must be more fully studied to comprehend the influences of Europeans and history on gender relationships and ideology. Kent (1984, 1990, 1995, 1998, 1999), unlike Janes, saw little value in incorporating a historical perspective and took a much stronger processual position that ethnoarchaeology needs to focus on cross-cultural generalizations rather than on specific historical contextual cases. Her search for gender in cross-cultural regularities and generalizations would seem at odds with the idea that gender is a cultural construction, and in fact her writings reflect this struggle. In one publication, Kent (1990:149) relinquished the cultural construction of gender and the visibility of gendered use of space to only more complex societies, as such less complex societies base gendered division of labor on sex. However, Kent (1998:40) later argued that behavior and thus gender are not biologically determined but rather that the sociopolitical organization of the culture system determined gender. These views do not necessarily represent a contradiction but a westernized evolutionary perspective that there are non-Western societies that are less complex and that base gender roles on biology/nature rather than culture. Interestingly, Kent (1999) specifically argued that her perspective is not Eurocentric even with the heavy evolutionary overtones. She stated that power in egalitarian societies is meaningless because no one has more power than another; it is Western ideology that has projected a higher value on hunting as more masculine and projected it onto foraging cultures, thus perpetuating the idea that there was a division of labor and space in past foraging societies. Kent, as one of the few researchers to dedicate her career to ethnoarchaeology, should also be commended for her life-long commitment to ethnoarchaeological studies of gender.

Contextual/interpretive ethnoarchaeology emphasized social practices and material culture as a specific system of signs that reflect the ideological structure (Hodder 1977, 1982, 1987; Schmidt 1978, 1983, 1997:23–44, 1998). The goal was to find not regularities but an understanding of meanings through material culture and its spatial distribution (i.e., context). Contextual ethnoarchaeology also stressed symbolic continuity through time by relying on structuralism, which outlines that there are universal binary oppositions, including male/female. While the male/female dichotomy may be a constant, what symbolizes this core binary opposition in ideology and practice was culture specific. As with cultural studies of gender, ethnoarchaeological contextual studies emphasized the differences that were produced by several different social processes. For example, Hodder (1977) and Herbich (1987) offered that homogeneous ceramic style may be produced by women potters in either patrilineal virilocal societies, where there are ideological pressures on women to conform in their married communities, or in matrilocal societies, where mother and daughter reside and produce pots together. Furthermore, according to Hodder (1982:83–84, 139–40), because of male dominance, women bonded and silently renegotiated their positions through the material world. Thus, Hodder viewed women as visible because women have a different ideology or worldview from men. David (1971) believed that men are invisible and that women are visible not because they silently bond through material culture but because most structures were built for women's activities. In contrast, based on her ethnoarchaeological research among the Endo of Kenya, Moore (1986:188) stated that men and women do not have a separate ideology and that materials do not reflect the true nature of gender relations. In Endo culture, males dominated and were represented obscuring male/female tensions. Donley-Reid's study of the Swahili (Donley 1982; Donley-Reid 1987, 1990a, 1990b) also emphasized male power as reflected in male control of female use of space. Lyons (1990, 1991, 1992) concurred that among her studies in northern Cameroon, space and materials in male-oriented societies are likely to reflect male dominance. However, Lyons states that ideology is not static and that through their activities and practices women make themselves known materially and spatially. Schmidt's (1996a, 1996b, 1997, 1998) work also emphasized the flexibility in gender ideology through time and space, indicating that anomalies and contradictions in male and female material and spatial representation are the key to understanding change in gendered relations as social constructions.

Proponents of evolutionary models insisted that all individuals (males and females) make their decisions on the basis of efficiency and effectiveness shaped by natural selection (Broughton and O'Connell 1999; O'Connell 1995:209). Several ethnoarchaeological studies of foragers in East Africa (Hawkes et al. 1997) and South America (Hurtado et al. 1985) by behavioral ecologists indicated that the activities that women do or do not engage in are a direct reflection of their biology and their need to enhance offspring survival, which results in their low-risk behavior. Likewise, essentialist feminists state that women are different from men because of their biology, specifically their secondary sex characteristics and reproduction system that extend to their visual-spatial ability, verbal ability, physical traits, and mental traits (Kirsch 1993; Rosser 1992). However, Gifford-Gonzalez (1993a) argued that behavioral ecological approaches have not gone far enough and fail to examine the contributions women make in hunting acquisition, transport, processing, and storage and how men, women, and children's contributions to a household together result in benefits.

Postmodern philosophers argue that Western culture has a limited perception of the world because it focuses on a center—an origin, a truth, or an ideal form (Bourdieu 1977; Derrida 1978). The presence of a center creates binary oppositions in which the privileged side (male) freezes the play marginalizing the other (female). At the forefront of this movement, feminists identified women as marginalized in past and present scientific theories, research questions, and analyses (Harding 1998; Stepan 1986). Cultural anthropologists in the past two decades have suggested that sex, like gender, is a social category and thus an entry point for understanding systems of meaning and power (Visweswaran 1997). While many ethnoarchaeological studies attempt to reveal women as the "marginalized other," none has examined gender outside the male/female dichotomy or explicitly examined their respective cultures in terms of either Western or non-Western notions of feminism.

Gender and Ethnoarchaeological Methodologies

There is little doubt that in the past decade, the focus on gender in the past has proliferated and often includes either reference to ethnohistorical documentation or cross-cultural regularities drawn from ethnographies in support of archaeological interpretations (e.g., Boismier 1991; Crass 2001; chapters in Frink et al. 2002; Galloway 1997; Spector 1983; chapters in Walde and Willows 1991). Ethnohistory, either written or oral, is an important part of ethnoarchaeological studies and is utilized to expose anomalies and change in symbolic systems related to gender (Schmidt 1997, 1998) and the impact of colonial markets and ideology on gender relations (Frink 2005; Jarvenpa and Brumbach 1995; Webley 1997, 2005). Archaeologists eager to incorporate women or gender into their interpretations rarely acknowledge the difficulties in assessing the historic and ethno-graphic records they use for their models. As exceptions, Kehoe (1983), Spector (1983), Larson (1991), and Gifford-Gonzalez (1998) pointed out that until the 1980s it was standard practice for men to be ethnographers with male informants. All acknowledge that it may have been difficult for male researchers to work with women participants because the latter may have anticipated disrespect. Thus, ear-lier text may inherently have a gendered bias that reflected the researcher's own cultural and gendered interests rather than representing the gender ideology, tasks, and roles of the community studied. Larson (1991) indicated that a careful reex-amination of the literature usually indicates the presence of women but that we need to be more careful with the language we use and more cognizant of how common knowledge and practice can mute variation and meaning. In Chase's (1991) attempt to sidestep this issue, she considered only works authored by women or husband-and-wife teams, reasoning that female ethnographers have improved access to female informants and would obtain more sincere informa-tion.

Most ethnoarchaeological studies that specifically focused on gender at the outset were conducted by women (e.g., Donley-Reid, Kent, Lyons, and Moore, with the exception of the work of Brumbach and Jarvenpa) with male researchers realizing the importance of gender in their works but not taking gender as the focal point (e.g., David, Hodder, Schmidt). In cultural anthropological studies, the sex of the interviewer and participant has been a topic of methodological discussion in the form of the questions: what is the experience of female research-ers, and should male researchers study only male participants and female only female participants (Flinn et al. 1998; Golde 1986b; Gregory 1984; Warren 1988; Wolf 1996). Researchers have argued that women are less threatening because of their biology or because women as oppressed citizens share a common experience and thus have greater insight into other women's lives (Golde 1986a; Hartsock 1987). Others suggested that a closer bond or friendship could lead to such an intimate rapport and bond that they had difficulty separating out what information they should ethically reveal (Stacey 1991). Female ethnographers also have indicated that women researchers may accrue an ambiguous status in fieldwork situations as asexual, honorary male, or pseudomale because of their race, class, and Western identity (Bujra 1975; Warren 1988:26). Women study-ing their own non-Western cultures found that they may receive access in a patri-archal society only through accompaniment by father, husband, and brothers and were expected to adhere more strictly to gender roles (Berik 1996; Gupta 1979). Interestingly, in order to cope with the presence of a female boss in a very patriar-chal society, my younger male assistants chose to refer to me as mother. Kent

(1984:17–19) indicated that she received the status of daughter or close friend in her ethnoarchaeological studies of the Navajo, Spanish American, and Euro-American households, enabling her to participate closely and relate on informal rather than formal terms; however, it also limited her participation in some male activities. Kent (1984:17) also stated that she chose the matrilineal Navajo as one of her study groups because "being a woman did not interfere with my observation and participation in most activities."

The sex and gender of translators/research assistants may also affect the access that researchers have to indigenous gender ideologies. Gould (1971), Brumbach and Jarvenpa (1990), and David and Kramer (2001) have all discussed the importance of research assistants for language translation, location of sites, and interpretation of artifacts and features. However, Lyons (1992:6–7) laments difficulties finding female translators/research assistants because educating women is not highly valued, and thus few speak nonindigenous languages. I experienced similar problems while working in southern Ethiopia, as few women attended school past the age of ten, and most had household and agricultural commitments and little time for wage labor. Thus, there were virtually no women to act as translators or research assistants. I found, however, that female participants seemed uninhibited by the presence of a male translator and even openly conveyed to me incidents concerning their personal lives that they did not share with foreign male researchers. Lyons (1992:7) stated that in her ethnoarchaeological study in northern Cameroon, she had difficulty interviewing female participants concerning household and grave construction because these areas belonged to the realm of men. However, she was able to interview women concerning craft production, marketing, beer making, and features concerning their activity areas.

Ethnoarchaeological studies of gender vary considerably in the amount of time spent from eleven days (Chang 1988) to eleven months (Lyons 1992) and into multi-year longitudinal studies (Janes 1983, 1989; Kent 1984, 1999; Schmidt 1978, 1997), broadly reflecting the duration of ethnoarchaeological studies in general. Janes (1989) reports that his longitudinal studies provided him with multiple observations of activities that varied over time and in space that he otherwise would not have ascertained. Regardless of the time spent in the field, the most common means of deriving spatial and material gendered evidence was through directed and open interviews and participant observation (Hodder 1982; Janes 1983; Jarvenpa and Brumbach 1995; Kent 1984; Lyons 1992; Schmidt 1997). Brumbach and Jarvenpa (1995, 1997a, 1997b) and Frink (2005) suggest that examining activities through the task system, where, via interviews and observation, the interviewer records each specific phase/stage, produces a more nuanced understanding of gendered activities. Constructing maps of activity areas also was a popular means for collecting information concerning gendered control and location of resources and activities (Chang 1988; Janes 1983; Kent 1984; Yellen 1977). Jarvenpa and Brumbach (1995; Brumbach and Jarvenpa 1997a, 1997b) showed their maps to participants who were asked to reveal the location of structures and activities at archaeological sites. Bowser and Patton (2004) combined their GPS-constructed maps locating distances between households against kinship and networking information to determine the strength of male and female alliances and their corresponding spatial representation. Similarly, I (Weedman 2005) compared household and village location against kinship and other forms of female alliance against stone-tool variation to examine the relationship between lithic variability and space. Several researchers considered life histories important for ascertaining changes in gender relationships related to stage of life (Hodder 1982:18; Jarvenpa and Brumbach 1995). Others, especially processual and behavioral ecologists, engaged in focal person studies in which the researcher followed and timed the activities of specific individuals to determine sex-specific activities and the time allocated to these activities (Chang 1988; Hawkes et al. 1997; Hurtado et al. 1985; Janes 1983).

Ethnoarchaeological writings rarely revealed the gender relationships, contrasts and similarities in ideologies, or ethical issues raised between the researchers, their assistants, and participants. However, the type of method used was more commonly found in articles related to gender than is seen overall in ethnoarchaeological literature (for a review, see Arthur and Weedman 2005). The latter may be a reflection on the predominance of female authors, who overall in archaeological studies have reported anxiety related to their work being disputed and tend to be more concerned with methods of data collection (Beaudry and White 1994; Ford and Hundt 1994; Lutz 1990). Ethnoarchaeologists need to be more explicit about their relationships, and this may serve not only to contextualize better the work but also to provide a more fluid opening into other realms of gender identity.

Gender in the Present Projected into the Past

In the past decade, the number of articles and chapters in edited volumes attempting to identify the presence of women and gender differences in the archaeological record has grown significantly. Primarily, gender is identified through space and specific material forms, burials, rock art, and figurines (see chapters in Claassen and Joyce 1997; Donald and Hurcombe 2000; Gero and Conkey 1991; Linduff and Sun 2004; Nelson and Rosen-Ayalon 2002; Wadley 1997; Wright 1996). The following section outlines the contributions of ethnoarchaeology to interpreting gender in the past. While there have been a few studies that focus on the visibility of gender in mortuary practices (David 1992a; Hodder 1982:163–84) and personal adornment (Hodder 1977, 1982:75–85; Lyons 1989, 1998), the majority of ethnoarchaeological studies examine the intersection of gender and the use of space and craft production.

Gendered Division of Labor and Use of Household Space

In Western society, we believe that there are differences between males and females and assign each sex with specific material culture, tasks/activities, and spaces, and this belief is so enculturated that we believe it to be natural. In 1984, Kent wrote the first ethnoarchaeological cross-cultural study of household activity areas and the gendered use of space, supporting the concept that Euro-Americans have sex-specific space and material culture. Kent offered that the differences between Euro-American, Spanish American. and Navajo households are related to sociopolitical complexity. Cultural anthropologist Maxine Margolis (2000) argued that the strict male:female division of labor and space (female/domestic:male/public) that we now view as natural in Euro-American culture is a result of industrialism. Interestingly, in Kent's study of Euro-American households, the head female had no full-time employment outside the household (one wife worked as a nurse part time on the weekends), while in the nine Navajo families (except one household where the woman was blind) and two Spanish American households, the women either produced crafts or worked outside the household. While I wish not to dispute Kent's results, which support our ideal of the "American dream household" where women stay at home, it is important to understand the magnitude with which historical and ideological contexts and our own Euro-American desires to idealize the past affect our perception of gender. In this shadow, archaeologists have overlain our Western ideology of male/competitive/public:female/docile/domestic on to the past. In this section, I address how ethnoarchaeological studies of the division of labor and use of space in non-Western societies broaden our understanding of gender visibility in the archaeological record.

FORAGERS   In prehistoric foraging societies, women were invisible because the materials associated with their gendered activities are perishable (Isaac 1989). Men as hunters and toolmakers were the only visible sex in the past; even at identified home bases or living floors (i.e., household contexts), women and children were immaterial. In the 1970s, feminist ethnographic studies of hunter-gatherers and the division of labor tended to counter the strict archaeological division of male/public/hunter/provider with female/domestic/gatherer/ nurturer and the emphasis on males and male activities as propelling human evolution (Bodenhorn 1990; Draper 1975; Ember 1978; Estioko-Griffin and Griffin 1975; Slocum 1975). These studies exposed women's participation in hunts and as the main food providers through gathering. In contrast, Draper's (1975) study of the !Kung San (Khoisan speakers) indicated that while men and women engaged in different but mutual activities, the space and materials they used for these activities overlapped as a result of the small amount of household space. Subsequent ethnoarchaeological studies of the !Kung of southern Africa concurred with Draper. For instance, Yellen's (1976, 1977:91–97) ethnoarchaeological study among the Dobe !Kung suggested that while men hunted and women gathered, these activities occurred outside the household and left few if any marks on the landscape. Furthermore, within !Kung households, activities and their products were intermixed, and there were no distinct separated gendered areas. Kent's (1990, 1998) studies of the Kutse San indicated that small-scale hunter-gatherers did not consistently segregate space or architecture by gender or by activity. Hence, men and women "without stigma" regularly collected wild plants, hunted small animals, collected water and firewood, and tended to small livestock. Kent (1999) argued that in Western society, hunting is associated with manliness, prestige, and danger, which is not a concept held by non-Western societies.

While Kent (1999:34) scoffed at the idea that hunting is more dangerous than gathering, Hurtado et al. (1985) and Hawkes et al. (1997; see also O'Connell et al. 1991) argued that females are gatherers because it minimizes risks to offspring, while enhancing male productivity. O'Connell et al.'s (1991) study of the Hadza of Tanzania (Khoisan speakers) revealed that behavior associated with refuse importantly reflects gendered activities, which are based on the female need to stay close to home to minimize risks to children. Males were more closely associated with weapons maintenance and its resulting refuse in peripheral communal areas, whereas women produced refuse associated with food processing and tool maintenance in the central communal areas and in households. Women swept the communal areas and households, which would result in male visibility in peripheral areas but female activity areas virtually void of material culture. Thus, in communal and household contexts, it would not be possible to distinguish sex-related activity areas. Hurtado et al.'s (1985) study of the Ache (Tupi speakers) of eastern Paraguay indicated that unlike the !Kung model, women did not provide most of the calories consumed by the group. Their research indicated that among the Ache, child care restraints were the primary means for the division of labor. Nursing women were less efficient foragers than nonnursing women, and as the number of weaned dependents increased, so did a woman's food production. They argued that because infant mortality was high, women began to choose less risky behavior that resulted in a lower mortality rate for infants. However, in the past, infant mortality may have been lower and women's contribution to food production higher. Hawkes et al. (1997) agreed that women participate in activities to enhance reproductive success; however, among the Hadza of Tanzania, nursing mothers did not spend either more or less time foraging than nonnursing mothers. However, because of the presence of a new child, more calories were needed. The authors offered that female relatives with an interest in survival of the children, including mother's mother, sisters, husband's mother, and great-grandmothers, increased their foraging time when a newborn arrives. Thus, the division of labor that rendered females as gatherers and child care providers, even after menopause, consisted of behaviors geared toward increasing survivorship.

Ethnoarchaeological studies of Arctic peoples disagree over the visibility of men and women in space and material culture. Binford's study of the Nunamiut (Eskimo-Aleut speakers) of Alaska (Binford 1978a, 1978b:152, 158–59) indicated that there were different areas associated with different activities and that both residential and male special purpose sites are visible, while women's activities of butchering, processing, and distributing were simply adjunct to men's. Janes's (1983:71–80, 1989) study of the Dene (Na-Dene speakers) of the Mackenzie Basin, Northwest Territories, Canada, supports Binford's work that it is safest to assume the presence of sex-specific activities at temporary hunting camps, which are predominantly male. Janes argued that because of differences in life experiences and because the same household spaces were used at different times for different tasks by males and females, the gendered use of space would not be visible in households. Chang's (1988) study of an Alaskan Inupiat fish camp also indicated that although men and women have separate tasks and equipment, there is not a spatial segregation of work. Brumbach and Jarvenpa's (1997a, 1997b; Jarvenpa and Brumbach 1995) studies of the Chipewyan (Na-Dene speakers) of Saskatchewan, Canada, disputed the idea that women are invisible in the Arctic and attempt to level the field by adding women. They used the task approach and life cycle approaches to look more closely at men and women's activities and the visibility of gender. While in agreement with Binford and Janes that bush-centered kill sites more often represent male activities, they believed that these types of sites are ephemeral. In contrast, transformation sites, where together men and women process animals, are more highly visible because of the types of material culture used and the length of occupation. Furthermore, women are the primary hunters of rabbits and other animals closer to home (within three to five kilometers), and their hunting activities may be more visible in village/settlement (village-centered hunting) context than those of men, who tend to kill a few large animals far removed from the village. Within village sites, there was also a distinct use of space representing female materials and female activities. Male activities tend to occur outside the village context, making their activities invisible in villages, though their materials for these external activities are stored in specific locations within a village. Their studies also indicated, like Hurtado et al. (1985), that women participate to different degrees in the different stages of hunting (locating, stalking, dispatching, butchering, and distributing), depending on their stage in the life cycle, and that most women outside of childbearing years participate in hunting. They used census data to indicate that before European contact, women bore fewer children and probably were involved more in hunting activities.

Finally, there have been two recent ethnoarchaeological studies of the division of labor in Asia, a region of the world where there are very few studies of gender in ethnoarchaeology. Although within Binford's (1987) and O'Connell's (1987) studies of site formation among the Alyawara (Australian speakers) of Australia we find embedded information concerning the sexual division of labor and space, there is either an emphasis on male activities (Binford) or a lack of details outlining differences between male and female space (O'Connell). Gargett and Hayden's (1991) research concerning the Pintupi (Australian speakers) of Australia indicated that because of the high value of female contribution to the diet (60 to 90 percent including protein), postmartial residence in this patrilineal society is initially matrilocal. Only after the death of a man's parents and in his elder years does he return to his clan estate. Thus, household aggregation is most commonly associated with mother–daughter relationships. Cooper's (1994, 2000) studies of the Onge (Andamanese speakers) hunter-gatherers of Little Andaman, India, explored interhousehold gender. The Onge live in fishing/hunting camps and temporary encampments, and as a result there are no archaeological habitation sites but rather shell refuse middens that also contain other types of material culture. She determined that while men were responsible mostly for heavier work associated with hunting, such as setting nets and building weirs and traps, women were also hunters and fishers. Furthermore, children also contributed significantly to the diet. Cooper suggested that the allocation of tasks according to sex and age is arranged to meet efficiency in production.

FARMERS   Ethnographers and archaeologists have argued that with the beginning of food production and increased sedentism (Bar-Yosef 1995; Draper 1975; Ehrenberg 1989) or with changes in forager economic and technological organization (Kent 1995), there is a more sharply defined sexual division of labor. Although women are quite clearly associated with plant gathering in forager societies, at the onset of agriculture either men or neutral agents are associated with food production. Again, much of this is a result of Western ideology, which envisions the male as farmer and the female as farmwife. The adherence and projection of our Western division of agricultural labor has already been demonstrated through the obscuring of women's roles in non-Western agriculture, leading to misunderstanding in education programs and loan agencies associated with development and aid organizations outside the West (Lewis 1984; Rubbo 1975; Spring 2000). For example, in an article that is labeled as ethnoarchaeological but that actually is ethnographic, Casey (1991) outlined the division of labor and gender roles in the agricultural society of Mamprugu in northern Ghana as strongly contrasting Western ideals. Casey points out that in Mamprugu society, women are not confined to the household and are expected to earn income, indicating that men and women are economically autonomous and that gender is not correlated with biological sex. Recent archaeological reconstructions have begun to acknowledge women as farmers (Ehrenberg 1989; Watson and Kennedy 1991), drawing into question the spaces and materials they used in prehistoric contexts. The ethnographic and ethnoarchaeological studies of agrarian division of labor and use of space are concentrated in Africa and Central and South America.

One of the most widely cited ethnographic works that described the gendered use of space in an agrarian patrilineal society is Bourdieu's "The Berber House" (1973). Bourdieu contends that the rectangular Algerian Berber (Afro-Asiatic speakers) house in Kabyle is a metaphor for organization of the universe, which is divided into homologous oppositions including male/public:female/private/ nature/darkness. But the house blurs this dichotomy because although the house is female/private as opposed to male/public, there are defined male and female objects and spaces within the house that are complementary, and the house is also a reversal of the order of the outside world, which is controlled by men. An earlier ethnoarchaeological study by David (1971) also examined an agrarian Muslim North African village for the gendered use of space but determined that men and children were mostly invisible in households, while women were visible. David studied thirty-six patrilineal Fulani (Niger-Congo speakers) households in the village of Bé in northern Cameroon to derive an archaeological model for population estimates. David suggested that the number of women in a village could be estimated on the basis of the number of structures with hearths and the number of water storage pots since only women cooked and collected water. Guest quarters and men's quarters were virtually devoid of materials, making men virtually invisible in the archaeological record, though males as heads of family may be counted by the number of granaries present.

Diane Lyons has been working on ethnoarchaeological studies of gender in agrarian West African societies for the past fifteen years. Lyons (1989, 1990, 1991, 1992, 1996, 1998) worked in the village of Dela in northern Cameron, comprised of four ethnic groups (the Mura, Urza, and the Muslim Shuw and Muslim Wandala of the Afro-Asiatic speakers). Her work outlined how women's symbolic and ideological status as daughters, wives, and cowives in different cultures and religions is practically expressed in household organization of space. In the Muslim households, men were expected to provide all resources for their wives and children (through hired labor); hence, women did not work in the fields or produce crafts as non-Muslim women in the region did. Each wife stored her resources within her own separate square dwelling, and there was little cooperation between wives. In the non-Muslim households, the roundhouses were arranged around a central area where there was cooperative family labor, storage of grains, and a family shrine. In households where there was husband–wife cooperation for economic and reproductive value, there also was sharing of space among cowives, whereas in households with cowife competition, there were restricted spaces. Lyons (1989) presented further evidence that there was a connection between the cultural construction of time, gender, and the separation of male and female household space. The patrilineal Mura's exogamous marriage patterns forced women to break continuity with their father's ancestors, denying them legitimate land rights and justifying their inferiority to men. Men spent their time cultivating ancestral fields and ensuring continuity of his patrilineage; hence, sexual relationships and the birth of children occurred in a man's house. His house was located facing east, where the sun rises, so that he would know when to rise to start working in the fields. Women spent their time cooking and with other household tasks that they performed in a separate structure. Female/ kitchen houses were located facing west, where the sun sets, so that a woman knew when to prepare the family meal. Furthermore, men buried medicine bundles, bones, and entrails of rooster at the threshold of the household entrance and sleeping hut and near their granaries to protect them from the witchcraft of other men and their own wives (Lyons 1989, 1998). There was no evidence that women buried items to protect themselves from their cowives. In addition, women prepared all food and beverages in decorated pots to protect men and guests from potential danger.

Donley-Reid's (1990a, 1990b; née Donley 1982, 1987) ethnoarchaeological study was situated in Muslim patrilineal households in East African societies. She stated that Swahili (Niger-Congo speakers) coral houses of the seventeenth to nineteenth centuries were organized in a manner to protect the purity of women, in turn securing the purity of the family line. Donley-Reid believed that the Swahili settlements of the seventeenth to nineteenth centuries along the coast were founded by Arabs marrying indigenous African women. The main architectural structures of coral houses and mosques were associated with the freeborn plantation owners and the traders of indigenous raw products. The freeborn occupied the upper levels of the house, the female servants lived on the lower levels where trade goods were stored, the household slaves lived on the ground floor, and the plantation slaves lived in thatched houses made of coconut leaves. Freeborn women lived in purdah and were therefore contained in their veils and houses, and having a wife in purdah gave a man higher status. Freeborn fathers built coral houses for their daughters as wedding presents, and such houses enhanced their value and made them more desirable as wives to Arab traders, who were usually the father's brother's son. Space in architecture was a means to control women by elite Swahili men; as women moved up in the social economic hierarchy, they moved from thatched houses toward the inner room of a coral house, and it was the men who decided who lived where.

Hodder (1982:125–42, 155–63) studied the agrarian southeastern Kadugli-Moro (patrilineal) and Mesakin Tiwal and Qisar (matrilineal) of Sudan (all three are Niger-Congo language speakers). In all three cultures, the household consisted of a ring of houses connected by a low stone wall. The Moro compounds were highly variable but at minimum consisted of a granary where the wife slept and another structure for the husband and children. The Mesakin household usually was composed of an entrance house where women and children slept, a male sleeping house, one grinding house, one storage house, and two granaries. The granaries faced each other, and one belonged to the wife located on the right and the other to the husband located on the left. Furthermore, they hung domesticated animal skulls on the granaries, which served as symbols of male purity and strength and thus protected men against the impurity of women, who were the main producers of grain and sources of pollution and danger. The houses were painted with symbols related to fertility so that the male symbols enclosed the female. These designs replicated the interconnectedness of males and females and reflected the desire to provide ritual protection for men against women's pollutive powers.

Moore (1986) studied the agrarian patrilineal Endo (Nilo-Saharan Sudanic speakers) of the Marakwet territory of Kenya. The earthen and thatch houses of a household compound consisted of a male sleeping area, female cooking house, goat structure, store area, compound rubbish area, ash and chaff waste dump, and animal dung heap. In public situations, males would firmly express male dominance and compare women to children, indicating that they are social and jural minors. It was common when men first married for the compound to consist of a single house and a separate cooking house. However, in some instances there were claims of insufficient resources to build a cooking house. A second house also may be built when the eldest daughter reached the age of eight, as a father can no longer sleep in the same house as his daughter. However, he may choose to sleep with the livestock or to allow his daughter to sleep with friends rather than building a separate structure. Men spent most of their time with other men making arrows and other objects or roasting meat and with their cattle. Men are closely associated with their cattle and animal fertility, and thus they are buried near the household dung heap. Women, in contrast, are identified with crops, so they are buried near household chaff heaps. Ash represents house, hearth, and cooking and is linked to female fertility and the powers of womanhood. However, even burial placement is variable, depending on the cause of death, household compound space, and age of the deceased. Moore believed that men and women shared the same dominate ideology, and thus one should not expect that men and women would present two different ideologies in material culture. The Endo view men and women as having separate roles, but the material and spatial expression can alter vastly with the family and individual life cycles. Thus, Moore argued that organization of space is not a direct reflection of culture codes and meanings representing the relationship between male and female but rather is developed through practice, which is highly variable.

In ethnographic studies of Bantu settlements, Schapera (1953) and Kuper (1982) associated the cattle byre with male authority, and the deceased male ancestors were buried in this location, while females and children associated with the domestic context were buried under or near the household. Numerous archaeologists have used this central cattle-byre pattern to outline the presence and spread of Bantu-speaking peoples from central to eastern and southern Africa (Denbow 1984; Huffman 1982; Phillipson 1977). Segobye (1998) brought into question the emphasis on cattle and iron by archaeologists reconstructing trends over broad spans of time and spaces and the secondary relegation of agricultural production, which was probably the main source of subsistence and related to women's production and daily activities. Davison (1988) studied a Mopondo (Niger-Congo speakers) homestead in Pondoland, Transkei, South Africa, to examine how gender and the use of space change through time in a Bantu community. Davison argued that meaning is not inherent in spatial order or in particular artifacts but in their context and association, which is produced through social action. She noted variation through time in the function of structures with storage structures becoming temporary sleeping structures for new wives, and the wives of the sons had neither their own sleeping houses nor hearths. The division of the household into a female left side and male right side was most strictly adhered to by the daughter-in-law, who must avoid her husband's senior male relatives.

Davison stated that archaeologists need to better understand and consider the archaeological context of materials as reflecting the active role of material culture in the negotiation of social relations.

Outside Africa, there have been two major ethnoarchaeological research projects in Latin America that focused on the gendered use of space. Hayden and Cannon (1984) studied three Mayan (Mayan speakers) villages (Chanal, San Mateo Ixtatan, and Aguacatenago) in the highlands of Guatemala. Among the patrilineal Maya, women cannot own or work land and have to depend on crafts and aid from males to survive economically; there are few female-only households. Hayden and Cannon examined if the ratio of artifact types would be affected by household sex ratio. They found no correlation and suggested that most tools are so essential to the operation of a household that no matter what the sex ratio, a household cannot do without them. Nelson et al. (2002) examined in more detail the scale of women's work among the Maya in San Mateo Ixtatan, Guatemala, and their representation in the spatial organization and composition of household assemblages. For the most part, kitchen and hearth areas were the domains of women, and the rest of the residential area was shared or dominated by men. Their study indicated that women's labor did not substantially contribute to increasing the wealth of a household. Generally, there were two household trends: one in which women engaged in pottery production and wage labor and another in which women made blouses and produced other craft items. Households that produced pottery tended to have more women in the household, probably because of the labor intensity of pottery production. There was no relationships between the scale of women's income from craft/wage production and the percentage of household space committed to women's use. Mayan women spent less than 10 percent of their time on crafts and did not need much space to store their products and materials.

Bowser and Patton (2004) studied the horticultural Achuar (Jivaroan speakers) and Quichua (Quechuan speakers) peoples in the village of Conambo, Ecuador. Their study of the strength of male and female alliances determined that women and men have different alliances and that women are better predictors of spatial arrangement (see also see Gargett and Hayden 1991). Women's alliances show more cross-cutting between Achuar and Quichua, and the authors suggested "that women are better situated to act as political brokers between groups" (168). Furthermore, women's kinship relationships better predict spatial distances between households than men's, probably because of the matrilocal postmarital residence patterns. Their pole-thatch and sawn-wood houses are divided into two parts: a public area where men spend their time and receive male guests and a private kitchen area where women prepare food and beer and receive female guests. Consequently, materials belonging to men, such as hunting equipment, basket-making materials, and machetes, are stored in the rafters of the public/ male area of the household. In contrast, materials for food and beer preparation are located in the private/female area as well as sleeping quarters. A woman's private space in the house is not open to visiting men but may be shared with her spouse and other male family members. There are clear boundary markers between the two areas indicated by architectural differences, decorated brewing pots (see the section "Ceramics and Calabashes" later in this chapter), and some-times a hearth that is used by men and women.

PASTORALISTS   Gifford-Gonzalez (1998) stated that most anthropological descriptions of pastoral society are androcentric, focusing on male relationships with one another and with domesticated stock. As a result, many pastoral ethno-graphies are missing much of the daily activities of women and children in camp and "participating in the rich web of socially contextualized work and experience" (119). Gendered studies of pastoralist societies and the use of space are seemingly limited and can be drawn mostly from ethnographies. For instance, Beck's (1978) ethnographic studies of the Shiite Muslim Qashqa'i pastoralist in Iran indicated that the domestic context was not divided into male and female sections as was commonly noted among other Middle Eastern nomadic peoples. Men and women used the encampment differently; while men were responsible for caring for the herd, sheering, branding, feeding, collecting firewood, and agriculture, women were responsible for milling and milk processing, weaving, care of small animals near the tent, lighting fires, bringing water, collecting wild plants, cook-ing, baking, and child care—they were mutually dependent on one another. While men and women engaged in different but mutual activities, the space and materials they used for these activities overlapped as a result of the small amount of space. In contrast, Dupire (1963) emphasized differences in space and material remains between the sexes among the Muslim Fulani of Niger. The Fulani con-sidered females and males opposite yet complementary, and the arrangement of the landscape and household space symbolically mirrored the principles of sex differentiation with women and female space following men's. Among the Fulani, women take care of stock located in the domestic context and are responsible for milking and making butter, building houses, decorating calabashes, tending to the hearth, drawing water, and cooking by boiling in pots, while men herd animals away from the household and roast meat. In stark contrast to Western culture, the Fulani women selected men at dance festivals for their gracefulness and beauty, and both young men and young women have complete sexual freedom.

These differences between pastoral groups are not resolved through ethnoarchaeological studies.

Ethnoarchaeological studies of gender and pastoralists have concentrated in Kenya among the Ilchamus (Nilo-Saharan speakers; Hodder 1987) and the Dassanetch (Afro-Asiatic speakers; Gifford-Gonzalez 1993a); both present positive evidence for the identification of gender in spatial arrangements and material culture. Hodder's (1987) study of the Ilchamus pastoralist of Kenya used a structural approach to argue the division of household space as it parallels gendered division of labor and ideology. A screen divided the Ilchamus household so that in the right/back portion of the house, female activities, which included cooking, storing calabashes, storing firewood, grain, sleeping, giving birth, breast feeding, and menstruating, were hidden from men. The left/front of the household was for men and visitors. Although men view themselves as providing, supporting, and controlling the home, in practice women were in control of the domestic context, and men had little access to the right/back portion of the household. Hodder offered that through practical action, women were renegotiating their power or control, which a woman lost when she married and entered the "control" of another patrilineage. Gifford-Gonzalez (1993a) studied the Dassanetch pastoralists of Kenya and suggested that women's cooking and processing activities have long been viewed as secondary and ignored by archaeologists as factors influencing site formation. Her study indicated that transverse fracturing and jagged breaks on animal bones are the direct result of breakage after cooking and may indicate the presence of female activities.

The ethnoarchaeological research outlined here points positively toward the identification of gendered social relationships through examining archaeological context and the use of space, especially in pastoral and farming societies. In foraging societies, the invisibility of women is contested only by Jarvenpa and Brumbach (1995), who argued that women as well as men were hunters and that they had specific identifiable tools and space within village contexts. Interestingly, the theoretical explanations for the invisibility of women in forager societies rest primarily on processual schools of thought, where function and activity are viewed as superseding social relationships. Most farmer and pastoral studies were conducted by contextual or postprocessual researchers who argued that meaning is culture and context specific. In addition, while forager studies focused primarily on the southern African, Asian, and Arctic peoples, studies of farming and pastoralists centered primarily on Africa and covered a wide range of cultural and linguistic groups. With few exceptions, most of the farmer and pastoral studies were among patrilineal societies and among Muslim populations in North and East Africa. In studies of agrarian societies, there also was exceptional diversity with some studies indicating the visibility of both men and women (Bourdieu 1973; Davison 1988; Hodder 1982, 1987; Lyons 1989, 1991, 1992, 1998) and others emphasizing male construction of female space with primarily female visibility (David 1971; Donley 1982, 1987; Donley-Reid 1990a, 1990b). Moore (1986) argued that gendered activities and spaces do not accurately reflect gender relations. Among the studies in South (Bowser and Patton 2004) and Central America (Hayden and Cannon 1984; Nelson et al. 2002), there also is disagreement over women's visibility. Still, there is much to be studied concerning space and gender. In most of these studies, it is unclear whether there are other village structures or places where men and women spend their time outside the household context, how their restriction to marginalized environments (especially among foragers) may affect the use of space, and how the spread of westernization, Christianity, and Islam and socioeconomic status (class, race, caste, and so on) have affected the presence of a binary male/female system and the idea of the women's space only within the domestic context. Thus far, Kent (1984, 1990, 1998) is the only ethnoarchaeologist who has examined the gendered use of space cross-culturally, concluding that societies that are highly stratified are more likely to have discrete areas of gendered activities than those representing low levels of stratification and a less strict division of labor and space.

Gender Specialized Occupations: Craft Production and Technology

In Western society, because of our historical background in which men are the industrial outside workers, we tend to ascribe the most labor-intensive, dull, and unskilled occupations with women, including craft production (Gifford-Gonzalez 1993b). Furthermore, these crafts are viewed as only meagerly contributing to household economic status and/or a means of obtaining status as compared to male activities (reinforced by at least one ethnoarchaeological study; see Nelson et al. 2002). Costin (1996) stated that despite the significance of the gendered division of labor in craft production for structuring social and power relations in complex society, there are few systematic sustained works ascribing gender in the studies of craft production. People use craft items not only in the domestic sphere but also to mediate social, economic, political, and ritual contexts (Costin 1998). As such, they are imbued with symbolic meaning and often serve as active or passive identity markers (Hodder 1982; Sackett 1990). Artisans have an essential role in creating meaning that is manifested in the objects they create (Costin 1998). Many of the items we recover in the archaeological deposits (ceramics, iron, stone tools, beads, basketry, wooden and stone figurines, and other objects) were created by specific artisans. Thus far, the ethnoarchaeological studies of gender and craft production are limited to iron, hide working, ceramics, and calabashes. The following sections review what these studies reveal to us when gender is taken as a focal point for exposing gender and political-economic status (kinds of good produced, access to resources, and extent of control over production and selling of products), gender and the type of craft production (household, household industry, workshop, village industry, and factory industry), and gender and social/ritual status (religion, kin, linguistic, and relations to noncraftspersons).

IRON   The studies of gendered iron production focus on Bantu Niger-Congo– and Cushitic Afro-Asiatic–speaking regions of Africa (Childs 1991; Goucher and Herbert 1996; Herbert 1993; Schmidt 1996a, 1996b, 1997, 1998; Schmidt and Mapunda 1997). Although African smelters are almost always men, women contribute significantly to the labor required to prepare for smelting. Women may collect the ore and produce the charcoal, but they do not make the furnace or the tuyeres. Biology unsatisfactorily explains the allocation of male and female work roles in metalworking, as women already perform most of the strength activities of lifting and carrying. On another level, metalworking has a strong connection to women through symbolic representations of gestation and reproduction. The furnace itself is analogous to the womb. In several cultures images of females giving birth may adorn the furnace, whose shape and name metaphorically imbue the idea of childbirth. The bellows and tuyeres of the furnace continue the metaphor as they enter the female womb of the furnace, thus representing male sexuality and even sexual movement. The bloom is the successful outcome of the interaction, as is a child. Schmidt (1996a, 1996b, 1997, 1998) outlined the symbolic meaning of iron smelting in central and eastern Africa among the Haya, Pangwa, Fipa, Lungu, and Barongo. Iron is used mainly to produce tools for agricultural production. A "fertile" furnace produced large amounts of iron, which, through use, increased the fertility of the land, in turn enhancing human reproduction. Iron served as a symbol of fertility in both agricultural and human domains. Cross-culturally, the symbolic meaning of iron is reproduced through the practice of iron smelting, the shape and attributes of the furnace, and the presence of medicine pots inside the furnace containing plants or clay liquids known to cure human infertility. Archaeologically, Schmidt (1997, 1998) has recovered similar material symbols of fertility associated with Iron Age furnaces. Although he recognized an ideological continuity relating smelting to fertility, he went further and noted differences in time and space affiliated with male or female symbols, outlining changes in the level of tension between genders as a concurrent reflection of changing economic and political spheres (Schmidt

1998). The prohibition of male smelters from sexual intercourse during the smelt may be related to lineage control over iron production and to ideologies forbidding males who are husbands to commit adultery (avoiding women "spies" who may want to steal knowledge for their own lineages). A successful "fertile" smelt is dependent on avoiding the presence of menstruating "fertile" women. The control of iron production and the resources to produce iron, including clay (Childs 1988, 1989), served as the primary means for power and accumulation of wealth since agricultural productivity was in part enhanced by iron tools. Political leadership and power is closely linked in Bantu-speaking Africa with ironworking and symbolic connections between power, reproduction, and fertility (de Maret 1985; Schmidt 1997).

HIDE WORKING AND STONE TOOLS   The early ethnoarchaeological studies of stone tools reflect a gendered bias toward male knappers (e.g., Binford 1986; Clark and Kurashina 1981; Gallagher 1977; Gould 1980; Hayden 1977, 1979; Nelson 1916). This occurred despite the fact that there were clearly female stone-tool makers represented in ethnohistoric, ethnographic, and even ethnoarchaeological studies (Bird 1993; Goodale 1971; Gorman 1995; Gould 1977:166; Hayden 1977:183–86; Holmes 1919:316; Mason 1889; Murdoch 1892; Tindale 1965:246). In these accounts, women made and used stone tools for shaving hair, tattooing, woodworking, fighting sticks, digging sticks, cutting tools, spear points, incising/decorating tools, and scraping hides. Unfortunately, other than hide production, there are no detailed ethnoarchaeological studies concerning women and stone tools. A cross-cultural ascription of hide production to women using stone tools is evident in the ethnohistorical and ethnoarchaeological literature from North America (Albright 1984; Hiller 1948; Mason 1889; Murdoch 1889; Nissen and Dittemore 1974), Asia (Beyries et al. 2001; D'iatchenko and David 2002), and Africa (Brandt and Weedman 1997, 2002; Brandt et al. 1996; Webley 1990). Hence, although women are acknowledged as stone-tool makers, there is a lack of focus on them as such. From these hide-worker studies, we learn about the presence of women as knappers and about the general hide production process, but we often learn little about the gendered aspect of hide working.

It was not until Frink and Weedman's *Gender and Hide Production* (2005) that the gender of the hide-working agent was considered in terms of one's status, identity, symbolism, and authority and one's potential visibility in materials and space. The ascription of hide-working stone tools to women is not insignificant; stone scrapers are among the earliest stone tools found in the archaeological record, and the processing of hides is probably one of the earliest known industries beyond hunting and gathering. Four of the chapters in this volume are ethnoarchaeological and examine hide working among the Cup'ik (Eskimo-Aleut speakers) of western Alaska (Frink 2005); the Plains, Plateau, and Rocky Mountain Native Americans of North America (Baillargeon 2005); the Namaqua Khoikhoen (Khoisan speakers) of South Africa (Webley 2005); and the Konso and Gamo (Afro-Asiatic speakers) of southern Ethiopia (Weedman 2005). Frink (2005) offers that because gender relationships change through time and space, we need a contextualized understanding of the hide production process that involves a detailed study of the different phases/stages and how they are gendered. Today, women process seal and men larger sea mammals and fox. In particular, Frink demonstrates, how with the onset of European trade and impinging ideology, women's production was devalued and replaced with male control over fur production, storage, distribution, and trade. While Frink (2005) hints that a gendered past might be accessible, Webley (1990, 1997, 2005) submits that since both men and women scrape hides among the Namaqua Khoikhoen of South Africa and there is no difference in the materials or spaces they use, it is difficult to determine the gender/sex of the hide production agent. The Namaqua are a pastoralist society in which women hold a high economic and social status as a result of the presence of a cross-descent naming system that weakens the patrilineal descent system. Women inherit livestock and resources from their parents and thus are owners of cattle and control most of the domestic economy. Webley agrees with Kent (1984, 1990, 1998) that in small-scale noncomplex societies, there is no differentiation of space based on gender or activity. I (Weedman 2005) also argue that female hide production may be indistinguishable from male production in terms of tool type and distribution based on my study of the Gamo and Konso peoples of southern Ethiopia. Among the Konso, women use high-quality raw materials from long-distance resources and produce formal tools, contesting recent archaeological scenarios searching for female visibility in stone tools (e.g., Casey 1998; Gero 1991; Sassaman 1992). Both Gamo male hide workers and Konso female hide workers are members of agrarian patrilineal patrilocal societies. The Gamo male hide workers learn how to produce their stone tools from their fathers, and since postmarital residence patterns are virilocal, a discrete village/lineage-based scraper style is discernible and statistically viable. The Konso female hide workers learn mainly from their mothers, but they move to their husband's village after they marry. This results in nondiscrete hide-working areas within the village context, unless there are clusters of related females in a village, in which case there tends to be a significant difference between scrapers on the village level. Women's voices are not silenced or demeaned in informal and poorly crafted tools, but unfortunately this means that their tools are probably indistinguishable from men's. Finally, Baillargeon (2005) adds significantly to our understanding of the cross-cultural ascription of hide working to females through a study of Native Americans from the Plains, Rocky Mountains, and Plateau regions. He illustrates that tanning is viewed as a spiritual and ritual art in which the animal is infused with power and energy and brought back to life in respect for the fact that it gave its life for humans. This process is gendered on the physical and spiritual planes since women work the hides and concomitantly channel the soul of the animal back into the hide, thus restoring order.

CERAMICS AND CALABASHES   Ethnoarchaeological studies of ceramic production, distribution, use, and style represent the largest body of literature in ethnoarchaeological studies (Arnold 1985; Arthur 2003, in press; Burns 1993; Deal 1998; DeBoer and Lathrap 1979; Hodder 1979; Kramer 1997; Longacre 1983; Skibo 1992; Stark 2003). The ceramic ethnoarchaeology literature illustrates that women are the primary producers of ceramics in North America, Africa, Southeast Asia, and the Pacific; that men control the craft in the Mediterranean, Aegean, Middle East, South Asia, and Japan; and that men and women are potters in parts of Africa, Latin America, and the Middle East (Kramer 1985). Even in regions of the world where women dominate ceramic production today, such as Africa, there persists an androcentrism either in the lack of assignment or in the assumption of male artisans in ceramic sculpture and production (Burns 1993). Generally, there have been three areas of focus concerning gender and pottery: style as reflecting female production and learning systems, power and politics, and style as symbolic of gender relations.

One emphasis has been to link style with uxorilocal residence, female production, and learning (Deetz 1968; Longacre 1968). These early works pilfered ethnographic descriptions to assign women to pottery production and associate style with cultural or ethnic identity. Longacre's (1981) later ethnoarchaeological work among the Kalinga seemed to support this hypothesis. However, a cursory cross-cultural survey suggests that skill and age (Lathrap 1983), nonkin influences (Stanislawski 1978), the individual (Deal 1998:33–36), and women's birth cohort (Graves 1985) also affect potter style. Hodder's (1977, 1982:41–42, 83–84) studies of the Tugen, Njemps, and Pokot (all Nilo-Saharan speakers) of Kenya indicated that even in patrilineal virilocal societies where women are potters, pottery style may remain homogeneous because of ideological pressures on women to conform in their married communities. Herbich's (1987) ethnoarchaeological work among the Luo (Nilo-Saharan speakers) of Kenya contradicted the commonly held assumption that ceramic manufacturing styles reflect matrilineal lines and mother–daughter production. Among the Luo, potting was a specialized craft that women learn from their mother-in-laws or cowives and tend to conform to their techniques and style of potting. The Luo highly valued a woman's ability to adapt to the expectations of senior cowives and the mother-in-law. Thus, local ceramic traditions can be perpetuated by women who are entirely recruited from outside the community as a result of patrilocal marital residence and mother-in-law/daughter-in-law learning pattern. However, Herbich also pointed out that there are incentives and instances in which one might slightly alter ceramic design, such as tension between cowives, consumer demand, and influence from potter friends. Dietler and Herbich (1989, 1993) indicated that women are able to distinguish their own pots from others, including an assessment of the quality of the work, raw materials, forms, proportion, and decoration. They demonstrated through an operational sequence of production that style resides in rather than is added to material culture and that pots were decorated to target other women, particularly the women the potter knows. Visibility of the decoration was not related to their social display as indicated by the fact that beer drinking pots, the most socially visible vessel, tended to be less decorated than other pots in some Luo areas. Similarly, Hodder (1982:68–69) also argued that women's decoration on calabashes of the Njemps of Kenya lacked conformity to an ethnic symbol but rather reflected local relationships, especially those between women in opposition to older men as a form of "silent discourse."

In contrast to Dietler and Herbich's (1989, 1993) study, which suggested that women create signals in pottery but not on socially/public visible pots, are studies by La Violette (1995) and Bowser (2000; Bowser and Patton 2004) that emphasize women as active agents empowered with the ability to represent their identity and rearticulate gender roles through ceramic design. La Violette's (1995) research among the Mande of Mali (Niger-Congo speakers) revealed two linguistic and ethnically distinct endogamous groups of potters. The women of each of these groups actively represented their identity through different pottery production techniques, tempers, designs, and marketing strategies. Although artisans were endogamous, often Muslim Somono (fishers and farmers) women married into one of the artisan groups and became potters. Women more easily crossed cultural boundaries through marriage into artisan families and through other social and economic alliances than men. Bowser's (2000) ethnoarchaeological research among the Achuar- and Quichua-speaking peoples of Ecuador found that women made two types of pots: large pots for fermenting and storing manioc beer and bowls for consuming beer. These vessels were highly visible in the public sphere of the household and were used to bridge public/private and political/domestics contexts. The designs on the vessels reflected women's political affiliation and divisions, and they were detectable and recognized by other women. Bowser effectively resolved the androcentric argument that although women make pottery that marks identity (ethnic, political, and so on) boundaries, they are not viewed as active participants in politics. Bowser's work revealed that women whose pottery designs strongly reflect their political alliances intend to strengthen their relationships within particular groups, while women whose symbolic representation on pots is ambiguous often serve as mediators. Thus, women actively and intentionally demonstrate their political intentions and affiliations through ceramic design.

Ceramic and calabash studies also have pointed to the use of design as protective power against powerful spirits (David et al. 1988) and against women's pollutive powers (Donley-Reid 1990a; Hodder 1982). Sterner's (1992; David et al. 1988) studies of the Mandara region in northern Cameroon (Afro-Asiatic speakers) offers that although men conduct rituals, women make and create the rare ceramic vessels and their designs that are used for communicating to the spirit world. Women's power is located in their control over ceramic decoration, and this serves to protect either the people using the pottery or the contents of the vessel from spirits. Among the peoples of Nuba, Sudan, especially among the matrilineal Mesakin, there is a concern with female pollution and abilities to contradict male dominance and control (Hodder 1982:142–50). Material culture is frequently used in purification, especially at boundaries of interaction. Men decorated calabashes and gave them to women as marriage gifts or used them at feasts where women served men drinks. All the decorations on the calabashes are male in the sense that they are similar to the scarification marks seen on men that serve as protection against female power. Conversely, pottery made by women and generally used by women features designs based on female scarification, and these designs also may be related to the desire to provide ritual protection against male power. Donley-Reid (1990a) demonstrated that in early Swahili society when Arab men married African women, women were considered polluted because they brought the Arab line into question. Women's pollution was considered in relationship to birth, sexual activities, death, and food preparation, reducing their status and posing them as a powerful threat against men. Among the Swahili, decorative ceramics were used as protective devices against women's pollution. In Swahili culture, pots that held food or medicine that women cooked or transformed for men were also decorated to protect men. Furthermore, the Swahili placed porcelain plates and glass-bead plates in wall niches where they served as decoration and protection from the evil eye and malevolent spirits. Sherds were also taken off archaeological sites and used in the construction of house walls for protection. Ceramics and beads were placed in the rooms where the most polluting activities of birth and sexual intercourse took place.

Other ceramic studies demonstrate how pottery is symbolic of the human body and serves to mediate gender roles (Kreamer 1994; Welbourn 1984). Wel-bourn's (1984) studies of the Endo Marakwet (Nilo-Saharan speakers) pottery in Kenya indicated that in their mundane and ritual contexts, ceramic forms and designs represent the sexual division of labor. The cooking pots represented the world of women and cereal production and contrasted with men's beer pots, which symbolized bee husbandry and ritual blessing at ceremonies. Men controlled the public ritual world and viewed themselves as opposite to women, whose power was muted but practical as it was asserted in the everyday actions of providing sustenance and through reproducing new clan members. Material culture was used to enhance the boundary between male and female aspects of social existence. Similarly, Kreamer (1994) studied with the Moba of Togo (Niger-Congo speakers), among whom both men and women are potters, but each have specialization in techniques and types of object produced based on the sexual division of labor and spatial domains. Women were full-time specialists closely associated with domestic pottery for food and drink preparation and storage, representing women's space and domain in the domestic context and in gardens. Men were part-time potters/farmers and exclusively made beer pots. Men made beer pots because they were transportable and moved beyond the domestic context into social/public spaces, and men control the social and ritual uses of beer libations for ancestors. However, women made beer from millet grown by men and supplemented it by ingredients grown in women's gardens. Women had control over the production and distribution of beer, and the profits added considerably to the household income and to women's status. Kreamer suggested that the gendered pottery production among the Moba represented the struggle for economic and social power between men and women.

The ethnoarchaeological studies of gender and craft production reveal, as Costin (1996) noted in her ethnographic search, that the gendered division of labor in craft production is strong and that the allocation of tasks is remarkably idiosyncratic. Certainly, studies by Kreamer concerning ceramics and by myself concerning lithics emphasized that both men and women are capable of producing highly stylized and well-made items. Yet contextualized studies of symbolic infused materials suggest that gender status and power relationships are visible in craft materials. Changes in ethnic and gender relationships through time in Bantu-speaking Africa were actively symbolized through the practices (restricted male access, open male access, and male and female access) and material culture (form and types of symbolic male/female mediums) associated with iron smelting. In studies of hide working, researchers noted that Euro-American market demands and gender ideologies often served to undermine indigenous women's control of resources, production, and distribution. Ethnoarchaeological studies of potter societies emphasized how women used pottery form and design actively to communicate their social relationships with men and other women and their political alliances to the public. One seemingly universal point is the symbolism associating iron, ceramic, and hide production with human sexuality, fertility, and transformation regardless of whether there was male, female, or male and female control of production. In some societies, the association of fertility and power transcended into the use of materials culture to protect men from female powers and men and women from spiritual power. In many of these studies, the socioeconomic status of artisans is evaluated as part of their identity because, often within the cultural groups described, they were members of specific endogamous and ritual groups. However, few if any of these works, such as those focusing on use of space, consider how the influx of Western products or westernization, Christianity, and Islam have effected changes in artisan procurement, production, storage, and distribution (for an exception, see Frink 2005).

Ethnoarchaeology and the Current Level of Gender Integration

Wilma Flintstone and Betty Rubble would feel very comfortable in most ethnoarchaeological portrayals of material and spatial entanglements with gender. However, whether we can easily stipulate that this is a result of the influences and spread of westernization through colonialism and globalism is yet to be determined.

Ethnoarchaeological studies rarely define gender, explore women's lives in broader societal and historical contexts, incorporate non-Western or even Western interpretations of feminism, or explore the similarities and differences in gender between the researchers and the culture studied in their works. Because of the absence in defining gender, it can only be assumed that most studies reflect already entrenched Western ideals that gender reflects biological sex. The ethnoarchaeological studies, with few exceptions, discuss primarily the gender of labor within households or in terms of craft production where women are sifted into the previously excavated and discussed archaeological matrix. In many instances, especially in earlier work, gender appears not to be the initial focus of the research but merely a by-product of trying to understand "larger" issues of style, site activity and structure, and the male place in the world. Even in later studies and with few exceptions (Bowser, Lyons, and Schmidt), the focus is on what women do and how they do it and the material and spatial by-products rather than looking more closely at how women articulate themselves in the wider societal context.

With the exception of Kent (1984, 1990, 1995, 1998, 1999), there also is a reluctance to stipulate how and whether the ethnoarchaeological-derived interpretations can be applied to engender the past. Many have criticized ethnoarchaeological studies for their failure to conduct research that will be useful to archaeologists (Simms 1992). I believe that most of these criticisms come from researchers who wish to be handed specific cultural formulas that the archaeologists can plug into her or his material and spatial data, resulting in a final truth rather than an interpretation. Most ethnoarchaeologists who have focused on gender in the past two decades are interpretive/contextual postprocessualists. Thus, while they adhere to a universal male/female dichotomy, they also acknowledge the immense diversity with which this binary is reflected in spatial patterning and material culture. In summation, it is not possible to state, on the basis of current ethnoarchaeological research, whether throughout all times and spaces gender is visible in material culture and spatial arrangements.

Much frustration will arise from those who have attempted to find ethnoarchaeological research focused on gender. A great deal of this literature, including works by well-established and highly recognized authors such as Susan Kent, Ian Hodder, Nicholas David, and Peter Schmidt (note that most are male), is located in dissertations, in second- or third-tiered journals, and abundantly in edited volumes. Furthermore, many of the publications, outside of gendered titled edited volumes, use titles that obscure their gendered or ethnoarchaeological focus (or both) and instead focus on activity areas, households, power, crafts, and so on. Exceptions to this may be Bowser's (2000; Bowser and Patton 2004) work, which may demonstrate a growing acceptance of gendered studies into mainstream archaeological discourse. Still, ethnoarchaeologists focusing on gender need to make more concerted efforts (myself included) to publish their studies in mediums with wide readership. In many cases, this may still require a bit of persistence, as gender is still viewed as an aside to reconstructing past lifeways, as evident in our need to have special conference sessions, journal issues, and edited volumes. Gender is not fully integrated into ethnoarchaeological or archaeological reconstructions in academic writings, textbooks, and the classroom.

I believe that ethnoarchaeological research has made important strides in reaching the third to fourth stages necessary for creating gender friendly translations of the past (Rosser 1997:3–5). We have gone beyond the time when women were not noted (stage 1) and recognizing that most archaeologists and past visible agents are male (stage 2). We are currently struggling to identify the barriers that prevent incorporating women into the past (stage 3) and revealing their unique contributions to our past (stage 4). However, there are few studies that begin with taking women as the focal point for understanding the past through ethnoarchaeology (stage 5). Certainly, a gendered past and gendered ethnoarchaeological studies that fully incorporate both men and women is still missing (stage 6, the final stage). Writing this chapter has been an enlightening adventure, as it has exposed to me (and I hope to others) the well-worn paths in the ethnoarchaeological studies of gender and the missed crossroads. Ethnoarchaeology has great potential as the arbitrator between cultural and archaeological studies and as an instigator for developing new theories and methods concerning unique gender ideologies and the material world. It is now up to us to create longitudinal research projects that begin with socially oriented and gendered questions and to make concerted efforts to publish them.

References

Albright, Sylvia
    1984   *Tahltan Ethnoarchaeology.* Vancouver: Department of Archaeology, Simon Fraser University.
Arnold, Dean E.
    1985   *Ceramic Theory and Cultural Process.* Cambridge: Cambridge University Press.
Arthur, John W.
    2003   Beer, Food, and Wealth: An Ethnoarchaeological Use-Alteration Analysis of Pottery. *Journal of Archaeological Method and Theory* 9:331–55.
    In press   *Living with Pottery: Ceramic Ethnoarchaeology among the Gamo of Southwestern Ethiopia.* Salt Lake City: University of Utah Press.
Arthur, John, and Kathryn Weedman
    2005   Ethnoarchaeology. In *Handbook of Archaeological Methods.* Herbert Maschner and Christopher Chippendale, eds. Pp. 216–69. Walnut Creek, CA: AltaMira Press.
Baillargeon, Morgan
    2005   Hide Tanning: The Act of Reviving. In *Gender and Hide Production.* Lisa Frink and Kathryn Weedman, eds. Pp. 89–104. Walnut Creek, CA: AltaMira Press.
Bar-Yosef, Ofer
    1995   Earliest Food Producers: Pre-Pottery Neolithic (8000–5500). In *The Archaeology of Society in the Holy Land.* T. E. Levy, ed. Pp. 190–201. New York: Facts on File.
Beaudry, Mary, and Jacquelyn White
    1994   Cowgirls with the Blues? A Study of Women's Publication and the Citation of Women's Work in Historical Archaeology. In *Women in Archaeology.* Cheryl Claassen, ed. Pp. 138–58. Philadelphia: University of Pennsylvania Press.
Beck, Lois
    1978   Women among Qashqa'I Nomadic Pastoralists in Iran. In *Women in the Muslim World.* L. Beck and N. Keddie, eds. Pp. 352–73. Cambridge, MA: Harvard University Press.

Berik, Günseli
   1996   Understanding the Gender System in Rural Turkey: Fieldwork Dilemmas of
           Conformity and Intervention. In *Feminist Dilemmas in Fieldwork*. Diane L. Wolf,
           ed. Pp. 56–71. Boulder, CO: Westview.
Beyries, Sylvie, Sergev A. Vasil'ev, Francine David, Vladimir I. D'iachenko, Claudin Kar-
lin, and Youri V. Chesnokov
   2001   Uil, a Paleolithic Site in Siberia: An Ethnoarchaeological Approach. In *Ethno-
           Archaeology and Its Transfers*. Sylvie Beyries and Pierre Pétrequin, eds. Pp. 9–21.
           Moyen Âge: CNRS-UNSA.
Binford, Lewis R.
   1978a   Dimensional Analysis of Behavior and Site Structure: Learning from an
           Eskimo Hunting Stand. *American Antiquity* 43:330–61.
   1978b   *Nunamiut Ethnoarchaeology*. New York: Academic Press.
   1986   An Alyawara Day: Making Men's Knives and Beyond. *American Antiquity*
           51:547–62.
   1987   Researching Ambiguity: Frames of Reference and Site Structure. In *Method and
           Theory for Activity Area Research: An Ethnoarchaeological Approach*. Susan Kent, ed. Pp.
           449–512. New York: Columbia University Press.
Bird, C. F. M.
   1993   Woman the Tool Maker: Evidence for Women's Use and Manufacture of
           Flaked Stone-Tools in Australia and New Guinea. In *Women in Archaeology: A
           Feminist Critique*. Hilary du Cros and Laurajane Smith, eds. Pp. 22–30. Can-
           berra: Australian National University.
Bodenhorn, Barbara
   1990   I'm Not the Great Hunter, My Wife Is: Inupiat and Anthropological Models
           of Gender. *Etudes/Inuit Studies* 14(1–2):55–74.
Boismier, William A.
   1991   Site Formation among Subartic Peoples: An Ethnohistorical Approach. In
           *Ethnoarchaeological Approaches to Mobile Campsites: Hunter-Gatherer and Pastoralist Case
           Studies*. C. S. Gamble and W. A. Boismier, eds. Pp. 189–214. Ann Arbor, MI:
           International Monographs in Prehistory 1.
Bourdieu, Pierre
   1973   The Berber House. In *Rules and Meaning*. Mary Douglas, ed. Pp. 98–110. Lon-
           don: Penguin.
   1977   *Outline of a Practice of Theory*. Cambridge: Cambridge University Press.
Bowser, Brenda J.
   2000   From Pottery to Politics: An Ethnoarchaeological Study of Political Faction-
           alism, Ethnicity, and Domestic Pottery Style in the Ecuadorian Amazon. *Jour-
           nal of Archaeological Method and Theory* 7(3):219–48.
Bowser, Brenda J., and John Q. Patton
   2004   Domestic Spaces as Public Places: An Ethnoarchaeological Case Study of

Houses, Gender, and Politics in the Ecuadorian Amazon. *Journal of Archaeological Method and Theory* 11(2):157–81.

Brandt, Steven A., and Kathryn J. Weedman

1997 The Ethnoarchaeology of Hideworking and Flaked Stone-Tool Use in Southern Ethiopia. In *Ethiopia in Broader Perspective: Papers of the XIIth International Conference of Ethiopian Studies*. Katsuyoshi Fukui, Elsei Kurimoto, and Masayoshi Shigeta, eds. Pp. 351–61. Kyoto: Shokado Book Sellers.

2002 The Ethnoarchaeology of Hideworking and Stone-Tool Use in Konso, Southern Ethiopia: An Introduction. In *Le travail du cuir de la préhistoire à nos jours*. Frédérique Audoin-Rouzeau and Sylvie Beyries, eds. Pp. 113–30. Antibes: Editions APDCA.

Brandt, Steven A., Kathryn J. Weedman, and Girma Hundie

1996 Gurage Hideworking, Stone-Tool Use and Social Identity: An Ethnoarchaeological Perspective. In *Essays on Gurage Language and Culture: Dedicated to Wolf Leslau on the Occasion of His 90th Birthday November 14, 1996*. Grover Hudson, ed. Pp. 35–51. Wiesbaden: Harrassowitz Verlag.

Broughton, Jack M., and O'Connell, James F.

1999 On Evolutionary Ecology, Selectionist Archaeology, and Behavioral Archaeology. *American Antiquity* 64:153–65.

Brumbach, Hetty Jo, and Robert Jarvenpa

1990 Archaeologist-Ethnographer-Informant Relations: The Dynamics of Ethnoarchaeology in the Field. In *Powers of Observation: Alternative Views in Archaeology*. S. M. Nelson and A. B. Kehoe, eds. Pp. 39–46. Archaeological Papers of the American Anthropological Association 2. Washington, DC: American Anthropological Association.

1997a Ethnoarchaeology of Subsistence Space and Gender: A Subartic Dene Case. *American Antiquity* 62:414–36.

1997b Woman the Hunter: Ethnoarchaeological Lessons from Chipewyan Life-Cycle Dynamics. In *Women in Prehistory*. Cheryl Claassen and Rosemary A. Joyce, eds. Pp. 17–32. Philadelphia: University of Pennsylvania Press.

Bujra, Janet

1975 Women and Fieldwork. In *Women Cross-Culturally: Change and Challenge*. Ruby Rohrlich-Leavitt, ed. Pp. 551–57. The Hague: Mouton.

Bunzel, Ruth L.

1929 *The Pueblo Potter: A Study of the Creative Imagination in Primitive Art*. Columbia University Contributions to Anthropology 8. New York: Columbia University Press.

Burns, Marla C.

1993 Art, History and Gender: Women and Clay in West Africa. *African Archaeological Review* 11:129–48.

Butler, Judith P.

1990 *Gender Trouble: Feminism and the Subversion of Identity*. New York: Routledge.

Casey, Joanna

1991 One Man No Chop: Gender Roles in the Domestic Economy in Northern Ghana, West Africa. In *The Archaeology of Gender*. Proceedings of the 22nd Annual Chacmool Conference. Dale Walde and Noreen Willows, eds. Pp. 137–43. Calgary: Department of Archaeology, University of Calgary.

1998 Just a Formality: The Presence of Fancy Projectile Points in a Basic Tool Assemblage. In *Gender in African Prehistory*. S. Kent, ed. Pp. 83–104. Walnut Creek, CA: AltaMira Press.

Chang, Claudia

1988 Nauyalik Fish Camp: An Ethnoarchaeological Study in Activity-Area Formation. *American Antiquity* 53(1):145–57.

Chase, Sabrina

1991 Polygyny, Architecture and Meaning. In *The Archaeology of Gender*. Proceedings of the 22nd Annual Chacmool Conference. Dale Walde and Noreen Willows, eds. Pp. 1150–58. Calgary: Department of Archaeology, University of Calgary.

Childs, S. Terry

1988 Clay Resource Specialization in Ancient Tanzania: Implications for Cultural Process. In *Ceramic Ecology Revisited*. Charles Kolb, ed. Pp. 1–31. BAR International Series 436. Oxford: British Archaeological Reports.

1989 Clay to Artifacts: Resource Selection in African Early Iron Age Iron-Making Technologies. In *Pottery Technology*. G. Bronitsky, ed. Pp. 139–64. Boulder, CO: Westview.

1991 Style, Technology and Iron Smelting Furnaces in Bantu-Speaking Africa. *Journal of Anthropological Archaeology* 10:332–59.

Claassen, Cheryl, and Rosemary A. Joyce, eds.

1997 *Women in Prehistory: North America and Mesoamerica*. Philadelphia: University of Pennsylvania Press.

Clark, J. Desmond, and Hiro Kurashina

1981 A Study of the Work of a Modern Tanner in Ethiopia and Its Relevance for Archaeological Interpretation. In *Modern Material Culture: The Archaeology of Us*. R. A. Gould and M. B. Schiffer, eds. Pp. 303–43. New York: Academic Press.

Clark, John Graham D.

1953 Archaeological Theories and Interpretation: Old World. In *Anthropology Today: Selections*. Sol Tax, ed. Pp. 104–21. Chicago: University of Chicago Press.

Colton, Harold S.

1953 *Potsherds*. Bulletin 25. Flagstaff: Museum of Northern Arizona.

Conkey, Margaret W., and Joan M. Gero

1997 Programme to Practice: Gender and Feminism in Archaeology. *Annual Review of Anthropology* 26:411–37.

Cooper, Zarine
    1994   Abandoned Onge Encampments and Their Relevance in Understanding the
            Archaeological Record in the Andaman Islands. In *Living Traditions: Studies in
            the Ethnoarchaeology of South Asia*. Bridget Allchin, ed. Pp. 235–63. New Delhi:
            Oxford University Press and IBH Publishing.
    2000   The Enigma of Gender in the Archaeological Record of the Andaman
            Islands. In *In Pursuit of Gender: Worldwide Archaeological Approaches*. Sarah M. Nel-
            son and Myrian Rosen-Ayalon, eds. Pp. 173–86. Walnut Creek, CA: Alta-
            Mira Press.
Costin, Cathy Lynne
    1996   Exploring the Relationship between Gender and Craft in Complex Societies:
            Methodological and Theoretical Issues of Gender Attribution. In *Gender and
            Archaeology*. Rita P. Wright, ed. Pp. 111–40. Philadelphia: University of Penn-
            sylvania Press.
    1998   Introduction: Craft and Social Identity. In *Craft and Social Identity*. Cathy Lynne
            Costin and Rita P. Wright, eds. Pp. 3–18. Archaeological Papers of the
            American Anthropological Association 8. Washington, DC: American
            Anthropological Association.
Crass, Barbara
    2001   Gender and Mortuary Analysis: What Can Grave Goods Really Tell Us. In
            Gender and the Archaeology of Death. Bettina Arnold and Nancy L. Wicker, eds.
            Pp. 105–18. Walnut Creek, CA: AltaMira Press.
Cunningham, Jeremy
    2003   Transcending the "Obnoxious Spectator": A Case for Processual Pluralism in
            Ethnoarchaeology. *Journal of Anthropological Archaeology* 22:389–410.
Cushing, Frank H.
    1886   *A Study of Pueblo Pottery as Illustrative of Zuni Culture Growth*. Washington, DC:
            Bureau of American Ethnology. Annual Report 4:467–521.
David, Nicholas
    1971   The Fulani Compound and the Archaeologist. *World Archaeology* 3(2):111–31.
    1992a   The Archaeology of Ideology: Mortuary Practices in the Central Mandara
            Highlands, Northern Cameroon. In *An African commitment; Papers in honor of Peter
            Lewis Shinnie*. Judy Sterner and Nicholas David, eds. Pp. 181–210. Calgary:
            University of Calgary Press.
    1992b   Integrating Ethnoarchaeology: A Subtle Realist Perspective. *Journal of Anthropo-
            logical Archaeology* 11:330–59.
David, Nicholas, and Carole Kramer
    2001   *Ethnoarchaeology in Action*. Cambridge: Cambridge University Press.
David, Nicholas, Judy Sterner, and Kodzo Gavua
    1988   Why Pots are Decorated. *Current Anthropology* 29:365–89.
Davison, Patricia
    1988   The Social Use of Domestic Space in a Mpondo Homestead. *South African
            Archaeological Bulletin* 43:100–108.

de Maret, Pierre
    1985   The Smith's Myth and the Origin of Leadership in Central Africa. In *African Iron Working: Ancient and Traditional*. Randi Haaland and Peter Shinnie, eds. Pp. 73–87. Oslo: Norwegian University Press.
Deal, Michael
    1998   *Pottery Ethnoarchaeology in the Central Maya Highlands*. Salt Lake City: University of Utah Press.
DeBoer, Warren R., and Donald W. Lathrap
    1979   The Making and Breaking of Shipibo-Conibo Ceramics. In *Ethnoarchaeology: Implications of Ethnography for Archaeology*. Carol Kramer, ed. Pp. 102–38. New York: Columbia University Press.
Deetz, James
    1968   The Inference of Residence and Descent Rules from Archaeological Data. In *Pursuit of the Past*. Sally R. Binford and Lewis R. Binford, eds. Pp. 41–48. Chicago: Aldine.
Denbow, James
    1984   Cows and Kings: A Spatial and Economic Analysis of a Hierarchical Early Iron Age Settlement System in Eastern Botswana. In *Frontiers: Southern African Archaeology Today*. BAR International Series 207. M. Hall, M. G. Avery, D. M. Avery, M. L. Wilson, and A. J. B. Humpreys, eds. Pp. 24–39. Oxford: British Archaeological Reports.
Derrida, Jacques
    1978   Structure, Sign and Play in the Discourse of the Human Sciences. In *Writing and Difference*. Alan Bass, trans. Pp. 278–93. London: Routledge.
di Leonardo, Micaela
    1991   Introduction: Gender, Culture, and Political Economy. In *Gender at the Crossroads of Knowledge: Feminists Anthropology in the Postmodern Era*. Micaela di Leonardo, ed. Pp. 3–45. Berkeley: University of California Press.
D'iatchenko, Vladimir I., and Francine David
    2002   Le Préparation traditionnelle des peaux de poissons et de mammifères marins chez les populations de l'Extrême-Orient sibérien de langue toungouze par. In *Le Travail du Cuir: de la Préhistoire à nos jours*. Frédérique Audoin-Rouzeau and Sylvie Beyries, eds. Pp. 175–91. Antibes: Editions APDCA.
Dietler, Michael, and Ingrid Herbich
    1989   Tich Matek: The Technology of Luo Pottery Production and the Definition of Ceramic Style. *World Archaeology* 21:148–64.
    1993   Ceramics and Ethnic Identity. In *Terre Cuite et Societe: Le ceramique, document technique, economique, culturel*. Juan-les-Pins, ed. Pp. 459–72. Antibes: Editions APDCA.
Donald, Moira, and Linda Hurcombe
    2000   Gender and Material Culture in Archaeological Perspective. New York: St. Martin's Press.

Donley, Linda W.

1982   House Power: Swahili Space and Symbolic Markers. In *Symbolic and Structural Archaeology*. I. R. Hodder, ed. Pp. 63–73. Cambridge: Cambridge University Press.

1987   Life in the Swahili Town House Reveals the Symbolic Meaning of Spaces and Artefact Assemblages. *African Archaeological Review* 5:181–92.

Donley-Reid, Linda W.

1990a   The Power of Swahili Porcelain, Beads and Pottery. In *Powers of Observation: Alternative Views in Archaeology*. S. M. Nelson and A. B. Kehoe, eds. Pp. 47–59. Archaeological Papers of the American Anthropological Association 2. Washington, DC: American Anthropological Association.

1990b   The Swahili House: A Structuring Space. In *Domestic Architecture and Use of Space*. Susan Kent, ed. Pp. 114–26. Cambridge: Cambridge University Press.

Draper, Patricia

1975   !Kung Women: Contrasts in Sexual Egalitarianism in Foraging and Sedentary Context. In *Toward an Anthropology of Women*. Rayna Reiter, ed. Pp. 77–109. New York: Monthly Review Press.

Dupire, Marguerite

1963   The Position of Women in a Pastoral Society. In *Women in Tropical Africa*. D. Paulme, ed. Pp. 47–92. Berkeley: University of California Press.

Ehrenberg, Margaret R.

1989   *Women in Prehistory*. London: British Museum Publications.

Ember, Carol

1978   Myths about Hunter-Gatherers. *Ethnology* 18:439–48.

Estioko-Griffin, Agnes, and P. Bion Griffin

1975   Woman the Hunter: The Agta. In *Woman the Gatherer*. Frances Dahlberg, ed. Pp. 121–40. New Haven, CT: Yale University Press.

Flinn, Juliana, Leslie Marshall, and Jocelyn Armstrong

1998   *Fieldwork and Families*. Honolulu: University of Hawai'i Press.

Ford, Anabel, and Anna Hundt

1994   Equity in Academia—Why the Best Men Still Win: An Examination of Women and Men in Mesoamerican Archaeology. In *Equity Issues for Women in Archaeology*. M. C. Nelson, S. M. Nelson, and A. Wylie, eds. Pp. 147–56. Archaeological Papers of the American Anthropological Association 5. Washington, DC: American Anthropological Association.

Foucault, Michel

1978   *The History of Sexuality*. New York: Vintage Books.

1980   *Herculine Barbin*. New York: Pantheon.

Frink, Lisa

2005   Gender and the Hide Production Process in Colonial Western Alaska. In *Gender and Hide Production*. Lisa Frink and Kathryn Weedman, eds. Pp. 89–104. Walnut Creek, CA: AltaMira Press.

Frink, Lisa, Rita S. Shepard, and Gregory A. Reinhardt, eds.
2002   *Many Faces of Gender.* Boulder: University Press of Colorado.
Frink, Lisa, and Kathryn Weedman
2005   *Gender and Hide Production.* Walnut Creek, CA: AltaMira Press.
Gallagher, James P.
1977   Contemporary Stone-Tool Use in Ethiopia: Implications for Archaeology. *Journal of Field Archaeology* 4:407–14.
Galloway, Patricia
1997   Where Have All the Menstrual Huts Gone? The Invisibility of Menstrual Seclusion in the Late Prehistoric Southeast. In *Women in Prehistory.* Cheryl Claassen and Rosemary A. Joyce, eds. Pp. 33–47. Philadelphia: University of Pennsylvania Press.
Gargett, Rob, and Brian Hayden
1991   Site Structure, Kinship, and Sharing in Aboriginal Australia. In *The Interpretation of Archaeological Spatial Patterning.* Ellen M. Kroll and Timothy D. Price, eds. Pp. 11–32. New York: Plenum.
Gero, Joan
1991   Genderlithics: Women's Roles in Stone-Tool Production. In *Engendering Archaeology: Women and Prehistory.* Joan M. Gero and Margaret W. Conkey, eds. Pp. 163–93. Oxford: Blackwell.
Gero, Joan M., and Margaret W. Conkey, eds.
1991   *Engendering Archaeology: Women and Prehistory.* Oxford: Blackwell.
Gifford-Gonzalez, Diane P.
1993a   Gaps in the Zooarchaeological Analyses of Butchery: Is Gender an Issue? In From Bones to Behavior: Ethnoarchaeological and Experimental Contributions to the Interpretation of Faunal Remains. J. Hudson, ed. Pp. 181–99. Occasional Paper 21. Carbondale: Center for Archaeological Investigations, Southern Illinois University.
1993b   You Can Hide, but You Can't Run: Representation of Women's Work in Illustrations of Paleolithic Life. *Visual Anthropology Review* 9(1):22–41.
1998   Gender and Early Pastoralist in East Africa. In *Gender in African Prehistory.* Susan Kent, ed. Pp. 115–38. Walnut Creek, CA: AltaMira Press.
Golde, Peggy
1986a   Introduction. In *Women in the Field.* Peggy Golde, ed. Pp. 1–18. Berkeley: University of California Press.
1986b   *Women in the Field.* Berkeley: University of California Press.
Goodale, Jane C.
1971   *Tiwi Wives.* Seattle: University of Washington Press.
Gorman, Alice
1995   Gender, Labour, and Resources: The Female Knappers of the Andaman Islands. In *Gendered Archaeology: The Second Australian Women in Archaeology Confer-*

ence. Jane Balme and Wendy Beck, eds. Pp. 87–91. Canberra: Australian National University.

Goucher, Candice L., and Eugenia W. Herbert

1996   The Blooms of Banjeli: Technology and Gender in West African Iron Making. In *The Culture and Technology of African Iron Production.* Peter R. Schmidt, ed. Pp. 40–57. Gainesville: University Press of Florida.

Gould, Richard A.

1971   The Archaeologists as Ethnographer: A Case Study from the Western Desert of Australia. *World Archaeology* 3:143–77.

1974   Some Current Problems in Ethnoarchaeology. In *Ethnoarchaeology.* C. William Clewlow Jr., ed. Pp. 29–48. Berkeley: University of California Press.

1977   Ethnoarchaeology: Or Where Do Models Come From. In *Stone-Tools as Cultural Markers.* R. V. S. Wright, ed. Pp. 162–68. Canberra: Australian Institute of Aboriginal Studies.

1980   Living Archaeology. Cambridge University Press, Cambridge.

Graves, Michael

1985   Ceramic Design Variation within a Kalinga Village: Temporal and Spatial Process. In *Decoding Prehistoric Ceramics.* B. A. Nelson, ed. Pp. 9–34. Carbondale: Southern Illinois University Press.

Gregory, James R.

1984   The Myth of the Male Ethnographer and the Woman's World. *American Anthropologist* 86:316–27.

Gupta, Khadija Ansari

1979   Travels of a Woman Fieldworker. In *The Fieldworker and the Field.* M. N. Srinivas, A. M. Shah, and E. A. Ramaswamy, eds. Pp. 103–14. Delhi: Oxford University Press.

Harding, Sandra

1998   *Is Science Multicultural? Postcolonialisms, Feminisms, and Epistemologies.* Bloomington: Indiana University Press.

Hartsock, Nancy

1987   The Feminist Standpoint: Developing the Ground of a Specifically Feminist Historical Materialism. In *Feminism and Methodology.* Sandra Harding, ed. Pp. 157–80. Bloomington: Indiana University Press.

Hawkes, Kristen, James F. O'Connell, and Nicholas G. Blurton Jones

1997   Hadza Women's Time Allocation, Offspring Provisioning, and the Evolution of Long Postmenopausal Life Spans. *Current Anthropology* 38(4):551–77.

Hayden, Brian

1977   Stone Tool Functions in the Western Desert. In *Stone Tools as Cultural Markers.* R. V. S. Wright, ed. Pp. 178–88. Canberra: Australian Institute of Aboriginal Studies.

1979   Paleolithic Reflections. Atlantic Highlands, NJ: Humanities Press.

Hayden, Brian, and Aubrey Cannon
    1984   The Structure of Material Systems: Ethnoarchaeology in the Maya High-
            lands. Society of American Archaeology Papers, no. 3. Washington, DC:
            Society of American Archaeology.
Herbert, Eugenia W.
    1993   Iron, Gender, and Power: Rituals of Transformation in African Societies. Bloomington:
            Indiana University Press.
Herbich, Ingrid
    1987   Learning Patterns, Potter Interaction and Ceramic Style among the Luo of
            Kenya. African Archaeological Review 5:193–204.
Hiller, Wesley R.
    1948   Hidatsa Soft Tanning of Hides. Minnesota Archaeologists 14:4–11.
Hodder, Ian
    1977   The Distribution of Material Culture Items in the Baringo District, Western
            Kenya. Man 12:239–69.
    1979   Pottery Distributions: Service and Tribal Areas. Pottery and the Archaeologists
            4:7–23.
    1982   Symbols in Action: Ethnoarchaeological Studies of Material Culture. Cambridge: Cam-
            bridge University Press.
    1987   The Meaning of Discard: Ash and Domestic Space in Baringo. In Method and
            Theory in Activity Area Research. Susan Kent, ed. Pp. 424–49. New York: Colum-
            bia University Press.
Hollimon, Sandra E.
    1997   The Third Gender in Native California: Two Spirit Undertakers among the
            Chumash and Their Neighbors. In Women in Prehistory. Cheryl Claassen and
            Rosemary A. Joyce, eds. Pp. 173–88. Philadelphia: University of Pennsylva-
            nia Press.
Holmes, William H.
    1919   Handbook of Aboriginal American Antiquities Part I. The Lithic Industries. Bulletin 60.
            Washington, DC: Bureau of American Ethnology.
Huffman, Thomas
    1982   Archaeology and Ethnohistory of the African Iron Age. Annual Review of
            Anthropology 11:133–50.
Hurtado, Ana Magdalena, Kristen Hawkes, Kim Hill, and Hillard Kaplan
    1985   Female Subsistence Strategies among the Ache Hunter-Gatherers of Eastern
            Paraguay. Human Ecology 13(1):1–27.
Isaac, Glynn
    1989   The Archaeology of Human Origins. Cambridge: Cambridge University Press.
Jaggar, Alison M.
    1983   Feminist Politics and Human Nature. Totowa, NJ: Rowman & Allanheld.
Janes, Robert R.
    1983   Archaeological Ethnography among Mackenzie Basin Dene, Canada. Techni-
            cal Paper 28. Calgary: Arctic Institute of North America.

1989   The Organization of Household Activities at a Contemporary Dene Hunting Camp—Ten Years in Retrospect. In *Households and Communities*. Proceedings of the 21st Annual Chacmool Conference. A. S. MacEachern, D. J. W. Archer, and R. D. Garvin, eds. Pp. 517–24. Calgary: Department of Archaeology, University of Calgary.

Jarvenpa, Robert, and Hetty J. Brumbach
1995   Ethnoarchaeology and Gender: Chipewyan Women as Hunters. *Research in Economic Anthropology* 16:39–82.

Kehoe, Alice
1983   The Shackles of Tradition. In *The Hidden Half: Studies of Plains Indian Women*. Patricia Albers and Beatrice Medicine, eds. Pp. 53–76. Lanham, MD: University Press of America.

Kent, Susan
1984   *Analyzing Activity Areas: An Ethnoarchaeological Study of the Use of Space*. Albuquerque: University of New Mexico Press.
1990   A Cross-Cultural Study of Segmentation, Architecture, and the Use of Space. In *Domestic and Architecture and the Use of Space*. Susan Kent, ed. Pp. 127–52. Cambridge: Cambridge University Press.
1995   Does Sedentization Promote Gender Inequality? A Case Study for the Kalahari. *Journal of the Royal Anthropological Institute* 1:513–36.
1998   Invisible Gender—Invisible Foragers: Hunter Gatherer Spatial Patterning and the Southern African Archaeological Record. In *Gender in African Prehistory*. Susan Kent, ed. Pp. 39–69. Walnut Creek, CA: AltaMira Press.
1999   Egalitarianism, Equality, and Equitable Power. In *Manifesting Power: Gender and the Interpretation of Power in Archaeology*. Tracy L. Sweely, ed. Pp. 30–48. London: Routledge.

Kirsch, Gesa E.
1993   *Women Writing the Academy*. Carbondale: Southern Illinois University Press.

Kosso, Peter
1991   Method in Archaeology: Middle Range Theory as Hermeneutics. *American Antiquity* 56:621–27.

Kramer, Carol
1985   Ceramic Ethnoarchaeology. *Annual Reviews in Anthropology* 14:77–102.
1997   Pottery in Rajasthan: Ethnoarchaeology in Two Indian Cities. Washington, DC: Smithsonian Institution Press.

Kreamer, Christine M.
1994   Money, Power and Gender: Some Social and Economic Factors in Moba Male and Female Pottery Traditions (Northern Togo). In *Clay and Fire: Pottery in Africa*. Iowa Studies in African Art: The Stabley Conferences at the University of Iowa 4. Christopher D. Roy, ed. Pp. 189–212. Iowa City: School of Art and Art History, University of Iowa.

Kuper, Adam
   1982   *Wives for Cattle*. London: Routledge.
Larson, Mary Ann
   1991   Determining the Function of a "Men's House." In *The Archaeology of Gender*.
           Proceedings of the 22nd Annual Chacmool Conference. Dale Walde and
           Noreen Willows, eds. Pp. 165–75. Calgary: Department of Archaeology,
           University of Calgary.
Lathrap, Donald
   1983   Recent Shipibo-Conibo Ceramics and Their Implications for Archaeological
           Interpretation. In *Structure and Cognition in Art*. D. K. Washburn, ed. Pp. 25–
           39. New York: Cambridge University Press.
La Violette, Adrien J.
   1995   Women Craft Specialists in Jenne: The Manipulation of Mande Social Cate-
           gories. In *Status and Identity in West Africa: Nyamakalaw of Mande*. D. C. Conrad
           and B. E. Frank, eds. Pp. 170–81. Bloomington: Indiana University Press.
Lewis, Barbara
   1984   The Impact of Development Policies on Women. In *African Women South of
           the Sahara*. Margaret Jean Hay and Sharon Stichter, eds. Pp. 170–82. Essex:
           Longman.
Linduff, Katheryn M., and Yan Sun
   2004   *Gender and Chinese Archaeology*. Walnut Creek, CA: AltaMira Press.
Longacre, William A.
   1968   Some Aspects of Prehistoric Society in East-Central Arizona. In *Pursuit of
           the Past*. Sally R. Binford and Lewis R. Binford, eds. Pp. 89–102. Chicago:
           Aldine.
   1981   Kalinga Potter: An Ethnoarchaeological Study. In *Pattern of the Past*. Ian Hod-
           der, Glynn Isaac, Norman Hammond, eds. Pp. 49–66. Cambridge: Cam-
           bridge University Press.
   1983   *Ethnoarchaeology of the Kalinga*. Westong: Pictures of Record.
Lutz, Catherine
   1990   The Erasure of Women's Writing in Sociocultural Anthropology. *American
           Ethnologists* 17:611–27.
Lyons, Diane E.
   1989   Deliver Us from Evil: Protective Materials Used in Witchcraft and Sorcery
           Confrontation by the Mura of Doulo, Northern Cameroon. In *Cultures in
           Conflict: Current Archaeological Perspectives*. Proceedings of the 20th Annual Chac-
           mool Conference. D. C. Tkaczuk and B. C. Vivian, eds. Pp. 297–302. Cal-
           gary: Archaeological Association of the University of Calgary.
   1990   Men's Houses: Women's Spaces: The Spatial Ordering of Households in
           Doulo, North Cameroon. In *Households and Communities*. Proceedings of the
           21st Annual Chacmool Conference. Scott MacEachern, David J. W. Archer,

and Richard D. Garvin, eds. Pp. 28–34. Calgary: Department of Archaeology, University of Calgary.

1991   The Construction of Gender, Time and Space. In *The Archaeology of Gender*. Proceedings of the 22nd Annual Chacmool Conference. D. Walde and N. Willows, eds. Pp. 108–14. Calgary: Department of Archaeology, University of Calgary.

1992   Men's Houses: Women's Spaces: An Ethnoarchaeological Study of Gender and Household Design in Dela, North Cameroon. Ph.D. dissertation, Simon Fraser University.

1996   The Politics of House Shape: Round versus Rectilinear Domestic Structures in Déla, Northern Cameroon. *Antiquity* 70(268):351–67.

1998   Witchcraft, Gender, Power and Intimate Relations in Mura Compounds in Déla, Northern Cameroon. *World Archaeology* 29(3):344–62.

Margolis, Maxine L.

2000   *True to Her Nature: Changing Advice to American Women*. Prospect Heights, IL: Waveland.

Mason, Otis

1889   *Aboriginal Skin Dressing*. Washington, DC: Smithsonian Institution Press.

Matthews, Keith

2000   The Material Culture of the Homosexual Male: A Case for Archaeological Exploration. In *Gender and Material Culture in Archaeological Perspective*. Moira Donald and Linda Hurcombe, eds. Pp. 2–19. London: Macmillan.

Moore, Henrietta L.

1986   *Space, Text and Gender: An Anthropological Study of the Marakwet of Kenya*. Cambridge: Cambridge University Press.

Morris, Rosalind C.

1995   All Made Uo: Performance Theory and the New Anthropology of Sex and Gender. *Annual Review of Anthropology* 24:567–92.

Moser, Stephanie

1993   Gender Stereotyping in Pictorial Reconstructions of Human Origins. In *Women in Archaeology: A Feminist Critique*. Hillary du Cros and Laurajane Smith, eds. Pp. 75–91. Canberra: Australian National University.

Murdoch, John

1892   *Ethnological Results of the Point Barrow Expedition*. Washington, DC: Smithsonian Institution Press.

Murray, Margaret

1949   *The Splendor That Was Egypt*. London: Sidgwick and Jackson.

Nelson, Margaret, Donna Glowacki, and Annette Smith

2002   The Impact of Women on Household Economies: A Maya Case Study. In *In Pursuit of Gender: Worldwide Archaeological Approaches*. Sarah Milledge Nelson and Myriam Rosen-Ayalon, eds. Pp. 125–54. Walnut Creek, CA: AltaMira Press.

Nelson, Nels
1916   Flint Working by Ishi. In *Holmes Anniversary Volume*. Frederick W. Hodge, ed. Pp. 397–402. New York: American Museum of Natural History.

Nelson, Sarah M., and Myriam Rosen-Ayalon
2002   *In Pursuit of Gender: Worldwide Archaeological Approaches*. Walnut Creek, CA: AltaMira Press.

Nissen, Karen, and Margaret Dittemore
1974   Ethnographic Data and Wear Pattern Analysis: A Study of Socketed Eskimo Scrapers. *Tebiwa* 17:67–87.

O'Connell, James F.
1987   Alyawara Site Structure and Its Archaeological Implications. *American Antiquity* 52:74–108.
1995   Ethnoarchaeology Needs a General Theory of Behavior. *Journal of Archaeological Research* 3:205–55.

O'Connell, James, Kristen Hawkes, and N. G. Blurton Jones
1991   Distribution of Refuse Producing Activities at Hadza Residence Base Camps: Implications for Analyses of Archaeological Site Structure. In *The Interpretation of Archaeological Spatial Patterning*. Ellen M. Kroll and Timothy D. Price, eds. Pp. 61–76. New York: Plenum.

Orme, Bryony
1981   *Anthropology for Archaeologists*. Ithaca, NY: Cornell University Press.

Ortner, Sherry B.
1974   Is Female to Male as Nature Is to Culture? In *Women, Culture and Society*. Michelle Z. Rosaldo and Louise Lamphere, eds. Stanford, CA: Stanford University Press.

Phillipson, David
1977   *The Later Prehistory of Eastern and Southern Africa*. New York: African Publishing.

Power, Camilla, and Ian Watts
1997   The Woman with the Zebra's Penis: Gender, Mutability and Performance. *Journal of the Royal Anthropological Institute* 3:537–60.

Rosser, Sue V.
1992   *Biology and Feminism*. New York: Twayne Publishers.
1997   *Re-Engineering Female Friendly Science*. New York: Teachers College Press.

Rubbo, Anna
1975   The Spread of Capitalism in Rural Colombia: Effects on Poor Women. In *Toward an Anthropology of Women*. Rayna Reiter, ed. Pp. 358–71. New York: Monthly Review Press.

Sackett, James
1990   Style and Ethnicity in Archaeology: The Case for Isochrestism. In *The Uses of Style in Archaeology*. M. W. Conkey and C. A. Hastorf, eds. Pp. 32–43. Cambridge: Cambridge University Press.

Sassaman, Kenneth E.
1992   Lithic Technology and the Hunter-Gatherer Sexual Division of Labor. *North American Archaeologist* 13:249–62.

Schapera, Isaac
1953   *The Tswana*. London: Kegan Paul International.

Schmidt, Peter R.
1978   *Historical Archaeology: A Structural Approach in African Culture*. Westport, CT: Greenwood Press.

1983   An Alternative to a Strictly Materialist Perspective: A Review of Historical Archaeology, Ethnoarchaeology, and Symbolic Approaches in African Archaeology. *American Antiquity* 48:62–81.

1996a Cultural Representation of African Iron Production. In *The Culture and Technology of African Iron Production*. Peter R. Schmidt, ed. Pp. 1–28. Gainesville: University Press of Florida.

1996b Reconfiguring the Barongo: Reproductive Symbolism and Reproduction among a Work Association of Iron Smelters. In *The Culture and Technology of African Iron Production*. Peter R. Schmidt, ed. Pp. 74–127. Gainesville: University Press of Florida.

1997   Iron Technology in East Africa: Symbolism, Science, and Archaeology. Bloomington: Indiana University Press.

1998   Reading Gender in the Ancient Iron Technology of Africa. In *Gender in African Prehistory*. Susan Kent, ed. Pp. 139–62. Walnut Creek, CA: AltaMira Press.

Schmidt, Peter R., and Bertram B. M. Mapunda
1997   Ideology and the Archaeological Record in Africa: Interpreting Symbolism in Iron Smelting Technology. *Journal of Anthropological Archaeology* 16:73–102.

Segobye, Alinah
1998   Daughters of Cattle: The Significance of Herding in the Growth of Complex Societies in Southern Africa. In *Gender in African Prehistory*. Susan Kent, ed. Pp. 227–34. Walnut Creek, CA: AltaMira Press.

Simms, Steven R.
1992   Ethnoarchaeology: Obnoxious Spectator, Trivial Pursuit, or the Keys to a Time Machine? In *Quandaries and Quests: Visions of Archaeology's Future*. LuAnn Wandsnider, ed. Pp. 186–98. Occasional Paper 20. Carbondale: Center for Archaeological Investigations, Southern Illinois University.

Skibo, James
1992   *Pottery Function*. New York: Plenum.

Slocum, Sally
1975   Woman the Gatherer: Male Bias in Anthropology. In *Toward and Anthropology of Women*. Rayna Reiter, ed. Pp. 36–50. New York: Monthly Review Press.

Spector, Janet D.
1983   Male/Female Task Differentiation among the Hidatsa: Toward the Development of an Archaeological Approach to the Study of Gender. In *The Hidden*

Half. Patricia Albers and Beatrice Medicine, eds. Pp. 77–99. Washington, DC: University Press of America.

Spring, Anita, ed.
2000   *Women Farmers and Commercial Ventures: Increasing Food Security in Developing Countries.* Boulder, CO: Lynne Rienner.

Stacey, Judith
1991   Can There Be a Feminist Ethnography? In *Women's Words.* S. B. Gluck and D. Patai, eds. Pp. 111–19. New York: Routledge.

Stanislawski, Michael B.
1978   If Pots Were Mortal. In *Explorations in Ethnoarchaeology.* Richard. A. Gould, ed. Pp. 201–28. Albuquerque: University of New Mexico Press.

Stark, Miriam T.
2003   Current Issues in Ceramic Ethnoarchaeology. *Journal of Archaeological Research* 11:193–242.

Stepan, Nancy L.
1986   Race and Gender: The Role of Analogy in Science. *Isis* 77:261–77.

Sterner, Judy A.
1992   Sacred Pots and "Symbolic Reservoirs" in the Mandara Highlands of Northern Cameroon. In *An African Commitment: Papers in Honor of Peter Lewis Shinnie.* Judy Sterner and Nicholas David, eds. Pp. 171–79. Calgary: University of Calgary Press.

Stone, Linda, and Nancy P. McKee
1998   *Gender and Culture in America.* Englewood Cliffs, NJ: Prentice Hall.

Tindale, Norman B.
1965   Stone Implement Making among the Nakako, Ngadadjara, and Pitjandjara of the Great Western Desert. *Records of the South Australian Museum* 1965:131–64.

Trigger, Bruce G.
1989   *A History of Archaeological Thought.* Cambridge: Cambridge University Press.

Visweswaran, Kamala
1997   Histories of Feminist Ethnography. *Annual Review of Anthropology* 26:591–621.

Voss, Barbara
2000   Feminism, Queer Theories, and the Archaeological Study of Past Sexualities. *World Archaeology* 32(2):180–92.

Wadley, Lynn
1997   *Our Gendered Past.* Johannesburg: Witwatersrand University Press.
1998   The Invisible Meat Providers: Women in the Stone Age of South Africa. In *Gender in African Prehistory.* Susan Kent, ed. Pp. 69–82. Walnut Creek, CA: AltaMira Press.

Walde, Dale, and Noreen Willows, eds.
1991   *The Archaeology of Gender.* Proceedings of the 22nd Annual Chacmool Conference. Calgary: Department of Archaeology, University of Calgary.

Warren, Carol A. B.
1988   *Gender Issues in Field Research.* Beverly Hills, CA: Sage.
Watson, Patty Jo, and Mary C. Kennedy
1991   The Development of Horticulture in the Eastern Woodlands of North America: Women's Roles. In *Engendering Archaeology.* Joan M. Gero and Margaret W. Conkey, eds. Pp. 255–75. Oxford: Blackwell.
Webley, Lita
1990   The Use of Stone Scrapers by Semi-Sedentary Pastoralist Groups in Namaqualand, South Africa. *South African Archaeological Bulletin* 45:28–32.
1997   Wives and Sisters: Changing Gender Relations among Khoi Pastoralists in Namaqualand. In *Our Gendered Past: Archaeological Studies of Gender in Southern Africa.* Lyn Wadley, ed. Pp. 167–99. Johannesburg: Witwatersrand University Press.
2005   Hideworking among Descendants of Khoekhoen Pastoralist in the Northern Cape, South Africa. In *Gender and Hide Production.* Lisa Frink and Kathryn Weedman, eds. Pp. 153–74. Walnut Creek, CA: AltaMira Press.
Weedman, Kathryn
2004   Are Wilma Flintstone and Betty Rubble Archetypes for Stone Age Women? An Ethnoarchaeological Model of Women Stone-Tool Makers from Ethiopia. Paper presented at the meeting of the Society of American Archaeology, Montreal, April.
2005   Gender and Stone-Tools: An Ethnographic Study of the Konso and Gamo Hideworkers of Southern Ethiopia. In *Gender and Hide Production.* Lisa Frink and Kathryn Weedman, eds. Pp. 175–96. Walnut Creek, CA: AltaMira Press.
Welbourn, Alice
1984   Endo Ceramics and Power Strategies. In *Ideology, Power and Prehistory.* D. Miller and C. Tilley, eds. Pp. 17–24. Cambridge: Cambridge University Press.
Willey, Gordon R.
1953   Archaeological Theories and Interpretation: New World. In *Anthropology Today: Selections.* Sol Tax, ed. Pp. 170–94. Chicago: University of Chicago Press.
Wolf, Diane L.
1996   *Feminist Dilemmas in Fieldwork.* Boulder, CO: Westview.
Wright, Rita P.
1996   *Gender and Archaeology.* Philadelphia: University of Pennsylvania Press.
Wylie, Alison
2000   Questions of Evidence, Legitimacy, and the (Dis)Unity of Science. *American Antiquity* 65:227–37.
Yellen, John
1976   Settlement Patters of the !Kung: An Archaeological Perspective. In *Kalahari Hunter-Gatherers: Studies of the !Kung San and Their Neighbors.* Richard B. Lee and Irvin DeVore, eds. Pp. 47–72. Cambridge, Mass.: Harvard University Press.
1977   *Archaeological Approaches to the Present.* New York: Academic Press.

Feminist Gender Research in Classical Archaeology

9

SUZANNE M. SPENCER-WOOD

T
HIS CHAPTER SURVEYS THE DEVELOPMENT of different feminist approaches to gender research in classical archaeology. However, most gender research in classical archaeology does not specify its theoretical approach, and some gender research is not feminist. To be feminist, gender research must use feminist concepts or theory either implicitly or explicitly. Since most gender research in classical archaeology does not specify its theoretical approach, I have analyzed the feminist theoretical approaches implicit in the gender research.

Although this survey covers a number of major themes in the development of feminist classical archaeology, it is far from comprehensive. An initial problem I had in conducting this review is the definition of classical archaeology since some artifact analyses are considered archaeology, while others are considered art history. In contrast to historical archaeology, the field of classics is separated into textual analyses, classical archaeology, and art history. A number of studies use textual analysis to provide cultural context for interpretations of material culture. Some of these studies, although they are called art history, are included here because they are similar to artifactual studies in archaeology.

This chapter first outlines the early development of feminist classical archaeology within its multiple contexts. The rest of the chapter is organized according to the development of feminist theory in a process I call peeling the androcentric onion. Androcentrism can be metaphorically understood as an onion with multiple layers of reinforcing biases, from the surface of supposedly ungendered discourse through binary gender stereotypes to deeper biases in methods, paradigms, concepts, and language (Spencer-Wood 1995).

The development of feminist classical archaeology generally followed the development of feminist theory in peeling the androcentric onion. First, feminist critique of ungendered discourse revealed how women were made invisible. Then the first wave of feminist theory made historic women visible and researched the importance of women's public and domestic roles (Spencer-Wood 1995). Starting in the 1970s, the second wave of feminist theory analyzed patriarchy and as a result often just added women explicitly to stereotypic binary constructions of the past that emphasized gender difference (Bunch 1987:140). The third wave of feminist theory, starting in the 1990s, critiqued binary constructions of classical gender systems, differentiated gender ideology from practice, and analyzed the diversity of both in relationship to the complex intersections between gender, class, race, and ethnicity in classical cultures (Lorber 2001; Spencer-Wood 1995).

The Development of Feminist Classical Archaeology

Although classical archaeology is similar to prehistoric and historical archaeology in remaining largely ungendered, feminism has been developing within classics since the turn of the twentieth century. Feminist classical textual analysis developed much earlier than feminist classical archaeology. The influence of first-wave feminism in reconstructions of Roman and Greek culture from texts can be seen as early as 1909, when Frank Abbott highlighted women's increasing public roles in Roman society as a first step to telling the story of the "emancipation" of Roman women (Abbott 1909:41). Books on women in antiquity increased in the 1960s, some of which drew on the early second-wave feminist tome *The Second Sex* by Simone de Beauvoir (e.g., Cartledge 1993:64).

Gender research in classical archaeology/art history developed earlier than gender research in historical archaeology, possibly because classical archaeology is an older field. Perhaps the earliest gender research in classical archaeology was Helen Clees's (1920) book *A Study of Women in Attic Inscriptions*. As one of the first generation of female classical archaeologists, Clees undertook remedial research to make women visible in a field where the focus on men had made women largely invisible.

Since the 1960s, feminist classical archaeology developed as a result of the influences of women's studies, feminist theory, and feminist anthropology and prehistoric archaeology. Of the three stages of feminist research outlined by Wylie (1991b:31–32), feminist classical archaeology has included a few first-stage critiques of androcentrism (e.g., Brown 1993, 1997; Pomeroy 1975; Richlin 1992:xii). Pomeroy (1975) made a first-wave feminist analysis of women's public and private lives primarily from classical texts but also from some material culture. In the 1980s, first-wave feminist critiques and theory led to some further analyses of women's public roles from material culture and texts (e.g., Havelock

1982; Kampen 1982, 1991). Starting in the 1970s, the second wave of feminism led to an increase in analyses of classical texts to reveal information on women's domestic lives that was still being ignored. Second-wave feminist analyses of the material evidence of women's domestic roles still predominate (e.g., Clarke 1998; Keuls 1983; Walker 1983; Williams 1983). However, women are often only added to preceding androcentric reconstructions of classical cultures (Lyons, critiqued by Koloski-Ostrow 1997:2).

Most feminist classical archaeology is in Wylie's second stage of remedial research to recover women's lives that have been overlooked by men's reconstructions of the past (Brown 1993:257–58). Only since the mid-1980s has feminist theory been used to reconceptualize the treatment of classical Greco-Roman gender systems in classical archaeology (e.g., Koloski-Ostrow and Lyons 1997; Richlin 1992:xiii). In the 1990s, a number of joint volumes by classicists, archaeologists, and art historians have conducted more complex analyses of women as social actors from synthetic analyses of material culture and documents (e.g., Archer et al. 1994; Fantham et al. 1994; Reeder 1995). Postmodern feminist classical archaeology has begun to develop and critique the limits of second-wave feminist approaches (e.g., Goldberg 1999). Postmodern feminist theory underlies the increase in analyses of sexuality and masculinity (e.g., Richlin 1992). In general, analyses of material culture in cultural context have increased (Brown 1993:258). However, textual analysis dominates the field of feminist classics as it does the field as a whole (e.g., Cameron and Kurht 1993; duBois 1988; Hallett and Skinner 1997; McClure 2002; Pomeroy 1975).

Although the study of women in antiquity has become a subfield of classics since the 1970s, it is still not widely accepted as legitimate (Richlin 1992:xiii). Classical archaeology has been slow to adopt feminist frameworks for analyzing the importance of material culture in reinforcing the construction and maintenance of gender as a fundamental social institution. Classics as a field remains male dominated, resulting in refusals to accept symposia on feminist classical archaeology at the American Institute for Archaeology meetings as recently as 1996. An increasing interest in gender research in classical archaeology has recently developed in conjunction with the acceptance of postmodern multicultural and anticolonialist perspectives that are related to postmodern feminist theoretical approaches and postprocessualism (Brown 1997:13).

Feminist Critiques of Male Biases in Supposedly Ungendered Research

Feminist classicists have pointed out how women were excluded from ungendered ancient Greek history (Pomeroy 1975), art history (Lyons and Koloski-Ostrow

1997), and classical archaeology (e.g., Brown 1993:257; Richlin 1992:xiii). Major works in the classics have not included index entries for women. Classical archaeology draws on the traditional supposedly ungendered descriptions of cultures as monolithic wholes both in archaeology and in history.

Ungendered discourse in classics has been similar to historical archaeology in addressing ethnic and class differences before gender, which is at least as foundational to culture and society (e.g., Brown 1993:257). The traditional exclusion of women in classics led to absurd reconstructions of only two unenfranchised classes in ancient Greece: resident aliens and slaves. The fact that women could not vote was ignored because women as a whole were devalued and disappeared from the past as insignificant to men's history (Pomeroy 1975:xii). Men's accounts are usually presented as the ungendered normative experience, behavior, and viewpoint of the entire society. Classical texts were interpreted in the exclusively male academies since the Renaissance, editing out author "biases" in order to construct an idealized androcentric origin for European culture that valorized (male) public activities as the ungendered norm and devalued and subsumed women's domestic activities as subsidiary to the important public events of (men's) political history (Gutzwiller and Michelini 1991).

Classical archaeology initially developed largely to illustrate textual interpretations and often uncritically generalizes androcentric historic texts written by men as the universal meaning of material culture, including architecture and features as well as artifacts (Gutzwiller and Michelini 1991). The focus on public archaeological remains was given impetus by the focus of classical history on public events, politics, and wars (Pomeroy 1975). Thus, classical archaeology has often illustrated only a degendered men's history. Methodologically, women have been disappeared from the past by the classical archaeological practice of projecting the androcentric view in modern and classical cultures that men's public history is important while women's domestic activities are not (Gazda 1991).

Feminists have critiqued the focus of ungendered classical archaeology on large-scale public monuments and buildings as the only significant cultural remains. Although not stated in ungendered archaeology, textual sources identified public constructions and space exclusively with men. Thus, the supposedly ungendered focus of archaeology on public monuments and buildings was actually an androcentric focus on men's public accomplishments (e.g., Alcock 2002). The strength of the tradition of ungendered language is attested to by Ault and Nevett's (1999) ungendered feminist critique of the favoring of classical Greek public sites and the neglect of household archaeology. Houses were often ignored because of their devaluation as women's domestic domain. When houses were analyzed, it often was in terms of the status of the male head of household.

Feminist Critiques of Androcentric Methods in Classical Archaeology

The ability of feminists to engender classical archaeology has been hampered by the traditional focus of the field on formal stylistic classification and chronology, as critiqued by Brown (1993:257–58). The ungendered analysis of classical men's monuments and buildings has often focused on formal stylistic attributes used for chronological dating of structures to reconstruct the temporal development of the male-public parts of cities (e.g., Alcock 2002). Classical archaeologists and art historians traditionally classified pots in large historically meaningless Eurocentric etic categories such as "geometrical" and "nongeometrical" for classical Greece (e.g., Boardman 1998).

In art history, individual artifacts, such as statues of gendered human forms and pots with gendered paintings, were traditionally analyzed in a modern aesthetic framework that imposed Western interpretations and meanings on the artifacts (Broude and Garrard 1982:14; Richlin 1992:xii). The Eurocentric definition of some types of art and images as inherently "good" art and superior to other "bad" art has inhibited reflexive scholarly criticism (Lyons and Koloski-Ostrow 1997:12). Traditionally, no attempt was made to understand the meaning of artifacts from their archaeological context (Brown 1993:257–58). For instance, major classical art historians identified different Greek vase painters on the basis of variation in styles and quality of execution of the paintings, with no analysis of historical context or content (e.g., Boardman 1998, critique of approach by Robertson 1992:3).

Feminist Critiques of Androcentric Methods of Constructing Households

House sites in classical Greece and Rome have traditionally been analyzed mainly in terms of ungendered issues of architectural chronology and construction sequences on individual sites (critiqued by Nevett 1999:26). More recently, analyses of Roman houses have analyzed how they expressed the social status of the male head of household who legally owned the house site and all its occupants (Clarke 1991; Gazda 1991; Wallace-Hadrill 1994). The focus on men's display of public power through their houses emerges from ungendered language with the use of male pronouns, such as: "The design of individual rooms and the overall organization of a building, taken together, emphasized the power of its owner and provided a prestigious background against which he played his assigned social role" (Thébert 1987:392–93). In ungendered language, shared androcentric assumptions are revealed in male pronouns and ungendered terms that represent males, as when specialized household rooms were considered to reflect "the aristocrat's desire to present himself in an impressive setting" (Gazda 1991:14). One book chapter was titled "Power, Architecture, and Décor: How the Late Roman Aristocrat Appeared to His Guests" (Ellis 1991).

The Roman house was androcentrically viewed both as the center of the ungendered but assumed male owner's public civic and political activity and as "the private living quarters of the owner" (Gazda 1991:7; see also Dwyer 1991:26–29, 34). Methodologically, women, children, and slaves often have been subsumed in the term "familia," or "family," in ungendered analyses of households focusing on wealth differences attributed to the male head of household (e.g., Wallace-Hadrill 1994:91–118, 143–75). Families, especially wives and children, have traditionally been described in their relationships to the male head of household (e.g. Gazda 1991:4–5).

Classical texts that name houses for the male head of household have been reified through the archaeological practice of naming domestic sites for the surname of the male head of household and frequently providing information only about his public uses of household spaces (e.g., Dwyer 1991; Ellis 1991; Gazda 1991). Naming house sites for the male head of household subsumes and disappears the other members of the household, including women, children, and slaves. Naming sites for men reifies married women's ideal seclusion in the household under their husband's authority in both classical Greece and Rome. Women's subordinate status and lack of civil rights and formal education resulted in few records by or about women, contributing to the focus on men's more frequently documented behaviors (Nevett 1999:15).

Household spaces have usually been archaeologically interpreted according to the structuralist gender dichotomy as exclusively *either* public *or* private in ungendered discourse or *either* male-public *or* female-private in explicitly gendered accounts. Curiously, the analysis of households in classical archaeology is most often not explicitly gendered, even sometimes by feminists (cf. Meadows 1999; Nevett 1999). Most analyses of household spaces and artifacts use only the code words of "domestic" and "public" without mentioning men or women or their social relationships encoded in domestic spaces, features such as floor mosaics and painted designs on pots (e.g., Allison 1999; Ault and Nevett 1999; Gazda 1991).

Feminist Critiques of Androcentric Gender Research in Classical Archaeology

Since the Renaissance, the patriarchal gender systems of classical Greece and Rome have been described on the basis of the few surviving men's texts that androcentrically address topics such as marriage and family. Until recent post-modern feminist critiques, these texts were considered to describe actual gender practices rather than ideals. Many histories of classical Greece and Rome present gender roles as static universal norms conforming to the dominant patriarchal gender ideology in each culture (e.g., Cowell 1980). The elite patriarchal gender ideologies of classical Greece and Rome accorded women no legal rights. As in the later femme covert laws of Europe, women belonged to their fathers until they married, and then they belonged to their husbands. However, feminist research has revealed that the treatment of Greek and Roman women by their husbands was often controlled by the wife's family through the practice of retaining rights to her dowry in the event of mistreatment and resulting divorce, which appears to have been easier than in eighteenth- to nineteenth-century Europe, at least for the middle class (cf. Goldberg 1998:109; Millett 1970; Pomeroy 1975).

In classical archaeology and contextual art history, sculpture, Greek vase paintings, and Greek household spaces have been unproblematically interpreted to conform to the gender ideals and myths in classical men's texts (e.g., Boardman 1974:205–34). While the depiction of idealistic myths in Greek vase paintings and Roman wall paintings are recognized, feminists have critiqued the unproblematic interpretation of other images as descriptive of actual gender practices rather than ideals. Goldberg (1999) has argued that Greek vase paintings of elite women performing domestic tasks should be interpreted as idealistic rather than necessarily realistic since slaves performed many domestic tasks for the elite.

The dominant classical patriarchal gender ideologies were developed by elite men and do not represent the full diversity of gender ideologies or actual gender practices even among elite women and much less among middle- and working-class women. All women had some public roles that were accepted in classical cultures but ignored in the patriarchal gender ideology that dichotomized the world into opposed mutually exclusive male-public versus female-private domains (Katz 1998). As with most ideologies, the Greek and Roman patriarchal gender ideologies were idealistic overgeneralizations that overlooked how actual gender practices and alternative gender ideologies deviated from dominant ideals (Spencer-Wood 1999:168–69).

The gender dichotomy was assumed in classical Greek Aristotelian dominant gender ideology, which strongly influenced Roman gender ideology and thus later European gender ideology through Roman conquest, and the fourteenth-century rediscovery of classical Roman texts and monuments as the foundation of Renaissance academies (Lerner 1993). Feminists have critiqued how Victorian men legitimated their patriarchal gender ideology by tracing it back to the Greeks, ignoring the diversity in gender ideologies and actual practices in ancient Greece (Spencer-Wood 1999:167–68). Yet recent androcentric classical archaeology continues to uncritically interpret material culture through the lens of modern patriarchal ideology that is projected as isomorphic with classical cultures (Keuls 1985).

For instance, in classical archaeology, Stewart (1990:78) unreflexively analyzed classical nude sculptures of Aphrodite only in terms of a stereotypic binary male response. Thus, he described a "high" response in analyzing one sculpture of Aphrodite covering her pubis as modest, beautiful, and ladylike. Stewart showed a typical Victorian sensibility in his asexual response to the sculpture identified as a respectable woman. At the other extreme, Stewart described a "low" male response to less modest Aphrodite sculptures, calling them "trivially coquettish," "overripe," and "whores" (Brown 1993:257–58). Stewart androcentrically projects modern binary heterosexual stereotypes of the lady versus the whore in his voyeuristic descriptions of the Aphrodite sculptures and does not recognize that he is ethnocentrically responding to them outside of their cultural context.

Feminist Critiques of Androcentrism in the Theoretical Paradigms

The theoretical paradigm of structuralism constructs cultures in supposedly deep inherent binary structures based on the gender dichotomy. Binary gender stereotypes have been used to dichotomize classical sites and household spaces as exclusively *either* male-public *or* female-private (Lyons and Koloski-Ostrow 1997:3). Actual gender practices have been constructed to conform to the dominant classical patriarchal gender ideologies. Stewart (1990) further projected onto classical Greek sculptures of the goddess Aphrodite the Victorian binary categorizations of women, and of men's responses to women.

Goldberg (1998:109) has critiqued the construction of classical cultures in ungendered dichotomies that are implicitly gendered. Further, she analyzed how the Western gender dichotomy led to the assumption that the supposedly ungendered public sphere was exclusively male in classical archaeology. Classical archaeology uses male-defined ungendered paradigms, viewpoints, categories of analysis, theories, and cultural language, all of which exclude women's experiences and views. With this framework identifying men as exclusively public, women's contributions to public life have been ignored, and men's contributions to domestic life have been ignored (Spencer-Wood 1999). The result has been an androcentric emphasis on the importance of men's houses for their public social and civic roles as well as an emphasis on the ways that men performed public interactions in their houses (Dwyer 1991:34).

Introduction to Feminist Theories Used in Gender Research in Classical Archaeology

Although a variety of feminist theoretical approaches have been simultaneously and usually implicitly used in classical archaeology, they will be discussed in the chronological order of the development of feminist theory. The historical development of feminist theory is simplified into three "waves," following normative practice despite the recognition that this tremendously oversimplifies the complex development of feminist theory (Nelson 2002).

Although feminists define the waves of feminist theory in a variety of ways, this chapter will use the broadest framework, one in which liberal egalitarian feminist theory is recognized to have developed out of the fifteenth-century feminist arguments for women's intellectual and educational equality, followed by movements for women's suffrage, equal pay, and other equal rights (Lerner 1993). Second-wave feminist theory developed out of nineteenth-century cultural feminism that valorized women's domesticity while analyzing the oppression of women in patriarchy (Donovan 2001:47–79). The second wave is usually identified with Betty Friedan's *Feminine Mystique* (1963), although it actually has precedents from the mid-nineteenth century. The third wave of feminist theory started with critiques of the second wave in the 1980s (Lorber 2001).

First-Wave Feminist Egalitarian Liberal Theory

Liberal egalitarian feminist theory critiques the patriarchal gender ideology that devalues women and conducts research demonstrating that women held diverse important roles in both 1) the public sphere and 2) the domestic sphere. Liberal feminist theory and research demonstrates that gender stereotypes were not universally practiced through these two different kinds of research paradigms concerning the ways that women are and historically have been social agents as much as men (Donovan 2001:17–79).

Research on the Importance of Women's Public Roles

Some feminist classical archaeologists have taken a first-wave liberal egalitarian theoretical approach to critique the universal identification of all public roles and spaces as inherently masculine with evidence that classical women also had public activities, roles, and spaces, some of which were as important as men's public activities, roles, and spaces. In many cases, the invisibility of women's public actions and roles is due to the classification of women's public roles as domestic, such as women's public marketing of domestic products or their dismissal as insignificant exceptions to the norm of domestic women (e.g., Cowell 1980:111, critiqued in Wallace-Hadrill 1994:138). The liberal egalitarian paradigm is important in showing that women's public activities and roles were not occasional and cannot be dismissed as exceptions even if they deviated from dominant gender norms or ideals. Although this paradigm does not challenge the higher status accorded the public sphere compared to the domestic sphere, it does importantly undermine the legitimation of men's dominance in the public sphere as universal, natural, and biological (Spencer-Wood 1995).

In contrast to the few elite classical Greek men's texts that have been interpreted to indicate the universal seclusion of women in their separate domestic quarters, feminist classicists and archaeologists have found both documentary and archaeological evidence that women of all classes held a variety of public roles. Women were responsible primarily for funeral rituals and acted as public mourners. Funerary vase paintings depict women as public mourners (e.g., Havelock 1982). Citizen's wives and daughters had primary roles in a number of major state religious festivals. For instance, maidens bearing a variety of ritual objects headed the public sacrificial procession in honor of the birthday of Athena, the city's tutelary deity. Girls also washed the statue of Athena and wove her robe, which is depicted on part of the Parthenon frieze. Many vase paintings illustrate the birth of Athena that women celebrated at the Panathenaea festival. Women had primary roles in rituals for goddesses who protected Athenian grain crops, Kore and Demeter. The largest public festival for Demeter, the Thesmophoria, was exclusively celebrated by citizens' wives over three days in late October. Women also celebrated the public Haloa festival in honor of Demeter and Dionysus in January and a threshing festival called Skira in July. Women's cycle of religious festivals celebrated their agricultural processing roles and were important in ritually ensuring the success of men's agricultural fieldwork. Some vase paintings illustrate women celebrating a ritual dance to Dionysus, performing a ritual at the altar to a god or goddess, and the third day of the Anthesteria festival (Buxton 1998:333–35; Katz 1998:101–8).

Archaeological reconstruction of roads and public buildings was used by Goldberg (1999) in conjunction with documentary records to map the path of women's ritual processions from shrines to goddesses. She was able to reconstruct the angle of vision and perspective that the women in the procession would have had in viewing public buildings and the landscape as they passed through it. Goldberg noted the cemeteries that the women's procession would pass. Women's ritual procession through the Athenian landscape sheds new light on the reasons for children's cemeteries to be located on roads leading to women's cult shrines, as noted by Houby-Nielsen (2000:161).

Feminists have also found neglected texts that discuss powerful public women, including queens, priestesses, a magistrate, and female warriors and leaders of armies in the Hellenistic period (Cantarella 1987:52–61; Pomeroy 1975:124). Texts note women's public importance as priestesses to goddesses and as oracles for two leading male gods, Zeus at Dodona, and the most important classical oracular shrine to Apollo at Delphi. Priestess was the only public office open to women, and women were priestesses for more than forty major cults in classical Athens. Further, the priestess of Athena Polias, Athens' patron deity, officiated at the most important of the state festivals and at times had the power to influence political decisions, as did the female oracles (Blundell 1995:134–35, 160–65). These texts identify women with public monuments and temples, such as the Parthenon and the large complex on Mount Olympus, where men went to get political predictions from the female oracle.

Classical Greek myths about Amazons defeating men could be empowering for Greek women, although vase paintings more often show men defeating Amazons. Herodotus's accounts of Amazons have been supported by weapons found in large numbers of female graves excavated in the Caucasus and Scythia. Among the Sauromatians in the Caucasus, 20 percent of the burials were of female warriors with weapons and battle injuries, and forty female warrior graves have been found in Scythia. A couple of female graves also include tall headdresses, portable altars, mirrors, and other items that suggest they were priestesses (Davis-Kimball 1997; Rolle 1989:88–89).

The importance of the Amazons as well as Athena for women's empowerment is suggested by their use to decorate a knee guard used in working wool. A painting on one side of the knee guard depicts Amazons preparing for battle by taking up shields and weapons, suggesting an analogy with preparing for wool working by donning the knee guard as shield. The other side depicts women working wool, interpreted as embodiments of the goddess Athena Ergane, the worker (Katz 1998:101). The analogy between Amazons at war and women working wool indicates that both may have been viewed as heroic public roles by the classical Greeks.

Although there was no public education for Athenian girls as there was for boys (Adkins and Adkins 1997:218, 153–55), documents and vase paintings show that many elite women did learn to read and write and keep household accounts (Katz 1998:130). Further, a number of Greek women were unusual in gaining an academic education and becoming renowned Greek poets and philosophers. Four vases and two coins from the island of Lesbos have been found depicting the famous poet Sappho by name, although she is not depicted reading her poetry (Snyder 1997). Female philosophers were accepted by men of the

Socratic school, which held that women could be intellectual equals of men, in support of the legendary female scholar and hetaera Aspasia (Keuls 1985:198–99). Some female philosophers practiced their egalitarian beliefs in relationships with male egalitarian philosophers or with women. In contrast to misogynist philosophers such as Aristotle, the Cynics and Pythagoreans took the revolutionary position that women and men had the same virtues so that women had the capacity to participate in public governance of society (Cantarella 1987:63–76, 91–93). In addition, Pythagorus founded and operated his famous school with his wife and accepted female as well as male students.

According to Katz's calculations, the majority of classical Greek citizen's wives engaged in small businesses, whether as wool workers, tavern keepers, or petty traders of foodstuffs such as bread or items such as garlands and perfumes. One vase painting depicts a woman selling perfume to a slave who then gives it to her mistress. Women's business transactions were restricted by law to small amounts no more than three times the daily wage of skilled workmen. As a result, women were petty traders of perfume, while men owned large perfume businesses (Katz 1998:117–18). Inscriptions on funerary monuments have identified a few Greek women doctors (Kampen 1982:70). Some court documents record that women worked the agricultural fields when necessary, such as in times of war. Some documents and vase paintings show that women were nurses and midwives (Nevett 1999:16).

Some vase paintings show women drawing water at public fountains. These women have problematically been identified as courtesans rather than citizens' wives on the basis of a few elite men's texts stating that (elite) women were secluded in houses and the typical hetaera names given the women on one vase, such as "yielding," "hither," and "little snub-nose" (Williams 1983:103–5). However, Keuls (1985:235–40) found literature recording complaints by citizens' wives about problems with unsavory characters encountered when drawing water in fountain houses. She also notes that foreign wives, called *metics*, were paid to go to the public fountains to draw water.

The only potentially lucrative area of trade largely under classical Greek women's control was the sex trade. Courtesans, called hetaerae, were learned female companions hired by men for symposia discussions. Courtesans could charge one hundred times the daily wage of a skilled workman. *Pornai*, or ordinary prostitutes, were mostly slaves who were paid about the same amount as a skilled workman and worked in brothels most often run by a man but also some women. Vase paintings illustrate both graphic sex scenes of naked prostitutes and men and other scenes of dressed women interpreted as hetaerae at men's parties called symposia, relaxing, and receiving men (Katz 1998:117–19; Sutton 1992; Williams 1983).

Roman archaeology does not provide the amount of vase painting of ordinary life that is available for classical Greece. Feminist Roman archaeologists have found carvings and documents showing that Roman women held a variety of public occupations. Documents record some women taking public political action to get sumptuary legislation passed and then to establish a women's court concerned with questions of dress and women's use of carriages. Some middle-class women operated businesses, including a large brick business producing bricks marked with the name of the woman owner and her daughter. Tomb inscriptions are dedicated to some famous late Roman female singers, composers, mimes, and flute players. Other inscriptions mention that some Roman women were in charge of large estates or were weavers, costumers, seamstresses, washwomen, fishmongers, and barmaids. The most frequent inscriptions involved a variety of trades connected with making and repairing clothing (Abbott 1909:45–51, 96–99).

Classical Roman relief carvings outside stores and on temples and funerary monuments have been found showing women in public roles, including doctors, obstetricians, midwives, nurses, hairdressers, artisans, textile producers, metalworkers, and sellers of produce in public markets. While saleswomen and salesmen appear to have the same status because of similarity in clothing and size, female doctors are not depicted as gods as are male doctors, and female textile producers and artisans are usually depicted as mythological rather than real. Roman women's work is more fully documented in texts and inscriptions than in art, which expressed the emphasis on women's domestic roles in the dominant ideology rather than women's diverse public roles in actual practice (Kampen 1982:70–74, 64–68).

Research on the Importance of Women's Domestic Roles

In this paradigm, feminists seek evidence of the importance of women's social agency in domestic roles to correct androcentric devaluations of women's domestic work. Feminists seek and find evidence that women's domestic roles in many cases either are as important as men's public roles or are significant to men's public roles or the culture in general. This paradigm derives from cultural feminist theory valorizing women's domestic roles (Donovan 2001:47–78).

Both documentary data and archaeological data indicate the importance of women's domestic production to classical cultures. Goldberg (1998:109) has pointed to the importance of the house as the primary locus of all production in the agriculturally based classical cultures. One classical Greek man's text portrayed marriage as a partnership and pointed out that a wife who was a prudent household manager could contribute more than half the income of a household of the wealthiest class (Pomeroy 1998:185).

Many of classical Greek women's household agricultural products were essential to the classical Greek economy, including production of textiles, bread and other foodstuffs, and processing vegetables, all of which some women sold in public markets. A female figurine making bread has been found (Katz 1998:133). The high value placed on women's textiles is evident in vase paintings of women spinning, weaving, and wearing clothes with woven designs, as well as the Parthenon frieze depicting preparation of a garment for the statue of Athena by women and men. Women's fine cloth was a gift to the gods (Blundell 1995:60–61; Nevett 1999:14).

In contrast to the exclusive identification of men with public roles in much classical archaeology, some texts and material culture show men performing domestic tasks in public. The importance of women's textile production is emphasized by a carving on the Parthenon frieze showing the folding of cloth by a bearded man and a child. Younger (1997) identified the child as a boy because of his exposed buttocks, which was not permitted for respectable girls, although other classicists have argued that it is a girl because textiles were women's work. However, men could commercialize women's domestic tasks into public businesses. By the end of the fifth century, a number of men were famous as bakers who sold their products in specialized Athenian bread markets (Katz 1998:133–35; Keuls 1985).

In Roman culture, women's household textile production was also important to the culture as a whole. Bread production shifted from women in the home to commercial businesses controlled by men in later Roman times (Cowell 1980:86) In Roman houses in Pompeii, Allison (1999:60–61) argued that the forecourts, which had previously been considered exclusively male public spaces, actually housed cupboards holding (women's) domestic utensils.

Research on Mothering and Child Rearing

Reconstructions of lifeways in classical cultures based on historic texts usually stress marriage and the family. In patriarchal classical Greece and Rome, women who bore sons were praised, while more than one daughter was not valued. Husbands had the power of life and death over family members, and female infanticide or sale was not uncommon (Cowell 1980:35). Babies in classical Greek vase paintings are almost invariably depicted naked and male in scenes showing slaves handing the baby to his elite mother, whose high status was depicted in having provided a male child (Keuls 1985:110–13). Recent gender research on classical artifacts has addressed previously neglected topics of mothering and childhood.

Classical Greek literary texts portray mothers' frequent deaths in childbirth as analogous to the heroic death of men in battle. Tomb carvings portray these mothers holding, but not suckling, naked male babies (Keuls 1985:138–41). Material representations of mothers and others nursing infants have been analyzed and problematized by Bonfante (1997). She found that representations of mothers nursing were rare in the formal art of both Greek and Roman civilization. Classical texts revealed that nursing was considered animalistic, primitive, and therefore uncivilized. Therefore, formal Greek and Roman art often represented animals nursing people, including the iconic statue of the twins who founded Rome nursing from a she-wolf. Neither the Greek gods nor elite or respectable bourgeois Greek or Roman women suckled their infants but instead had wet nurses. Terra-cotta figurines of wet nurses portray them as big breasted, old, and ugly, in contrast to statues and vase paintings of elite women as small breasted and pretty. Classical Greek art valorizes the young boyish-looking female body in parallel with its focus on boys. Greek documents record the practice of mothers binding their daughters' breasts to conform to the slender ideal. Elite women from the classical cultures through the Renaissance and the nineteenth century sought to preserve their youthful figures by not breast-feeding. Although formal Roman art generally copied Greek formal art, including the rarity of depictions of nursing women, Bonfante found more portrayals of nursing mothers in classical Italy because of the longevity of a goddess cult.

Conceptions of childhood are suggested by a number of classical Greek artifacts that have been interpreted as toys, including miniature four-wheeled platforms carrying horses, a wheeled mule with rider and amphorae, and a miniature beehive, granary, or pot with holes at the pointed end for use as a pendant (Williams 2000). Reilly's (1997) research has critiqued the Western ethnocentric interpretation of miniature female images carved on Athenian girls' gravestone reliefs as dolls. She differentiates terra-cotta dolls that have little breast development and jointed arms and legs from the sexually adult miniature female images that usually do not have arms or lower legs. Reilly concludes that the miniature adult female torsos presented to or held by girl children in grave bas-reliefs were votive figures representing the girl's participation in a socioreligious custom designed to form her character and body into proper and healthy femininity. The dedication of such votive figures became very popular in mid-fifth-century B.C. healing cults and made a statement that the girl buried in the grave was being brought up to become a proper feminine woman, in contrast to the popular Greek myth that girls who did not achieve menarche would become mad, refuse to

marry, and attempt suicide. Houby-Nielson (2000) found that children's cemeteries in classical Athens were located close to city gates and roads that led to
female cult shrines.

Second-Wave Feminist Theoretical Projections
of Patriarchal Gender Ideology

The second wave of feminist theory, starting in the 1970s, involved projecting
modern or historically dominant patriarchal gender ideology onto other cultures
to interpret women's roles as universally domestic and subordinate to men's universally public roles (e.g., Ortner 1974; Rosaldo 1974; Rosaldo and Lamphere
1974). Rosaldo (1980) reflexively critiqued how she and others projected Victorian gender ideology to construct gender systems in other cultures as simplistic
asymmetrical dichotomies.

Second-wave feminist gender research uncritically accepts classical men's
accounts of a binary gender system as actual historic practice and reads the gender
dichotomy into archaeological data. Second-wave feminist classical archaeologists
have divided house spaces into exclusively *either* women's spaces *or* men's spaces
(e.g., Fantham et al. 1994, critiqued by Goldberg 1999; Walker 1983).

On the basis of a number of documents, women were associated with rooms
with hearths, storerooms with amphorae and other large jars, and workrooms
with loom weights used in weaving cloth. Women's sleeping quarters are not
often identified because one account specified that they were on the second story
and thus are seldom preserved (Walker 1983:84, 91). Vase paintings of well-
dressed women performing domestic chores such as spinning, weaving, relaxing,
taking nude male babies from servants, and eating alone behind closed doors have
been interpreted as depicting the women's quarters (Keuls 1983:215).

The *andron*, where men met for parties, called symposia, with hetaerae, has
been ideally identified as the largest, most elaborately decorated room with a
mosaic floor, close access to the public street, and an off-center door to accom-
modate masonry benches along two walls to support the wooden couches where
men traditionally reclined for their symposia (Walker 1983:91). In some cases,
the *andron* and an adjacent room or courtyard with paved or mosaic floor have
been identified as the men's quarters (Keuls 1985:210–15; Walker 1983:84).
Vase paintings of men holding wine cups reclining on couches with well-dressed
women who sometimes play flutes or other instruments have been interpreted as
depictions of symposia in the *andron* (Keuls 1985:212–13).

Third-Wave Postmodern Feminist Theoretical Approaches to Gender Research

Postmodern feminist theory critiques the second-wave structuralist approach of uncritically projecting elite Western patriarchal gender dichotomies as the universal reality of actual gender practices (e.g., Amos and Parmer 1984; Mohanty 1988; Spelman 1988). In postmodern feminist theory, gender ideologies are distinguished from the diversity of actual practices (Spencer-Wood 1992, 1991:243–44; 1994:182; 1999:168–69, 173). Postmodern multicultural feminism, queer theory, and masculinity theory destabilize the heterosexist gender dichotomy by theorizing gender and sexuality as fluid multiple identities, practices, and performances at the intersections of gender, class, race, ethnicity, religion, and other social variables (Butler 1990; Hill 1990; Lorber 2001:203; Nicholson 1990).

Diversity in Classical Gender Ideologies

In contrast to the second-wave analysis only of the elite patriarchal gender ideology, some feminist classicists and classical archaeologists have researched the diversity in the classical gender ideologies of men and indications of alternative gender ideologies materialized by some women. Feminists have critiqued the modern interpretation of Aristotle's misogynist Stoic school as the dominant gender ideology. The dominance of this ideology of gender dichotomy was constructed by Victorian men to legitimate their separate spheres of gender ideology (Spencer-Wood 1999:167–68). Feminist research has recovered a number of neglected philosophical schools with more egalitarian gender ideology, including the Socratic school, which held that women could be the intellectual equals of men, and the Cynic and Pythagorean schools, which held that women were capable of governing society because they had the same virtues as men. In contrast, Aristotelian philosophy argued that women's virtues were domestic and physical, while men's virtues included rational thought and the ability to govern, justifying the legal exclusion of women from education and formal politics (Cantarella 1987:52–61). Aristotelian gender ideology was used to legitimate misogynist gender ideology and practices from classical Greek times through much of the nineteenth century in Western cultures.

There is some documentary and archaeological evidence of Greek women's alternative gender ideologies that valorized women and their roles. Women's diverse cultic shrines and their already mentioned control of some major religious festivals indicate that women controlled ideologies that were materialized to celebrate women's powers. Archaeological excavations on the island of Lesbos have found structures with caches of female figurines that have been interpreted as women's rituals and religion at a temple.

Postmodern Gendered Household Research in Contrast to Classical Patriarchal Gender Ideology

Classical household archaeology has progressed from second-wave structuralist constructions of household spaces to embody the dominant patriarchal gender ideology to postmodern analyses of variability in the gendered use of household spaces. Allison (1999) has critiqued the use of historic texts to interpret Roman household spaces and artifacts according to the mutually exclusive dichotomy of male-public versus female-domestic. She made a feminist ungendered critique of the assumption, based on a few men's texts, that all household courtyards were male-controlled spaces with chests for storing valuables and gold that belonged to Roman male household heads. Instead, Allison found textual references to the use of courtyard chests for storing domestic equipment. On the basis of texts by Vitruvius, recent research has recognized the oversimplification involved in previous analyses of Roman houses into public versus private family areas (Longfellow 2000:25). Both feminists and nonfeminists have concluded that rooms in Roman houses had multiple flexible uses and cannot be exclusively associated with *either* men *or* women (Allison 2004:156). Roman house rooms blended public and private functions, blurring the ideal boundary (Wallace-Hadrill 1994:9, 138).

Laurence (1994:127, 131) has agreed that there was no gendered dichotomy in the identification of elite Roman household spaces. However, instead of interpreting temporal change in gendered room use as fluidity and lack of mutually exclusive gender spaces, Laurence has analyzed a gender dichotomy in the use of spaces that was temporal rather than spatial. Laurence interprets household reception and dining spaces as used exclusively by men for public-political activities in the mornings and evenings. When the male head of house went out to transact business or politics in the forum and the public baths in the middle of the day, household spaces became exclusively female spaces used for domestic tasks.

Goldberg (1999) critiqued the inadequacy of the previous structuralist paradigm used to universally interpret classical Greek house spaces to conform to the patriarchal gender dichotomy (e.g., Vernant 1983). She critiqued Hoepfner and Schwander's (1994:22–50:fig. 33) uniform reconstruction of a block of classical Athenian houses with women's quarters on the second floor and a hearth in the main living room of every house despite the lack of archaeological evidence for the women's quarters or hearths in all the houses. Goldberg pointed out that one of the houses analyzed into separate spaces by Walker was identified as two houses by the excavator. Keuls (1985:210) states in her analyses of a house floor plan in Athens and two in Olynthus that these were among the few houses where the floor plan could be determined, raising issues concerning the breadth of applicability of her binary gendered analysis of these floor plans. One wonders whether the clarity of the floor plans analyzed by Keuls (1985) and by Walker (1983) are more the result of their reconstruction and representation rather than an accurate depiction of the actual arrangement of more ambiguous archaeological remains.

Goldberg critiqued the second-wave focus on a universalized cultural gender dichotomy and a lack of consideration of intermediary categories as well as individual social agency in manipulating cultural ideals. She critiqued the failure to consider how class, age, religion, and status of women would mediate and alter the applicability of elite patriarchal ideals (Versnel 1987). Further, she critiqued the projection of elite gender ideology to construct fixed gender boundaries rather than address how these boundaries were negotiated (e.g., Sanders 1990).

Goldberg (1999) analyzed the diversity and fluidity in the use of household spaces over time due to variables such as household size, composition, family life cycle, and variation in daily activities. She found documentary references showing the ease with which room functions were altered. Artifacts only occasionally indicated gendered room use, as in the case of loom weights used by women that were found concentrated in one room in only two Athenian houses (Jameson 1990:186, cited in Goldberg 1999:149). In contrast to the frequent identification of house courtyards as male public space (e.g., Keuls 1985; Walker 1983), loom weights associated with women have sometimes been found in courtyards. Nevett (1994) and Jameson (1990) have argued that women worked in house courtyards preparing raw grains and vegetables as well as weaving. Goldberg points out that the devaluation of domestic sites in classical archaeology led to poor records of the locations of finds within many excavated houses.

Goldberg (1999) discusses the evidence that excavated Athenian houses did not all have a room with the distinctive features identified as the *andron* for men's symposia, including a mosaic floor and stone benches for couches. One court document recorded that the *andron* in his house was moved upstairs when the bedroom was moved downstairs, demonstrating that it was not always a fixed space. Goldberg differentiates men's idealistic statements about gender-segregated spaces such as the *andron*, from its actual mixed-gender use, involving women who prepared the space and brought food and drink, as well as the hetaerae who lounged there with the men.

In contrast to the few elite men's documents claiming that women were secluded in a women's quarters or *gunaikonitis*, Goldberg (1999) notes that excavated house sites have not yielded any particular rooms with concentrations of artifacts identified with women, such as mirrors or jewelry. Further, Goldberg pointed out that some documents record changes in room functions, in one case involving the wife's bedroom being shifted from upstairs to downstairs to facilitate caring for a new baby. Clearly there were no fixed women's quarters in that house. Vase paintings of women engaged in a range of domestic activities need to be interpreted not as literally showing a fixed women's quarters but rather as economically depicting women's typical actions

Goldberg constructs classical Greek household spaces as fluid in their gendered uses and functions. Although for much of the day men may have been out of the house farming or politicking, leaving the house to women and their work, Goldberg points out that courtyards were used by women as well as men. Therefore, strange men and women entering the house at the courtyard would have seen women, who were supposed to be secluded in the women's quarters, according to a few classical men's texts. Further, strangers often had to walk across the courtyard to reach the *andron*. Goldberg postulates that strangers may have ignored women working in the courtyard or that the women may have veiled their faces.

Nevett (1999) also critiqued the fixed structuralist identification of domestic spaces in classical Greek houses as *either* male *or* female. Instead, she compared a large number of house structures in different time periods and regions to show change through time and a high degree of variability in house size that probably related to wealth and social position. Variability in house structure and room access suggested control of social interaction between family and outsiders and possibly between genders or kin. Further, Nevett analyzed locations of artifacts in context to discuss possible gendered uses of household space. She found evidence that women and men used most areas of houses to differing degrees or frequencies. Evidence was found of segregation of sets of rooms in some houses, which could be interpreted as the women's quarters in the inner house, segregated from the men's quarters with an entrance onto the street. However, the configurations of rooms could also be explained by the desire to segregate family from strangers and visitors. Nevett pointed to the importance of the outside door to the house separating the household from nonhousehold people and the interior door in some houses separating private family space from public space. Goldberg (1999:154–55) has further pointed out that the off-center location of some house doors meant that outsiders could not see directly into the courtyard, while in other houses the door location meant that they could see people in the courtyard, which might well include women who, according to the elite gender ideology, were not to be seen by strangers.

Feminist Material Analyses of Sexual Identities and Practices in Classical Cultures

Classical archaeologists may have been the first to analyze material evidence of sexuality, including diversity in sexualities, sexual identities, and sexual practices, due to depictions of both homosexual and heterosexual sex acts and sexuality on classical Greek and Roman artifacts, from vases and sculptures to floor mosaics and wall paintings. However, discourse on sexuality was long taboo in the classics, and many of the few studies conducted before the 1970s were written in Latin (Richlin 1992:xiii). Dover's (1978) seminal *Greek Homosexuality* drew on images as well as texts but retained a male gaze. Groundbreaking feminist research on sexuality and aggression in Roman humorous texts (Richlin 1983) was followed by a radical feminist theoretical approach to research on classical Greek images and texts concerned with male sexual domination (Keuls 1985). In the 1990s, a number of studies of sexuality in classical Greece and Rome combined structuralist approaches of Detienne, Vernant, and Foucault with a more contextual anthropological approach positing that sexual experiences in antiquity were radically different from those in modern Western cultures (e.g., Halperin 1990; Halperin et al. 1990; Winkler 1990).

One of the earliest feminist analyses, by Williams (1983:97–100), proposed to unreflectively learn about Greek women's lives from Athenian painted vase designs portraying women and men in a variety of activities. She identifies vases picturing nude hetaerae learning to dance from a dressed madam and another of hetaerae washing at a fountain. A more questionable identification is made of a dressed hetaerae receiving two men, the first of whom has a bag apparently of money that she interpreted as payment for sex either for himself or for his son behind him. However, it is not clear what the woman is being paid for, and the other side of the vase shows the man paying another woman interpreted as his wife (Keuls 1985:153–87). Williams importantly questions whether dressed women need always be interpreted as respectable women. She notes that hetaerae could be depicted on two vases showing clothed women relaxing and playing the harp, one including the child-sized god Eros. Williams points out that the pottery district in Athens was also renowned for its brothels, so the male potters had a lot of opportunity to observe and paint the lives of the often wealthy hetaerae. Finally, Williams argues that the vases were made by men from and for the male gaze. As she put it, "Athenian vase painting was essentially a man's view of a man's point of view" (Williams 1983:105). Williams's research interestingly shifts from an apparently unreflectively first-wave feminist reading of vase paintings as evidence of women's lives to raising postmodern issues about the identity of the vase painters and the clothed women they painted. Finally, she discusses the male view of the vase painters in creating scenes from a male viewpoint or gaze.

Feminist classical archaeologists may have been the earliest to explicitly apply postmodern feminist theory to analyze the diversity in material depictions of sexual activities, sexuality, and sexual identities due to complex intersections of gender and class as well as temporal changes. Richlin (1992) edited *Pornography and Representation in Greece and Rome* with an introduction combining postmodern theoretical approaches of textual analysis and representation with second-wave radical feminist theorizing about the connections between pornography, sexual identities, and the oppression of women through objectification and violence. Richlin (1992:xiv–xviii) also discusses the feminist pro-pornography backlash, which includes a liberal defense of individual rights, and the lesbian sadomasochists who argue against legislating sexuality. Richlin and other authors in her volume discuss the diversity in sexual acts, sexuality, and sexual identities depicted in classical Greek and Roman paintings and texts.

Richlin's analysis of the feminist debate over pornography resonates with the debate among classical archaeologists about whether different sexual images were pornographic for the Greeks and Romans. Chapters in Richlin range from those considering all sexual themes on classical Greek vases as pornography (Sutton 1992) to those considering pornography too strong a word for some Greek images (Shapiro 1992) to questioning the classification of Roman heterosexual images as pornography (Myerowitz 1992).

Sutton (1992:7–31) analyzes sexual themes painted on fourth- to sixth-century Greek vases from a woman's viewpoint. However, he ethnocentrically describes as "hard-core" pornography the 575–450 B.C. explicit images of misogynistic heterosexual sex acts, including forcing women to have various types of sex. Keuls (1985:187–97) discusses not only these vase paintings but also others that depicted hetaerae and prostitutes in affectionate poses with customers, which she ethnocentrically labels as the myths of the happy hooker, noble prostitute, or whore with the golden heart. Sutton ethnocentrically describes the later courting and wedding scenes as "soft-core" pornography, including both homosexual pederastic courting scenes with partially clothed or nude boys, popular from 550 to 480 B.C., and heterosexual courting scenes (480–450 B.C.) and wedding scenes (450–400 B.C.), both with fully clothed women. He points out that abuse is extremely rare in the pederastic homosexual courting scenes and are absent in the romantic heterosexual courting, wedding, and abduction scenes involving respectable women. Sutton discusses how the targeted audience and gaze for the vases shifts from showing a male-centered viewpoint on sex to depictions of heterosexual courting in which women have the power to choose and even initiate gift giving and female-centered depictions of domestic scenes, including women preparing for weddings.

Shapiro (1992:61–63, 70) focuses on classical Greek vase paintings of courting scenes involving pederastic homosexual men pursuing or giving gifts to partially clothed or naked boys whom he androcentrically calls "coy" and "playful." He makes an ethnocentric analogy between the way the boys are portrayed and modern pinup girls, which he does not consider to be pornographic. By the mid-fifth century, homosexuality was viewed as the old-fashioned antidemocratic and elitist sexuality, and images of the god Eros shift from depicting him pursuing boys to pursuing girls.

Williams's earlier interpretations of vase paintings raise questions about whether the women are interpreted as respectably preparing for weddings just because they are clothed and whether they could rather be hetaerae preparing for symposia. One of the vase paintings Sutton shows could also be interpreted as a lesbian scene since it involves four women, one of whom is standing and supporting or pushing the miniature male god Eros toward a seated woman facing her and playing the harp. Sutton interpreted this woman as a bride without clear reason.

Finally, Sutton (1992:21–24) interprets the development of vase paintings of nude bathers in the second half of the fourth century as due to the innovative and iconoclastic nude sculpture of Aphrodite of Knidos. Sutton discussed how the paintings of nude bathers shifted from being painted for men on the inside of wine cups to being painted for women because they are on vases that were usually used by women. Sutton questions whether paintings of all nude women can be identified as hetaerae and states that some of these painted vases were meant for use by respectable women. However, he also mentions that the water vases with nude bathers would have been used in the public baths, which were akin to modern massage parlors, implying that these vases might have been used by less respectable women.

Other research has analyzed women's sexual powers from classical Greek documents and paintings. A number of documents record the wealth that powerful hetaerae could achieve, and vase paintings include depictions of men coming to brothels to pay for hetaerae (Keuls 1985:153–87). Some statues depict women or hermaphrodites who in myths lifted their skirts to expose their genitals as a source of power, following the model of men, who are most often depicted on vases and in sculpture with exposed genitals signaling their social dominance (Ajootian 1997). Vases further depict women exposing their genitals as a source of sexual power to arouse men or centaurs (Cohen 1997:70). Bonfante (1997) discusses the awe and terror that the bared breast evoked for the Greeks because of its magical sexual and maternal powers connected to life and death. Cohen (1997) researched how sculptures and vase paintings express the power of women outside the norm to disrupt the social order, indicated by the exposed breasts of Amazons, the goddess Athena in battle, women in Bacchic dancing, divine lovemaking, and prostitutes as well as women's exposed breasts as loss of power in the social disruption of rape scenes. In literature, mothers exposed their breasts to inspire their sons to defend them in war. Some vase paintings depict women with bared breasts attacking men or gods (Keuls 1985:380).

Myerowitz (1992:137–54) questions whether Roman wall paintings of heterosexual sex acts are pornographic. She argues that these scenes are not pornographic because no sadism or abuse of women is shown and women and men are equally objectified and have equal social agency as sexual actors. Further, women were shown only in profile rather than the full frontal display for the gaze of the male spectator and voyeur, which is found in later European art. Finally, the paintings were not hidden away for private male voyeurism but were publicly displayed on house walls, especially in bedrooms, where women as well as men viewed them. Myerowitz (1992:151) argues that Romans viewed sex as part of women's domain of pregnancy and childbirth.

Myerowitz (1992:151–52) critiques the problem of applying modern feminist theories to anachronistically interpret Roman material culture. At the same time, she understands Susanne Kappeler's feminist analysis in arguing that all representation is sexist when men hold the mirror and control the viewpoint objectifying women. Myerowitz herself at one point interprets Roman wall paintings of sex acts as the transformation of sexuality from female nature to masculine culture, which is a second-wave feminist binary structuralist construction of gender. She points out that women wrote books instructing women on how to objectify themselves for the male gaze through sexual positions preferred by men (Myerowitz 1992:136).

In contrast to Myerowitz, Koloski-Ostrow (1997) uses the popularity of the theater in Nero's time to interpret mythological scenes painted on the walls of Pompeiian houses as theatrical stage sets meant for voyeurism. Koloski-Ostrow found mythological scenes of men and gods controlling passive women, as when Paris is shown persuading Helen to go with him to Troy. In another scene, Cassandra is shown powerless in attempting to warn the Trojans about the Trojan horse. However, in another scene, a man is about to be killed by dogs for viewing a goddess naked. The mythological scenes portray gendered asymmetries of power in contrast to the sex scenes analyzed by Myerowitz. It could be further noted that many of the Roman myths were actually Greek myths that were adopted and that brought with them the gender divisions and conflicts in classical Greek culture that were expressed in myths.

Clarke (1998:13–17, 276–78) has attempted to eliminate ethnocentrism by taking an anthropological approach in analyzing the meaning of sexual images to Romans on the basis of the contexts in which the images of sex acts are displayed as well as contemporary texts concerning sex. He found a variety of sexual identities and relationships depicted according to class, status, and ethnic differences. He argues against assuming that Roman images of sex are self-evident and can be read from our cultural viewpoint. Clarke cautions against projecting modern Western values to create anachronistic distorted interpretations of the past. At the same time, he recognizes his use of the term "lovemaking," for sex acts could be understood as a nonneutral term that romanticizes sex from a Western perspective.

Clarke (1998:13, 195, 278) asks for whom Roman images of sex were erotic and points out that this depends on the cultural context. He found that Roman laws against premarital sex and adultery were only to address the elite concerns over legitimate heirs and did not apply to sex with people of lower status. There was no uniform Christian moral standard and no Christian guilt over sex for enjoyment. A wide variety of sex acts were displayed in public spaces and houses, where they were seen by women and children as well as men. Frescoes in public baths displayed sex acts undertaken not only for men but also for women, such as cunnilingus and lesbian sex. A brothel, called a lupanar, was identified from the small cubicles or cribs with built-in stone plastered beds and depictions of sex scenes that were often exaggerated and more crudely painted than the small sexually explicit paintings found in a few rooms in houses. It would seem that Romans addressed sex more openly than Christians. Further, children as well as women were permitted to view a variety of sex acts based on the sexual identities of people from different classes, ethnic groups, and sexual orientations. Clarke does the most to destabilize and "queer" Western heterosexist interpretations of Roman depictions of sex acts.

Applications of Masculinity Theories in Classical Archaeology

Feminist masculinity theories have analyzed the Western cultural construction of a normative heterosexual hypermasculinity that valorizes and institutionalizes male domination through violence. Hypermasculinity would seem to be illustrated in Greek vase paintings of myths and men's misogynistic treatment of prostitutes, showing rape, forced sex, and beatings (Keuls 1985:47–55, 180–86; Sutton 1992:11–13).

The ideology of hypermasculinity has been contrasted with postmodern research demonstrating diversity in masculine identities, experiences, behaviors, and actual performance of masculine roles. Feminist masculinity theory and research further addresses how men's institutionalized privileges and domination benefit all men—and particular groups of men more than others. Feminist masculinity research has demonstrated the institutionalization of dominance by some groups of men not only over educational and economic resources but also over other men as well as women (Lorber 2001:163–78).

Classical Greek vase paintings depict an ideology of masculinity valorizing homosexuality (575–480 B.C.). The valorization of homosexuality is interpreted from the affection shown in pederastic courting scenes of older bearded men giving gifts to and pursuing unbearded youths. Homosexuality was further legitimated in vase paintings of the main god Zeus pursuing the boy-god Gannymead (Shapiro 1992). The valorization of homosexuality provides a new perspective on Greek men's texts defining ideal masculinity as the "same-mindedness" and interdependence of autonomous citizen men (Morris 2000:155), while women were excluded from being citizens because they lacked male virtues according to Aristotle (Pomeroy 1975).

Classical Greek vase paintings depict a shift in the ideology of masculinity to valorizing male deference to clothed respectable women in courting and wedding scenes (480–400 B.C.). Vase paintings depicting women's domestic work behind closed doors in the women's quarters or women entering the half-opened door to a bedroom (Keuls 1983, 1985:98–129) both represent men's control over women that was valorized in idealistic documents associating masculinity with the responsible pious male citizen head of household, who was married with children and a self-sufficient farmer who owned his own land (Hanson 1995:87–88; Morris 2000:115–49). Second-wave feminist classical archaeologists projected the ideal of masculine control of women to divide excavated foundations of houses into segregated male-public spaces and women's private quarters that had no access to the outside and that restricted access to the rest of the house (e.g., Keuls 1985; Walker 1983).

The Romans shared some similar masculine ideals as heads of households controlling their wives, children, and slaves. In fact, Roman men had the power to put members of their family to death, which was more power than Greek men had, except for female infanticide. Roman freemen also shared masculine ideals as citizens and as warriors for the state. However, classical Roman explicit sexual scenes are more often egalitarian than Greek sex scenes (Myerowitz 1992).

Roman sex scenes showed women as well as men willingly participating, in contrast to Greek scenes. Rome borrowed the Greek gods and goddesses and as a result depicted the same mythological scenes of rape.

The Future

Feminist classical archaeology has generally followed the development of feminist theory. Therefore, it can be hoped that second-wave analyses projecting the dominant historic patriarchal ideology as the universal actual gender practice will be increasingly replaced with third-wave feminist analyses of the diversity and fluidity in classical gender systems. A start has been made in constructing a richer picture of the complexity and change in classical gender systems. Most research so far has addressed class differences in gendered household spaces and consumer choices. Clarke (1988) has shown that it is also possible to address ethnic differences in houses in classical Roman culture. Perhaps it would also be possible to find ethnic areas in classical Greek cities that would reveal some ethnic differences in house design or artifacts. It is hoped that research on the negotiation and fluidity of gender identities and sexual orientations will continue to develop.

The explicit use of feminist theory in the classics has increased from Pomeroy (1975) to Keuls (1985), Richlin (1992), and Lyons and Koloski-Ostrow (1997). It is hoped that this review has demonstrated that further insight can be gained by the explicit application of feminist theory in gender research in classical archaeology.

Acknowledgments

I would like to thank the following colleagues for their generous assistance in providing me with information on gender research in feminist classical archaeology: Pim Allison, Marilyn Goldberg, Claire Lyons, and Lynn Meskell. My deepest thanks to Sarah Nelson for encouraging me to write this chapter. Of course, any errors are mine.

References

Abbott, Frank F.
    1909   *Society and Politics in Ancient Rome: Essays and Sketches*. New York: Scribner's.
Adkins, Lesley, and Roy A. Adkins
    1997   *Handbook to Life in Ancient Greece*. New York: Facts on File.
Ajootian, Aileen
    1997   The Only Happy Couple: Hermaphrodites and Gender. In *Naked Truths:*

Women, Sexuality and Gender in Classical Art and Archaeology. A. O. Koloski-Ostrow and C. L. Lyons, eds. Pp. 220–43. London: Routledge.

Alcock, Susan E.

2002   *Archaeologies of the Greek Past: Landscape, Monuments, and Memories.* Cambridge: Cambridge University Press.

Allison, Penelope M.

1999   Labels for Ladles: Interpreting the Material Culture of Roman Households. In *The Archaeology of Household Activities.* Penelope M. Allison, ed. Pp. 57–78. London: Routledge.

2004   *Pompeian Households: An Analysis of Material Culture.* Monograph 42. Los Angeles: Costen Institute of Archaeology, University of California, Los Angeles.

Amos, Valerie, and Pratibha Parmer

1984   Challenging Imperial Feminism. *Feminist Review* 17(autumn):3–19.

Archer, L. J., S. Fischler, and M. Wyke, eds.

1994   *Women in Ancient Societies: "An Illusion of the Night."* New York: Routledge.

Ault, Bradley A., and Lisa C. Nevett

1999   Digging Houses: Archaeologies of Classical and Hellenistic Greek Domestic Assemblages. In *The Archaeology of Household Activities.* Penelope M. Allison, ed. Pp. 43–57. London: Routledge.

Blundell, S.

1995   *Women in Ancient Greece.* London: British Museum Press.

Boardman, John

1974   *Athenian Black Figure Vases.* London: Thames and Hudson.

1998   *Early Greek Vase Painting: 11th–6th Centuries b.c.* London: Thames and Hudson.

Bonfante, Larissa

1997   Nursing Mothers in Classical Art. In *Naked Truths: Women, Sexuality and Gender in Classical Art and Archaeology.* A. O. Koloski-Ostrow and C. L. Lyons, eds. Pp. 174–97. London: Routledge.

Broude, N., and M. Garrard, eds.

1982   *Feminism and Art History: Questioning the Litany.* New York: Harper and Row.

Brown, Shelby

1993   Feminist Research in Archaeology: What Does It Mean? Why Is It Taking so Long? In *Feminist Theory and the Classics.* Sorkin Rabinowitz and Amy Richlin, eds. Pp. 238–71. New York: Routledge.

1997   "Ways of Seeing" Women in Antiquity: An Introduction to Feminism in Classical Archaeology and Ancient Art History. In *Naked Truths: Women, Sexuality and Gender in Classical Art and Archaeology.* A. O. Koloski-Ostrow and C. L. Lyons, eds. Pp. 1243. London: Routledge.

Bunch, Charlotte

1987   *Passionate Politics: Essays 1968–1986—Feminist Theory in Action.* New York: St. Martin's Press.

Butler, Judith
1990   *Gender Trouble: Feminism and the Subversion of Identity.* London: Routledge.
Buxton, Richard
1998   Religion and Myth. In *The Cambridge Illustrated History of Ancient Greece.* Paul Cartledge, ed. Pp. 320–45. Cambridge: Cambridge University Press.
Cameron, Averil, and Amélie Kuhrt
1993   *Images of Women in Antiquity.* Detroit: Wayne State University Press.
Cantarella, Eva
1987   *Pandora's Daughters: The Role and Status of Women in Greek and Roman Antiquity.* Baltimore: The Johns Hopkins University Press.
Cartledge, Paul
1993   *The Greeks: A Portrait of Self and Others.* New York: Oxford University Press.
Clarke, John R.
1991   *The Houses of Roman Italy 100 B.C.–A.D. 250: Ritual, Space and Decoration.* Berkeley: University of California Press.
1998   *Looking at Lovemaking: Constructions of Sexuality in Roman Art 100 B.C.–A.D. 250.* Berkeley: University of California Press.
Clees, Helen
1920   *A Study of Women in Attic Inscriptions.* New York: Columbia University Press.
Cohen, Beth
1997   Divesting the Female Breast of Clothes in Classical Sculpture. In *Naked Truths: Women, Sexuality and Gender in Classical Art and Archaeology.* A. O. Koloski-Ostrow and C. L. Lyons, eds. Pp. 66–93. London: Routledge.
Collins, Patricia Hill
1990   *Black Feminist Thought: Knowledge, Consciousness, and the Politics of Empowerment.* Boston: Unwin Hyman.
Cowell, Frank R.
1980   *Life in Ancient Rome.* New York: Putnam.
Davis-Kimball, Jeannine
1997   Sauro-Sarmatian Nomadic Women: New Gender Identities. *Journal of Indo-European Studies* 25:327–44.
Donovan, Josephine
2001   *Feminist Theory: The Intellectual Traditions.* 3rd ed. New York: Continuum.
Dover, K. J.
1978   *Greek Homosexuality.* Cambridge, MA: Harvard University Press.
duBois, Page
1988   *Sowing the Body: Psychoanalysis and Ancient Representations of Women.* Chicago: University of Chicago Press.
Dwyer, Eugene
1991   The Pompeian Atrium House in Theory and in Practice. In *Roman Art in the Private Sphere: New Perspectives on the Architecture and Décor of the Domus, Villa, and*

Insula. E. K. Gazda, ed., assisted by A. E. Haeckl. Pp. 25–49. Ann Arbor: University of Michigan Press.

Ellis, Simon P.

1991   Power, Architecture, and Décor: How the Late Roman Aristocrat Appeared to His Guests. In *Roman Art in the Private Sphere: New Perspectives on the Architecture and Décor of the Domus, Villa, and Insula.* E. K. Gazda, ed., assisted by A. E. Haeckl. Pp. 117–35. Ann Arbor: University of Michigan Press.

Fantham, E., H. P. Foley, N. B. Kampen, S. B. Pomeroy, and H. A. Shapiro, eds.

1994   *Women in the Classical World: Image and Text.* New York: Oxford University Press.

Gazda, Elaine K.

1991   Introduction. In *Roman Art in the Private Sphere: New Perspectives on the Architecture and Décor of the Domus, Villa, and Insula.* E. K. Gazda, ed., assisted by A. E. Haeckl. Pp. 1–25. Ann Arbor: University of Michigan Press.

Goldberg, Marilyn Y.

1998   Deceptive Dichotomy: Two Case Studies. In *Redefining Archaeology: Feminist Perspectives.* Mary Casey, Denise Donlon, Jeanette Hope, and Sharon Welfare, eds. Pp. 107–13. Canberra: ANH Publications, Research School of Pacific and Asian Studies, Australian National University.

1999   Spatial and Behavioural Negotiation in Classical Athenian City Houses. In *The Archaeology of Household Activities: Gender Ideologies, Domestic Spaces and Material Culture.* Penelope M. Allison, ed. Pp. 142–62. London: Routledge.

Gutzwiller, Kathryn J., and Ann N. Michelini

1991   Women and Other Strangers: Feminist Perspectives in Classical Literature. In *(En)Gendering Knowledge: Feminists in Academe.* Joan E. Hartman and Ellen Messer-Davidow, eds. Pp. 66–85. Knoxville: University of Tennessee Press.

Hallett, Judith P., and Marilyn B. Skinner, eds.

1997   *Roman Sexualities.* Princeton, NJ: Princeton University Press.

Halperin, David M.

1990   *One Hundred Years of Homosexuality.* New York: Routledge.

Halperin, David M., John J. Winkler, and Froma Zeitlin, eds.

1990   *Before Sexuality: The Construction of Erotic Experience in Ancient Greece.* Princeton, NJ: Princeton University Press.

Hanson, V. D.

1995   *The Other Greeks: The Family Farm and the Agrarian Roots of Western Civilization.* New York: Free Press.

Havelock, Christine M.

1982   Mourners on Greek Vases: Remarks on the Social History of Women. In *Feminism and Art History: Questioning the Litany.* Norma Broude and Mary D. Garrard, eds. Pp. 45–63. New York: Harper and Row.

Hoepfner, W., and Schwander, E. L.

1994   *Haus und statdt im klassischen Griechenland.* Munich: Deutscher Kunstverlag.

Houby-Nielsen, Sanne
  2000   Child Burials in Ancient Athens. In *Children and Material Culture*. Joanna S.
          Derevenski, ed. Pp. 151–67. London: Routledge.
Jameson, M.
  1990   Domestic Space in the Greek City-State. In *Domestic Architecture and the Use of
          Space*. Susan Kent, ed. Pp. 92–113. Cambridge: Cambridge University Press.
Kampen, Natalie B.
  1982   Social Status and Gender in Roman Art: The Case of the Saleswoman. In
          Feminism and Art History: Questioning the Litany. Norma Broude and Mary D.
          Garrard, eds. Pp. 63–79. New York: Harper and Row.
  1991   Between Public and Private: Women as Historical Subjects in Roman Art. In
          Women's History and Ancient History. Sarah Pomeroy, ed. Pp. 218–48. Chapel
          Hill: University of North Carolina Press.
Katz, Marilyn
  1998   Women, Children and Men. In *The Cambridge Illustrated History of Ancient Greece*.
          Paul Cartledge, ed. Pp. 100–39. Cambridge: Cambridge University Press.
Keuls, Eva
  1983   Attic Vase-Painting and the Home Textile Industry. In *Ancient Greek Art and
          Iconography*. Warren G. Moon, ed. Pp. 209–30. Madison: University of Wis-
          consin Press.
  1985   *The Reign of the Phallus: Sexual Politics in Ancient Athens*. New York: Harper and
          Row.
Koloski-Ostrow, Ann Olga
  1997   Violent Stages in Two Pompeian Houses: Imperial Taste, Aristocratic
          Response, and Messages of Male Control. In *Naked Truths: Women, Sexuality and
          Gender in Classical Art and Archaeology*. A. O. Koloski-Ostrow and C. L. Lyons,
          eds. Pp. 243–67. London: Routledge.
Koloski-Ostrow, Ann Olga, and Claire L. Lyons, eds.
  1997   *Naked Truths: Women, Sexuality and Gender in Classical Art and Archaeology*. New
          York: Routledge.
Laurence, Ray
  1994   *Roman Pompeii: Space and Society*. London: Routledge.
Lerner, Gerda
  1993   *The Creation of Feminist Consciousness: From the Middle Ages to Eighteen-Seventy*. New
          York: Oxford University Press.
Longfellow, Brenda
  2000   A Gendered Space? Location and Function of Room 5 in the Villa of the
          Mysteries. In *The Villa of the Mysteries in Pompeii*. Elaine K. Gazda, ed. Pp. 24–
          38. Ann Arbor: Kelsey Museum of Archaeology and the University of Michi-
          gan Museum of Art.
Lorber, Judith
  2001   *Gender Inequality: Feminist Theories and Politics*. 2nd ed. Los Angeles: Roxbury.

Lyons, Claire L., and Olga Koloski-Ostrow
    1997   Introduction. In *Naked Truths: Women, Sexuality and Gender in Classical Art and Archaeology*. A. O. Koloski-Ostrow and C. L. Lyons, eds. Pp. 1–12. London: Routledge.
McClure, Laura K., ed.
    2002   *Sexuality and Gender in the Classical World: Readings and Sources*. Oxford: Blackwell.
Meadows, Karen
    1999   The Appetites of Households in Early Roman Britain. In *The Archaeology of Household Activities: Gender Ideologies, Domestic Spaces and Material Culture*. Penelope M. Allison, ed. Pp. 101–21. London: Routledge.
Millett, Kate
    1970   *Sexual Politics: A Surprising Examination of Society's Most Arbitrary Folly*. Garden City, NY: Doubleday.
Mohanty, Chandra T.
    1988   Under Western Eyes: Feminist Scholarship and Colonial Discourse. *Feminist Review* 30(autumn):61–88.
Morris, Ian
    1994   *Classical Greece: Ancient Histories and Modern Archaeologies*. Cambridge: Cambridge University Press.
    2000   *Archaeology as Cultural History: Words and Things in Iron Age Greece*. London: Blackwell.
Myerowitz, Molly
    1992   The Domestication of Desire: Ovid's *Parva Tabella* and the Theater of Love. In *Pornography and Representation in Greece and Rome*. Amy Richlin, ed. Pp. 131–58. New York: Oxford University Press.
Nelson, Sarah M.
    2002   Gender in Archaeology: The Professional Is Political. Paper presented at the 2002 Centennial Meetings of the American Anthropological Association, New Orleans.
Nevett, Lisa C.
    1994   Separation or Seclusion: Towards an Archaeological Approach to Investigating Women in the Greek Household in the Fifth to Third Centuries B.C. In *Architecture and Order: Approaches to Social Space*. M. Parker Pearson and C. Richards, eds. Pp. 98–112. London: Routledge.
    1999   *House and Society in the Ancient Greek World*. Cambridge: Cambridge University Press.
Nicholson, Linda J., ed.
    1990   *Feminism/Postmodernism*. New York: Routledge.
Ortner, Sherry B.
    1974   Is Female to Male as Nature Is to Culture? In *Woman, Culture and Society*. Michelle Z. Rosaldo and Louise Lamphere, eds. Pp. 67–88. Stanford, CA: Stanford University Press.

Pomeroy, Sarah B.
   1975   *Goddesses, Whores, Wives and Slaves: Women in Classical Antiquity.* New York: Schocken Books.
   1998   The Contribution of Women to the Greek Domestic Economy: Rereading Xenophon's Oeconomicus. In *Feminisms in the Academy.* Donna C. Stanton and Abigail J. Stewart, eds. Pp. 180–99. Ann Arbor: University of Michigan Press.
Reeder, E., ed.
   1995   *Pandora: Women in Classical Greece.* Princeton, NJ: Princeton University Press.
Reilly, Joan
   1997   Naked and Limbless: Learning about the Feminine Body in Ancient Athens. In *Naked Truths: Women, Sexuality and Gender in Classical Art and Archaeology.* A. O. Koloski-Ostrow and C. L. Lyons. Pp. 154–74. London: Routledge.
Richlin, Amy
   1983   *The Garden of Priapus: Sexuality and Aggression in Roman Humor.* New Haven, CT: Yale University Press.
   1992   Introduction. In *Pornography and Representation in Greece and Rome.* Amy Richlin, ed. Pp. xi–xxiv. New York: Oxford University Press.
Robertson, Charles M.
   1992   *The Art of Vase-Painting in Classical Athens.* Cambridge: Cambridge University Press.
Rolle, Renate
   1989   *The World of the Scythians.* F. G. Walls, trans. Berkeley: University of California Press. Originally published in German in 1980.
Rosaldo, Michele Zimbalist
   1980   The Use and Abuse of Anthropology: Reflections on Feminism and Cross-Cultural Understanding. *Signs* 5(3):389–417.
   1974   Woman, Culture, and Society: A Theoretical Overview. In *Woman, Culture and Society.* Michelle Z. Rosaldo and Louise Lamphere, eds. Pp. 17–42. Stanford, CA: Stanford University Press.
Rosaldo, Michele Z., and Louise Lamphere
   1974   Introduction. In *Woman, Culture and Society.* Michelle Z. Rosaldo and Louise Lamphere, eds. Pp. 1–16. Stanford, CA: Stanford University Press.
Sanders, D.
   1990   Behavioral Conventions and Archaeology: Methods for the Analysis of Ancient Architecture. In *Domestic Architecture and the Use of Space.* Susan Kent, ed. Pp. 43–72. Cambridge: Cambridge University Press.
Shapiro, H. A.
   1992   Eros in Love: Pederasty and Pornography in Greece. In *Pornography and Representation in Greece and Rome.* Amy Richlin, ed. Pp. 53–73. New York: Oxford University Press.

Snyder, Jane M.
   1997   Sappho in Attic Vase Painting. In *Naked Truths: Women, Sexuality and Gender in Classical Art and Archaeology*. A. O. Koloski-Ostrow and C. L. Lyons, eds. Pp. 108–20. London: Routledge.
Spelman, Elizabeth
   1988   *Inessential Woman: Problems of Exclusion in Feminist Thought*. Boston: Beacon Press.
Spencer-Wood, Suzanne M.
   1991   Toward an Historical Archaeology of Domestic Reform. In *The Archaeology of Inequality*. R. McGuire and R. Paynter, eds. Pp. 231–86. Oxford: Basil Black-well.
   1992   A Feminist Program for a Non-Sexist Archaeology. In *Quandaries and Quests: Visions of Archaeology's Future*. LuAnn Wandsnider, ed. Pp. 98–113. Occasional Paper 20. Carbondale: Center for Archaeological Investigations, Southern Illinois University.
   1994   Diversity in 19th Century Domestic Reform: Relationships among Classes and Ethnic Groups. In *"Those of Little Note": Gender, Race and Class in Historical Archaeology*. Elizabeth Scott, ed. Tucson: University of Arizona Press.
   1995   Toward the Further Development of Feminist Historical Archaeology. *World Archaeological Bulletin* 7:118–36.
   1999   The World Their Household: Changing Meanings of the Domestic Sphere in the Nineteenth Century. In *The Archaeology of Household Activities: Gender Ideologies, Domestic Spaces and Material Culture*. Penelope M. Allison, ed. Pp. 162–89. London: Routledge.
Stewart, Andrew
   1990   *Greek Sculpture: An Exploration*. New Haven, CT: Yale University Press.
Sutton, Robert F., Jr.
   1992   Pornography and Persuasion on Attic Pottery. In *Pornography and Representation in Greece and Rome*. Amy Richlin, ed. Pp. 3–36. New York: Oxford University Press.
Thébert, Y.
   1987   Private Life and Domestic Architecture in Roman Africa. In *A History of Private Life: I. From Pagan Rome to Byzantium*. P. Veyne, ed. Pp. 313–410. Cambridge, MA: Belknap Press.
Vernant, J. P.
   1983   Hestia-Hermes: The Religious Expression of Space and Movement in Ancient Greece. In *Myth and Thought*. J. P. Vernant, ed. Pp. 127–75. London: Routledge and Kegan Paul.
Versnel, H. S.
   1987   Wife and Helpmate: Women of Ancient Athens in Anthropological Perspective. In *Sexual Asymmetry*. J. Blok and P. Mason, eds. Pp. 59–86. Amsterdam: Gieben.

Walker, Susan
  1983   Women and Housing in Classical Greece: The Archaeological Evidence. In *Images of Women in Antiquity*. Averil Cameron and Amélie Kuhrt, eds. Pp. 81–91. Detroit: Wayne State University Press.
Wallace-Hadrill, Andrew
  1994   *Houses and Society in Pompeii and Herculaneum*. Princeton, NJ: Princeton University Press.
Williams, Dyfri
  1983   Women on Athenian Vases: Problems of Interpretation. In *Images of Women in Antiquity*. Averil Cameron and Amélie Kuhrt, eds. Pp. 92–107. Detroit: Wayne State University Press.
  2000   Of Geometric Toys, Symbols and Votives. In *Periplous: Papers on Classical Art and Archaeology Presented to Sir John Boardman*. G. R. Tsetskhladze, A. N. J. W. Prag, and A. M. Snodgrass, eds. Pp. 388–97. London: Thames and Hudson.
Winkler, John J.
  1990   *The Constraints of Desire: The Anthropology of Sex and Gender in Ancient Greece*. New York: Routledge.
Wylie, Alison
  1991   Gender Theory and the Archaeological Record: Why Is There No Archaeology of Gender? In *Engendering Archaeology: Women and Prehistory*. J. M. Gero and M. W. Conkey, eds. Pp. 31–54. Oxford: Basil Blackwell.
Younger, John G.
  1997   Gender and Sexuality in the Parthenon Frieze. In *Naked Truths: Women, Sexuality and Gender in Classical Art and Archaeology*. A. O. Koloski-Ostrow and C. L. Lyons, eds. Pp. 120–54. London: Routledge.

Index

domestic group, 141
domesticity, controversy over, 146–48
Domesticity, Cult of, 48, 52
domestic roles of women: classical archaeology on, 277–78; combined with public,
research on, 40–43; reform ideologies
and, 49–50; research on, 37–38
Dreaming Tracks, 179
dress: and burial rituals, 86–87; and heterarchy, 202–7, *203*, 210n2; in Iron Age,
122–25; material culture and, 87–90. *See
also* ornaments
dwelling area, 141

Early Bronze Age: dress in, 89; material culture of, 81–82
Egyptian society: divine images in, 172–73;
gender attributions and, 13; representational art of, 11
embodiment, 6; gendered, of landscape,
171–74; material culture and, 83–84;
and space, 93–94
enculturation, archaeology and, 217–18
Endo society: ceramic production in, 245;
ethnoarchaeology and, 222, 233–34
engendered mortuary analysis: approaches to,
111–22; case study in, 122–25; future
directions for, 125–28; history of,
108–10; levels of, 112
epistemology: androcentric, critiques of,
33–34; feminist, issues in, 17n1
Eros, 285, 287
essentialist feminism: and ethnoarchaeology,
223; second-wave theory and, 43
ethnoarchaeology, 217–64; definition of,
218; gender integration in, 246–48;
methodologies in, 223–26; research in,
finding, 247
ethnography: sex of researcher in, 224–25;
uses of, 5–6
ethnohistory: and gender attributions, 12;
uses of, 5–6
evidence: multiple lines of, for gender attri-

bution, 12; types of, and gender archaeology, 7–14

family, term, 270
farmers, ethnoarchaeology on, 230–36
feasting: equipment, in hoards, 204; and gender attribution, 13; households and, 156
Female Invalidism, Cult of, 47
female warriors, 115–16, 275
feminist archaeology: methodologies in,
1–28. *See also* gender archaeology
feminist classical archaeology, 265–99;
development of, 266–67; research directions for, 291
feminist epistemology, issues in, 17n1
feminist theory: in classical archaeology, 273;
development of, 30–31, 35–36, 265–66;
in historical archaeology, 29–74
fertility, mortuary evidence on, 118–19
fibulae, 90
first-wave feminist theory: and classical
archaeology, 266, 273–80; definition of,
36, 266, 273; and historical archaeology,
36–43
Five Points area, 37, 39–41, 54
The Flintstones, 217–18
fluidity, in gender systems, 52–54
foragers, ethnoarchaeology and, 223,
227–30
Fort Ross, households in, 142
Fulani society, 219; households in, 231, 236
funerary archaeology. *See* mortuary analysis

Gaia, 171
Gamo society, tool production in, 241
Gannymead, 290
gardens, naming of, 34, 40
gaze: gendered, and landscapes, 170–71;
male, representational art and, 11, 285
gender: experience of, methodologies and,
6–7; issues in, vii; objects as reflection of,
76–78; versus sex, 113; single-frame
analysis of, 4–5; uses of, 110–11. *See also*

mortuary analysis, 107–40; and gender
archaeology, 8–10, 85–87; heterarchy
and, 193; and living population, 107; and
material culture, 81. *See also* engendered
mortuary analysis
Mother Earth/Nature, 171–72
mothering: classical archaeology on, 278–80;
ethnoarchaeology on, 228–29; historical
archaeology on, 39–40; third-wave feminist theory on, 47
multiple burials, 116
Mura society, households in, 232

Namaqua Khoikhoen society, tool production in, 241
naming, androcentric practices in, 34, 40,
270
Native American societies: divine images in,
172; tool production in, 242. See also *specific group*
Natufian society, skeletal analysis and, 117
Navajo society, divine images in, 172
Near Eastern archaeology, engendered mortuary analysis in, 109
negotiations: in gender systems, 52–54;
household studies and, 142; material culture and, 80, 82
Nelson, Sarah Milledge, vii–xi
Neolithic societies, marking gender in,
178–79
neutral burial category, 122
Njemp society, calabash production in, 243
norms, material culture and, 82–87
North American archaeology: engendered
mortuary analysis in, 110. *See also* historical archaeology
Norwegian society: gendered landscapes in,
180; material culture of, 77
Nuba society, ceramic production in, 244
Nunamiut society, division of labor in, 229
nunneries, 95; architecture of, 93

occupations, gender specialized, 238–46
Olmec society, representational art of, 11

Onge society, division of labor in, 230
oracles, 275
ornaments, 90; and gender attribution,
12–13; and heterarchy, 202–7, *203*,
210n2; in Iron Age, 122–25. *See also* dress

Pachamama, 172
painting, and landscapes, 170
Paleolithic societies, rock art in, 177–78
Panathenaea, 274
past. *See* projection of present values on past
pastoralists, ethnoarchaeology and, 236–38
Peirce, Melusina Fay, 44
people-object relations, 85
performance, 110; material culture and, 83
phenomenological studies in archaeology, 6
Pintupi society, division of labor in, 230
politics, scholarship and, 1–2
postcolonial feminist theory, 44–45
postmodern feminist theory, 46; and classical
archaeology, 267, 281–84; and historical
archaeology, 46–55
power: in households, 156–57; legitimization of, material culture and, 80; mortuary analysis and, 120–21; spatial relations
and, 92
prestige, in households, 156–57
prism metaphor, viii
production: engendering, 152; heterarchy
and, 197
projection of present values on past: androcentrism in, 32; classical archaeology and,
271–72, 280; ethnoarchaeology and,
226–46; *The Flintstones* and, 217–18; pre-
cautions with, 126–27
public roles of women: classical archaeology
on, 273–77; combined with domestic,
research on, 40–43; research on, 36–39
Pueblo society: representational art of, 10;
variability in, 2
Pythagorean philosophy, 276, 281

Qashqa'i society, households in, 236
Qisar society, households in, 233

About the Contributors

Bettina Arnold is an associate professor in the Department of Anthropology at the University of Wisconsin–Milwaukee. Her area of expertise is Early Iron Age Europe, but she has also participated in archaeological projects ranging from the Middle Bronze Age through the Roman period. Her research interests include European prehistory generally, Celtic Europe, the archaeology of gender, mortuary analysis, material culture as a system of communication, and ethical issues in archaeology, including the use and abuse of the past for political purposes. She is the coeditor, with Nancy L. Wicker, of *Gender and the Archaeology of Death* (2001) and *From the Ground Up: Beyond Gender Theory in Archaeology* (1999).

Wendy Ashmore is a professor of anthropology at the University of California, Riverside. Since receiving her Ph.D. from the University of Pennsylvania, attention to gender has joined study of settlement patterns, households, landscapes, and other aspects of space in antiquity as focus for her research and teaching, particularly with respect to the ancient Maya and their neighbors. Her publications include *Archaeologies of Landscape: Contemporary Perspectives* (coedited with A. Bernard Knapp, 1999).

Elizabeth M. Brumfiel is a professor of anthropology at Northwestern University. She holds a Ph.D. in anthropology at the University of Michigan. For the past eighteen years, she has pursued archaeological research at Xaltocan, a hinterland Aztec site in the basin of Mexico. Her edited volumes include *The Economic Anthropology of the State* (1994) and *Factional Competition and Political Development in the New World* (with J. W. Fox, 1994).

Julia A. Hendon is an associate professor of anthropology in the Department of Sociology and Anthropology at Gettysburg College. A specialist in Mesoamerican archaeology with interests in household archaeology, gender, economic specialization, landscape, and the development of complex societies, her fieldwork and research has concentrated on the Classic period Maya and neighboring complex societies in northern Honduras. She is coeditor of *Mesoamerican Archaeology: Theory and Practice* (2004) and has published articles in *American Anthropologist, Annual Review of Anthropology, Latin American Antiquity,* and *Cambridge Archaeological Journal.*

Janet E. Levy is an associate professor of anthropology at the University of North Carolina at Charlotte, where she has taught since 1980. She earned a B.A. in anthropology from Brown University and a Ph.D. in anthropology from Washington University—St. Louis. She has also taught in Illinois, Oregon, England, and Finland. In addition to gender, her interests include the prehistory of western Europe, the southeastern United States, ethics in archaeology and anthropology, and archaeometallurgy. She has served in the governance of the American Anthropological Association and Society for American Archaeology.

Sarah Milledge Nelson is a John Evans Professor at the University of Denver. She works mostly in Asian archaeology. Her current project is in Liaoning Province, China, where she is surveying sites of the Hongshan period. Books include *Korean Social Archaeology* (2004) and *Gender in Archaeology, Analyzing Power and Prestige* (2nd ed., 2004). Edited books include *Ancient Queens* (2003) and *The Archaeology of the Russian Far East* (with Y. V. Kuzmin, R. Bland, and A. Derivanko, 2006).

Marie Louise Stig Sørensen earned her Ph.D. from the University of Cambridge. She is University Senior Lecturer at the Department of Archaeology, University of Cambridge, teaching and specializing in Bronze Age Europe, archaeological theory (especially gender), and archaeological heritage studies. Publications include *Gender Archaeology* (2000) and *Excavating Women: A History of Women in European Archaeology* (edited with M. Diaz-Andreu, 1998).

Suzanne M. Spencer-Wood is an associate professor of anthropology at Oakland University and an associate, Peabody Museum of Archaeology and Ethnology, Harvard University, specializing in applying feminist theory in historical archaeology and analyzing gender, class, and ethnic interactions at turn-of-the-century reform women's institutions. She organized the first two conference symposia on feminist historical archaeology in 1989 and has published in *Historical Archaeology, International Journal of Historical Archaeology,* and *The Landscape Journal* as well as a number of chapters in edited volumes, most recently a chapter in *Gender and Hide Production* (2005).

Kathryn Weedman is a visiting assistant professor at the University of South Florida, St. Petersburg. She received her Ph.D. from the University of Florida, where she focused her ethnoarchaeological studies in Ethiopia on the relationship between social group membership and stone tool production and use. She has coedited *Gender and Hide Production* (with Lisa Frink, 2005).